Dictionary of Lexicography

Anyone who has ever handled a dictionary will have wondered how it was put together, where the information has come from, and how and why it can benefit so many of its users. The *Dictionary of Lexicography* addresses all these issues.

The *Dictionary of Lexicography* examines both the theoretical and practical aspects of its subject, and how they are related. In the realm of dictionary research the authors highlight the history, criticism, typology, structures and use of dictionaries. They consider the subjects of data-collection and corpus technology, definition-writing and editing, presentation and publishing in relation to dictionary-making. English lexicography is the main focus of the work, but the wide range of lexicographical compilations in other cultures also features.

The *Dictionary* gives a comprehensive overview of the current state of lexicography and all its possibilities in an interdisciplinary context. The representative literature has been included and an alphabetically arranged appendix lists all bibliographical references given in the more than 2,000 entries, which also provide examples of relevant dictionaries and other reference works.

The authors have specialised in various aspects of the field and have contributed significantly to its astonishing development in recent years. **Dr R. R. K. Hartmann** is Director of the Dictionary Research Centre at the University of Exeter, and has founded the European Association for Lexicography and pioneered postgraduate training in the field. **Dr Gregory James** is Director of the Language Centre at the Hong Kong University of Science and Technology, where he has done research into what separates and unites European and Asian lexicography.

Dictionary of
Lexicography

R. R. K. Hartmann
and Gregory James

London and New York

First published 1998
by Routledge
11 New Fetter Lane, London EC4P 4EE

Simultaneously published in the USA and
Canada
by Routledge
29 West 35th Street, New York, NY 10001

© 1998 R. R. K. Hartmann and Gregory James

Typeset in Times by Florencetype Ltd,
Stoodleigh, Devon
Printed and bound in Great Britain by
TJ International Ltd, Padstow, Cornwall

*British Library Cataloguing in Publication
Data*
A catalogue record for this book is available
from the British Library

*Library of Congress Cataloging in Publication
Data*
Hartmann, R. R. K.
  Dictionary of lexicography / R.R.K.
Hartmann and Gregory James.
      p.   cm.
  Includes bibliographical references.
  ISBN 0–415–14143–5 (hc). – ISBN
  1. Lexicography–Dictionaries. I. James,
Gregory. II. Title.
P327.H37 1998   97–34079
413′.028–dc21   CIP

ISBN 0–415–14143–5

Acknowledgements

We owe a deep debt of gratitude to the very many people who have helped us along our way in the compilation of this dictionary.

The University of Exeter and the Hong Kong University of Science and Technology provided congenial environments within which we were able to work. We benefited greatly from the study leave granted to RRKH, which allowed him an extended period in Hong Kong, sponsored by the British Council and by the Language Centre at HKUST, where we were able to work together face to face.

We are extremely fortunate to have had excellent office back-up both at Exeter and HKUST. We should like to thank Cathy Pantry for secretarial assistance at the Dictionary Research Centre at Exeter; and at the Language Centre, HKUST, Ada Fan Shui-fun for secretarial assistance, Candice Poon Wai-yi for executive assistance, and Forward Hui Kam-chun and Terence Chow Chi-wai for technical assistance.

Our professional colleagues have helped us in a variety of ways, and we should like to record our appreciation especially to: (at Exeter) Steven McGill for the database design and transfer, Alan Wakelam for the initial design of the panels, Trevor Learmouth for assistance with 'library' matters and entries, John Wilkins for references for 'Classics'; (at HKUST) John Milton for assistance with 'computer' matters and entries, and the staff of the University Library for general helpfulness.

We should like to thank the postgraduate students at Exeter, especially the 1994–5 cohort, who helped us in our initial item search; in particular Martin Stark made a great contribution to our wordlist by his very thorough sifting of available sources. Li Lan and her fellow doctoral students helped us greatly in our search for references.

We are grateful to colleagues far and wide for their willingness to answer our queries: especially A. D. de V. Cluver on terminology, Edward Gates on the DSNA, Andrew Taylor on textbooks; others commented very substantially on our text, in particular Adelia Carstens, Amy Chi Man-lai, Turki Diab, Tom McArthur and Daan Prinsloo. We ought to mention, too, the anonymous reviewers of our first draft: their constructive observations on our entries were extremely helpful to us.

We have drawn upon the ideas of many colleagues, both from their published work and from informal personal contacts; we should like to thank, in this regard, Henning Bergenholtz, Rufus Gouws, Colin Yallop and Jacques van Keymeulen, as well as several Visiting Scholars at Exeter.

We appreciate very much the assistance of Rosalind Fergusson, our perspicacious copy-editor, who made significant contributions to the final form of the text. Our editors at Routledge deserve our thanks too, for their care and attention to our work.

We should like to thank the many publishers who responded to our requests for catalogues and other information; and the colleagues and students who answered our initial questionnaire, which persuaded us to see our proposed project to fruition.

We hope that all those who made contributions, large and small, to the final product will be forgiving of our sins of commission and omission, for which we alone remain responsible.

Finally, we should like to thank our families for putting up with our prolonged hibernation in our offices, and general absent-mindedness at home while entries were germinating in our heads.

R. R. K. Hartmann
Exeter

Gregory James
Kowloon

Introduction

Theory and practice

A dictionary of lexicography? A dictionary of dictionary-making? Indeed, 'lexicography' is commonly understood in a narrow sense as the theory and practice, or the 'art and craft' (Landau 1984), of dictionary-making, the compilation and preparation of reference texts for publication. However, in the latter half of this century, the importance of a second strand to the discipline, namely the scholarly field of dictionary research, has become increasingly recognised. With the very rapid advances in the technologies and formats of reference materials, particularly as a result of the development of electronic media, the horizons of lexicography have extended, and we are witnessing the emergence of a more global academic domain of 'reference science' in the modern context of the widespread availability of, and ever-increasing needs for rapid access to, all forms of information.

Lexicography, often misconceived as a branch of linguistics, is *sui generis*, a field whose endeavours are informed by the theories and practices of information science, literature, publishing, philosophy, and historical, comparative and applied linguistics. Sister disciplines, such as terminology, lexicology, encyclopedia work, bibliography, terminography, indexing, information technology, librarianship, media studies, translation and teaching, as well as the neighbouring disciplines of history, education and anthropology, provide the wider setting within which lexicographers have defined and developed their field.

The boundaries between the professional activity and the academic field of lexicography are fluid, and several associations, e.g. the DSNA (the Dictionary Society of North America, est. 1975), the Lexicographical Society of India (est. 1975), EURALEX (the European Association for Lexicography, est. 1983), AUSTRALEX (the Australasian Association for Lexicography, est. 1990), the Lexicographical Society of China (est. 1992), AFRILEX (the African Association for Lexicography, est. 1995), and ASIALEX (the Asian Association for Lexicography, est. 1997), have been formed to act as bridges between dictionary makers and academic lexicographers. Professional training, regular national and international conferences, seminars and workshops, and academic publications have served to mature lexicography into an independent field with its own principles and practices, purposefully making use of, and qualifying, the findings of other disciplines.

Dictionary typology

The core material of lexicography is the 'dictionary', or 'wordbook', the commonest variety of reference work, at once the subject of lexicographical theory (dictionary research) and the product of lexicographical practice (dictionary-making). The dictionary *qua* dictionary encompasses many genres, or types, which can be structurally classified. For example, a *phenomenological typology*, or categorisation based on formal features, might take account of such compositional characteristics as size ('pocket dictionary', 'abridged dictionary', 'concise dictionary' etc.) or coverage of the content of the work ('general dictionary', 'specialised dictionary' etc.). A *presentational*, or *tectonic*, typology would focus on the format ('alphabetical', 'classified', 'thematic' etc.) or medium ('manuscript', 'print', 'electronic' etc.) of the dictionary. A *functional typology*, or categorisation based on the contextual uses of the dictionary, would focus on the information categories provided ('pronunciation', 'spelling', 'etymological' etc.), and the ways these are presented ('explanatory', 'pedagogical', 'terminological' etc.) within the perspective of the target user ('scholarly', 'learner's', 'translator's' etc.). A *linguistic typology* would be based on the language(s) of the dictionary ('monolingual', 'bilingual', 'bilingualised' etc.).

These different types of dictionary have developed over a considerable period, in response to linguistic and cultural demands, and as a result of changes in the use and availability of communicative media. McArthur (1986a:4ff.) discusses four major 'shifts' in the process of the development of human communication: (i) the consolidation of speech and gesture; (ii) the development of writing; (iii) the advent of print technology; and (iv) electronic computation. In several lexicographical traditions, e.g. Arabic, Persian and Sanskrit, many early manifestations of lexical reference works were in metrical format. For example, the thematically-arranged synonymies of the Sanskrit tradition (called *nighaṇḍus*) emerged at the time of advanced development of pre-literate speech and the beginning of the development of writing. These reference tools were at first unwritten, and were passed from generation to generation in oral mode. To facilitate memorisation, they incorporated mnemonic devices such as rhythm, rhyme and perhaps music, and some were extremely sophisticated in their structure. The later emergence in the same tradition of thesauruses with letter-order arrangement demonstrates the second 'communicative shift', from total reliance on speech to a formalised and exclusive codification in the written medium, and involving a tactical reformulation of the dictionary consultation process. This shift of the basis of the process of dictionary compilation from spoken medium to script has implications for, and implies alterations in, at least four 'factors of dictionary use': (i) *information*: considerations of the written medium – ordering of items, spelling, legibility, development and preservation of writing materials – now supersede those of sound; (ii) *operations*: the nature of the consultation of the dictionary, i.e. reading not memorising, will be extended as the information is offered in differently accessible formats and literacy will assume enhanced social and referential functions; (iii) *users*: the users will be those who are functionally literate, and the oral traditions of memorisation and recitation will become inadequate; and (iv) *purposes*: the contexts of dictionary use will be extended as their content and format change, for example they may serve as repositories of knowledge, and develop a role as arbiters in matters of orthography and other areas of usage.

From print to computerisation

The third of McArthur's 'communicative shifts', that from writing to print, permitted the mass production of dictionaries, and a change in users' attitudes towards the social and educational purpose of the dictionary, which because of its stability in print format assumed the role of an authority and a judge in language. All of the major European languages can claim their 'own' dictionaries, many of them monumental pioneering scholastic enterprises, either as individual initiatives or under the auspices or sponsorship of an academy, and all of which served, in various ways, to codify their respective languages: such examples are the *Vocabolario degli Accademici della Crusca* (Venice, 1612) for Italian, the *Dictionnaire de l'Académie française* (Paris, 1694) for French, the Spanish Academy's *Diccionario de la lengua Castellana* (Madrid, 1726–39) for Spanish, Jacob and Wilhelm Grimm's *Deutsches Wörterbuch* (Leipzig, 1854–1961) for German, the *Tolkovyi slovar' zhivago velikorusskogo yazyka* (St Petersburg, 1863–66) by Vladimir Ivanovich Dal' for Russian, James Murray *et al.*'s *New English Dictionary on Historical Principles*, which became the *Oxford English Dictionary* (Oxford, 1884–1933) for English, and the *Novo Dicionário da Língua Portuguesa* (Lisbon, 1899) by Cândido de Figueiredo for Portuguese.

The widespread use of these and other European languages, and the historical and political circumstances of their dissemination, have meant that the lexicographical traditions of languages in other parts of the world have often been somewhat neglected outside their own spheres. In China, for example, lexicography has a distinguished pedigree. The first thesaurus made its appearance during the early Qin dynasty (221–207 BC), and the 49,000-entry character dictionary, *Kāngxī zìdiǎn*, commissioned by the Qing Emperor Kangxi in the early eighteenth century, eclipses anything produced in Europe up to that period.

The fourth 'communicative shift' proposed by McArthur, that of electronic computation, has revolutionised lexicography not only with respect to the stages of the dictionary-making process (e.g. the automatic retrieval of lexical evidence from large corpora of texts, and on-screen text processing), but also in the conception and treatment of reference systems (e.g. in the use of multimedia, and the varied possibilities of search and access methods). From the hand-held electronic spelling dictionary to the multimedia encyclopedia on CD-ROM, lexicography is an area of academic and commercial enterprise that has turned computerisation to account in a variety of novel ways. In particular the development of the relational database as a design feature has served to corrode traditional organisational access structures, such as alphabetisation. In print format, the structure and composition of the material collected by the lexicographer determined the access path taken by the user: alphabetically organised headwords would be looked up alphabetically, the ordering of senses determined a sequence of search strategies to locate the sense sought, etc.

Computerisation has radically transformed these relationships. The output can now be specified by the user in a variety of ways, which are not necessarily determined by the internal organisation of the dictionary or the structure of the input. For example, material may be accessed and retrieved in alphabetical order, in reverse alphabetical order, by chronology, by definition keywords, by grammatical function, or by a wide variety of different configurations of information categories, irrespective of the way they have been organised as input to the database. Thus it is the user who can stipulate the limits of the information sought, and retrieve that information according to a designated reference scheme, avoiding redundancies. The emphasis is less on following a predetermined pathway through the dictionary structure, more on navigating relationships across and within entries, via a choice of, often invisible, programmed links.

The user perspective

One of the principal advances in lexicography in recent years has been the focus on the user perspective, that is the realisation that different users have different reasons for using a dictionary, and that the dictionary can, and should, respond to these. Whilst dictionaries have usually tried to satisfy the overall perceived needs of large classes of users, there has often been little attention to the specific needs of smaller groups or individuals, or to the fact that users differ in their needs depending on the immediate context of dictionary use. Users may not, for example, have adequate reference skills to follow the structure of a printed dictionary entry, and may need explicit assistance to locate and extract the information they seek. One very common reason for recourse to a dictionary

is for translation from one language to another, and this need has spawned an abundance of bilingual and multilingual dictionaries of all sorts and sizes, over many hundreds of years. A speaker of English and a speaker of French, for example, translating a non-specialist English text into French, might use a general English–French dictionary. It is only recently that there has emerged a general recognition of the fact that the needs of these users will be different, and that a simple 'English–French' compilation may not respond to both equally well. User-oriented research takes account of the profiles of dictionary users; the various contexts of dictionary use; the functions of the dictionary in its many situations of use; and the skills necessary for, and brought to bear on, dictionary use. There now exists a body of investigatory techniques, which are constantly being improved upon, and a considerable cumulation of findings of enquiries carried out in many different language communities around the world, which provide valuable information for the incorporation of a user perspective into dictionary conception and design.

The response to the potential needs of users has implications for the teaching of dictionary use, an area of education that was somehow taken for granted, and either neglected or, at best, skimpily treated, in the past. Specifically, more attention is now being paid to the abilities needed, and the behaviours associated with those abilities (or lack of those abilities), on the part of the dictionary user to locate the information being sought. The complex operations involved in the dictionary consultation process are being investigated and analysed, and there is a conscious attempt in many dictionaries to relate the conventions of the dictionary text (e.g. abbreviations, codes, labels) to these operations. One example is the increasing use of full-sentence definitions, pioneered by the COBUILD dictionaries, in learners' dictionaries. Nowadays we are also witnessing the growth and extension of explicit instruction in dictionary use, in the form of the inclusion of 'dictionary skills' in school syllabuses and 'the teaching of dictionary skills' in teacher-training syllabuses, all directly informed by the findings of research.

The computer provides the latest user-determined type of retrieval system, but even very early dictionaries in different cultures were compiled with specific purposes in mind. For example, one of the oldest dictionary traditions in China – where dictionaries have been known for over 3,000 years

– was that of examination preparation. The development of dictionaries of Chinese was closely tied to the civil service examination system. Indeed, most of the dictionaries before the establishment of the Republic in 1911 were compiled by members of the élite scholar–official class associated in one way or another with these examinations, which tested literary erudition and written composition through mastery of intricate rhyme patterns and a knowledge of Chinese characters. In India, on the other hand, dictionaries developed within an oral tradition, the earliest being cumulative synonymies composed in poetical format. The metrical structure of these dictionaries facilitated memorisation and oral recitation. The dictionaries were composed as aids to oral composition of poetry, and for the teaching and understanding of religious texts. The very different types of dictionary which developed within these two traditions – China and India – were a function of the different cultural milieux, and the different purposes for which they were required. But in both traditions, there was an authoritarian perspective. The dictionary was a resource of what was considered to be the 'best' or 'correct' language. This perspective has carried on to our own day, and there is a very deep-seated public attitude, shared among many language communities across the globe, that 'the dictionary' is supposed to represent some form of final authority in matters of lexical meaning and use. The academy dictionaries typically exert considerable influence – sometimes upheld by legal sanction – in protecting a language from what are perceived as unacceptable or corrupting pressures, for example, excessive borrowing from other languages. The acceptance of the authority of the dictionary has also often been brought to bear in litigation, where meanings and judicial interpretations of words have been determined or elucidated by reference to 'standard' dictionaries.

The dictionary and linguistic evidence

In 1961, the compilers of the third edition of *Webster's New International Dictionary of the English Language* adopted a new criterion by explicitly breaking with the authoritarian tradition. In its indications of pronunciations, in its definitions, and in its selection of words, *Webster's Third* abandoned any claim to be a lexical canon, and discarded all puristic tendencies (cf. Bolinger 1975:585). But in its shattering the image of the dictionary as a linguistic arbiter, this lexicographical *cause célèbre* engendered a controversy which lasted for several years. The public, even some literary editors, did not want a dictionary that recorded even careless (albeit generalised) pronunciations, or meanings felt to be 'incorrect'. It was not, in the view of some, the dictionary's place to describe, but to prescribe. However, the replacement in *Webster's Third* of a normative, attitudinal approach to dictionary-making by one based on objectively observed facts about language was in tune with the currents of linguistic thought of the time, and indeed within a tradition that had begun with Samuel Johnson's *Dictionary of the English Language* (1755). Johnson's initial aim had been to compile a definitive dictionary for English along the prescriptive model of the Académie française's national French dictionary. However, realising that change was inherent in language, and that 'fixing' English in this way was an unrealistic proposition, he sought to show sufficient grounds for his definitions by supplementing them with illustrative citations from 'the best writers'. Thus, he hoped to temper the process of what was at the time perceived as degeneration of the language, rather than attempt a stabilisation of an unrealisable 'ideal'. Johnson's appeal to usage rather than etymology in defining words was as innovative as it was controversial. His methodology of using citations to corroborate definitions, however, has provided the model for the dictionaries of our day. Nevertheless, Johnson was not entirely objective, especially in his selection of words to be defined, and he omitted those he considered would offend the sensibilities of the polite society of his day. In a similar way, conscious choices are sometimes made in our own time. In the context of the new South Africa, for example, a decision was made by the compilers of the *Woordeboek van die Afrikaanse Taal* to omit racial slurs, both as headwords and in illustrative citations.

Whilst the dictionary, therefore, can properly reflect change, it thereby also legitimises it. The ready availability of huge banks of electronic data have provided hitherto unobtainable evidence of language use, indicating subtle discriminations only suspected before. For example, many dictionaries of English have defined (and still define) *big* in terms of *large*, and *vice versa*. The evidence from concordances of occurrences of these adjectives in extensive modern text archives, however, demonstrates convincingly that although they do overlap in some contexts, they are differentiated systematically in many others, and that an important concomitant of these differentiations lies in their different collocational patterns, an area of usage that is now attracting greater attention of lexicographers than has been the case in the past.

The compilation of large-scale (not *big-scale*!) corpora can enable the recording and documentation of language change in progress. For example, the language of computing has given us backformations such as *input* and *output* as verbs. In the Hong Kong University of Science and Technology's (HKUST) 1,000,000-word corpus of English in Computer Science (James *et al.* 1994), verbal usage constitutes about five per cent of the total occurrences of these forms. However, the evidence is that there is variability in the formation of the past tenses (*input/output* or *inputted/outputted*?). Nevertheless, the derivational influence remains strong, and the weight is still towards *input/output* (the only forms accepted by, for example, the revised third edition of the *Collins Concise Dictionary*, which advertises itself as 'the authority on current English'). But the use of *input/output* as the past form can cause confusion, as the participular-adjectival usage of *input/output* can thus have two senses, proactive (e.g. *input data* = 'data to be input') and retroactive ('data which has been input'). This example demonstrates the uncertainty that can occur when a novel creation conflicts with the language system. New verbal formations in English characteristically attract the morphological increments of weak verbs (*-ed*); in the case of strong verb compounds, largely confined to 'special language' contexts, the resultant instability of competing forms can create linguistic insecurity. This can be mitigated by corpus data, which can thus be brought to bear on the process as well as the product of language change, and documented in dictionaries in a way that has hitherto been impossible.

Interestingly, whereas in the name of descriptive lexicography, *Webster's Third* reported variant pronunciations for words – even some considered 'unacceptable' by certain speakers – a similar liberality was not exercised with respect to spelling, and the *Third* remains, as does every other dictionary of English, as authoritarian as ever in this regard. This is a reflection of the mood of the English language communities: speakers of English tolerate wide variations in pronunciation, but variations in spelling are codified (*centre* and *center*, for example, are accepted in different contexts, largely determined by regional prove-

nance, but *accomodation* for *accommodation*, or *principle* in the sense of *principal*, are considered errors despite their widespread 'careless' use). A diversification in pronunciation is an indicator of coefficiency of individuals' identities; standardisation in spelling is what unites the language across the different communities of its speakers.

Dictionary compilation

How, then, is the dictionary compiled? Dictionary-making *per se* comprises those operations which contribute to the production of dictionaries. In addition to preliminary activities such as surveying the potential market, planning the dictionary, training and recruiting the staff etc., three principal stages in the dictionary-making process may be isolated: data gathering, editing and publishing.

Computerisation has motivated the creation of dictionary databases by publishers, to assist in dictionary compilation. These databases are of two kinds: the *language resource database* (or *citation database*) and the *entry database*. The former is used as the authority for the dictionary entries, and ideally consists of corpora, text archives, individual citations etc. from a very wide range of published and unpublished (e.g. spoken) sources. Creating such a database was once a very onerous task – the compilation of the citation files of the *Oxford English Dictionary*, through a reading programme which involved many people in all walks of life, took some 22 years – but nowadays computerisation and the rapid access to electronic texts have meant that very large resources, extensive in scope, can be established relatively quickly. The *British National Corpus*, for example, consists of some 100,000,000 words, ten per cent of which are transcribed from natural spoken language, and the *Bank of English*, which is used for the CO-BUILD dictionary series, comprises in excess of 320,000,000 words, and is continually being extended. Linguistic archives can also incorporate the findings of fieldwork, that is, the collection and documentation of information obtained by interviews, and, indeed, this form of data-gathering is essential in the compilation of dialect, slang and other special-purpose dictionaries.

The entry database includes the headwords, definitions and other information categories (e.g. pronunciation, syntactic functions, usage labels). This database also includes formatting codes, page layout instructions, cross-references and links across entries, which enable rapid updating of information, and easy extraction of specific entries or parts of entries from the database for, for example, the production of an abridged or compact edition of a larger dictionary.

The central stage in the dictionary-making process is the writing and editing of the entries in the entry database. Lexicographers may be assisted in this task by professional and technical consultants and groups of advisers (called *usage panels*) to whom they can turn for recommendations on lexical meaning and use, particularly in specialised domains. The editing is preceded by a pre-editing phase, when certain decisions as to the structure and format of the dictionary will have been taken, e.g. whether senses are to be listed chronologically, that is with the earliest known uses and senses given first, as in the *Oxford English Dictionary*, or according to frequency (usually based on evidence from a language resource archive), with the most frequently occurring modern senses given first, as in the *Collins COBUILD English Language Dictionary*. Editors can call upon the resources of large corpora, particularly via concordance programs, to validate their user judgements, both in the area of sense discrimination as well as in syntactic function and use (e.g. collocational features). For example, in the HKUST corpus of English in Computer Science, 299 of the 307 occurrences of *interrupt* are, perhaps surprisingly, nominal or adjectival ('. . . the interrupt arrives while the system is busy . . .', '. . . it may be necessary to turn off the interrupt feature of the printer . . .'). An editor would need to make a decision as to whether to include this use in a general dictionary, by comparing and contrasting the evidence with data from other sources. (Such formations, for example, as *interrupt enable*, *compile time*, *document view* and *instruction fetch* are still felt to be restricted to the domain of Computer Science, and as such do not feature in general dictionaries of English.)

The final stage in the dictionary-making process is the production, distribution, marketing and sale of the dictionary. Intense competition in the publishing industry, and the almost insatiable public demand for reference materials, have led to an explosion in the number of dictionaries and other reference works on the world market, and sometimes technical quality may give way to commercial appeal.

Coverage and quality

Claims to comprehensiveness of coverage, for example, are common in dictionary advertising materials. But 'comprehensiveness' itself is a relative term. The real extent of a dictionary's coverage is very difficult to determine, especially when claims of absolute numbers (cf. '70,000 words', '40,000 synonyms and antonyms', '85,000 explanatory pronunciations', '125,000 references', '16,000 encyclopedic entries') are cited, and when compilers take different attitudes towards the treatment of, for example, homonyms and polysemes, or hyphenated forms and derivatives: what occurs as a headword in one dictionary may be a run-on entry in another. Comparisons of coverage across dictionaries are often unmanageable. Moreover, the depth of penetration of the vocabulary of a language in any particular dictionary is a matter of subjective decision which may depend as much on commercial as professional interests.

General and specialised dictionaries abound: there are dictionaries for almost every conceivable lexical requirement, and it is probably impossible to compile – nor, perhaps would one ever need – a truly accurate, comprehensive descriptive dictionary of a language. Nevertheless, it is not uncommon to find in the preface of a dictionary the compiler's or editor's justification for the work. (We explain our own working methods in the next section below.) Often this takes the form of a less than modest claim that previous dictionaries in the field have, in some way, been 'deficient'. Rarely do the writers elaborate on the alleged inadequacies of their predecessors' works, but the reader is encouraged in the view that in the new compilation the defects of its antecedents are, in some measure, remedied. However, there are no internationally agreed standards as to what constitutes a good dictionary, and, as we have noted, many new types are emerging (cf. Crystal 1986). Nonetheless, there is a growing theoretical underpinning for the practice of dictionary criticism, which allows for the systematic analysis of the technical qualities of a dictionary rather than judgements on mere commercial attractiveness. For example, the appropriateness of the component structures of dictionaries can be analysed from the points of view of the *macrostructure* and *microstructure*. The former refers to the overall access format of the dictionary. Historical and socio-political circumstances have led to the widespread acceptance of alphabetisation as the archetypal dictionary access structure, although there are many other ways of ordering headwords (e.g. by theme or topic, by chronology, by frequency). The macrostructure is supplemented by outside matter such as the front matter (e.g. preface, user's guide), middle matter (e.g. panels, plates, illustrations) and back matter (lists of names, weights and measures, abbreviations etc.), the totality of which may be called the *megastructure*. The microstructure refers to the format of the entry, how information about the headword is provided and presented, and the appropriateness of the discourse structure of the entry for the benefit of the anticipated user.

Lexicographical research has been pioneered by the various Dictionary Research Centres which have been established in several academic institutions around the world, sometimes on individual initiative, sometimes through the good offices of interested publishers, sometimes in response to governmental demand. These Centres offer professional consultation services, engage in training, and co-ordinate and manage studies of, and investigations into, the many aspects of lexicographic theory and practice. We envisage a day when these Centres will form into a coherent pan-continental research association, contributing to the development of a 'world lexicography'.

Until comparatively recently, lexicographical endeavour was often the domain of the brilliant amateur, the self-deprecating dilettante with a love of words, an eye for detail and a passion for 'ordered profusion' (Finkenstaedt & Wolff 1973). Such a person was often schooled in one of the great classical traditions of education – occidental or oriental – and trained in literature, philosophy and rhetoric. Many of the best crafted and best respected dictionaries are eloquent testimonies to the virtuosity of the instinctive lexicographer. But the technological revolution, and the advances in descriptive linguistic and lexicographical techniques which this has afforded, no longer allow us to rely on intuitive handiwork of the 'harmless drudge'.

Over time, printers, and later publishers, evolved traditions of dictionary design and format, and the training of editorial staff came to be perceived as part of the publisher's task. Some publishing houses have directly employed and catechised teams of lexicographers, whose products have seen many editions, occasionally without even any acknowledgement. Conventional wisdom is still that good dictionaries can only be produced by teams of in-house lexicographers, sponsored by publishers, but who, like the copy-editor, often remain the anonymous back-room boys (or girls).

Dictionary compilers have to exercise judgement, and informed subjectivity and a feel for the language should allow educated guesses to be made as, for example, to the likely permanent or ephemeral status of current and contemporary forms. A similar procedure has had to be adopted for orthographical variants, where a primary form may have to be selected as a headword. Explicit preferences offer implicit information, and it is only a keen sensitivity and a responsiveness to the social, political and linguistic forces being exerted on a language that enable lexicographers to reconcile the institutional or symbiotic and the communicational aspects of a language in their definitions and classifications. Dictionary compilation is a cultural activity, and a sympathetic appreciation not only of the cultural environment but also of the impact a dictionary will have, as well as the information it seeks to impart, is a *sine qua non* in editorial qualification.

An increasing demand for recognition of the professionalism of the discipline of lexicography has stimulated vocational training within the current academic framework. More and more, the universities are responding to the needs of the marketplace by offering courses, generally at postgraduate level, in the precepts of lexicography. In Africa, Australasia, China, Europe and India, expert programmes are now available in the theory and practice of dictionary-making and dictionary use. An innovative feature of some of these courses is the provision for students to gain direct experience of the workplace by spending part of their study period on a 'placement', for example as an assistant in the editorial office of a dictionary publisher. Other courses involve international co-operation, through which students can prepare for their qualification through studying for different periods in different countries, thus widening their cultural and linguistic horizons. The orientations of the various training courses on offer around the world differ, but most, we predict, will involve some aspects of linguistics (including especially semantics, psycholinguistics, sociolinguistics and corpus linguistics), language in education, specific language study (especially vocabulary analysis), computer technology and social science research methods. Other aspects which may be covered include the history and development of lexicographic traditions, the principles of editing, and creative writing. The human element is not lost. Today's lexicographer still needs a good general education, an enquiring disposition, an appreciation of precision and objectivity, and a flair for language. The specialist training serves to capitalise on these attributes to produce an informed and accomplished professional who can command respect in today's competitive world.

Working methods used in this Dictionary

Given that there was little precedent for this work, we feel we ought to explain our methodology. After having obtained the publisher's agreement to our proposal, we conducted a structured user survey amongst academics, professional lexicographers, students and others, both by correspondence and personal contact. The responses informed our initial decisions concerning the content and layout of our entries and the principles of cross-referencing.

Our sources have included glossaries, textbooks and specialist works on lexicography (e.g. Zgusta 1971, Hartmann 1983, Landau 1984, Cluver 1989b, ISO 1990, Kabdebo 1992, McArthur 1992, Svensén 1993, Bergenholtz & Tarp 1995 and Prytherch 1995, all of which are cited in the Bibliography); conference proceedings of associations such as EURALEX and DSNA; journals (e.g. the *International Journal of Lexicography*); monographs and edited collections of studies; a vast number of dictionaries and other lexicographical works in a variety of languages; and two recent major reference publications in lexicography: the comprehensive three-volume *Wörterbücher/Dictionaries/Dictionnaires. An International Encyclopedia of Lexicography*, edited by F. J. Hausmann, O. Reichmann, H. E. Wiegand and L. Zgusta (Berlin, 1989–91) and J. M. de Sousa's *Diccionario de lexicografía práctica* (Barcelona, 1995). One further relevant work, the *Nordisk leksikografisk ordbok* edited by H. Bergenholtz, I. Cantell, R. Vatvedt Fjeld, D. Gundersen, J. Hilmar Jónsson and B. Svensén (Oslo, 1997), appeared after we had completed the bulk of our manuscript.

Our first list of entries was compiled by extracting topics from the major sources which we consulted, supplemented by suggestions from colleagues, and items which we felt, from our own experience, should be included. We also formulated certain principles for exclusion, omitting very rare or idiosyncratic terms (e.g. *glossem*, *lexicographal*), common terms with no particular lexicographical denotation (e.g. *appendix*, *page*), terms with no immediate direct relevance to the general theme, for example from descriptive linguistics (e.g. *aphesis*, *double-headed nominal group*) or printing (e.g. *bullet*, *font*), or names of languages and regionalisms. We wished to confine our headwords to nominal and adjectival forms, illustrating terminology relevant to contemporary aspects of the discipline of lexicography, and we decided therefore not to include such encyclopedic items as biographies of famous lexicographers, descriptions of well-known dictionaries or histories and traditions of lexicography in different cultures. We have, however, included the names of the principal professional bodies associated with lexicography, as well as perhaps lesser-known items such as prizes and medals awarded for lexicographical endeavour of distinction.

The list was gradually refined, through various iterations involving many deletions and additions, to eliminate repetitions and to incorporate cross-references. We hope thereby to have achieved a cohesion in presentation which will enhance the utility of the work.

We have provided brief definitions for each major entry, and cross-references where we have felt it appropriate to do so. Inevitably, we have taken a stand on some theoretically divergent terms (e.g. *lemma*), and on terms whose significations differ in the literature (e.g. *base, canonical form, entry, recursive definition*). The degree of standardisation that exists in the vocabulary of 'terminology' does not exist in other areas of lexicography. We have aimed for a judicious balance, representative of a consensus of opinion, at the same time attempting to inject a measure of coherence into what is still an unstable terminological area.

Entry style

We have endeavoured as far as possible to preserve a formulaic definition style, e.g. 'A complex of activities concerned with . . .', 'A word or phrase which . . .'. Entries are, in many cases, supplemented by bibliographical references (indicated by 📖) to works published in English, generally within the last two decades. We have restricted our bibliography to English-language publications, since we appreciate that a list of works in a multiplicity of languages would not be accessible to most readers. This is not in any way to denigrate the very significant scholarship that has been published in different languages around the world, from Afrikaans and Chinese to Norwegian and Tamil, some of which we were ourselves indeed fortunate to be able to consult in our own search for enlightenment, but we wished our references to be an immediately practical source of information for as wide a readership as possible. Many references to non-English-language works can be found in the bibliographies of the publications we have cited.

Some of the entries are complemented by examples of works (indicated by 📑), which serve to illustrate the application of the headword concept in lexicographical practice. No value judgement attaches to the selection of these publications: they have merely been selected as exemplars in each case. We have also added, in relevant contexts, cross-references to electronic data or to Internet websites (indicated by 💻).

We have tried to bring lexicography to life by showing connections, for example between dictionary 'design' and dictionary 'use', and by illustrating lexicographical theory in our own entries. A typical entry is structured in this way:

---

[1] abbreviation

[2] A shortened form of a word, phrase or term which represents its full form. [3] Abbreviations can be subdivided into 'clippings' ([4] *vet* for *veterinary surgeon*), 'contractions' (*don't* for *do not*), 'acronyms' (*EURALEX* for *European Association for Lexicography*), 'initialisms', 'acrophones' or 'alphabetisms' (*DRC* for *Dictionary Research Centre*, *VIP* for *very important person*) and 'blends' (*brunch* for *breakfast/lunch*). Reference works vary in their treatment of abbreviations. In general dictionaries, they may be given [5] HEADWORD status, or be covered in separate lists in the front or back matter.

Abbreviations are often used in dictionaries to indicate a word's grammatical role (e.g. *vt* for *transitive verb*) or morphological features (e.g. *m* or *masc* for *masculine*) or to label a particular usage (e.g. *obs* for *obsolete*). Annotated lists of the abbreviations used are normally given in the USER'S GUIDE or elsewhere.

[6] ⇨ CODE (2), EXPANSION, TEXT COMPRESSION.

[7] 📖 Landau 1984, Cannon 1990, ISO 1990, McArthur 1992, Svensén 1993.

[8] 📑 *Acronyms, Initialisms and Abbreviations Dictionary* (J. E. Towell), Detroit MI, 1989; *The Oxford Dictionary of Abbreviations*, Oxford, 1992.

[9] 💻 *WWW Acronym and Abbreviation Server*: www.ucc.ie/info/net/acronyms/index.html

[1] *Headword*
[2] *(Formulaic) definition*
[3] *Elaboration*
[4] *Examples*

[5] *In-text cross-reference to another headword in the Dictionary.*

[6] *Further cross-references to related notions, in alphabetical order.*
[7] *References to English-language publications by (first) author, in date order: full details are given in the Bibliography.*
[8] *Sample reference works in date order illustrating the lexicographical application of the headword concept.*
[9] *Reference to electronic data, e.g. an Internet site.*

A

abbreviation

A shortened form of a word, phrase or term which represents its full form. Abbreviations can be subdivided into 'clippings' (*vet* for *veterinary surgeon*), 'contractions' (*don't* for *do not*), 'acronyms' (*EURALEX* for *European Association for Lexicography*), 'initialisms', 'acrophones' or 'alphabetisms' (*DRC* for *Dictionary Research Centre*, *VIP* for *very important person*) and 'blends' (*brunch* for *breakfast/lunch*). Reference works vary in their treatment of abbreviations. In general dictionaries, they may be given HEAD-WORD status, or be covered in separate lists in the front or back matter.

Abbreviations are often used in dictionaries to indicate a word's grammatical role (e.g. *vt* for *transitive verb*) or morphological features (e.g. *m* or *masc* for *masculine*) or to label a particular usage (e.g. *obs* for *obsolete*). Annotated lists of the abbreviations used are normally given in the USER'S GUIDE or elsewhere.

⇨ CODE (2), EXPANSION, TEXT COMPRESSION.

📖 Landau 1984, Cannon 1990, ISO 1990, McArthur 1992, Svensén 1993.

📄 *Acronyms, Initialisms and Abbreviations Dictionary* (J. E. Towell), Detroit MI, 1989; *The Oxford Dictionary of Abbreviations*, Oxford, 1992.

💻 *WWW Acronym and Abbreviation Server*: www.ucc.ie/info/net/acronyms/index.html

ABC

The first three letters of the LATIN ALPHABET, often found in the titles of primers or introductory works on any subject, as a synonym of 'introductory dictionary'.

⇨ XYZ.

📄 *A.B.C. of English Usage* (H. A. Treble & G. H. Vallins), Oxford, 1936; *ABC of Plain Words* (E. Gowers), London, 1951.

ABC order

⇨ ALPHABETICAL ORDER.

abecedarian

An archaic term for one who engages in the study or design of ALPHABETS.

abecedary

An archaic general term for 'alphabet primer' or 'dictionary'.

abridged (dictionary)

A shortened version of a larger dictionary in a DICTIONARY FAMILY, which is made by omitting from the fuller (UNABRIDGED) version items such as older or less frequently used words or phrases, etymologies or examples.

⇨ DERIVATIVE DICTIONARY.

📖 Burnett 1988.

📄 *Shorter Slang Dictionary* (E. Partridge/rev. R. Fergusson), London & New York NY, 1993; *The New Shorter Oxford English Dictionary on Historical Principles* (L. Brown), Oxford, 1993.

absolute synonym

⇨ SYNONYMY (1).

absolute synonymy

⇨ SYNONYMY (1).

abstracting service

The comprehensive documentation of the published literature in a subject field by means of alphabetically or systematically arranged summaries at regular intervals, e.g. the *Linguistics Abstracts*, published in Oxford five times a year since 1985.

💻 *Linguistics and Language Behavior Abstracts* [annual], Norwood MA, 1993.

abusage
The use of a word or phrase deprecated as incorrect.
⇨ USAGE GUIDE.
▨ *Usage and Abusage* (E. Partridge), London, 1942.

abuse
1 With respect to levels of correctness, ⇨ ABUSAGE.
2 With respect to insults, ⇨ TERM OF ABUSE.

academic dictionary
⇨ SCHOLARLY DICTIONARY.

academic lexicography
An approach to LEXICOGRAPHY which is concerned with DICTIONARY RESEARCH and the bringing to bear of theory on practice.
⇨ DICTIONARY RESEARCH CENTRE, GENERAL LEXICOGRAPHY, THEORY OF LEXICOGRAPHY, TRAINING.
▨ Ilson 1986a.

Academy
An official body established to promote and maintain the 'best' uses of a language and to protect it from what are considered unacceptable and unwelcome influences. Academies typically exert control by sponsoring prescriptive GRAMMARS and ACADEMY DICTIONARIES, through which the rules of the language are authoritatively defined.
⇨ STANDARD (1).

Academy dictionary
A type of DICTIONARY created under the auspices or sponsorship of an ACADEMY. The first such dictionaries in Europe were the *Vocabolario degli Accademici della Crusca* (Venice, 1612), the *Dictionnaire de l'Académie française* (Paris, 1694) and the Spanish Academy's *Diccionario de la lengua castellana* or *Diccionario de autoridades* (Madrid, 1726–39). For English, such an Academy dictionary does not exist, although Samuel Johnson had started his *Dictionary of the English Language* (London, 1755) with the idea of 'fixing' the language.
⇨ AUTHORITY, NATIONAL DICTIONARY.

accent
1 Prominence in the pronunciation of a syllable (e.g. stress) achieved by increased loudness or duration, or by alteration of pitch.

2 Aspects of pronunciation which are characteristic either intralingually of a speaker's regional or social DIALECT, or interlingually of a speaker's first or dominant language.
3 A DIACRITIC.

acceptability
An aspect of USAGE by which members of a given speech community characterise a word or phrase as normal and authentic. The suitability of an expression to a particular situational context is sometimes referred to as APPROPRIATENESS, while suitability in a particular verbal context is called GRAMMATICALITY.
▨ Greenbaum 1988.

acceptability rating
The evaluation of a term within a technical field, on a scale from 'deprecated' to 'admitted' to 'preferred' to 'standardised'.
▨ ISO 1990.

acceptance
The sociolinguistic approval of a word or phrase by virtue of its inclusion in an authoritative reference work such as a USAGE GUIDE or an ACADEMY DICTIONARY. Those who do not approve of expressions which have not found their way into dictionaries can find themselves in a dilemma, because such items will not appear in descriptive dictionaries until espoused by general USAGE.
⇨ DESCRIPTIVE LEXICOGRAPHY.

access
The relative ease with which INFORMATION can be located in a REFERENCE WORK. In a general dictionary this may be the alphabetical order in which HEADWORDS appear; in a thesaurus it may be the arrangement of items in thematic groups; in a DATABASE or retrieval system it may be the route along which the computer leads the user.
⇨ LEMMA, MACROSTRUCTURE.

access alphabet
The organisation of a reference work, which allows the compiler and user to locate a particular information category under a LEMMA. This may not coincide entirely with the conventional sequence of the script used, and may include abbreviations, letters from other scripts, numbers and ALPHANUMERIC COMBINATIONS, or signs such as apostrophes, hyphens and obliques.
▨ Hausmann & Wiegand 1989.

access profile

The totality of devices that facilitate ACCESS in a particular reference work. In addition to the format, such as ALPHABETICAL ORDER in a general dictionary, this may include the TABLE OF CONTENTS and instructions for use (USER'S GUIDE) in the front matter, as well as special appendices and/or INDEXES in the back matter.

⇨   ORDERING DEVICE.

  Hausmann & Wiegand 1989.

access structure

Those component parts of the overall design of a REFERENCE WORK which allow the user to search for a particular item of information. The prototypical 'external' (or 'outer') access structure in the general dictionary is the ALPHABETICAL ORDER of headwords. Such dictionaries are called 'monoaccessible' if there is only one access in the form of the alphabetical WORD-LIST; in 'polyaccessible' dictionaries there are additional access structures, such as an INDEX. The prototypical 'internal' (or 'inner') access structure is the BASE STRUCTURE.

⇨   RADICAL, SEARCH PATH.

  Hausmann & Wiegand 1989.

ACL

Abbreviation for ASSOCIATION FOR COMPUTATIONAL LINGUISTICS.

acrolect

⇨   CREOLE.

acronym

⇨   ABBREVIATION.

acrophone

⇨   ABBREVIATION.

active dictionary

A type of DICTIONARY designed to help with encoding tasks, such as the production of a text. In monolingual lexicography, the typical example of an active dictionary is the THESAURUS, whose main function is to provide vocabulary choice for the writer; in bilingual lexicography the function addressed is translation into the foreign language. The PASSIVE DICTIONARY, by contrast, is aimed primarily at decoding tasks such as reading.

⇨   ACTIVE VOCABULARY.

  Svensén 1993, Rundell & Ham 1994, Berkov 1996.

Gradus ad Parnassum, Paris, 1666; *Longman Language Activator* (M. Rundell), Harlow, 1993.

active vocabulary

The VOCABULARY available to a native speaker or a learner for encoding purposes such as speaking, writing, or translating from the native into a foreign language. Estimates suggest that this is considerably smaller than the PASSIVE VOCABULARY associated with decoding tasks such as listening and reading, hence the need for ACTIVE DICTIONARIES.

  Laufer & Nation 1995.

addendum

⇨   SUPPLEMENT.

address

1   The component part of the entry (usually the HEADWORD) to which various INFORMATION CATEGORIES refer. The address signals the TOPIC which is elaborated on (in the form of a COMMENT) by the information provided on it, e.g. spelling, pronunciation, grammar, definition, etymology. Because of the high degree of text compression inside dictionary entries it is not always made explicit which item is actually addressed. Thus, in the extract illustrated in the panel 'Microstructure' on page 94, the etymological information given on the verb *energize* is addressed to both of its senses, but the usage label ('arch.') applies only to its second sense, namely the one marked 'v.i.'.

  Hausmann & Wiegand 1989.

2   ⇨   FORM OF ADDRESS.

adjective

A PART OF SPEECH which serves primarily to specify an attribute or quality of a noun or a noun phrase.

⇨   GRAMMATICAL INFORMATION.

Cassell Dictionary of Appropriate Adjectives (E. H. Mikhail), London, 1994.

admitted term

A technical TERM accepted by the practitioners in a subject field as a suitable synonym for a PREFERRED TERM, e.g. *technical dictionary* for *terminological dictionary*.

⇨   ACCEPTABILITY RATING.

  ISO 1990.

adverb
A PART OF SPEECH which serves primarily to modify a verb, adjective or other adverb.
⇨ GRAMMATICAL INFORMATION.

advisory panel
A group of consultants whose opinions are sought in the compilation of a REFERENCE WORK.
⇨ USAGE PANEL.

affective meaning
⇨ CONNOTATION.

affix
A bound morphological element which may be added to a base or stem of a word. An affix added to the beginning of a base or stem is a 'prefix'; one added to the end of a base or stem is a 'suffix'; and one added within a base or stem is an 'infix'. An affix used to form new words is a derivational affix; an inflectional affix, by contrast, is used to indicate different grammatical forms of the same word. Dictionaries do not always recognise affixes, particularly inflectional affixes, as HEADWORDS, even in languages whose syntactic relationships are expressed primarily by AFFIXATION.
⇨ CANONICAL FORM.
📖 ISO 1990, Svensén 1993.

affixation
The process of morphological modification in which AFFIXES are added to a base or stem, either for deriving new words or for forming inflections, or both.
⇨ MORPHOLOGY.
📖 Bwenge 1989.

African Association for Lexicography
A professional society, founded at the University of Stellenbosch in 1995. It holds annual conferences and sponsors the journal *LEXIKOS*.

AFRILEX
Acronym for AFRICAN ASSOCIATION FOR LEXICOGRAPHY.

agnonym
A word or phrase in the native or second/foreign language which is not in a given speaker's ACTIVE VOCABULARY or PASSIVE VOCABULARY, but may be found in a specialised reference work such as a dictionary of NEOLOGISMS.
📖 Morkovkina 1996.

AILA
Acronym for ASSOCIATION INTERNATIONALE DE LINGUISTIQUE APPLIQUÉE.

alignment of texts
⇨ PARALLEL TEXTS.

aljamiado principle
⇨ DIGRAPHIA.

allusion
A literary or other cultural reference, typically in the form of an intertextual QUOTATION. It is often oblique and not usually assigned to its source.
📖 Makkai 1980.
📗 *Brewer's Dictionary of Phrase and Fable* (E. C. Brewer/rev. A. Room), London, 1870/1995; *Allusions. Cultural, Literary, Biblical, and Historical: A Thematic Dictionary* (L. Urdang), Detroit MI, 1982.

almanac(k)
A type of REFERENCE WORK published regularly, usually once a year, which contains historical, geographical, technical or other encyclopedic information arranged in chronological or thematic format.
⇨ CALENDAR.
📗 *Whitaker's Almanack 1997* (H. Marsden), London, 1996.

alphabet
An inventory of graphic symbols (LETTERS) used to represent speech. Ideally, each letter stands for one speech sound, though in practice there is rarely a total one-to-one correspondence.
⇨ ALPHABETICAL ORDER, WRITING.
📖 Healey 1990, McArthur 1992.
📗 *Handbook of Scripts and Alphabets* (G. L. Campbell), London, 1996.

alphabetarian
An archaic term for one who engages in the study or design of ALPHABETS.

alphabetic(al) arrangement
⇨ ALPHABETICAL ORDER.

alphabetic(al) fragmentation
The separation of semantically linked words or phrases when they are listed in alphabetically ordered reference works. An example would be the scattering of various 'furniture' lexemes such as *chair*, *table* and *sofa* in different sections of the dictionary WORD-LIST. To counteract this,

lexicographers treat such items conceptually and provide links, either by cross-references between them or by using alternative formats, such as the thematically arranged THESAURUS, or by using lists and/or displays.
📖 Jackson 1988, Béjoint 1994.

alphabetic(al) index
⇨ INDEX.

alphabetic(al) order
The conventional sequence of the letters of an ALPHABET. In languages whose script is based on the LATIN ALPHABET, arrangement of entries by the orthographic form of the HEADWORDS allows compilers and users of reference works to locate INFORMATION.
📖 ISO 1990, McArthur 1992.

alphabetic(al) organisation
The principled use of ALPHABETICAL ORDER for the placing and retrieval of information in REFERENCE WORKS. Even among those languages in which the LATIN ALPHABET is used to represent speech, there is considerable variation in the number and sequencing of LETTERS (e.g. with or without DIACRITICS) and in the methods employed to design the MACROSTRUCTURE of the dictionary. The arrangement of headwords and entries can vary according to whether word boundaries are recognised or ignored (WORD-BY-WORD ALPHABETISATION versus LETTER-BY-LETTER ALPHABETISATION), whether the direction of the script is followed or reversed ('ab initio' versus 'a tergo'), and whether sub-entries are allocated to single or separate text blocks ('clustering' versus 'listing').

In most alphabetic systems, it took centuries for dictionary makers to develop alphabetisation from ordering by the first letter only, to second-letter ordering, third-letter ordering and beyond.
⇨ ORGANISATION.
📖 Osselton 1989a, Zgusta 1989b, Spears 1990, Svensén 1993, van der Meer 1996a.

alphabetic(al) sequence
⇨ ALPHABETICAL ORDER.

alphabetic(al) writing
A WRITING SYSTEM based on the representation of speech sounds (PHONEMES) by letters (GRAPHEMES). The prototype is the LATIN ALPHABET used for most European and many non-European languages.

📑 *Handbook of Scripts and Alphabets* (G. L. Campbell), London, 1996.

alphabetisation
1 With reference to the ordering principle, ⇨ ALPHABETICAL ORGANISATION.
2 With reference to script transfer, ⇨ TRANSCRIPTION.

alphabetism
⇨ ABBREVIATION.

alphabetist
One who engages in the study or design of ALPHABETS.

alphanumeric combination
A word or phrase consisting of numerals and letters, e.g. *3-D*, *4-ply*. In reference works, such items may be arranged sequentially according to the spelling of the numerals concerned (thus *3-D* would be alphabetised where it would be expected to appear if written as *three-D*) or they may be placed initially under each letter (thus *3-D* would occur at the beginning of the entries under the letter *T*).

alternative lexicography
A collective term for those activities concerned with the compilation of reference works outside the framework of conventional LEXICOGRAPHY. This includes dictionaries made by amateurs without reference to professional principles, such as informal in-house glossaries, computer-generated lists of specialised words or phrases offered on the INTERNET, or even literary texts masquerading under the title DICTIONARY.
⇨ ANTIDICTIONARY, REFERENCE PROFESSIONAL.
📑 *Index. The Catalogue Shop* (Littlewoods Mail Order), 1997.
💻 *The on-line hacker Jargon File*, version 2.9.4, 1991.

ambiguity
A condition in which a word or phrase is capable of different interpretations because of insufficient context, or any instance of this, e.g. *We had granny for tea* (where *had* is ambiguous: 'had as a visitor' or 'had as a meal').
⇨ IDIOM, METAPHOR, SENSE DISCRIMINATION.

amelioration
⇨ SEMANTIC CHANGE.

American Library Association

A professional society, based in Chicago IL, founded in 1876 to represent LIBRARIANS. One of its eleven divisions is devoted to Reference and Adult Services.

⇨ DARTMOUTH MEDAL, LIBRARY ASSOCIATION.

🖥 Website: www.ala.org

American Society of Indexers

A professional society, based in Seattle WA, founded in 1968 to represent INDEXERS.

⇨ INDEX, SOCIETY OF INDEXERS.

🖥 Website: www.well.com/user/asi

anagogical meaning

A secondary SENSE or CONNOTATION of a word or phrase, which is mystical or spiritual.

📖 James 1991.

anagogy

The process of interpretation of the mystical or hidden spiritual senses or connotations of words.

anagram

A word or phrase formed by rearranging the letters of another word or phrase, e.g. *emits – times*. 'Palindromes' are types of anagrams which can be read in both directions, e.g. *Able was I ere I saw Elba*. Anagrams feature commonly in crossword puzzles, for which specialised dictionaries of anagrams have been compiled.

⇨ WORD GAME.

📖 Towner 1995.

📑 *Bloomsbury Anagram Finder* (J. Daintith), London, 1993.

analects

A type of REFERENCE WORK containing sayings by famous people.

📑 *The Analects of Confucius*, New York NY, 1997.

analogical dictionary

A type of DICTIONARY which contains information such as collocations, synonyms or confusable words.

📑 *Cassell Guide to Related Words* (S. I. Hayakawa/rev. E. Ehrlich), London, 1971/94.

analytical definition

The classical DEFINITION formula which is used to explain the meaning of a word or phrase by reference to a generic term (GENUS PROXIMUM) and at least one distinguishing feature (DIFFERENTIA SPECIFICA).

anecdote

A short, entertaining account of an event.

📑 *Thesaurus of Anecdotes* (E. Fuller), New York NY, 1942; *British Literary Anecdotes* (R. Hendrickson), New York NY, 1990.

anisomorphism

A mismatch between a pair of languages due to their semantic, grammatical and cultural differences. This leads to a relative absence of direct, one-to-one translation EQUIVALENTS.

⇨ CONTRASTIVE LINGUISTICS, TRANSLATION.

📖 Sundström 1992.

annotation

Comments on a portion of a text, e.g. critical remarks on items listed in a BIBLIOGRAPHY.

⇨ REFERENCE (4).

antedating

Evidence of the occurrence of a word or phrase prior to the date given in a HISTORICAL DICTIONARY.

📖 Schäfer 1980.

anthroponym

⇨ PERSONAL NAME.

antidictionary

A REFERENCE WORK which deviates from the expected norm in content (humour), style (satire) or format (non-alphabetic arrangement). The *Anticrusca* by Paolo Beni (1612) was a critical analysis of the Italian Academy dictionary, the *Vocabolario degli Accademici della Crusca* (Venice, 1612); R. F. Gillet's *Le Porte-feuille* (Madrid, 1762) was notorious for its negative evaluation of dictionaries and their compilers, and Ambrose Bierce's *Devil's Dictionary* (1906) for its sarcastic definitions of controversial issues. Because of its non-alphabetic arrangement, it is possible to refer to a thematic THESAURUS as an antidictionary.

⇨ REVERSE DICTIONARY.

📖 Béjoint 1994.

antiquating dictionary

⇨ ARCHAISING DICTIONARY.

antonym

A member of a pair of words or phrases characterised by ANTONYMY.

📑 *The Penguin Dictionary of English Synonyms and Antonyms* (R. Fergusson), London, 1992.

antonymy

The SENSE RELATION obtaining between words or phrases of opposite meaning. Antonymy can be 'complementary', with one member of a pair implying the negation of the other: *alive* = not *dead*; 'conversive' or 'reciprocal', with the meaning of one member of a pair presupposing that of the other: *buy* / *sell*; or 'graded' ('gradable'), with two concepts being compared: *clean* versus *dirty*, *bigger/better than*. . . . The term can also be used to refer to the phenomenon of one word having two opposite senses, e.g. *sanction* 'permit' or 'penalise'.

⇨ CONVERSENESS, INCOMPATIBILITY, OPPOSITION, SYNONYMY (1).

📖 Jackson 1988.

apostil

A note, comment or other annotation made in the margin of a book or manuscript.

⇨ GLOSS.

applied linguistics

An approach to LANGUAGE problems which seeks practical solutions in an interdisciplinary setting. The field of LANGUAGE TEACHING, for example, has profited from applied linguistic analysis of its basic premises (which skills are to be learned and how they are best learned) and practices (which pedagogical approaches and methods work the best in different contexts). Applied linguists have also been instrumental in utilising theoretical and descriptive work, e.g. from phonetics, grammar, semantics and text linguistics, in addressing specific issues of language acquisition, language planning, speech therapy, translation etc.

There is some debate as to whether LEXICO‒GRAPHY should be considered an applied linguistic discipline; certainly, a range of notions from LINGUISTICS are relevant to practical DICTIONARY-MAKING, such as semantics in definition writing, grammar in part-of-speech specification, and discourse analysis in the layout of the dictionary text.

⇨ ASSOCIATION INTERNATIONALE DE LINGUISTIQUE APPLIQUÉE, COMPUTATIONAL LINGUISTICS, LANGUAGE ARTS, LANGUAGE ENGINEERING, PEDAGOGICAL LEXICOGRAPHY.

📖 Biber *et al.* 1994, Hartmann 1996a, Mills 1996.

📑 *Longman Dictionary of Language Teaching and Applied Linguistics* [2nd edition] (J. C. Richards *et al.*), Harlow, 1992.

🖥 *Applied Linguistics* (journal) website: www.oup.co.uk./applij/

appropriacy

⇨ APPROPRIATENESS.

appropriateness

An aspect of USAGE which stresses the communicative suitability of a word or phrase in a given context. Like ACCEPTABILITY and GRAMMATICALITY, appropriateness is often the subject of prescriptive reference works such as USAGE GUIDES.

⇨ CORRECTNESS.

aptronym

A name derived from a person's characteristics (e.g. *Redhead*) or occupation (e.g. *Baker*).

⇨ ONOMASTIC INFORMATION.

archaic

A USAGE LABEL indicating that a word or phrase is felt to be characteristic of an earlier period rather than part of the contemporary modern language.

⇨ DIACHRONIC INFORMATION.

archaising dictionary

A dictionary which gives preference in its selection and treatment to those words and phrases whose use is associated with earlier periods of the language, e.g. in the works of classical authors.

⇨ MODERNISING DICTIONARY.

📖 Zgusta 1989a.

archaism

A word or phrase (or one of its senses) which is no longer in current use except in fixed contexts, such as legal documents, nursery rhymes, poetry or prayers, or for humorous effect. Archaisms are often marked by a USAGE LABEL, and included in general or specialised dictionaries.

📑 *The Archaicon. A Collection of Unusual, Archaic English* (J. E. Barlough), Metuchen NJ, 1974.

archilexeme

A word or phrase which covers the meaning of all the members in a SEMANTIC FIELD, e.g. *cook* which can act as a substitute for all 'cooking' verbs.

archive

1   An assembly of dictionaries, either in a REFERENCE DEPARTMENT within a library or as a specialised COLLECTION, such as the Cordell Collection at Indiana State University.

Gates 1994.

Catalog of Dictionaries, Word Books, and Philological Texts, 1440–1900 (D. E. Vancil), Westport CT, 1993.

2 An unstructured collection of texts.
⇨ CORPUS, DATA ARCHIVE.

archivist
One who engages in the administration of an ARCHIVE.

argot
A SPECIAL-PURPOSE LANGUAGE used by certain groups of speakers to indicate membership of the group and to disguise the meanings of words and phrases to outsiders. The vocabulary of an argot, or 'cant', may include novel terms, or ordinary words of a language in novel senses, and its use is often associated with such sub-cultures as criminal groups or secret societies.
⇨ SLANG.

Spears 1987, 1989.

A Dictionary of the Underworld. British and American (E. Partridge), London, 1949; *Slang and Euphemism* (R. A. Spears), Middle Village NY, 1981.

arrangement
A cover term for the various ways in which the WORD-LIST can be ordered in a reference work, e.g. ALPHABETICAL ORGANISATION, CHRONOLOGICAL ORDER, CLASSIFIED ORDER, RHYME, SYSTEMATIC ORDER, THEMATIC ORDER. A 'mixed' arrangement is one in which two or more of these are combined (HYBRID).
⇨ ORGANISATION.

Zgusta 1989b, ISO 1990.

article
1 The basic REFERENCE UNIT in an encyclopedia or encyclopedic dictionary; in a dictionary, this is more often called ENTRY.
⇨ MICROSTRUCTURE.
2 In grammar, a function word, associated in English with the NOUN, which identifies a phrase as 'definite' (*the*) or 'indefinite' (*a, an*).
⇨ GRAMMATICAL INFORMATION.

Collins COBUILD English Guides 3: Articles (R. Berry), London, 1993.

artificial intelligence
An academic field concerned with the study of computers and their use in understanding and simulating processes of human knowledge and communication. In particular, SPEECH RECOGNITION, semantic DISAMBIGUATION and text CORPUS technology are of relevance to lexicography.
⇨ EXPERT SYSTEM, NATURAL LANGUAGE PROCESSING.

Butler 1990, Winston 1993.

The Artificial Intelligence Dictionary (E. Thro), London, 1990.

artificial language
The collective term for a number of systems developed for international communication or for a specific intellectual or scientific purpose. Examples are planned AUXILIARY LANGUAGES (such as Esperanto), computer programming languages, philosophical TAXONOMIES, SHORTHAND, BRAILLE and SIGN LANGUAGE, each with a range of published dictionaries.

An Esperanto–English–Chinese Dictionary (Z. Z. Wang), Qingdao, 1992.

artwork
⇨ GRAPHICS.

ASIALEX
Acronym for ASIAN ASSOCIATION FOR LEXICOGRAPHY.

Asian Association for Lexicography
A professional society, founded at the Hong Kong University of Science and Technology in 1997.
Website: www.anu.edu.au/linguistics/alex/asialex.html

assimilated word
A BORROWING which has been integrated into the native word-stock of a language, e.g. *coffee*, *café*, *Kaffee*, *koffie* etc. < Arabic /qahveh/ via Turkish.
⇨ LOAN-WORD.

Association for Computational Linguistics
A professional society, founded in 1962, for natural language processing and computing. It publishes a journal, *Computational Linguistics*, holds regular conferences, and has a special-interest group for lexical resources (SIGLEX).
SIGLEX website: www.cs.columbia.edu/~radev/newacl/information.html

Association internationale de linguistique appliquée
A professional society, founded in 1964, to represent APPLIED LINGUISTICS world-wide.

LEXICOGRAPHY and LEXICOLOGY form a section in the programme of its triennial international congresses.
💻 Website: ezinfo.ucs.indiana.edu/~emmerson

associations
Professional societies representing the interests of lexicographers and other REFERENCE PROFESSIONALS.

Applied linguists:
⇨ ASSOCIATION INTERNATIONALE DE LINGUISTIQUE APPLIQUÉE.
Archivists:
⇨ SOCIETY OF AMERICAN ARCHIVISTS, SOCIETY OF ARCHIVISTS.
Authors:
⇨ SOCIETY OF AUTHORS.
Computational linguists:
⇨ ASSOCIATION FOR COMPUTATIONAL LINGUISTICS.
Documentalists:
⇨ FÉDÉRATION INTERNATIONALE D'INFORMATION ET DE DOCUMENTATION.
Indexers:
⇨ AMERICAN SOCIETY OF INDEXERS, SOCIETY OF INDEXERS.
Lexicographers:
⇨ AFRICAN ASSOCIATION FOR LEXICOGRAPHY, ASIAN ASSOCIATION FOR LEXICOGRAPHY, AUSTRALASIAN ASSOCIATION FOR LEXICOGRAPHY, DICTIONARY SOCIETY OF NORTH AMERICA, EUROPEAN ASSOCIATION FOR LEXICOGRAPHY, LEXICOGRAPHICAL SOCIETY OF CHINA, LEXICOGRAPHICAL SOCIETY OF INDIA, NORDISK FORENING FOR LEKSIKOGRAFI.
Librarians:
⇨ AMERICAN LIBRARY ASSOCIATION, LIBRARY ASSOCIATION.
Onomasticians:
⇨ INTERNATIONAL COUNCIL OF ONOMASTIC SCIENCES.
Terminologists:
⇨ EUROPEAN ASSOCIATION FOR TERMINOLOGY.

associative meaning
⇨ CONNOTATION.

a tergo dictionary
⇨ REVERSE-ORDER DICTIONARY.

atlas
A type of REFERENCE WORK which provides geographical and other information in the form of systematically arranged MAPS, tables and text, often in combination with indexes of place names and/or the phenomena illustrated.
⇨ CULTURAL ATLAS, GAZETTEER, HYBRID, LINGUISTIC ATLAS.
📖 Chayen 1989.
📄 *Atlas sive cosmographicae meditationes de fabrica mundi* (G. Mercator), 1595; *The Times Atlas of the World*, New York NY & London, 1992.
💻 *The Times Electronic World Map and Database* [CD-ROM], Cheltenham, 1995.

attestation
⇨ AUTHENTICATION.

attitudinal information
⇨ DIAEVALUATIVE INFORMATION.

Australasian Association for Lexicography
A professional society, founded at Macquarie University in 1990. It publishes a newsletter and holds biennial meetings.
💻 Website: www.anu.edu.au/linguistics/alex

AUSTRALEX
Acronym for AUSTRALASIAN ASSOCIATION FOR LEXICOGRAPHY.

authentication
The collective term for the various means used by lexicographers to verify and document the words and phrases treated in the dictionary. These range from the careful selection of the WORD-LIST from representative sources (e.g. a text CORPUS) to the inclusion and labelling of quoted EXAMPLES, felt to be particularly important in HISTORICAL DICTIONARIES. The more authentic the EVIDENCE, the greater the AUTHORITY of the reference work.
⇨ ANTEDATING, CITATION.
📖 Gouws 1987, Osselton 1996.

author
1 One who engages in the COMPILATION of a reference work. The terminology of REFERENCE PROFESSIONALS is far from agreed, and LEXICOGRAPHERS and TERMINOLOGISTS, for example, do not always have their full AUTHORSHIP rights acknowledged.
2 One who engages in the composition of a literary work or other text and can be the subject of an AUTHOR'S DICTIONARY or DICTIONARY OF AUTHORS.
⇨ AUTHORS AND DICTIONARIES.

author dictionary

1 A dictionary of a single author, ⇨ AUTHOR'S DICTIONARY.
2 A dictionary of several authors, ⇨ DICTIONARY OF AUTHORS.

authority

The respect accorded to the dictionary (and other REFERENCE WORKS) by its users as an arbiter of linguistic STANDARDS. Public appreciation of such dictionaries as 'the Oxford', 'the Webster' or 'the Duden' is based on their role as repositories and transmitters of INFORMATION, linguistic as well as encyclopedic, especially by providing DEFINITIONS of 'hard' words of the language. This undifferentiated positive IMAGE of the dictionary as a linguistic authority often does not allow for the enormous variety of available reference works, from the GENERAL DICTIONARY to the more specialised USAGE GUIDES. Nor does the ordinary dictionary user recognise that authority must be earned, through the principled selection of source material (AUTHENTICATION), the sifting of EVIDENCE and the presentation of the material in formats appropriate to the REFERENCE NEEDS of users.
⇨ CITATION, CRITICISM.
📖 Creswell 1975, Algeo 1989b, Wadsworth 1989, Milroy & Milroy 1991, Willinsky 1994.

author lexicography

A complex of activities concerned with the design, compilation, use and evaluation of AUTHOR'S DICTIONARIES.

authors and dictionaries

Some literary authors are known for their fascination with dictionaries. The second edition of the *Oxford English Dictionary* [*OED*] (Oxford, 1989) cites several examples of archaic words last attested several centuries previously, which had been culled by James Joyce and W. H. Auden from the first edition of the *OED*.
⇨ AUTHOR LEXICOGRAPHY, COMPILER PERSPECTIVE, DICTIONARY OF AUTHORS, LEXICOGRAPHER, REFERENCE PROFESSIONAL.

author's concordance

⇨ AUTHOR'S DICTIONARY.

author's dictionary

A type of REFERENCE WORK which provides information on the vocabulary of a specific author.

The material is usually based on a text CORPUS of one, several or all of the works of the author, and often presented in alphabetical order, with examples or contexts (but not definitions) of the words cited. Author's dictionaries have a long tradition, from the glossarial CONCORDANCES of classical Greek and Roman writers through the philological INDEXES to the works of Dante, Chaucer and Shakespeare to the more contemporary, often computer-assisted, dictionaries of Goethe, Pushkin and others. Nevertheless, there is still no coherent framework for the principles of a general AUTHOR LEXICOGRAPHY.
📖 Karpova 1992.
📑 *Complete and Systematic Concordance to the Works of Shakespeare* (M. Spevack), Hildesheim, 1968–75.

authors' dictionary

1 A dictionary of several authors, ⇨ DICTIONARY OF AUTHORS.
2 A dictionary for authors, ⇨ STYLE MANUAL.

authorship

The acknowledged right of having produced a published document. This is not always fully granted to REFERENCE PROFESSIONALS such as lexicographers, particularly when they work in-house for a publisher in a team, e.g. on the basis of an inherited text such as a previous edition of a dictionary.
⇨ COPYRIGHT, CRIMINALITY.

author-specific dictionary

⇨ AUTHOR'S DICTIONARY.

author-specific lexicography

⇨ AUTHOR LEXICOGRAPHY.

automatic dictionary

⇨ ELECTRONIC DICTIONARY.

automatic disambiguation

DISAMBIGUATION by use of computational techniques.

automatic excerption

EXCERPTION by use of computational techniques.

automatic indexing

The production of an INDEX by use of computational techniques.

automatic lemmatisation

LEMMATISATION by use of computational techniques.

automatic lexicography

⇨   COMPUTATIONAL LEXICOGRAPHY.

automatic parsing

PARSING by use of computational techniques.

auxiliary language

1   An ARTIFICIAL LANGUAGE created for the purpose of international communication, such as Esperanto, Volapük, Ido and Interlingua. For Esperanto alone, a wide range of monolingual, bilingual and terminological dictionaries is available.

   📖   Large 1985, Moore 1994.

2   A natural language that serves as a LINGUA FRANCA, such as Swahili in eastern and southern Africa.

   ⇨   EXOGLOSSIC LANGUAGE.

auxiliary verb

A member of a closed set of VERBS used in many languages with a main verb to indicate grammatical categories such as voice and tense.

⇨   GRAMMATICAL INFORMATION.

A–Z

The first and last letters of the LATIN ALPHABET, used to mean the whole alphabet. The term is often found in the titles of primers or guides on any subject.

   📄   *An A to Z of British Life* (A. Room), Oxford, 1992.

B

back-derivation

⇨ BACK-FORMATION.

back-formation

A WORD-FORMATION process in which an element, usually an AFFIX, is removed from a word to create another, e.g. sorption from absorption/ adsorption.

back matter

Those component parts of a dictionary's MACRO-STRUCTURE which are located between the central WORD-LIST section and the end of the work. Examples of such 'subsidiaries' in general dictionaries may include: personal and place names; weights and measures; military ranks; chemical elements; alphabetic and numerical symbols; musical notation; quotations and proverbs; index.

⇨ OUTSIDE MATTER.

📖 Hausmann & Wiegand 1989, Svensén 1993.

Bank of English

A large CORPUS of English texts, initiated in 1991 at the University of Birmingham to support linguistic analysis and lexicographical projects, notably the COBUILD series. At over 320,000,000 words, this is the largest electronically accessible text archive of English, which has generated useful empirical EVIDENCE on grammar, semantics and other aspects of USAGE.

📖 Krishnamurthy 1996.

💻 Website: titania.cobuild.collins.co.uk/ boe_info.html

barbarism

An informal term for a word or phrase deprecated because it is felt to deviate from the NORM. Dictionaries and USAGE GUIDES mark such items on the grounds that they are 'ill-formed', e.g. because they mix word-formation elements borrowed from different languages, or are 'unnecessary', e.g. because they take the place of existing words perceived to be more suitable.

⇨ CORRECTNESS, FOREIGNISM, PURISM.

📄 *Ne dites pas … mais dites … barbarismes, solécismes, locutions vicieuses* (E. Le Gal), Paris, 1966.

base

A meaningful morphological element used to form words. Bases, which are common to the members of a WORD FAMILY, combine with one or more other elements, such as AFFIXES, to form STEMS, e.g. the base *hap-* as in *happy, unhappy, happiness, hapless* or *know* as in *unknown, knowable, knowledge, acknowledge, acknowledgement.*

⇨ MORPHEME, WORD.

📖 Denning & Leben 1995.

📄 *Collins COBUILD English Guides 2: Word Formation* (J. Bradbury), London & Glasgow, 1991.

base form

1 With reference to lemmatisation, ⇨ CANONICAL FORM.

2 With reference to morphology, ⇨ BASE.

base structure

In a hierarchical representation of the MICRO-STRUCTURE of dictionary entries, the branching of INFORMATION into formal details and semantic explanation. Both may be regarded as 'comments' on the 'topic' introduced by the HEADWORD, and depicted as a binary tree diagram, with further subdivisions: the 'formal comment' (as the left-core structure, consisting of information categories such as spelling, grammar and pronunciation) and the 'semantic comment' (as the right-core structure, consisting of information categories such as definition, etymology and usage).

⇨   Panel 'Microstructure' (page 94).

📖 Hausmann & Wiegand 1989.

base word

⇨   CANONICAL FORM.

basic form

⇨   CANONICAL FORM.

basic sense

The essential MEANING of a word or phrase selected for prominent treatment inside a dictionary entry. The issues of whether it is possible to isolate a basic sense and, if so, how to present it (e.g. in one or more DEFINITIONS) are still unsettled. Various approaches have been tried, by reference to such notions as ETYMOLOGY and FREQUENCY, but no satisfactory solution has yet emerged. Further complications arise when such semantic phenomena as HOMONYMY and POLYSEMY are considered. The collection of empirical evidence from CORPUS data, supplemented by native-speaker intuitions, may help to determine PROTOTYPE senses, but this has not yet been attempted on a sufficiently large scale to assist dictionary-makers.

⇨   SENSE.

📖 Swanepoel 1994.

basic vocabulary

Those words selected by FREQUENCY counts and similar means, which are considered essential for communication in a language and thus also for purposes of learning that language. This selection (variously called 'core' or 'elementary' or 'fundamental' or 'minimum' vocabulary) tends to focus on words which are statistically representative, stylistically neutral and semantically powerful while at the same time helping learners to cope in everyday communicative situations. The GENERAL DICTIONARY covers core words (as well as less frequent 'hard words'), and the LEARNER'S DICTIONARY concentrates on them; the FREQUENCY DICTIONARY provides statistical information.

⇨   CORE WORD, CORPUS, DEFINING VOCABULARY, THRESHOLD LEVEL.

📖 Pemberton & Tsang 1993.

▤   *The General Basic English Dictionary* (C. K. Ogden), London, 1940; *The Cambridge English Lexicon* (R. X. Hindmarsh), Cambridge, 1980; *Webster's Basic English Dictionary*, Springfield MA, 1990.

basic word

1 With reference to lemmatisation, ⇨ CANONICAL FORM.

2 With reference to vocabulary, ⇨ CORE WORD.

basilect

⇨   CREOLE.

bias-free vocabulary

Words or phrases which are considered appropriate as being non-discriminatory ('politically correct') in relation to such issues as age, gender, race, religion, politics or ecology.

⇨   CENSORSHIP, GENDERLECT, RACISM, SEXISM.

▤   *Dictionary of Bias-Free Usage* (R. Maggio), Boston MA, 1992.

bibliographical information

Details needed to describe and locate a published text, such as the author's name and the title, publisher and date of publication of the work.

⇨   BIBLIOGRAPHY.

bibliography

1 A list of publications, e.g. at the end of a book or dissertation. Some reference works, such as this *Dictionary of Lexicography*, have brief bibliographical details at the end of some entries and a comprehensive bibliography at the back. The systematic management of sources is one of the preconditions of reliable DICTIONARY-MAKING.

⇨   DICTIONARY CATALOGUE, REFERENCE (4).

📖   Congleton & Congleton 1984, Sheehy 1986, Wynar 1986, Brewer 1988, Zgusta 1988a, Ryan 1989, Cop 1990, Kabdebo 1992, Kister 1994.

2 A branch of LIBRARY SCIENCE concerned with the history, production, recording and classification of books and other DOCUMENTS.

⇨   WALFORD AWARD.

▤   *Harrod's Librarians' Glossary* (R. Prytherch), Aldershot, 1995.

bidirectional dictionary

A type of BILINGUAL DICTIONARY in which the translation equivalents can be accessed equally from each of the two languages. Thus a two-way English and French dictionary could be used by both English and French speakers because the equivalents can be consulted in either side or volume, provided that there is REVERSIBILITY. However, two-way directionality is difficult to achieve in practice, especially when the languages and cultures in question are very different and the purposes for which users look up words (reading or writing) diverge. Thus, the information a speaker of English needs for reading French texts (consulting a PASSIVE DICTIONARY) is not the same as that required by a French speaker writing an English text (using an ACTIVE DICTIONARY), and vice versa. The compiler's or publisher's interest in producing a single work for both target groups can therefore be in conflict with the requirements of a MONODIRECTIONAL DICTIONARY.

⇨ DIRECTIONALITY, FUNCTIONALITY.

📖 O'Neill & Palmer 1992.

bifunctional dictionary

A type of DICTIONARY designed to provide information which may be useful for two different purposes. An example would be a bilingual dictionary for both encoding ('active') and decoding ('passive') tasks such as translating into and out of the foreign language.

⇨ ACTIVE DICTIONARY, PASSIVE DICTIONARY.

bigraphism

⇨ DIGRAPHIA.

bilingual dictionary

A type of DICTIONARY which relates the vocabularies of two languages together by means of translation EQUIVALENTS, in contrast to the MONOLINGUAL DICTIONARY, in which explanations are provided in one language. This is at once its greatest advantage and disadvantage. By providing lexical equivalents, the bilingual dictionary helps language learners and translators to read or create texts in a foreign language. However, finding suitable lexical equivalents is a notoriously difficult task, especially in pairs of languages with different cultures. Nevertheless, in the lexicographic tradition of many languages, the production of bilingual dictionaries started early, e.g. for English and Latin before 1450, English and Welsh in 1547, English and French in 1570, even before the publication of the first monolingual English dictionary in 1604, but it took some time before they became truly BIDIRECTIONAL DICTIONARIES. Bilingual dictionaries can be distinguished as ACTIVE DICTIONARIES or PASSIVE DICTIONARIES, according to whether their purpose is to help with encoding (writing) or decoding (reading) activities. They also differ in their coverage of the vocabulary, and in the extent to which they concentrate on general words or specialised terms.

Computer technology is likely to improve existing bilingual formats and to develop new ones in future.

⇨ ELECTRONIC DICTIONARY, INTERLINGUAL DICTIONARY, LEARNER'S DICTIONARY, TERMINOLOGICAL DICTIONARY.

📖 Zgusta 1984, 1986a, Steiner 1986b, Heid 1992, Neubert 1992, Svensén 1993, Piotrowski 1994a, Atkins 1996.

📖 *Abecedarium Anglico–Latinum pro tyrunculis* (R. Huloet), London, 1552; *Collins Pons German–English English–German Dictionary* (P. Terrell *et al.*), Glasgow & Stuttgart, 1980; *Collins Robert French–English English–French Dictionary* (B. T. Atkins *et al.*), Glasgow & Paris, 1987.

bilingualisation

The adaptation of a monolingual REFERENCE WORK to a bilingual purpose by means of TRANSLATION.

bilingualised dictionary

A type of dictionary based on a MONOLINGUAL DICTIONARY whose entries have been translated in full or in part into another language. Such adaptations, motivated by the needs of foreign-language teachers and learners, have a fairly long history, but the most widely known are those based on EFL DICTIONARIES since A. S. Hornby's *Oxford Advanced Learner's Dictionary of Current English* (Oxford, 1948), bilingualised for speakers of Chinese and other languages, and the *Password* series published by Kernerman in Israel for a wide range of languages. Other genres such as pictorial dictionaries and thesauruses have also been bilingualised. The resulting HYBRIDS combine features of the monolingual dictionary (such as the definitions formulated in the target language) with those normally associated with the BILINGUAL DICTIONARY (translation equivalents of headwords and/or examples) for the benefit of learner–users, especially in decoding tasks such as reading.

⇨ BILINGUAL LEARNER'S DICTIONARY, INTERLINGUAL DICTIONARY, LEARNER'S DICTIONARY, SEMI-BILINGUAL DICTIONARY.

📖 Hartmann 1994, James 1994a, Laufer & Melamed 1994, Osselton 1995.

📖 *Le grand dictionaire françois & flamand* (P. Richelet/F. Halma), Amsterdam, 1717; *Orthographical Dictionary* (N. Bailey), London, 1727; *The Password English Dictionary for Speakers of French* (C. M. Schwartz & M. A. Seaton/M. Morin & G. J. Forgue), Tel Aviv, 1989; *Longman Lexicon of*

Contemporary English (English–Chinese edition) (T. McArthur/S. W. Chang), Hong Kong, 1992; *Longman Dictionary of Contemporary English (English–Chinese)* (D. Summers/Y. Zhu), Hong Kong, 1997.

bilingualism

⇨ NATIVE LANGUAGE.

bilingual learner's dictionary

A BILINGUAL DICTIONARY aimed at (foreign) language learners. The development of the monolingual LEARNER'S DICTIONARY, e.g. in the ENGLISH AS A FOREIGN LANGUAGE context, has contributed to a debate between lexicographers and language teachers as to which REFERENCE NEEDS should be met, and by what means. But a similar interaction has not yet affected the bilingual dictionary, which, in spite of its long tradition and continuing dominance of foreign-language learning, has remained basically conservative. However, the USER PERSPECTIVE has recently come under closer scrutiny, and new formats have been advocated for the benefit of learners, e.g. ACTIVE DICTIONARIES such as bilingual THESAURUSES to help with encoding tasks such as writing and translating into the foreign language.

⇨ BILINGUALISED DICTIONARY.

📖 Nakao 1989, Zöfgen 1991, Taylor & Poon 1994.

📕 *Merriam-Webster's Kenkyusha Japanese–English Learner's Dictionary* (S. Takebayashi), Springfield MA, 1993.

bilingual lexicography

A complex of activities concerned with the design, compilation, use and evaluation of BILINGUAL DICTIONARIES. Although there is a long tradition in the production of such reference works, and in some cultures they are considered the 'prototypical' dictionary, the field has lagged behind that of MONOLINGUAL LEXICOGRAPHY in terms of theory formation and professional standards, especially where the language pair in question does not include at least one major world language.

⇨ ANISOMORPHISM.

📖 Bartholomew & Schoenhals 1983, Kromann *et al.* 1991, Roberts 1992, Piotrowski 1994a.

binomial compound

In international scientific classifications, a two-part phrase consisting of a genus word (or GENERIC TERM) and a species word (or SPECIFIC TERM), e.g. the botanical name *Pinus sylvestris* 'Scotch fir'. In English technical taxonomies, the more specific part of the compound term usually precedes the genus word and is cited as the HEADWORD in dictionary entries, although the morphological composition and semantic connection between the two parts may not be obvious to the non-expert reader.

📖 Thomas, P. 1992.

binomial idiom

A two-part IRREVERSIBLE IDIOM, e.g. *bits and pieces*.

biographical dictionary

A type of REFERENCE WORK which provides descriptions of the lives and achievements of famous people. Some GENERAL DICTIONARIES may include such details on a limited scale, but there are more specialised genres, including the COMPANION and the WHO'S WHO, devoted to BIOGRAPHICAL INFORMATION.

⇨ DICTIONARY OF AUTHORS.

📖 McCalman 1996.

📕 *The Dictionary of National Biography* [Compact Edition] (L. Stephen *et al.*), Oxford, 1975; *The Cambridge Biographical Encyclopedia* (D. Crystal), Cambridge, 1994; *The Wordsworth Dictionary of Biography*, Ware, 1994; *The Kenkyusha Biographical Dictionary of English Linguistics and Philology*, Tokyo, 1995; *Lexicon Grammaticorum. Who's Who in the History of World Linguistics* (H. Stammerjohann), Tübingen, 1996.

biographical information

Details on the lives and achievements of famous people as included in BIOGRAPHICAL DICTIONARIES and ENCYCLOPEDIAS.

biographical lexicography

A complex of activities concerned with the design, compilation, use and evaluation of BIOGRAPHICAL DICTIONARIES.

bi-text

⇨ PARALLEL TEXTS.

blend

A word or phrase which is the result of a BLENDING process.

⇨ ABBREVIATION.

blending

A WORD-FORMATION process in which two words or phrases are fused, or 'telescoped', by overlapping their phonic and/or graphic shape, e.g. *breakfast + lunch > brunch*.

BNC
Abbreviation for BRITISH NATIONAL CORPUS.

bogey
⇨ GHOST WORD.

book of records
A type of REFERENCE WORK with information on ultimate achievements in all fields of activity.
▦ *The Guinness Book of Records* (N. McWhirter), London & New York NY, 1996.

borrowed concept
A CONCEPT transferred from one subject field to another, e.g. *affixation* from linguistics to lexicography and terminology.

borrowed term
A technical TERM transferred from one language or subject field to another, e.g. *thesaurus* from Latin to English, or from lexicography to terminology.

borrowed word
A word or phrase which is the result of BORROWING.
⇨ ASSIMILATED WORD.

borrowing
A WORD-FORMATION process in which a word or phrase is copied and transferred from one language (or subject field) to another. Borrowing is the natural result of bilingualism, translation and other forms of LANGUAGE CONTACT, which in its most intensive form leads to mixed vernaculars such as PIDGINS and CREOLES.
⇨ BORROWED CONCEPT, BORROWED TERM, DIAINTEGRATIVE INFORMATION, FOREIGNISM, INTERNATIONALISM, JARGON DICTIONARY, LOAN TRANSLATION, LOAN-WORD, NATIVE WORD, NEOLOGISM.
▦ Kirkness 1984, Poirier 1985, Jackson 1988, McArthur 1992.
▤ *A Lexicon of French Borrowings in the German Vocabulary (1575–1648)* (W. J. Jones), Berlin & New York NY, 1976.

bound morpheme
⇨ MORPHEME.

Braille
The collective term for a number of communication systems based on touch, devised originally by Louis Braille in 1824 to help the blind to read. Braille 'logograms' consist of cells with configurations of up to six raised dots to represent letters and words, and these are used to transliterate the text of ordinary print dictionaries and to produce new dictionaries of and in Braille.
▦ Caton 1991.
▤ *The Burns Braille Transcription Dictionary* (M. F. Burns), New York NY, 1991.

bridge dictionary
The collective term for a number of reference works intended to mediate between different cultures, or different ethnic groups in one country. In the widest sense this includes dictionaries which are the result of an adaptation by translation of an existing dictionary for speakers of different languages (BILINGUALISED DICTIONARY). More specifically the term has been used for dictionaries aimed at immigrants to help them adapt, e.g. the *Lexicon för Invandrare* (*Lexin*) series in Sweden, or for dictionaries which are based on lists of words produced in the study of 'indigenous languages' (FIELD DICTIONARY), e.g. aboriginal languages in Australia or Bantu languages in South Africa.
⇨ COMPARATIVE DICTIONARY, CULTURE-SPECIFIC VOCABULARY.
▦ Baker & Kaplan 1993.
▤ *Collins COBUILD Portuguese Bridge Bilingual Dictionary*, London, 1996.

British National Corpus
A CORPUS of English texts of some 100,000,000 words (90 per cent written, 10 per cent transcribed natural spoken language), based at Oxford.
▱ Website: info.ox.ac.uk/bnc/

broad transcription
⇨ TRANSCRIPTION.

browsing
Apparently aimless, but potentially pleasurable, casual reading of DICTIONARIES or other REFERENCE WORKS. Most computer TEXT-PROCESSING systems now include a so-called 'browsing function' for scrolling through texts.

buying guide
An annotated list of evaluated and recommended titles of reference works.

Dictionary Buying Guide. A Consumer Guide to General English-Language Wordbooks in Print (K. F. Kister), New York NY, 1977; *Which Dictionary? A Consumer's Guide* (B. Loughridge), London, 1990;

Kister's Best Encyclopedias: *A Comparative Guide to General and Specialized Encyclopedias* (K. F. Kister), Phoenix AZ, 1994.

C

caco-
A COMBINING FORM (< Greek 'bad') used to suggest 'incorrect' or 'inappropriate' usage, e.g. *caconym* 'a taxonomic name that is objectionable for sociolinguistic reasons'.

cacoepy
A pronunciation which is considered incorrect. Dictionaries are often consulted as arbiters in such cases.
⇨ CORRECTNESS, ORTHOEPY.

Cahiers de lexicologie
A periodical, published in France since 1959, devoted to topics in LEXICOLOGY and LEXICOGRAPHY.

calendar
A type of REFERENCE WORK which arranges the information provided in relation to the days of the year. In institutions of higher education, the term is often used for a CATALOGUE of academic programmes.
⇨ CHRONOLOGICAL ORDER.
▤ *Academic Calendar* (*The Hong Kong University of Science and Technology*), Hong Kong, 1997.

calepin(e)
A term used in the sixteenth and seventeenth centuries to mean a 'dictionary' or 'note-book', from the anglicised form of [Ambrosius] *Calepinus* (*c.* 1435–*c.* 1509), the author of *Ambrosii Calepini Bergomatis Dictionarium* (Reggio, 1502).

calque
⇨ LOAN TRANSLATION.

canonical form
The base form under which several variants of a word or phrase can be cited as a HEADWORD for a dictionary entry. Compilers and users of dictionaries follow standard conventions about which affixes may have to be removed from a word stem to determine the form under which the word can be cited or looked up. To take an English example, the word *arm(s)*, which occurs in a number of variants such as *arm*, *arms*, *arming* and *armed*, needs to be shorn of its inflectional endings before it can be established as a headword: *arm* (noun) 'body part' or *arm* (verb) 'to provide with weapons'. Dictionaries differ in their treatment of *arms* (pl. noun) 'weapons', regarding it either as a sub-sense of *arm* (noun) or giving it separate headword status.

In morphologically complex languages, the determination of the canonical form has to take account of such phenomena as 'mutation' (e.g. syntactically conditioned word-initial or word-medial variation) and 'sandhi' (phonologically conditioned orthographic variation).
⇨ LEMMATISATION.
▢ Landau 1984, Särkkä 1984, ISO 1990.

cant
⇨ ARGOT.

catachresis
The improper use of a word or phrase, particularly through inaccurate or inappropriate denotation. Dictionaries are often consulted as arbiters in cases of such alleged misuse.
⇨ DESIGNATION.

catalogue
A type of REFERENCE WORK giving, in alphabetic or thematic order, a set of items such as lists of objects with prices or bibliographical references in a library.
⇨ BIBLIOGRAPHY, DIRECTORY.
▤ *Stanley Gibbons Simplified Catalogue. Stamps of the World*, London & Ringwood, 1995.

catalogue raisonné

An annotated list of artistic creations, often associated with exhibitions or museum collections.

▤ *Édouard Manet, The Graphic Work: a Catalogue Raisonné* (J. C. Harris/rev. J. M. Smith), San Francisco CA, 1990.

catch-phrase

A memorable expression, especially one used by a well-known person or on the radio or television, e.g. *I'm only here for the beer!* Catch-phrases often become CLICHÉS or quickly go out of fashion.

▤ *Dictionary of Catch-Phrases* (E. Partridge/rev. P. Beale), London, 1977/91.

catch-word

1 In colloquial use, a CATCH-PHRASE.
2 In dictionary layout, a GUIDEWORD.
3 In library indexing, a KEYWORD.

category

1 ⇨ INFORMATION CATEGORY.
2 In the classification of the CONCEPTS of a subject field or of the DOCUMENTS in a library system, a class or facet which allows the grouping and subdivision of items, e.g. 'topic' or 'country of origin'.

CD-ROM

Acronym for 'compact disc read-only memory', a high-capacity medium for storing and retrieving both acoustic and graphic (digital) information. The technology has been applied to the production of reference works, such as large-scale dictionaries (the whole of the second edition of the twenty-volume *Oxford English Dictionary* fits on a single 12-cm CD), encyclopedias and directories as well as library catalogues.

⇨ CORPUS, DATABASE, ELECTRONIC DICTIONARY, HYPERTEXT, MULTIMEDIA, REFERENCE SHELF.

▢ Lemmens & Wekker 1990, Duval 1992.

▤ *CD-ROM Directory* [*The Multimedia Yearbook* 5th edition], London, 1996.

▭ *The OED on CD-ROM*, Oxford, 1987/92.

censorship

A reduction in the freedom to publish certain ideologically or politically 'incorrect' views. In lexicography, one form of censorship is PROSCRIPTION, e.g. the labelling of certain words or phrases in USAGE GUIDES as 'wrong' or 'substandard', or the banning of information from dictionaries altogether, examples being the exclusion from the GENERAL DICTIONARY of racial, sexual or religious vocabulary or the imposition of bias in definitions of political terms.

▢ Sands 1980–1, Landau 1984, Wierzbicka 1995.

census

A detailed account of the editions of a particular set of dictionaries from a given period or genre, sometimes with information on their location in specialised libraries.

⇨ DICTIONARY HISTORY.

▢ Starnes & Noyes 1946/91, Schäfer 1989.

central meaning

⇨ BASIC SENSE.

character

A graphic sign which stands for a sound, word or other linguistic unit. In alphabetic writing systems, the relationship between a speech sound and a character (LETTER) may or may not be one-to-one, while in logographic scripts such as Chinese, or Japanese 'kanji', the character represents one or more words which may be pronounced very differently. In Western dictionary-making, printing and computer-processing, the CHARACTER SET is based on the letters and alphabetical order of the LATIN ALPHABET; in some non-alphabetic scripts the characters are not only made up of several strokes (sometimes derived from pictorial symbols), but often combined with other characters so that the user needs to go through a series of steps to find the required headword.

⇨ CHARACTER DICTIONARY, RADICAL.

▢ Zgusta 1989b.

character dictionary

A type of REFERENCE WORK based on a logographic script, such as Chinese, in which words and phrases are represented by, and listed in order of, CHARACTERS. Such dictionaries are based either on single characters (*zìdiǎn*) or character combinations (*cídiǎn*).

▢ Xue 1982, Creamer 1991, Halpern 1992, Lai 1992.

▤ *NTC's New Japanese–English Character Dictionary* (J. Halpern), Lincolnwood IL, 1993.

characteristic

A property which can be used to classify or define an object: for example, with respect to dictionaries, 'gem', 'compact', 'concise', 'comprehensive' etc. What unites these defining features is the category 'size'.

⇨ TYPE (3).

📖 ISO 1990.

character set

An inventory of graphic signs used in typing, printing and text processing to represent spoken language, e.g. an ALPHABET or the ASCII code.

children's dictionary

A DICTIONARY aimed at children. While the transition between the dictionary for younger children and the SCHOOL DICTIONARY is fluid, the former is less bound by the conventions of the traditional, fully-fledged GENERAL DICTIONARY than the latter. It is based on a limited BASIC VOCABULARY and uses pictorial illustrations and 'stories' – often humorous – rather than formal definitions, to explain the meanings of the (predominantly concrete) words.

⇨ PICTURE DICTIONARY.

📖 Landau 1984, Svensén 1993, Cignoni *et al.* 1996.

▤ *Richard Scarry's Best Word Book Ever* (R. Scarry), New York NY, 1980; *Picture Dictionary* (S. Hewitt), St Albans, 1993.

Chinese Lexicography Prize

A biennial award given by the LEXICOGRAPHICAL SOCIETY OF CHINA for outstanding compilations in the field of Chinese dictionaries, bilingual and multilingual dictionaries, specialised dictionaries and encyclopedic dictionaries.

chrestomathy

A CORPUS of selected texts of one or more authors, used in language teaching and learning.

▤ *Chrestomathy of Arabic Prose Pieces* (R.-E. Brunnow), London, 1895.

Christian name

⇨ PERSONAL NAME.

chronolect

⇨ PERIOD.

chronological dictionary

A type of REFERENCE WORK in which the words or phrases are arranged in order of dates of their first occurrence in a language.

⇨ ALMANACK, CALENDAR.

📖 Landau 1984.

▤ *The Chronological English Dictionary* (T. Finkenstaedt *et al.*), Heidelberg, 1970; *Chronological Dictionary of Quotations* (E. Wright), London, 1993.

chronological order

The arrangement of material in a REFERENCE WORK by historical date rather than by alphabetical or thematic order. Some specialised dictionaries follow this principle to arrange the whole WORD-LIST in this way. In general and historical dictionaries, TEMPORAL LABELS are used to indicate the period with which a particular word or phrase is associated.

⇨ CHRONOLOGICAL DICTIONARY.

cídiǎn

⇨ CHARACTER DICTIONARY.

circular definition

A DEFINITION in which the key term or terms used are defined by the words which they serve to explain. Thus, the word *able* is defined in one general English dictionary as 'capable, competent . . .', *capable* as 'able, competent . . .', and *competent* as 'capable . . .', a practice which supports the case for a limited DEFINING VOCABULARY.

📖 Landau 1984, Svensén 1993.

circular reference

⇨ REFERENCE CIRCULARITY.

Císhū Yánjiù

The title (< Chinese 'Lexicographical Studies') of a periodical published in Shanghai since 1979.

citation

A source of lexicographical data, verified in the form of an extract from a text, to illustrate a particular USAGE of a word or phrase. Such details are stored either in an informal collection (CITATION FILE) or in database form, particularly when drawn from a CORPUS, and used as evidence or quoted as EXAMPLES inside the dictionary entry. Data based on spoken language is more difficult to maintain and record, especially when it is the result of fieldwork techniques such as ELICITATION. The quality and AUTHORITY of citations are enhanced if they meet the criteria of representativeness and prototypicality of use.

⇨ ANTEDATING, AUTHENTICATION, CONCORDANCE, COPYING IN DICTIONARIES.

📖 Landau 1984, Rundell & Stock 1992, Béjoint 1994.

citation database
⇨   DATABASE.

citation file
A collection of words and phrases, with their verbal contexts, used as raw material for DICTIONARY-MAKING. Depending on the type of dictionary, citation files can range from a simple list of references to sources in which the word or phrase occurs, to a collection of file-cards with full quotations and a systematic CORPUS of texts in the form of printed or on-screen concordances.
⇨   CITATION, DATABASE, EXCERPTION.
▭   Landau 1984, Sinclair 1987.

citation form
⇨   CANONICAL FORM.

citation index
A list of REFERENCES to published academic papers, used as an indicator of their significance or popularity.
⇨   INDEX.
▤   *Social Sciences Citation Index* (The Institute for Scientific Information), Philadelphia PA, 1966–.

class
The sum total of entities to which a CONCEPT refers. In a hierarchy of related concepts, the higher-ranking or 'generic' concepts refer to a larger class than the lower-ranking or 'specific' concepts.
⇨   CLASSIFICATION (1).
▭   ISO 1990.

classical compound
A WORD-FORMATION pattern in which both parts of a COMPOUND are based on classical Greek or Latin, sometimes in combination, e.g. *synonym dictionary*.
▭   McArthur 1992, van Niekerk 1992, Kirkness 1994.

classical definition
⇨   ANALYTICAL DEFINITION.

classical dictionary
A type of REFERENCE WORK with encyclopedic information on people, events and institutions of the ancient world, usually Greece and Rome.
▤   *The Oxford Classical Dictionary* (S. Hornblower & A. Spawforth), Oxford, 1949/96.

classicism
A word or phrase based on an ancient classical language such as Greek or Latin, e.g. *lexicography* or *Ides of March*.

classification
1 In encyclopedic, terminological and other thematic systems, the network of relationships between CONCEPTS. Such relationships have also been used in LIBRARIES for the cataloguing and shelving of documents, e.g. the Dewey Decimal Classification of subjects.
⇨   NOMENCLATURE, TAXONOMY.
▭   Bowker 1996.
2 ⇨   TYPOLOGY (1).

classified order
An arrangement of items by classes, e.g. words or terms in a thematic THESAURUS or documents in a systematic library CATALOGUE.

cliché
A word or phrase which has become weakened in meaning through overuse, e.g. *desirable residence* in an estate agent's brochure.
▤   *A Dictionary of Clichés* (E. Partridge), London, 1940; *Bloomsbury Dictionary of Clichés* (E. M. Kirkpatrick), London, 1996.

clipping
⇨   ABBREVIATION.

closed-class word
⇨   FUNCTION WORD.

clustering
The gathering together of several DERIVATIVES inside one entry in order to save space, in contrast to 'listing', where these items are given separate HEADWORD status. Thus in the *Chambers Twentieth Century Dictionary* (Edinburgh, 1983) the bold-faced **diathermal**, **diathermanous** and **diathermous** are included inside the entry **diathermic**, following the definition 'permeable by radiant heat' and introduced by the word *also*. By contrast, the *New Shorter Oxford English Dictionary* (Oxford, 1993) lists them in separate entries, with cross-references from **diathermal**, **diathermic** and **diathermous** to **diathermanous**, which is defined as 'transparent to infrared radiation'.
⇨   NESTING, NICHING.
▭   Landau 1984, Hausmann & Wiegand 1989.

COBUILD

Acronym for *Collins Birmingham University International Language Database*. A DICTIONARY FAMILY based on the *Collins COBUILD English Language Dictionary* (London & Glasgow, 1987) published as a result of the collaboration of a dictionary publisher with the Department of English at the University of Birmingham.
⇨ BANK OF ENGLISH, LEARNER'S DICTIONARY.
📖 Sinclair 1987.
🖥 Website: titania.cobuild.collins.co.uk/

code

1 A system of communication such as natural or artificial LANGUAGE, or language variety such as DIALECT or SOCIOLECT.
2 An abbreviated term or symbol used in REFERENCE WORKS as a LABEL to mark the provenance of a word or phrase. In terminological dictionaries, for example, the LANGUAGE CODE marks the language, the COUNTRY CODE the country, and the SOURCE CODE the texts with which a particular term is associated.
📖 ISO 1990.

codification

The presentation of linguistic information about USAGE in textbooks and reference works. There is no unified framework for this process, but the activity has a long tradition in the fields of pronunciation (ORTHOEPY), spelling (ORTHOGRAPHY), vocabulary (LEXICOGRAPHY) and technical terminology (TERMINOGRAPHY). Other fields potentially open to this approach include grammar ('grammatography'), idiomatic expressions and collocations ('phraseography') and style and discourse ('textography'). GENERAL DICTIONARIES and USAGE GUIDES fulfil an important role in codifying linguistic facts, but in the absence of EVIDENCE, prescription and PURISM often cloud the issue of AUTHORITY. Specialised dictionaries, e.g. for spelling, pronunciation and terminology, have contributed to the establishment of linguistic NORMS.
⇨ STANDARDISATION.
📖 Hartmann 1996b.

cognate

A member of a pair or group of words or phrases characterised by intralingual or interlingual genetic relationship.
⇨ DOUBLET, FALSE FRIEND.

cognitive meaning

⇨ DENOTATION.

co-hyponym

Two or more words or phrases sharing the same HYPERONYM, e.g. *arm* and *leg* in relation to *limb*.

coinage

⇨ ROOT-CREATION.

collateral term

⇨ COMPOUND TERM.

collection

1 The acquisition and archiving of DICTIONARIES and other reference works.
⇨ ARCHIVE (1).
2 The gathering of source material for the purpose of compiling REFERENCE WORKS.
⇨ CITATION, CORPUS, ELICITATION.
📖 Svensén 1993.

college dictionary

A type of DICTIONARY aimed at upper-secondary school and undergraduate students. College dictionaries are of intermediate ('desk') size and contain most of the information categories provided by the GENERAL DICTIONARY of which they are often ABRIDGED versions. In the USA, in contrast to Britain, the 'collegiate' dictionary is also used as a LEARNER'S DICTIONARY by students and teachers of English as a foreign language.
⇨ SCHOOL DICTIONARY, STANDARD DICTIONARY.
📖 Landau 1984, 1994, Algeo 1990, Béjoint 1994.
📑 *The American College Dictionary* (C. L. Barnhart), New York NY, 1947; *Webster's New World Dictionary (College Edition)*, New York NY & Cleveland OH, 1953; *The Random House College Dictionary* (L. Urdang), New York NY, 1975; *Merriam Webster's Collegiate Dictionary* [10th edition] (F. C. Mish), Springfield MA, 1996.

collegiate dictionary

⇨ COLLEGE DICTIONARY.

collocation

The semantic compatibility of grammatically adjacent words. Whether these patterns of co-occurrence between such words as adjective–noun *nice surprise*, noun–verb *panic broke out*, or verb–preposition *lecture on* are approached positively as 'solidarity relations' or negatively as 'selection restrictions' (*good surprise, *passion broke out, *lecture over*), the resulting collocations are more fixed than free combinations and less fixed than idioms. Since collocability is difficult for foreign-language learners, dictionaries need to specify such patterns, especially where translation equivalence is unpredictable. The double issue of which part of the collocation is more 'basic' than the other and under which the collocation should be entered in the dictionary has not been settled satisfactorily.

⇨ CONSTRUCTION, FIXED EXPRESSION, VALENCY.

  Benson 1989, Cop 1991, Svensén 1993, Béjoint 1994, Heid 1994, Bragina 1996, Fontenelle 1996, Grefenstette *et al*. 1996.

  BBI Combinatory Dictionary of English (2nd edition) (M. Benson *et al*.), Amsterdam, 1997.

  COBUILD English Collocations on CD-ROM, London, 1995.

colloquialism

A word or phrase normally used in the spoken language and considered more informal than written discourse. Dictionaries and USAGE GUIDES have had problems defining and labelling such items because of their inability to decide on which of several scales to place them: formality ('informal' in opposition to 'formal'), medium ('speech' in opposition to 'writing'), or social status ('slang' rather than 'genteel').

  Lovatt 1984.

  NTC's Dictionary of American Slang and Colloquial Expressions (R. A. Spears), Lincolnwood IL, 1989.

combining form

A WORD-FORMATION element with lexical content, which helps to create a new word but cannot usually stand alone, e.g. *lexico-* or *-graphy* versus the full compound *lexicography*.

⇨ BASE.

  McArthur 1992, Kirkness 1994.

comment

In a diagrammatic model of the BASE STRUCTURE of the dictionary entry, the INFORMATION supplied, in relation to the HEADWORD ('topic'). The new information on the topic can be subdivided into the 'formal' comment (spelling, grammar, pronunciation) and the 'semantic' comment (definition, etymology, usage). Often much of the comment on form is included in the typographical representation of the headword itself. Thus, the

following entry from *Collins Pons German–English English–German Dictionary* (Glasgow & Stuttgart, 1980), '**Allee** *f* -, **-n** [-eːən] avenue', tells the user of this bilingual dictionary the orthography, the pronunciation (explicit only for the plural form), stress (italicised second syllable), gender (feminine) and endings (genitive and plural). The comment on meaning is minimal here, consisting only of one translation equivalent, 'avenue'.

⇨ CORE STRUCTURE.

  Hausmann & Wiegand 1989.

commercial dictionary

A type of REFERENCE WORK produced primarily for financial gain, sometimes contrasted with SCHOLARLY DICTIONARY.

common core vocabulary

⇨ BASIC VOCABULARY.

communication

Interaction for the exchange of INFORMATION. The most basic means for human communication is verbal LANGUAGE, studied as a symbolic code in LINGUISTICS; the wider context of communication is the province of SEMIOTICS. Both are relevant to lexicography, as DICTIONARIES and other REFERENCE WORKS make use of various forms of communication through phonic, graphic and other means. The medium of the written TEXT imposes limits on what must and can be conveyed, however. Readability may be affected by layout and the use of genre-specific conventions. The semiotic perspective can not only extend linguistic awareness to a fuller understanding of the processes of REFERENCE (who looks for what information under what conditions) but adds the use of supplementary codes such as pictures, film and sound to provide a more satisfactory reference experience.

⇨ ACCESS, COMPILER PERSPECTIVE, CONSULTATION, DICTIONARIES AS DISCOURSE, INTERACTIVE DICTIONARY, USER PERSPECTIVE.

communicative shift

Any of the four major stages in the development of human COMMUNICATION, namely from non-communication to speech (*c*. 50,000 years ago), expanded by writing (*c*. 5,000 years ago), printing (*c*. 500 years ago) and computing and other media (contemporary). Each of these stages has associated with it a new reference technology, e.g. oral METRICAL DICTIONARIES, script-based

GLOSSARIES, the DICTIONARY as a book, and the ELECTRONIC DICTIONARY.

📖 McArthur 1986a, 1992.

compact dictionary

A reference work which is reduced either in physical size, e.g. *The Compact Edition of the Oxford English Dictionary* (Oxford, 1971), or in content, e.g. *Webster's Compact Dictionary* (Springfield MA, 1987).

compact disc

⇨ CD-ROM.

companion

A type of REFERENCE WORK which provides information in easily digestible form on a specific subject, in alphabetical, thematic or other order.

📖 McArthur 1989a.

▤ *The Oxford Companion to the English Language* (T. McArthur), Oxford, 1992.

comparable text

⇨ PARALLEL TEXTS.

comparative dictionary

A type of DICTIONARY which is compiled, sometimes on the basis of informal glossaries collected during linguistic fieldwork, for the purpose of contrastively evaluating the shared vocabulary of several languages.

📖 Key 1991, Naden 1993.

▤ *Dictionary of Selected Synonyms in the Principal Indo-European Languages* (C. D. Buck), Chicago IL, 1949; *Dictionary of Turkic Languages* (K. Öztopçu *et al.*), London, 1996.

comparative lexicography

1 A branch of GENERAL LEXICOGRAPHY which contrasts the dictionary traditions of various cultures, languages and countries with a view to distilling from them common principles, by considering the external factors that have led to divergent practices. Examples include issues such as how different scripts influence the format of reference works, which different genres predominate, and what constitutes good practice in DICTIONARY-MAKING and dictionary use.

⇨ CHARACTER DICTIONARY, COMPARISON OF DICTIONARIES, TYPOLOGY (1).

📖 Stein 1979, Zgusta 1980, Huang 1994, Kachru & Kahane 1995.

2 A complex of activities concerned with the design, compilation, use and evaluation of COMPARATIVE DICTIONARIES.

📖 Naden 1993.

comparative linguistics

⇨ PHILOLOGY.

comparison of dictionaries

The contrastive EVALUATION of two or more dictionaries or other reference works, e.g. for the purpose of dictionary CRITICISM or the study of DICTIONARY HISTORY.

⇨ COVERAGE.

📖 Hüllen 1990, Butler 1992, Thelen 1992, Laufer & Melamed 1994, Dickens & Salkie 1996, Herbst 1996.

compendium

1 A type of REFERENCE WORK which seeks to summarise knowledge of a subject in an easily accessible form; often used as a synonym of COMPANION or VADE-MECUM.

▤ *Compendium of the World's Languages* (G. L. Campbell), London, 1991.

2 ⇨ REFERENCE SHELF.

competence example

⇨ EDITORIAL EXAMPLE.

compilation

The collective term for the process or result of producing a REFERENCE WORK.

⇨ COMPILER PERSPECTIVE, DESIGN, DICTIONARY-MAKING.

compiler

One who engages in the COMPILATION of a REFERENCE WORK.

⇨ REFERENCE PROFESSIONAL.

compiler perspective

An approach that considers lexicography from the point of view of DICTIONARY-MAKING. Issues treated include the status, training and career structure of the compiler, the techniques and tools available for the production of REFERENCE WORKS, and the theoretical and practical limitations of their design, use and evaluation.

⇨ PROFESSIONAL RESOURCES, REFERENCE PROFESSIONAL, USER PERSPECTIVE, Panel 'Compiler and User Perspectives' (page 25).

📖 McGregor 1985, Ilson 1986a, Krishnamurthy 1987, James 1989, Whitcut 1989, Svensén 1993.

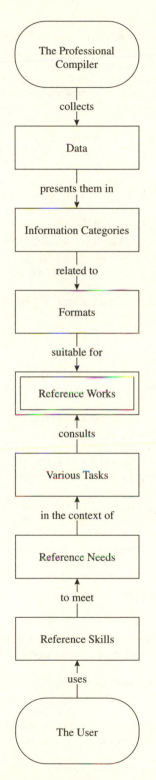

Compiler and User Perspectives

complementarity
⇨   ANTONYMY.

complete synonym
⇨   SYNONYMY (1).

complete synonymy
⇨   SYNONYMY (1).

complex term
A term formed from a SIMPLE TERM by the addition of one or more DERIVATIVES, e.g. *dictionary-making*.
⇨   COMPOUND TERM.
📖   ISO 1990.

complex word
A word formed from a SIMPLE WORD by the addition of one or more derivational AFFIXES, e.g. *facelessness*.
⇨   COMPOUND WORD.

component
1   In the design of REFERENCE WORKS, one of the constituent functional elements of the MACROSTRUCTURE or MICROSTRUCTURE.
2   In COMPONENTIAL ANALYSIS, the smallest distinctive feature of meaning.

componential analysis
An approach in SEMANTICS in which meanings are discussed in terms of sets of components. By extending the technique of analysing phonemes in terms of 'distinctive features' (such as voice, labiality or constriction) to the level of meaning, linguists have attempted to decompose LEXEMES into 'contrastive' semantic features or components, e.g. *man* into –FEMALE and +ADULT, *woman* into +FEMALE and +ADULT, *boy* into –FEMALE and –ADULT, and *girl* into +FEMALE and –ADULT. This method has been claimed to be useful in definition writing. However, it is debatable whether componential analysis can be applied to more than a few tightly structured SEMANTIC FIELDS such as kinship terms.
📖   Ayto 1983, Jackson 1988.

composition
⇨   COMPOUNDING.

compounding
A WORD-FORMATION process in which two or more SIMPLE WORDS are joined to form a new

word with a single meaning, e.g. *airport*, *dry-clean*.
⇨ BINOMIAL COMPOUND, CLASSICAL COMPOUND.
📖 Ten Hacken 1992.

compound term
A term formed by joining two or more SIMPLE TERMS, e.g. *dictionary reference skills*.
⇨ BINOMIAL COMPOUND, COMPLEX TERM.
📖 ISO 1990, Minaeva 1996.

compound word
A word formed by joining two or more SIMPLE WORDS, e.g. *airport*.
⇨ COMPLEX WORD.
📖 Zgusta 1989b, McArthur 1992, Thompson 1992a, Raadik 1996.

comprehensive concept
Also called 'integrative concept', a SUPERORDINATE CONCEPT in a PARTITIVE RELATION, e.g. 'house' in relation to 'gable', or 'reference work' in relation to 'microstructure'.
📖 ISO 1990.

comprehensive dictionary
A large, all-inclusive DICTIONARY.
⇨ DICTIONARY FAMILY.
📓 *A Comprehensive Dictionary of Measurement and Control* [3rd edition] (The Instrument Society of America), Research Triangle Park NC, 1995.

compression
1 The condensation or contraction of WORDS for ease of computer processing, e.g. by stripping DIACRITICS and eliminating blanks.
   📖 ISO 1990.
2 The condensation or contraction of TEXTS, e.g. to save space on the page of a reference work.
   ⇨ DICTIONARESE, TEXT COMPRESSION.

computational lexicography
A complex of activities concerned with the design, compilation, use and evaluation of ELECTRONIC DICTIONARIES. This ranges from the mechanisation of the main stages of the dictionary-making process (e.g. data-capture from a text CORPUS, computer-assisted DISAMBIGUATION, on-screen text processing and the use of printing technology) through the use of MACHINE-READABLE DICTIONARIES (e.g. in machine translation and natural language processing) to the design of entirely new reference systems (CD-ROM, multimedia encyclopedias and multilingual terminological databases).
⇨ WORK-STATION.
📖 DANLEX Group 1987, Urdang 1988, Dodd 1989, Knowles 1990, Neff & Cantor 1990, Kiefer *et al.* 1992, Meijs 1992, Byrd 1995, Sinclair 1996.

computational lexicology
The application of computer techniques to LEMMATISATION, DISAMBIGUATION, CORPUS design, TERMINOLOGY processing and similar topics.
📖 Atkins & Zampolli 1994, Walker *et al.* 1995.

computational linguistics
A branch of LINGUISTICS concerned with the application of computers to language research.
⇨ ASSOCIATION FOR COMPUTATIONAL LINGUISTICS.
📖 McNaught 1988, Butler 1990, McEnery 1992.
📓 *Elsevier's Dictionary of Mathematical and Computational Linguistics* (Y. Venev), Amsterdam, 1990.

computer-aided dictionary
⇨ ELECTRONIC DICTIONARY.

computer-assisted dictionary
⇨ ELECTRONIC DICTIONARY.

computer-assisted lexicography
⇨ COMPUTATIONAL LEXICOGRAPHY.

computer-based dictionary
⇨ ELECTRONIC DICTIONARY.

computer-based lexicography
⇨ COMPUTATIONAL LEXICOGRAPHY.

computer dictionary
⇨ ELECTRONIC DICTIONARY.

computer-enhanced lexicography
⇨ COMPUTATIONAL LEXICOGRAPHY.

computerised dictionary
⇨ ELECTRONIC DICTIONARY.

computerised lexicography
⇨ COMPUTATIONAL LEXICOGRAPHY.

computer lexicography
⇨ COMPUTATIONAL LEXICOGRAPHY.

computing

A result of the fourth major COMMUNICATIVE SHIFT, from printing to information technology. Together with other telecommunications media, the electronic computer has revolutionised the storage, presentation and transmission of INFORMATION, and thus contributed significantly to the generation of new types of reference works.

⇨ COMPUTATIONAL LEXICOGRAPHY, CORPUS.

concept

The basic notion which a TERM is designed to express. Within the systematic framework of a particular subject field, the unity between term and concept is considered an essential requirement of unambiguous communication, strengthened by definitions agreed by expert practitioners and the avoidance of synonyms. The term is occasionally used in semantics as an alternative for the MEANING (and in lexicography as an alternative for the SENSE) of a LEXEME.

⇨ HIERARCHICAL RELATION.

📖 ISO 1990, Svensén 1993, Meyer & Mackintosh 1994.

concept correspondence

The overlap in INTENSION or semantic content of two CONCEPTS in different theories, fields or languages. Concepts may be identical, similar or different according to how many characteristic features they share (ANTONYMY, HYPONYMY, PARTITIVE RELATION, SYNONYMY etc.). In TERMINOLOGY the aim is to delimit and define concepts so that unambiguous terms can be allocated to them.

📖 ISO 1990.

concept field

A thematically related set of CONCEPTS within a technical subject, e.g. classes of 'drinking vessels' in catering, or types of 'dictionaries' in lexicography.

⇨ SEMANTIC FIELD, SUBJECT FIELD.

📖 ISO 1990.

conceptual dictionary

⇨ ONOMASIOLOGICAL DICTIONARY.

conceptual index

⇨ THESAURUS (2).

conceptual relation

⇨ SENSE RELATION.

conceptual system

An ordered arrangement, usually in hierarchical sequence, of CONCEPTS, WORDS or TERMS. Examples are the linguistic analysis of words in SEMANTIC FIELDS, the thematic classification of vocabulary in a THESAURUS, or the logical (e.g. part–whole or generic–specific) networks within the technical TERMINOLOGY of particular subject fields.

📖 Cluver 1989a, ISO 1990, Sager 1990.

concise dictionary

In a DICTIONARY FAMILY, a reduced version of a larger reference work.

⇨ ABRIDGED DICTIONARY.

📑 *The Concise Oxford Dictionary of Current English* (R. E. Allen), Oxford, 1990.

concordance

A systematic list of the VOCABULARY which occurs in a text or an author's work, with a minimal verbal context provided for each word. Traditionally, concordances were associated with the Bible and other canonical texts, such as the works of classical and established authors. Since the concordance provides formal details about the words (spelling, grammar and citations, rather than meaning and definitions), it is sometimes called INDEX, especially when line positions rather than textual contexts are given. Advances in information technology and CORPUS design have given a new impetus to AUTHOR LEXICOGRAPHY (and dictionary-making in general) by allowing the rapid processing of large-scale text archives. Today's computer-generated KEYWORD-IN-CONTEXT concordances can display the words preceding (left of) or following (right of) the keyword in either frequency or alphabetical order, producing EVIDENCE on such aspects of USAGE as collocation, compounding and lemmatisation.

⇨ AUTHOR'S DICTIONARY.

📖 Knowles 1990, Tribble & Jones 1990, Sinclair 1991, 1997, Mills 1996.

📑 *A Concordance to the Poems of Samuel Johnson* (H. H. Naugle & P. B. Sherry), Ithaca NY, 1973; *Collins COBUILD Concordance Samplers 1: Prepositions* (A. Capel), London, 1993; *2: Phrasal Verbs* (M. Goodale), London, 1995; *3: Reporting* (G. Thompson), London, 1995; *4: Tenses* (M. Goodale), London, 1995.

condensation

⇨ COMPRESSION.

confusable words

⇨ CONFUSIBLE WORDS.

confusible words

An informal term for pairs or groups of words which may cause confusion in reception or production. This can refer to words similar in sound, written form, meaning or etymology.

⇨ DOUBLET, FALSE FRIEND, HOMONYM, PARONYM, SYNONYM (1).

▣ *Dictionary of Contrasting Pairs* (A. Room), London, 1988; *Collins COBUILD English Guides 4: Confusable Words* (E. Carpenter), London, 1993; *Dictionary of Differences* (L. Urdang), London, 1993; *NTC's Dictionary of Easily Confused Words* (D. K. Williams), Lincolnwood IL, 1995.

confusing words

⇨ CONFUSIBLE WORDS.

conjugation

The PARADIGM of a VERB, giving all its forms. In dictionaries of Ancient Greek and Latin, whose verbs are classified according to their morphological regularities, the CANONICAL FORM is traditionally the first person singular of the present tense, which does not necessarily give a clue as to the conjugation pattern. This is usually supplemented by an indication of the PRINCIPAL PARTS as a synopsis of the whole. In Romance language dictionaries, the citation form of a verb is usually that form which will indicate its conjugation pattern (e.g. the infinitive), and from which other forms can be predicted. In ambiguous instances, the word may be accompanied by a conventional label or number, or by an alternative form, as an indicator of the appropriate paradigm to which it belongs.

⇨ DECLENSION.

conjunction

A PART OF SPEECH which links words, phrases and more complex syntactic structures.

⇨ GRAMMATICAL INFORMATION.

connotation

An aspect of MEANING of a word or phrase associated with the subjective emotive overtones it evokes. Also called 'affective' or 'emotive' meaning, connotative associations are difficult to capture in dictionary DEFINITIONS, which therefore tend to concentrate on the more objective referential aspects (DENOTATION). However, con-notative meanings do play an important part in communication, and lexicographers attempt to mark them (not always consistently) by USAGE LABELS such as 'informal', 'derogatory', 'offensive' and 'ironic'.

▦ Landau 1984, Opitz 1992, Svensén 1993, Gouws 1996.

connotative meaning

⇨ CONNOTATION.

construction

The grammatical relationships of words in the context of phrases, and phrases in the context of sentences. The traditional GENERAL DICTIONARY for native speakers limited specification of syntactic constructions to PART-OF-SPEECH marking and verb sub-classification (e.g. 'transitive' versus 'intransitive'), supported by illustrative examples of subject–verb–object patterns.

⇨ COLLOCATION, EXPLANATORY DICTIONARY, GRAMMAR, VALENCY.

▦ Cowie 1989a, Kromann *et al.* 1991, McCorduck 1993, Heid 1994, Macleod *et al.* 1996.

consultant

One engaged in a dictionary project as an expert in an aspect of linguistic and/or technical knowledge.

⇨ ADVISORY PANEL, USAGE PANEL.

consultation

The act of using a REFERENCE WORK to look up (i.e. seek, find and retrieve) required information. Knowledge about the user's needs and skills (the USER PERSPECTIVE) is an important consideration in how to improve DICTIONARY-MAKING, but empirical research in this area has only begun relatively recently.

⇨ ACCESS, INFORMATION CATEGORY, SEARCH PATH, USER EDUCATION, WORKBOOK.

▦ Hartmann 1989.

contact language

⇨ CONTACT VERNACULAR.

contact variety

⇨ CONTACT VERNACULAR.

contact vernacular

The result of LANGUAGE CONTACT in the form of mixed and simplified vocabulary and grammar structures. Examples are 'foreigner talk', 'pidgin',

'creole' and learners' 'interlanguage', some of which are documented in specialised dictionaries.
⇨ CREOLE, FALSE FRIEND, INTERFERENCE.
📖 Romaine 1988, Görlach 1990.
📑 *Hobson-Jobson: A Glossary of Colloquial Indian Words and Phrases* (H. Yule & A. C. Burnell), Calcutta, 1886.

contemporary usage
The current language, in contrast to earlier periods. In dictionaries, this is the neutral variety, while ARCHAISMS and some NEOLOGISMS are marked with special labels.
⇨ DIACHRONIC INFORMATION.

content word
A word with predominantly lexical significance, such as a noun, a verb or an adjective, rather than grammatical value, such as a conjunction or a preposition.
⇨ FUNCTION WORD.

context
1 The part of a text where a particular WORD, PHRASE or TERM occurs (also called 'verbal context' or 'co-text').
   ⇨ CONCORDANCE.
2 The setting or circumstances with which a WORD, PHRASE or TERM is associated (also called 'situational context', 'context of use' or 'environment').
   ⇨ DISCOURSE ANALYSIS.

context of use
⇨ CONTEXT (2).

contextual definition
A DEFINITION which explains a word, phrase or term by means of an EXAMPLE in context.

context word
A LABEL used to mark the context with which a word or phrase is usually associated.

contraction
The process or result of shortening a word, phrase or text.
⇨ ABBREVIATION, COMPRESSION.

contrasting pairs
⇨ CONFUSIBLE WORDS.

contrastive feature
⇨ COMPONENTIAL ANALYSIS.

contrastive linguistics
A branch of LINGUISTICS concerned with the parallel description of two (usually contemporary) languages or language varieties for a practical purpose, such as foreign-language teaching or translation. Such studies, which can be carried out at every level (PHONOLOGY, GRAPHEMICS, LEXICOLOGY and DISCOURSE) can throw light on interlingual differences in the material to be included in BILINGUAL DICTIONARIES.
⇨ PARALLEL TEXTS.
📖 Heltai 1988, Hartmann 1991.

controlled defining vocabulary
⇨ DEFINING VOCABULARY.

convergence
In cases of partial TRANSLATION equivalence, the rendering of two or more words in one language by a single word in the other language. Thus the meanings of the two English words *slug* and *snail* are covered by the single Dutch word *slak*. (The opposite direction is called DIVERGENCE.) The BILINGUAL DICTIONARY must allow for such asymmetrical relations, in conjunction with the problem of the user orientation.
⇨ ANISOMORPHISM, BIDIRECTIONAL DICTIONARY.
📖 Kromann *et al.* 1991.

converseness
A bilateral SENSE RELATION between a pair of words involving symmetrical opposition in which the one implies the existence of the other, e.g. *give* versus *take*, *husband* versus *wife*, *over* versus *under*.
⇨ ANTONYMY.

conversion
1 A WORD-FORMATION pattern in which a word's function is changed through a shift in word-class or part of speech, e.g. *tape* (noun) 'recording' to *to tape* (denominal verb) 'to make a recording'; *to interrupt* (verb) to *interrupt* (deverbal noun) 'break in a computer program'.
   ⇨ SEMANTIC CHANGE.
2 The adaptation of one dictionary or dictionary type to create another, e.g. from a dictionary to a thesaurus, or from a Dutch–Russian dictionary to a Russian–Dutch one.
   ⇨ BILINGUALISATION, REVERSIBILITY.
   📖 Heid 1992, Honselaar & Elstrodt 1992.

conversive antonymy
⇨ CONVERSENESS.

co-occurrence
⇨ COLLOCATION.

co-ordinate concept
A CONCEPT which shares with another concept the same rank of a hierarchical sense relation with respect to a superordinate concept, e.g. 'dictionary' and 'thesaurus' in relation to 'reference work'.
📖 ISO 1990.

co-ordination
The SENSE RELATION between two CONCEPTS at the same rank of a hierarchy. Such concepts are said to be CO-ORDINATE CONCEPTS with respect to a superordinate concept, similar to two or more CO-HYPONYMS in relation to a hyperonym.
📖 ISO 1990.

copying in dictionaries
The reproduction or imitation of text from one existing dictionary to compile a new one. Lexicographers have made use of dictionaries as source material for centuries, in the belief that there is no COPYRIGHT on the words of the language. The increased availability of computer technology has made copying easier than ever.
⇨ AUTHORSHIP, CRIMINALITY, DERIVATIVE DICTIONARY.
📖 Burchfield 1984, Dolezal 1986, Spears 1987, Zgusta 1988b, Hausmann 1989, Williams 1992.

copyright
The legal right to use a TEXT for publication or storage. Copyright may be passed to a third party by agreement, often on payment of a ROYALTY. In reference works, the formulation of DEFINITIONS and TRADE NAMES (but not words, phrases and terms) are protected by copyright.
⇨ COPYING IN DICTIONARIES, DEPOSITORY LIBRARY.
📖 Landau 1984, Read 1984, Svensén 1993.

copyright infringement
The publication or storage of a TEXT without legal permission.
⇨ AUTHORSHIP, CRIMINALITY.
📖 Landau 1984, Williams 1992.

copyright library
⇨ DEPOSITORY LIBRARY.

core meaning
⇨ BASIC SENSE.

core structure
One of the two subdivisions in a diagrammatic model of the BASE STRUCTURE of dictionary entries. The left-core structure contains the 'comment on form' (spelling, pronunciation, grammar), the right-core structure contains the 'comment on meaning' (definition, etymology, usage information).
⇨ COMMENT.
📖 Hausmann & Wiegand 1989.

core vocabulary
⇨ CORE WORD, VOCABULARY.

core word
A word forming part of the common core of the BASIC VOCABULARY. Such words are the unmarked, most frequent items of the language shared by speech and writing, but not differentiated along such dimensions as technical usage, dialect and slang. In dictionaries, core words are usually not labelled as they are not restricted in USAGE, e.g. *hand* 'part of the human anatomy . . .', as opposed to such non-core words as *handbill* (theatre), *handicap* (golf) or *handsel* (dial. 'gift'). It has been argued that only core words should be used in the DEFINING VOCABULARY to make the explanation of meanings easier, but it is an awkward fact that such common words are also the most polysemous, e.g. *hand* has several SENSES: 'part of the human anatomy . . .', 'set of cards', 'clock pointer', 'worker', etc.
⇨ CORPUS, FREQUENCY.

corpora
The Latin plural form of CORPUS, interchangeable in English with *corpuses*.

corpus
A systematic collection of TEXTS which documents the USAGE features of a language or language variety. The practical uses of computers for data-processing and the theoretical advances of CORPUS LINGUISTICS have given lexicographers powerful tools for the storage and retrieval of (written and spoken) data to describe all aspects of language, especially VOCABULARY, and to present the results in dictionaries. For English, the BRITISH NATIONAL CORPUS, the BANK OF ENGLISH and a number of specialised corpora are

now available, as are the facilities of the INTER-NET, for collecting project-specific archives of discourse, even of PARALLEL TEXTS, multilingual material and author CONCORDANCES.

⇨   COMPUTATIONAL LEXICOGRAPHY, FREQUENCY, INTERNATIONAL COMPUTER ARCHIVE OF MODERN ENGLISH, MONITOR CORPUS, PARSING, SPOKEN CORPUS, TAGGING.

📖 Renouf 1987, Paikeday 1992, Rundell & Stock 1992, Svartvik 1992b, Flowerdew & Tong 1994, James *et al.* 1994, Calzolari 1996, Meijs 1996, Stubbs 1996.

📄 *Corpus of Formal British English Speech* (G. Knowles *et al.*), Harlow, 1996.

💾 *The ICAME Collection of English Language Corpora* [CD-ROM], Oslo.

corpus information
⇨   DIAFREQUENTIAL INFORMATION.

corpus linguistics
A branch of LINGUISTICS concerned with the application of computational CORPUS techniques to the solution of problems of large-scale description. Particularly relevant to lexicography are CONCORDANCES and other presentation devices, techniques for LEMMATISATION and DISAMBIGUATION, and various forms of grammatical, phonetic and semantic annotation in texts.

⇨   FREQUENCY DICTIONARY, *INTERNATIONAL JOURNAL OF CORPUS LINGUISTICS*, PARALLEL TEXTS.

📖 Aijmer & Altenberg 1991, Svartvik 1992a, James *et al.* 1994, Kirk 1994, McEnery & Wilson 1996, Meijs 1996, Kennedy 1997.

corpus-oriented lexicography
An approach to DICTIONARY-MAKING based on the tools and techniques of CORPUS LINGUISTICS.

⇨   COMPUTATIONAL LEXICOGRAPHY.

📖 Svensén 1993, Krishnamurthy 1996.

correctness
An aspect of USAGE which stresses adherence to linguistic NORMS.

⇨   ACCEPTABILITY, APPROPRIATENESS, ERROR ANALYSIS, GRAMMATICALITY, *ORTHO*-, PURISM, STANDARD (1), USAGE GUIDE.

📖 Landau 1984, Algeo 1989a.

co-text
⇨   CONTEXT (1).

counterfeiting
The fraudulent reproduction of a text for commercial gain.

⇨   COPYING IN DICTIONARIES, CRIMINALITY.

country code
An abbreviation or symbol used to LABEL the country associated with a particular word, phrase or term.

📖 ISO 1990.

country label
⇨   COUNTRY CODE.

country symbol
⇨   COUNTRY CODE.

coverage
The amount of material included in a REFERENCE WORK, usually in comparison with others. Claims in publishers' advertising literature are notoriously difficult to verify, e.g. when absolute numbers (of 'words', 'headwords', 'references', 'entries', 'definitions' etc.) are quoted. However, dictionary CRITICISM has failed so far to set reliable standards for the EVALUATION of the relative coverage of different publications.

⇨   COMPARISON OF DICTIONARIES, CRIMINALITY, SCOPE, SIZE.

cover term
⇨   GENERIC TERM.

credit
A line acknowledging COPYRIGHT in a publication, e.g. to an artist who owns the rights to an illustration.

creole
A CONTACT VERNACULAR based on a 'pidgin' which has become the mother tongue of a speech community. Linguists recognise a continuum from the variety nearest the standard language ('acrolect') to that most different ('basilect'), with an intermediate variety ('mesolect') which varies from speaker to speaker.

📖 Romaine 1988, Görlach 1990.

📄 *Haitian Creole–English, English–Haitian Creole Dictionary* (T. Charmant), New York NY, 1995.

criminality
Any form of fraud, including PLAGIARISM, perpetrated by an author, compiler, editor or publisher of a dictionary or similar reference work.

⇨ COPYRIGHT INFRINGEMENT.

📖 Hausmann 1989, Béjoint 1994.

criticism

A branch of DICTIONARY RESEARCH concerned with the description and evaluation of DICTIONARIES and other reference works. This may involve studies of the historical background of the work and/or its compiler(s), detailed comparisons of its contents with other products of its type (with or without an assessment of its value to its potential or actual users), and result in a REVIEW in a periodical publication.

⇨ ANTIDICTIONARY, AUTHORITY, CRIMINALITY, DICTIONARY ARCHAEOLOGY, EVALUATION, IMAGE OF THE DICTIONARY.

📖 Sledd & Ebbitt 1962, Tomaszczyk 1988, Osselton 1989b, Hartmann 1990, Steiner 1993, Allen 1996.

cross-classification

The treatment of a word or phrase in more than one SEMANTIC FIELD or technical subject, e.g. the different uses of the term *level* (with the sense 'layer in a hierarchical structure') in geology, sociology or linguistics.

cross-reference

A word or symbol in a REFERENCE WORK to facilitate access to related information. In this *Dictionary of Lexicography*, four such devices are used for this purpose: the right-pointing arrow (⇨) to refer the reader to relevant information covered in other entries; small capitals in the running text to highlight terms explained elsewhere; bibliographical references (📖) to cite published sources listed at the end of the book; and references to Panels where information is summarised in diagrammatic or tabular form.

⇨ CIRCULAR REFERENCE, CROSS-REFERENCE STRUCTURE.

cross-reference structure

The network of CROSS-REFERENCES which allows compilers and users of a reference work to locate material spread over different component parts. There are many different types of cross-references and typographical devices to support them (between or inside ENTRIES, within or outside the WORD-LIST, alphabetical or numerical, by lettering or punctuation etc.), and a framework for their systematic study ('mediostructure') is still to be developed.

⇨ TEXT COMPRESSION.

📖 Wiegand 1996.

crossword

A puzzle consisting of a number of clues the solutions to which are words or phrases to be written, horizontally or vertically, letter by letter, in squares on a given grid. A variation is the WORD GAME *Scrabble®* in which players compete to form words from individually lettered tiles, placing them advantageously on a board designed akin to a crossword grid, to maximise their scores.

📑 *The Official Scrabble® Players Dictionary* [2nd edition], Springfield MA, 1990; *Bloomsbury Crossword Solver*, London, 1997.

cultural atlas

A type of REFERENCE WORK which provides CULTURAL INFORMATION in the form of MAPS, illustrations and similar material about a country, region, or group of people.

📑 *The Cultural Map of Wisconsin* (R. Ostergren *et al.*), Madison WI, 1996.

cultural dictionary

The collective term for a range of REFERENCE WORKS which are both the result of cultural practice and agents of its promotion. During the early stages of a language community, NATIONAL DICTIONARIES can contribute to the development of a cultural identity, while DIALECT DICTIONARIES can document internal regional and social variety. General monolingual USAGE dictionaries can help to support a common linguistic STANDARD, thus benefiting education. ENCYCLOPEDIAS and similar reference works can help to raise the level of factual knowledge, and BILINGUAL DICTIONARIES can improve individual and public awareness of intercultural contact and contrast.

⇨ ALLUSION, BRIDGE DICTIONARY, DICTIONARY CULTURE.

📖 Collison 1982, Lara 1995, Steiner 1995.

📑 *Oxford Advanced Learner's Dictionary (Encyclopedic Edition)*, Oxford, 1992; *Longman Dictionary of English Language and Culture* (D. Summers), Harlow, 1992; *Oxford Illustrated Encyclopedia of Peoples and Cultures* (R. Hoggart), Oxford, 1992; *The Dictionary of Cultural Literacy* [2nd edition] (E. D. Hirsch *et al.*), Boston MA, 1993.

cultural information

Knowledge about the social, intellectual and artistic achievements of a particular group or civilisation as presented in REFERENCE WORKS. Such information is usually associated with ENCYCLOPEDIC DICTIONARIES, but other types also often contain cultural details.

⇨ CULTURAL ATLAS, CULTURAL DICTIONARY, CULTURE-SPECIFIC VOCABULARY.

📖 Nguyen 1980–81, Stock 1992, Williams 1996.

cultural lexicography

A complex of activities concerned with the design, compilation, use and evaluation of CULTURAL DICTIONARIES. There is no unified framework for this field, which can include national, dialect and historical dictionaries as well as encyclopedic reference works, but since they are all products and instruments of cultural development they share certain features worth studying in an interdisciplinary perspective.

⇨ DICTIONARY CULTURE, TYPOLOGY (1).

📖 Burchfield 1987b, Kachru & Kahane 1995.

culture-bound lexical items

⇨ CULTURE-SPECIFIC VOCABULARY.

culture-specific vocabulary

The words and phrases associated with the 'way of life' of a language community. In translation and the BILINGUAL DICTIONARY, these lexical items cause particular problems of EQUIVALENCE.

⇨ EXPLANATORY EQUIVALENT.

📖 Bartholomew & Schoenhals 1983, Schnorr 1986, Bool & Carter 1989, Benson 1990, Leemets 1992.

📰 *The Friendly German–English Dictionary (A Guide to German Language, Culture and Society through Faux Amis, Literary Illustration and other Diversions)* (F. Bridgham), London, 1996.

cumulated index

An INDEX in a periodical publication which includes references to earlier issues or volumes.

📰 *Who's Who 1997* [with cumulated index], London, 1996.

cumulative synonymy

A SYNONYM DICTIONARY or thesaurus in which expressions of similar meaning are listed and classified into semantic groups without definitions or SENSE DISCRIMINATION.

⇨ DISTINCTIVE SYNONYMY, SYNONYMY (1), SYNONYMY (2).

📰 *Thesaurus of English Words and Phrases* (P. M. Roget), London, 1852.

cumulative thesaurus

⇨ CUMULATIVE SYNONYMY.

currency

⇨ CONTEMPORARY USAGE.

currency label

⇨ TEMPORAL LABEL.

cut-down

An informal term for ABRIDGED DICTIONARY.

cybarian

One who engages in the operation of an electronic ('cyberspace') LIBRARY system.

cyclical incompatibility

⇨ INCOMPATIBILITY.

cyclopedia

⇨ ENCYCLOPEDIA.

D

Dartmouth Medal
An annual award by the AMERICAN LIBRARY ASSOCIATION for the most outstanding REFERENCE WORK published during the preceding year.

data
The raw material collected for the purpose of compiling a REFERENCE WORK. The type of data required is determined by the nature and scope of the work; thus the compilers of a new, large-scale dictionary may draw on a CORPUS of texts, supplemented by means of FIELDWORK interviews, while a smaller version is usually based on secondary SOURCES.
⇨ CITATION FILE, DATABASE, INFORMATION.
📖 DANLEX Group 1987, Thompson 1992b.

data archive
A specialised collection of research materials, e.g. that of computer-readable social-science census and survey data of the Economic and Social Science Research Council, based at the University of Essex.

databank
⇨ DATABASE.

database
A facility for the electronic storing and manipulation of linguistic and other DATA. The text of this *Dictionary of Lexicography* was compiled on *ClarisWorks 4.0* (Macintosh) using a predetermined number of fields for the component parts of ENTRIES, including 'headword', 'sense number', 'definition', 'elaboration', 'examples', 'cross-references' and 'bibliographical references'. Databases may contain lexical, terminological or encyclopedic INFORMATION which can be adapted to bilingual or multilingual uses. 'Relational databases' allow the tracing and use of complex relationships between different fields, such as the conceptual hierarchies between different terms. In DICTIONARY-MAKING, a 'language resource database', or 'citation database', comprises the corpora, text archives and individual citations from a range of published and unpublished sources, which constitute the EVIDENCE for dictionary entries. An 'entry database' includes the headwords, definitions and other INFORMATION CATEGORIES, as well as formatting codes, cross-references etc. of the dictionary entries.
⇨ CITATION FILE, CORPUS, TERMINOLOGICAL DATABASE, FIELD (2).
📖 DANLEX Group 1987, Miller 1990, Boguraev *et al.* 1992, Svensén 1993, Martin & Tamm 1996.
📕 *MLA International Bibliography* [annual], Norwood MA, 1988–.

data-capture
A cover term for those strategies, often computer-based, which are aimed at collecting data for the compilation of REFERENCE WORKS. These include techniques for gathering primary data (CITATION FILE, CORPUS, FIELDWORK) as well as reliance on secondary sources (e.g. copying from other dictionaries).
⇨ DATA-PROCESSING.
📖 Knowles 1990.

data collection
⇨ DATA-CAPTURE.

data gathering
⇨ DATA-CAPTURE.

data-processing
The electronic collection, manipulation and presentation of DATA.
📖 DANLEX Group 1987, Lemmens & Wekker 1990.

data retrieval
⇨   INFORMATION RETRIEVAL.

date
The year of publication of a book or other text. Modern publications allow, and COPYRIGHT law requires, accurate dating, but for earlier periods it is sometimes difficult to determine the origin of source material.
⇨   ANTEDATING, EDITION, ETYMOLOGY.
📖   Barnhart 1989, Berg 1993.

dead example
An EDITORIAL EXAMPLE not based on citation but invented to illustrate a particular construction type.
📖   Svensén 1993.

dead reference
A cross-reference to a HEADWORD which does not occur in the dictionary in question.
⇨   CHARACTER REFERENCE.

deaf language
⇨   SIGN LANGUAGE.

declension
The paradigm of an ADJECTIVE, NOUN or PRONOUN, giving all its forms. In dictionaries of Ancient Greek and Latin, whose nouns are classified according to the regularities of their paradigms, the CANONICAL FORM is traditionally the nominative singular. In ambiguous instances, the word may be accompanied by a conventional label or number, or by an alternative form, as an indicator of the appropriate paradigm to which it belongs.
⇨   CONJUGATION.

decoding
A linguistic activity involving receptive skills such as reading, listening or translating from a foreign language into a NATIVE LANGUAGE. The dictionary most suitable for this function is the PASSIVE DICTIONARY.

decoding dictionary
⇨   PASSIVE DICTIONARY.

definer
One who engages in the writing of DEFINITIONS.

definiendum
A word or phrase the meaning of which is to be explained in a DEFINITION.

definiens
The DEFINITION which explains the meaning of a word or phrase.

defining dictionary
A type of REFERENCE WORK which explains the meaning of the words and phrases by DEFINITIONS. The prototype of this dictionary is the monolingual alphabetical GENERAL DICTIONARY.
⇨   ENCYCLOPEDIC DICTIONARY, TERMINOLOGICAL DICTIONARY.

defining feature
⇨   CHARACTERISTIC.

defining style
⇨   DEFINITION STYLE.

defining thesaurus
⇨   DISTINCTIVE SYNONYMY.

defining vocabulary
The controlled use of VOCABULARY in DEFINITIONS. Restricting the number of words to those most frequent has become common practice in the compilation of the CHILDREN'S DICTIONARY and the LEARNER'S DICTIONARY, e.g. the 2,000-word *Longman Defining Vocabulary*, as listed in the *Longman Dictionary of Contemporary English* [3rd edition] (Harlow, 1995). The assumption is that explanations are easier to grasp when couched in 'simple language'. However, information on the FREQUENCY of words and phrases is not available even for all the major world languages, and the most common CORE WORDS are not necessarily the easiest to learn, since they tend to be polysemous. Thus, *head* and *run* each have many different SENSES in addition to being used as either nouns or verbs. Which of these senses is coming into play if *manager* or *manage* is defined in terms of *head* and *run*?
⇨   VOCABULARY CONTROL.
📖   Landau 1984, Fox 1989, Neubauer 1989.
📖   *An International Reader's Dictionary, Explaining the Meaning of over 24,000 Items within a Vocabulary of 1,490 Words* (M. West), London, 1965.

definition
A component part in the MICROSTRUCTURE of a REFERENCE WORK which gives an explanation of the meaning of a word, phrase or term. The definition provides an essential function: it is the place where compilers locate and users find semantic

information. The monolingual general dictionary provides definitions in a prominent position at the beginning of entries (it is therefore also often called DEFINING DICTIONARY or EXPLANATORY DICTIONARY), usually in the form of a 'comment' on the 'topic' introduced by the HEADWORD. The relationship between the word to be explained ('definiendum') and the explanation ('definiens') is complex and depends on the purpose of the definition and the DEFINITION STYLE used.

A distinction can be made between the lexicographic definition as formulated in general dictionaries and the ENCYCLOPEDIC DEFINITION, which explains by providing factual information about the item in question within a specific subject-matter context. The traditional ('analytical', 'classical', 'formal' or 'logical') definition formula 'X is a member of the class Y distinguished from other members by the feature(s) N' works well for nouns which are core items of the vocabulary in restricted lexical domains, but is less suitable for defining verbs and adjectives or more specialised CONCEPTS.
⇨ CIRCULAR DEFINITION, DEFINING VOCABULARY, RECURSIVE DEFINITION.
📖 Landau 1984, Hanks 1987, Jackson 1988, Stock 1988, ISO 1990, Dolezal 1992, Wiegand 1992, Svensén 1993.

definitional dictionary
⇨ DEFINING DICTIONARY.

definition style
The approach taken and the type of language chosen to provide a DEFINITION. Depending on the nature and scope of the REFERENCE WORK and its intended users, compilers can select (or combine) one or more defining styles which may also be influenced by the theoretical model of 'meaning' they are committed to. Thus the traditional definition formula 'X is a type of Y which . . .' presupposes a knowledge of the SENSE RELATIONS between words, e.g. as members of HYPERONYM or HYPONYM chains. Such definitions specify conceptual links between lexical items, while 'encyclopedic' definitions tend to describe objects in physical or pictorial terms. Some words or phrases are easier to define by a GLOSS or SYNONYM, particularly when they form sets in SEMANTIC FIELDS; others, especially verbs, are more amenable to a 'whole-sentence' approach, e.g. from *Collins COBUILD English Dictionary* (London, 1995): 'If you **define** a word or expression, you explain its meaning, for example in a dictionary.'

⇨ CONTEXTUAL DEFINITION, ENCYCLOPEDIC DEFINITION, EXPLANATION, EXTENSIONAL DEFINITION, FOLK DEFINITION, FORMULAIC DEFINITION, HUMOROUS DEFINITION, IMPLICIT DEFINITION, INTENSIONAL DEFINITION, OSTENSIVE DEFINITION, SEMANTICS.
📖 Frawley 1982, Landau 1984, Wierzbicka 1985, Ilson 1986a, Hanks 1987, Markowitz & Franz 1988, Stock 1992, Walter 1992, Svensén 1993, Béjoint 1994.

degrees in lexicography
⇨ TRAINING.

demotic language
Words and phrases associated with the 'low' rather than the 'high' variety of a language. In dictionary-making, DIASYSTEMATIC LABELLING can be used to classify demotic usage as 'slang' (in opposition to 'genteel'), as 'speech' (in opposition to 'writing'), or as 'vernacular' (in opposition to 'learned').
⇨ DIGLOSSIA.

denotation
An aspect of MEANING that relates a word or phrase to the objective REFERENT it expresses. Also called 'referential' or 'cognitive' meaning, this is the usual topic of the explanation of words (DEFINITION), while the more subjective or emotive aspects (CONNOTATION) are difficult to agree upon and capture in the dictionary.
📖 Landau 1984, Jackson 1988, Svensén 1993, Gouws 1996.

denotative meaning
⇨ DENOTATION.

denotatum
The meaning distilled from a REFERENT by a process of perception.
⇨ DENOTATION.

depository library
A LIBRARY of central or national importance where all books published in a country must be deposited by law.

deprecated term
A technical TERM rejected by the practitioners in a subject field as a less suitable synonym for designating a particular CONCEPT.
⇨ ACCEPTABILITY RATING.
📖 ISO 1990.

derivation

1 The origin and early history of a word or phrase.
   ⇨ ETYMOLOGY.
2 The creation of a new word, typically by adding an AFFIX to a BASE or STEM.
   ⇨ WORD FORMATION.

derivational morpheme

A MORPHEME added to a BASE or STEM to form a new word.
⇨ INFLECTIONAL MORPHEME.

derivational morphology

⇨ MORPHOLOGY.

derivative

A word which is the result of DERIVATION, e.g. *lexical, lexically, lexicalise, lexicalisation, delexicalise < lex-*. Such words form paradigms (WORD FAMILIES). In GENERAL DICTIONARIES, they are not always given headword status in separate entries, but added as RUN-ON ENTRIES or subentries under the HEADWORD from which they are assumed to be derived (e.g. *lexis* or *lexical*).
⇨ CLUSTERING.
📖 Berg 1993.
📑 *The Latin Elements in English Words. A Handook of Derivation* (L. Lee), New York NY, 1959.

derivative dictionary

A DICTIONARY closely based on another, of which it may be an abridged version or a copy.
⇨ BILINGUALISED DICTIONARY, COPYING IN DICTIONARIES, DICTIONARY FAMILY.
📑 *Webster's New Young American Dictionary* [based on *Merriam-Webster's Elementary Dictionary*], New York NY, 1995.

derogatory

A USAGE LABEL in a dictionary to mark a word or phrase as 'offensive' or 'disparaging', one extreme example being the racial slur.
⇨ BIAS-FREE VOCABULARY, RACISM.

descriptive dictionary

⇨ DESCRIPTIVE LEXICOGRAPHY.

descriptive grammar

⇨ GRAMMAR.

descriptive lexicography

An approach to DICTIONARY-MAKING which is based on the observed facts about a language or language variety rather than attitudes on how it should be used (PRESCRIPTIVE LEXICOGRAPHY). Nowadays, with the availability of CORPUS evidence, the collection of DATA on actual USAGE is no longer so difficult, expensive and time-consuming as in the past. Even if it were possible to produce a truly comprehensive and accurate 'descriptive dictionary', it would, in turn, be regarded by its users as an AUTHORITY on 'correctness'.
⇨ MONITOR CORPUS, NORM, STANDARD (1).
📖 Zgusta 1989a, Svensén 1993, Béjoint 1994.

design

The overall principles that govern the production of efficient REFERENCE WORKS, taking into account not only features of content (INFORMATION CATEGORIES) and presentation (ARRANGEMENT), but also the reference needs and skills of the USER.
⇨ ACCESS STRUCTURE, LAYOUT, STRUCTURE.
📖 Mufwene 1984, Hausmann & Wiegand 1989, Stark 1996.

designation

The expression of a meaning or CONCEPT by a word or TERM.
📖 ISO 1990.

designatum

The aspect of meaning identified for expression by a word or phrase.
⇨ DESIGNATION.

desk dictionary

A general-purpose dictionary similar in scope and size to the COLLEGE DICTIONARY and the STANDARD DICTIONARY. In the North American tradition, it usually contains ENCYCLOPEDIC INFORMATION.
📖 Landau 1984, Algeo 1990, Svensén 1993.
📑 *Merriam Webster's Medical Desk Dictionary*, Springfield MA, 1986.

desktop publishing

⇨ PUBLISHING.

determiner

A FUNCTION WORD associated with a noun, to express quantity, possession etc.
📑 *Collins COBUILD English Guides 10: Determiners* (R. Berry), London, 1997.

diachronic dictionary

A dictionary which traces the origins and developments of words through one or more periods in the history of the language, in contrast to a SYNCHRONIC DICTIONARY, which concentrates on the contemporary language.
⇨ ETYMOLOGICAL DICTIONARY, HISTORICAL DICTIONARY, PERIOD DICTIONARY.
📖 Landau 1984, Svensén 1993.

diachronic information

A usage feature which associates a word or phrase with a particular PERIOD in the history of a language. Such information can be marked in dictionaries by temporal USAGE LABELS on a chronological scale from 'archaic' through 'obsolescent' to contemporary (the unmarked neutral, synchronic zone) and 'new'.
⇨ ARCHAISM, HISTORICAL DICTIONARY, NEOLOGISM.

diachronic markedness

Labelled DIACHRONIC INFORMATION in a dictionary.

diaconnotative information

⇨ DIAEVALUATIVE INFORMATION.

diaconnotative markedness

⇨ DIAEVALUATIVE MARKEDNESS.

diacritic (mark)

A graphic sign placed above, below, beside or through a LETTER or CHARACTER, often to indicate a particular phonological exponent (e.g. nasalisation, palatalisation, lengthening, lip-rounding, stress or tone).
⇨ TRANSCRIPTION.

diaevaluative information

A usage feature which associates a word or phrase with a particular attitude or evaluation. Such information can be marked in dictionaries by USAGE LABELS on a scale of emotiveness from 'appreciative' through neutral (the unmarked zone) to 'derogatory' and 'offensive'.

diaevaluative markedness

Labelled DIAEVALUATIVE INFORMATION in a dictionary.

diafrequential information

A usage feature which associates a word or phrase with a particular FREQUENCY of occurrence. Such information can be marked in dictionaries by USAGE LABELS ranging from 'very frequent' to frequent (the unmarked neutral zone) to 'becoming rare' and 'very rare'.
⇨ BASIC VOCABULARY, CORPUS, FREQUENCY DICTIONARY.

diafrequential markedness

Labelled DIAFREQUENTIAL INFORMATION in a dictionary.

diaintegrative information

A usage feature which associates a word or phrase with a particular degree of integration into the native word-stock of the language. Such information can be marked in dictionaries by USAGE LABELS on a scale of indigenisation ranging from 'foreign' and 'borrowed' through 'assimilated' to native (the unmarked neutral zone).
⇨ CREOLE, FOREIGNISM.

diaintegrative markedness

Labelled DIAINTEGRATIVE INFORMATION in a dictionary.

dialect

A variety of a language, sometimes contrasted with STANDARD, and often with a negative connotation. The term has had wide application, ranging from very localised forms (e.g. in a village) to extensive language communities (e.g. the varieties of Chinese). 'Prestige dialects' are those which have gained status through social or political developments. Linguists prefer to use specific terms to refer to specialised aspects of language variety, e.g. SOCIOLECT, GENDERLECT, IDIOLECT, and TECHNOLECT.
⇨ DIALECT DICTIONARY, DIALECTOLOGY, LANGUAGE VARIETY, REGIONALISM.
📖 Wakelin 1987, McArthur 1992.

dialect atlas

⇨ LINGUISTIC ATLAS (1).

dialect dictionary

A type of REFERENCE WORK containing information about one or more DIALECTS of a language. There is a very long tradition of specialised glossaries listing the vocabulary of local dialects, and many general dictionaries include a selection of REGIONALISMS. However, it was not until nineteenth-century historical-comparative linguists and folklorists carried out systematic fieldwork that DIALECTOLOGY became established in many countries, leading to the development of a special dictionary genre. Since J. Wright's *English Dialect Dictionary* (Oxford, 1898–1905), many of the local (or 'provincial') dialects of Britain and the USA and the national (or 'metropolitan') varieties of English have been codified in dictionaries. However, their coverage is uneven, and there are considerable differences in methodology from one country and language to another. In recent years there has been a marked shift from geographical to social dialects, producing new dictionary types, e.g. for SLANG and CREOLE.

⇨   LINGUISTIC ATLAS (1), REGIONAL DICTIONARY.

📖   Wakelin 1987, Kuhn 1988, Görlach 1990, McArthur 1992, Svensén 1993.

📰   *Survey of English Dialects. The Dictionary and Grammar* (C. Upton *et al.*), London, 1994.

dialect geography

A branch of DIALECTOLOGY concerned with regional (rather than social) dialects.

⇨   LINGUISTIC ATLAS (1).

dialect label

⇨   REGIONAL LABEL.

dialect lexicography

A complex of activities concerned with the design, compilation, use and evaluation of DIALECT DICTIONARIES. General dictionaries mark language variation (and other features such as style, formality and technicality) by means of USAGE LABELS, but these do not systematically describe any particular regional or social DIALECTS. On the basis of fieldwork techniques, traditional dialectology plotted differences in vocabulary, pronunciation and grammar on maps (LINGUISTIC ATLAS (1)), and it is information of this kind which is presented in specialised dictionaries. There is still no unified framework, and dialect dictionaries can range from the popular-amateurish to the philological-scholarly, with considerable differences between various linguistic and cultural traditions.

📖   Fischer & Ammann 1991.

dialectology

An academic discipline concerned with the study of DIALECTS. When the emphasis is on local or regional varieties of a language, the term DIALECT GEOGRAPHY may be appropriate; when the emphasis is on social varieties (also called

SOCIOLECTS), dialectology shades into SOCIOLINGUISTICS.

⇨   DIALECT DICTIONARY, REGIONAL DICTIONARY.

diamedial information

A usage feature which associates a word or phrase with a particular channel of communication. Such information can be marked in some dictionaries by USAGE LABELS for the 'written' or 'spoken' media, while items shared by both are usually left unmarked.

diamedial markedness

Labelled DIAMEDIAL INFORMATION in a dictionary.

dianormative information

A usage feature which associates a word or phrase with a particular degree of deviation from a cultural STANDARD. Such information can be marked in dictionaries by USAGE LABELS on a scale from correct (the unmarked neutral zone) to 'substandard' or 'illiterate'.

⇨   CORRECTNESS, HYPERCORRECTION.

dianormative markedness

Labelled DIANORMATIVE INFORMATION in a dictionary.

diaphasic information

A usage feature which associates a word or phrase with a particular REGISTER of a language. Such information can be marked in dictionaries by USAGE LABELS on a scale of formality from 'elevated' and 'formal' through neutral (the unmarked zone) to 'informal' and 'intimate'. There is often an overlap with DIASTRATIC INFORMATION.

diaphasic markedness

Labelled DIAPHASIC INFORMATION in a dictionary.

diary

1   A type of REFERENCE WORK using the style of a periodicised record.

     ⇨   ALMANACK, CALENDAR.

2   In research on dictionary use, a user's personal record of his/her experience in consulting various reference works during or after specific activities such as writing or translating.

     ⇨   USER PERSPECTIVE, USER RESEARCH.

     📖   Nuccorini 1992.

diastratic information

A usage feature which associates a word or phrase with a particular social group. Such information can be marked in dictionaries by USAGE LABELS on a scale from neutral (the unmarked zone) to 'demotic' or 'slang'. In some cultures, such as the Indian caste system, there may be an extension of the scale towards the 'high' varieties. There is often an overlap with DIAPHASIC INFORMATION.
⇨ SLANG DICTIONARY, SOCIOLECT.

diastratic markedness

Labelled DIASTRATIC INFORMATION in a dictionary.

diasystematic labelling

A unified way of specifying the restrictions on the USAGE of the word or phrase being explained, through a range of interrelated USAGE LABELS.
⇨ Panel 'Usage Labels' (page 151).
📖 Hausmann & Wiegand 1989, Ilson 1990, Thomsen 1994.

diatechnical information

A usage feature which associates a word or phrase with a particular SUBJECT FIELD. Such information can be marked in dictionaries by USAGE LABELS for a range of technical specialities, e.g. 'Law', 'Music', 'Chemistry'. The CORE WORDS common to non-technical language varieties are usually left unmarked, as is non-specific, 'vague' vocabulary.
⇨ SUBJECT-FIELD DICTIONARY, TERMINOLOGICAL DICTIONARY.

diatechnical markedness

Labelled DIATECHNICAL INFORMATION in a dictionary.

diatextual information

A usage feature which associates a word or phrase with a particular discourse type or GENRE. Such information can be marked in dictionaries by USAGE LABELS on a scale of textuality from 'poetic' to 'conversational', with the shared neutral items remaining unmarked. There is often an overlap or combination with DIAPHASIC and DIASTRATIC INFORMATION.
⇨ COLLOQUIALISM, DISCOURSE ANALYSIS, TEXT LINGUISTICS.

diatextual markedness

Labelled DIATEXTUAL INFORMATION in a dictionary.

diatopic(al) information

A usage feature which associates a word or phrase with a particular DIALECT or regional language variety. Such features can be marked in dictionaries by USAGE LABELS on a continuum of regionality from 'local' or 'provincial' dialects to 'metropolitan' and even 'international' varieties. The neutral zone of the 'home' variety (e.g. British English in a British dictionary or American English in an American dictionary) may be left unmarked.
⇨ DIALECT DICTIONARY, REGIONAL DICTIONARY, REGIONAL LABEL.

diatopic(al) markedness

Labelled DIATOPICAL INFORMATION in a dictionary.

dictionarese

The language and other conventions in reference works, which often puzzle users, e.g. ABBREVIATIONS and symbols, USAGE LABELS, CROSS-REFERENCES, DEFINITION formulae and GRAMMAR codes.
⇨ DICTIONARIES AS DISCOURSE.

dictionarian

An archaic term for one (usually an amateur) who engages in the compilation of dictionaries.
⇨ LEXICOGRAPHER.

Dictionaries

The title of the journal of the DICTIONARY SOCIETY OF NORTH AMERICA, published annually since 1979.

dictionaries as discourse

The textual features of dictionaries and other reference works and their relative user-friendliness, which have rarely been the subject of systematic critical evaluation. The requirements of the genre, i.e. maximum information in minimum space, often lead to a degree of TEXT COMPRESSION which may conflict with those of clarity and transparency.
⇨ CRITICISM, DESIGN, EVALUATION.
📖 DeMaria 1986, Dolezal 1989, Wiegand 1990.

dictionarist

An archaic term for one who engages in the compilation of dictionaries.
⇨ LEXICOGRAPHER.

dictionary

The most common type of REFERENCE WORK, first used as a TITLE in the Latin–English *Dictionary of Syr Thomas Elyot knyght* (London, 1538), and the monolingual *English Dictionarie: or, An Interpreter of Hard English Words* by Henry Cockeram (London, 1623).

Since the sixteenth century the title *dictionary* has been used for an increasingly wider range of alphabetic (but also thematic), general (but also specialised), monolingual (but also bilingual and multilingual) reference works, from the polyglot to the historical and the pedagogical dictionary. At the same time there has been a tendency for other terms to be used as designations for more specialised dictionary genres, e.g. THESAURUS, ENCYCLOPEDIA and TERMINOLOGY. To describe and evaluate the structural components of dictionaries, terms like MACROSTRUCTURE (the overall WORD-LIST and its organisation) and MICROSTRUCTURE (the information categories presented inside entries) have been developed in the literature.

⇨ BIBLIOGRAPHY (1), BUYING GUIDE, COMPILER PERSPECTIVE, LEXICOGRAPHY, TERMINOLOGICAL DICTIONARY, USER PERSPECTIVE, WORDBOOK.

📖 Landau 1984, Stein 1985, Bailey 1987, Jackson 1988, Zgusta 1988a, Hausmann *et al.* 1989–91, James 1989, Svensén 1993, Béjoint 1994, Osselton 1995, Green 1996.

📖 *Dictionary of Dictionaries* (T. Kabdebo), London, 1992.

dictionary archaeology

The uncovering of links between different dictionaries by studying their contents, history and genetic affiliations.

⇨ CRITICISM, DICTIONARY HISTORY.

📖 Dolezal 1986, Ilson 1986b.

dictionary archive

⇨ ARCHIVE (1).

dictionary article

⇨ ENTRY.

dictionary automation

⇨ COMPUTATIONAL LEXICOGRAPHY.

dictionary awareness

⇨ DICTIONARY CULTURE.

dictionary bibliography

⇨ BIBLIOGRAPHY (1).

dictionary buying guide

⇨ BUYING GUIDE.

dictionary catalogue

1 A list of dictionaries and other reference works forming part of a REFERENCE DEPARTMENT in a library, or a separate publication providing bibliographical details. As the AUTHORSHIP of such works is often difficult to determine, the items may be entered in a single INDEX of both authors'/compilers' names and titles, with subdivisions by subject, country or language.

⇨ BIBLIOGRAPHY (1).

📖 *Dictionary of Dictionaries* (T. Kabdebo), London, 1992; *The Encyclopedia of Dictionaries Published in Japan* (T. Okimori *et al.*), Tokyo, 1996.

2 A CATALOGUE published in A–Z format.

dictionary category

⇨ TYPE (1).

dictionary collection

⇨ COLLECTION (1).

dictionary compiler

⇨ COMPILER.

dictionary component

⇨ COMPONENT (1).

dictionary criminality

⇨ CRIMINALITY.

dictionary criticism

⇨ CRITICISM.

dictionary culture

The critical awareness of the value and limitations of DICTIONARIES and other reference works in a particular community. This can vary according to the status of the language used, the availability of dictionaries and the standards of DICTIONARY-MAKING, dictionary CRITICISM and dictionary use.

⇨ CULTURAL LEXICOGRAPHY, EVALUATION, IMAGE OF THE DICTIONARY, TRAINING.

dictionary-cum-atlas

⇨ HYBRID.

dictionary-cum-encyclopedia

⇨ HYBRID.

dictionary-cum-grammar
⇨ HYBRID.

dictionary-cum-thesaurus
⇨ HYBRID.

dictionary-cum-usage guide
⇨ HYBRID.

dictionary definition
⇨ DEFINITION.

dictionary entry
⇨ ENTRY.

dictionary family
The range of dictionaries from 'unabridged' through 'concise' to 'pocket' and 'gem' (or a related set of reference works, including encyclopedic and technical) produced under the same publisher's IMPRINT.
⇨ HYBRID.
   Ilson 1986b, Burnett 1988.
   The Oxford English Dictionary [2nd edition] (J. A. Simpson & E. S. C. Weiner), Oxford, 1989; *The New Shorter Oxford English Dictionary on Historical Principles* [4th edition] (L. Brown), Oxford, 1993; *The Concise Oxford Dictionary of Current English* [8th edition] (R. E. Allen), Oxford, 1990; *The Pocket Oxford Dictionary of Current English* [8th edition] (D. Thompson), Oxford, 1992.

dictionary for foreign-language learners
⇨ LEARNER'S DICTIONARY.

dictionary function
⇨ FUNCTION.

dictionary genre
⇨ TYPE (1).

dictionary grammar
The GRAMMATICAL INFORMATION in the dictionary included as a separate component arranged in systematic or alphabetical order, usually in the FRONT MATTER rather than integrated into the entries in abbreviated form.
⇨ GRAMMAR DICTIONARY.
   Haraldsson 1996.

dictionary history
A branch of DICTIONARY RESEARCH concerned with the chronological development of diction-

aries and their compilers within a sociocultural context.
   Starnes & Noyes 1946/91, Friend 1967, Collison 1982, Dolezal 1985, Stein 1985, Hartmann 1986, Ilson 1986b, McArthur 1986a, Steiner 1986a, Osselton 1990, Zgusta 1992, Green 1996.

dictionary index
1 An INDEX provided in addition to the alphabetically arranged central WORD-LIST of a dictionary, usually as part of the BACK MATTER, to help the user find supplementary INFORMATION such as illustrations, names, events, defining vocabulary, archaisms or neologisms.
2 An INDEX published in A–Z format.
   Indexionary. A Dictionary-index in which Words are Grouped Alphabetically According to their Functional Elements (B. Kasravi), Santa Barbara CA, 1990.

dictionary information
The INFORMATION CATEGORIES presented by the compiler and consulted by the user of a dictionary or other reference work. The information can be linguistic (e.g. spelling, meaning, pronunciation) or encyclopedic (facts and figures).

dictionary journal
A periodical publication containing information of relevance to DICTIONARY-MAKING, e.g. *The Barnhart Dictionary Companion* (established 1991), which lists English NEOLOGISMS from various fields of activity.

dictionary look-up form
⇨ CANONICAL FORM.

dictionary maker
⇨ REFERENCE PROFESSIONAL.

dictionary-making
The practical aspects of LEXICOGRAPHY, concerned with the professional activity of compiling REFERENCE WORKS. Depending upon the complexity and scale of a dictionary project and the historical, organisational and technical context in which it is implemented, a number of stages or phases may be distinguished, from planning and staff training to printing and marketing. Most projects involve three basic operations: FIELDWORK, or gathering and recording of raw DATA; description, or EDITING the text; and presentation, or

PUBLISHING the final product. The old debate as to whether practical lexicography is a science or an art is now being resolved by an increased emphasis on professional TRAINING and computerisation, supported by complementary DICTIONARY RESEARCH.

⇨ COMPILER PERSPECTIVE, COMPUTATIONAL LEXICOGRAPHY, DATABASE, Panel 'Lexicography: Theory and Practice' (page 86).

📖 Landau 1984, Burchfield 1987a, Krishnamurthy 1987, Jackson 1988, Algeo 1990, Svensén 1993, Béjoint 1994.

dictionary manual
⇨ WORKBOOK.

dictionary of authors
A type of REFERENCE WORK providing literary, biographical and sometimes encyclopedic information about a selection of authors from a country, language, period or genre.

⇨ BIOGRAPHICAL DICTIONARY.

📘 *The Cambridge Guide to Literature in English* (I. Ousby), Cambridge, 1988; *The Oxford Companion to Twentieth-Century Literature in English* (J. Stringer), Oxford, 1996.

dictionary order
⇨ ARRANGEMENT.

dictionary range
⇨ DICTIONARY FAMILY.

dictionary research
The theoretical aspects of LEXICOGRAPHY, concerned with the academic study of such topics as the nature, history, criticism, typology and use of DICTIONARIES and other REFERENCE WORKS.

⇨ METALEXICOGRAPHY, REFERENCE SCIENCE, Panel 'Lexicography: Theory and Practice' (page 86).

📖 Bailey 1987, Hausmann *et al.* 1989–91, Hartmann 1996a.

Dictionary Research Centre
An academic institute concerned with the investigation of such topics as the nature, history, criticism, typology and use of DICTIONARIES and other reference works. Such centres exist at the University of Exeter (UK), the University of Erlangen-Nürnberg (Germany), the Australian National University, Macquarie University (Australia), Nanjing University (China), Yonsei University (Korea), the University of Montreal (Canada) and elsewhere. In addition to research, these centres are active in documentation as well as TRAINING and organising conferences in LEXICOGRAPHY.

🖥 Australian National University website: www.anu.edu.au/andc; Exeter website: www.ex.ac.uk/coverpage/lex; Macquarie website: www.macnet.mq.edu.au

dictionary review
⇨ REVIEW.

dictionary skills
⇨ REFERENCE SKILLS.

Dictionary Society of North America
A professional society established at Indiana State University in 1975. It holds meetings every two years and publishes a newsletter and the journal *DICTIONARIES*. Together with the EUROPEAN ASSOCIATION FOR LEXICOGRAPHY, the Dictionary Society of North America co-sponsors the *INTERNATIONAL JOURNAL OF LEXICOGRAPHY* and the double series *LEXICOGRAPHICA* (*Series Maior* and *International Annual*).

🖥 Website: www.csuohio.edu/dsna/

dictionary software
⇨ SOFTWARE.

dictionary structure
⇨ STRUCTURE.

dictionary style
The content and form of a dictionary that are appropriate to the reference needs and skills of the user.

⇨ DICTIONARESE, TYPOLOGY (1).

📖 Zgusta 1991.

dictionary title
⇨ TITLE.

dictionary type
⇨ TYPE (1).

dictionary typology
⇨ TYPOLOGY (1).

dictionary use
⇨ USE OF REFERENCE WORKS.

dictionary user
⇨ USER.

dictionary-using skills
⇨ REFERENCE SKILLS.

dictionary war
Acrimonious rivalry between competing dictionary compilers, publishers or critics. Examples include the original 'war of the dictionaries' between Noah Webster and Joseph Worcester in the 1830s about how to represent pronunciation in the American dictionary; the critical reception of *Webster's Third New International Dictionary* in the early 1960s; and the recent competition among British publishers in the LEARNER'S DICTIONARY market.
📖 Read 1986, Haebler 1989, Algeo 1990, Béjoint 1994, Morton 1994, Allen 1996.

dictionary workbook
⇨ WORKBOOK.

didactic dictionary
⇨ PEDAGOGICAL DICTIONARY.

differentia specifica
In the classical DEFINITION formula, the second part, or one or more of the characteristic features which distinguish the word to be explained from the generic term of which it is considered a specific instance. Thus, the English word *fir* can be defined as 'a kind of tree with evergreen needles'. The phrase *with evergreen needles* is the differentia specifica which sets *fir* off from *tree*, the GENUS PROXIMUM.
📖 Svensén 1993.

diglossia
The presence in a language of two competing STANDARDS, such as the *katharevusa* ('high' or archaising) and *dhimotiki* ('low' or popular) varieties of Modern Greek.
📖 Britto 1986.

digraph
1 In alphabetic writing systems, the combined use of two letters to represent a single speech sound, e.g. English *th* for /θ/. When they are conjoined, as in *æ*, they are known as 'ligatures'.
    ⇨ ALPHABETICAL ORGANISATION.
2 In syllabic writing systems such as that used for Tamil, two conjoined characters which represent a syllable, e.g. தி.

📖 Zgusta 1989b.
📘 *Handbook of Scripts and Alphabets* (G. L. Campbell), London, 1996.

digraphia
The co-existence in one language of two writing systems ('bigraphism') for the representation of speech, e.g. kana and kanji in Japanese. A special case of digraphia, known as the 'aljamiado principle' is the use by Muslims of the Perso-Arabic script for a number of languages normally written in different scripts.
⇨ ROMANISATION.
📖 Hegyi 1979.

diplomas in lexicography
⇨ TRAINING.

direct entry
The listing of a MULTI-WORD EXPRESSION under its first (rather than last) constituent.
⇨ INVERTED ENTRY.

directionality
The user orientation of the BILINGUAL DICTIONARY according to the direction of the look-up operation.
⇨ BIDIRECTIONAL DICTIONARY, MONODIRECTIONAL DICTIONARY, SOURCE LANGUAGE, TARGET LANGUAGE.
📖 Steiner 1986b, Kernerman 1994.

directory
A type of REFERENCE WORK which gives information, usually in alphabetical order of names, on contact addresses and specialisations of the people, organisations or products listed.
⇨ TELEPHONE DIRECTORY, YELLOW PAGES.
📘 *The CHEST Directory 1996/97* [of IT products for the education and research communities] (T. Jones), Bath, 1996; *Who's Who in Lexicography. An International Directory of EURALEX Members* (S. McGill), Exeter, 1996.

disambiguation
The (typically electronic) recognition and separation of words similar in form either by their grammatical shapes or by their meanings.
⇨ LEMMATISATION, SENSE DISCRIMINATION.

discography
A CATALOGUE of music and other sound recordings in alphabetical and/or thematic order, giving details on titles, composers, performers etc.

▣ *Music Master CD Catalogue* (G. Rankin), London, 1991.

discourse analysis

A branch of LINGUISTICS concerned with language not as words or sentences, but as (spoken as well as written) text in context. Discourse analysis focuses on conversational and other face-to-face interaction (and is thus close to SOCIO-LINGUISTICS), while TEXT LINGUISTICS is more associated with the study of written and printed text and the factors that contribute to its structural cohesion. Both approaches profit from the evidence provided by CORPUS LINGUISTICS, and both have potential application to lexicography, e.g. in the analysis of the complexity and transparency of dictionary entries.

⇨ DICTIONARIES AS DISCOURSE, TEXT COMPRESSION.

▣ Dolezal 1989, Hausmann & Wiegand 1989, Stubbs 1996.

discourse information

⇨ DIATEXTUAL INFORMATION.

discriminating synonymy

⇨ DISTINCTIVE SYNONYMY.

discrimination of meaning

⇨ SENSE DISCRIMINATION.

discussion

A device used to explain the meaning of words or phrases, such as the formula 'is used for . . .' in defining FUNCTION WORDS in general or learners' dictionaries.

⇨ DEFINITION STYLE.

▣ Ilson 1990.

distinctive feature

A CHARACTERISTIC which can be used to explain the meaning, or define the concept, of a word or term.

⇨ ANALYTICAL DEFINITION, COMPONENTIAL ANALYSIS.

distinctive synonymy

A SYNONYM DICTIONARY or THESAURUS in which expressions of similar meaning are not only listed and grouped into semantic sets, but also defined and set apart by SENSE DISCRIMINATION.

⇨ CUMULATIVE SYNONYMY, SYNONYMY (1), SYNONYMY (2).

▣ Hausmann 1990.

▣ *The British Synonymy* (H. T. Piozzi), London, 1794; *The Oxford Thesaurus. An A–Z Dictionary of Synonyms* (L. Urdang), Oxford, 1991.

distinctive thesaurus

⇨ DISTINCTIVE SYNONYMY.

divergence

In cases of partial TRANSLATION equivalence, the rendering of a word in one language by two or more words in the other language. Thus the meaning of the English word *aunt* is expressed in Danish by two words, *moster* 'maternal aunt' and *faster* 'paternal aunt'. (The opposite direction is called CONVERGENCE.) The BILINGUAL DICTIONARY must allow for such asymmetrical relations, in conjunction with the problem of the user orientation.

⇨ ANISOMORPHISM, BIDIRECTIONAL DICTIONARY.

divided indexing

⇨ SINGLE INDEXING.

document

A TEXT (such as a book, map, sound recording or electronic disk) which is the object of treatment (e.g. in TEXT PROCESSING or a CORPUS) or collection (e.g. in a LIBRARY or BIBLIOGRAPHY).

⇨ STANDARD GENERALIZED MARK-UP LANGUAGE.

documentalist

One who engages in the collection, processing and distribution of DOCUMENTS and the information contained in them.

⇨ FÉDÉRATION INTERNATIONALE D'INFORMATION ET DE DOCUMENTATION, REFERENCE PROFESSIONAL.

documentation

The totality of activities concerned with the collection, maintenance and exploitation of SOURCES in the compilation of REFERENCE WORKS.

⇨ CITATION, DATA.

▣ Schäfer 1980.

domain

Alternative term for FIELD.

doublespeak

A euphemistic word, phrase or style of discourse used to disguise the true meaning of a TEXT.

⇨ EUPHEMISM.

📄 *A Dictionary of Euphemisms and other Doubletalk* (H. Rawson), New York NY, 1981.

doubletalk
⇨ DOUBLESPEAK.

doublet
One of a pair of words or phrases similar in form and/or meaning and sharing a common origin, such as the English words *regal* and *royal*, which are both derived from Latin (via French) *regalis*.
⇨ COGNATE, CONFUSIBLE WORDS.

downward reference
A CROSS-REFERENCE from a general to a more specific (less comprehensive) heading in a CATALOGUE.

DSNA
Abbreviation for DICTIONARY SOCIETY OF NORTH AMERICA.

dual-language dictionary
⇨ BIDIRECTIONAL DICTIONARY.

Duke of Edinburgh English Language Competition Award
A set of prizes, including a section for dictionaries, awarded annually by the English Speaking Union (London) for the most outstanding English teaching materials.

dysphemism
A word or phrase used disparagingly.
⇨ EUPHEMISM.

E

EAFT
Abbreviation for EUROPEAN ASSOCIATION FOR TERMINOLOGY.

ECHO
The *European Commission Host Organisation* which provides access to European Union information, such as the terminological database EURODICAUTOM, by computer link.
⌨ Website: www2.echo.lu/

editing
The central stage in the DICTIONARY-MAKING process.
📖 Landau 1984, Reddick 1990.

edition
The particular version of a DOCUMENT such as a book or dictionary at the DATE of its publication. Depending on the frequency of its reissue and the nature of the changes made to the original text, it may be an identical 'impression' (REPRINT) or a substantially revised ('new' or 'second', 'third' etc.) or abridged edition.
⇨ FACSIMILE EDITION, RECENSION, REVISION.
📖 Ravin *et al.* 1990, Snell-Hornby 1990.

editor
One who engages in the preparation of TEXT for publication, one of several titles available for REFERENCE PROFESSIONALS, especially those in positions of authority and responsibility in a SCHOLARLY DICTIONARY.
📖 McGregor 1985, Berg 1993.

editorial example
An EXAMPLE used in a dictionary or other reference work, based on the introspective judgement (or 'competence') of a compiler rather than on a CORPUS or FIELDWORK evidence.
📖 Fox 1987, Svensén 1993.

EFL
Abbreviation for ENGLISH AS A FOREIGN LANGUAGE.

EFL dictionary
A LEARNER'S DICTIONARY designed for students of ENGLISH AS A FOREIGN LANGUAGE or ENGLISH AS A SECOND LANGUAGE.
⇨ COLLEGE DICTIONARY.
📖 McArthur 1989b, Stein 1989, Herbst 1990, McCorduck 1993, Béjoint 1994, Allen 1996.
📑 *Cambridge International Dictionary of English* (P. Procter), Cambridge, 1995; *Collins COBUILD English Dictionary* (J. Sinclair), London, 1995; *Longman Dictionary of Contemporary English* [3rd edition] (D. Summers), Harlow, 1995; *Oxford Advanced Learner's Dictionary* [5th edition] (J. Crowther), Oxford, 1995.

EFL lexicography
A complex of activities concerned with the design, compilation, use and evaluation of EFL DICTIONARIES.

ELC
Abbreviation for the EUROPEAN LANGUAGE COUNCIL.

electronic bilingual dictionary
A BILINGUAL DICTIONARY in electronic form.
📖 Atkins 1996.

electronic dictionary
A type of REFERENCE WORK which utilises computers and associated technology to present information on-screen. Examples include spelling checkers and thesauruses built into word processors, multi-volume dictionaries and encyclopedias on CD-ROM, multilingual terminological databanks and translation systems (e.g. EURODICAUTOM),

research corpora, hypertext and the INTERNET. Further progress will depend on the price, compatibility and user-friendliness of products and the ability of compilers and publishers to satisfy the reference needs of specific users.

⇨ COMPUTATIONAL LEXICOGRAPHY, INTERACTIVE DICTIONARY, MACHINE-READABLE DICTIONARY, POCKET ELECTRONIC DICTIONARY.

📖 DANLEX Group 1987, Sinclair 1987, Meijs 1992, Calzolari 1996.

💻 *The OED on CD-ROM* [2nd edition], Oxford, 1992. www.bucknell.edu/~rbeard/diction.html

electronic lexicography
⇨ COMPUTATIONAL LEXICOGRAPHY.

electronic publishing
⇨ PUBLISHING.

elementary dictionary
An informal term for a dictionary aimed at relative beginners.

📑 *Merriam Webster's Elementary Dictionary*, Springfield MA, 1986.

elicitation
A method of collecting linguistic DATA by FIELDWORK.

⇨ CITATION.

📖 Béjoint 1983.

ELT
Abbreviation for English Language Teaching.

ELT dictionary
⇨ EFL DICTIONARY.

ELT lexicography
⇨ EFL LEXICOGRAPHY.

-eme
A COMBINING FORM used in LINGUISTICS to refer to a number of distinct units at the level of speech (PHONEME), writing (GRAPHEME), morphology (MORPHEME) and vocabulary (LEXEME).

emotive meaning
⇨ CONNOTATION.

encoding
A linguistic activity involving productive skills such as writing, speaking or translating from the NATIVE LANGUAGE into a foreign language. The dictionary most suitable for this function is the ACTIVE DICTIONARY.

encoding dictionary
⇨ ACTIVE DICTIONARY.

encyclopedia
A type of REFERENCE WORK which presents factual information in a wide range of subject disciplines. This information is collected from expert consultants and arranged in a combination of systematic and alphabetical order for the benefit of the general educated reader. ENCYCLOPEDIC DEFINITIONS are more detailed and less vague than the meaning explanations offered in GENERAL DICTIONARIES. However, because of their price and bulk, encyclopedias can be less user-friendly. HYPERTEXT and CD-ROM technology is likely to bring new multimedia encyclopedic works that can be more easily produced and used via computer.

Many different approaches have been used even within the Western tradition, from Denis Diderot and Jean d'Alembert's French *Encyclopédie* (Paris, 1751–80) and Friedrich Brockhaus' German *Konversations-Lexikon* (Wiesbaden, 1809–11) to the *Encyclopaedia Britannica* (first published in Scotland 1768–71, and now edited and regularly updated from Chicago [15th edition, 32 volumes, 1974/85]).

⇨ BUYING GUIDE.

📖 Collison & Preece 1974, Haiman 1980, Landau 1984, Ryan 1989, McArthur 1992, Kister 1994.

📑 *Encyclopaedia cursus philosophici* (J. H. Alsted), Herborn, 1608; *The Cambridge Encyclopedia of the English Language* [2nd edition] (D. Crystal), Cambridge, 1997.

💻 *Microsoft Encarta Multimedia Encyclopedia*, Redmont WA, 1993; *Hutchinson Multimedia Encyclopedia*, Oxford 1997.

encyclopedic content
⇨ ENCYCLOPEDIC INFORMATION.

encyclopedic database
⇨ DATABASE.

encyclopedic definition
A DEFINITION which reflects encyclopedic knowledge (about facts) rather than linguistic knowledge (about words). Usually these two aspects overlap – ENCYCLOPEDIC INFORMATION often being difficult to distinguish from LINGUISTIC INFORMATION

– and dictionaries attempt to capture both in the explanation of meaning: a *tabla* is an 'Indian drum played in pairs by hand at variable pitch', but only a fully encyclopedic (and perhaps illustrated) description can demonstrate what it looks and sounds like, and how the effect is achieved.

📖 Wiegand 1992.

encyclopedic dictionary

A type of REFERENCE WORK which shares features of the GENERAL DICTIONARY and the ENCYCLOPEDIA. There is a tension between LINGUISTIC INFORMATION (e.g. on the etymology, spelling, pronunciation, grammar and meaning of the lexical items treated) and ENCYCLOPEDIC INFORMATION (e.g. facts and figures on the technical terms and names included, often with pictorial illustrations), which explains the HYBRID or compromise status of this dictionary type.

📖 Landau 1984, Stark 1996.

📖 *The Century Dictionary and Cyclopedia* (W. D. Whitney), New York NY, 1889–91; *Cambridge Encyclopedia* (D. Crystal), Cambridge, 1992; *Longman Dictionary of English Language and Culture* (D. Summers), Harlow, 1992.

encyclopedic information

One of the INFORMATION CATEGORIES presented by the compiler and consulted by the user of a reference work, based on factual knowledge. In contrast with LINGUISTIC INFORMATION, encyclopedic material is more concerned with the description of objective realities than the words or phrases that refer to them. In practice, however, there is no hard and fast boundary between factual and lexical knowledge. Many GENERAL DICTIONARIES contain encyclopedic items either in the entries (usually as part of a so-called ENCYCLOPEDIC DEFINITION) or outside the word-list (as part of the FRONT MATTER or BACK MATTER). SPECIALISED DICTIONARIES typically have more encyclopedic content.

The ENCYCLOPEDIA is the general-knowledge work of reference *par excellence*, usually published in multi-volume systematic formats with one or more alphabetical INDEXES, and involving consultants from a number of broadly based disciplines supplying facts and figures.

⇨ ENCYCLOPEDIC DICTIONARY, ENCYCLOPEDIC LEXICOGRAPHY.

📖 Roe 1978, Landau 1984, Svensén 1993.

encyclopedic lexicography

A complex of activities concerned with the design, compilation, use and evaluation of ENCYLOPEDIAS and ENCYCLOPEDIC DICTIONARIES and similar reference works. There is no unified framework, as such works vary considerably in scope,

ENCYCLOPEDIC LEXICOGRAPHY		GENERAL LEXICOGRAPHY
Emphasis on things (facts)	**Orientation of compiler**	Emphasis on words (language)
Multi-expert knowledge-base	**Compiling method**	Small-scale database
Factual information	**Scope**	General vocabulary
Specialist texts	**Corpus data used**	Non-specialist texts
'Encyclopedic' reflecting specialist conceptual systems	**Definition style**	'Linguistic' reflecting semantic distinctions in regular usage
Library use by educated readers	**Functionality**	Multi-purpose general users
Systematic order, with index	**Arrangement of macrostructure**	Script-based order
Provision of real-world knowledge	**Overall aim**	Explanation of meanings
Relatively common	**Pictorial illustration**	Relatively rare

Encyclopedic versus General Lexicography

content and presentation, and there are very different encyclopedic traditions.
⇨ Panel 'Encyclopedic versus General Lexicography' (page 49).
📖 Haiman 1980, Stark 1996.

encyclopedic material
⇨ ENCYCLOPEDIC INFORMATION.

encyclopedist
One who engages in the compilation of an ENCYCLOPEDIA.

ending
A word-final AFFIX.

end matter
⇨ BACK MATTER.

end-of-entry note
A paragraph at the end of a dictionary entry, for example with ENCYCLOPEDIC INFORMATION or details on USAGE, SYNONYMS or ETYMOLOGY.
⇨ USAGE NOTE.

endoglossic language
A language spoken as a NATIVE LANGUAGE by the majority of people in a given geographic region, e.g. French in France.
⇨ EXOGLOSSIC LANGUAGE.

English as a foreign language
Those varieties of English which are used by learners for whom it is not the NATIVE LANGUAGE, usually outside a country where it is the dominant language.
⇨ EFL DICTIONARY, LEARNER'S DICTIONARY.

English as a second language
Those varieties of English which are used by speakers for whom it is not the NATIVE LANGUAGE, usually in a country where it is the endoglossic, or dominant language, or in countries where it has an acknowledged function.
⇨ EFL DICTIONARY, LEARNER'S DICTIONARY.

English for specific purposes
⇨ LANGUAGE FOR SPECIFIC PURPOSES.

entry
The basic REFERENCE UNIT in a dictionary or other reference system such as a library catalogue. A wide range of formats (MICROSTRUCTURE) is possible. In the DICTIONARY, depending on its content and purpose, these component parts are common: the LEMMA (which allows the compiler to locate and the user to find the entry within the overall word-list); the formal COMMENT on the 'topic' introduced by the lemma (spelling, pronunciation, grammar); and the semantic 'comment' (definition, usage, etymology). In case of multiple meanings of the lemma, the entry is subdivided into (usually numbered or otherwise marked) sections called 'sub-entries' or 'sub-senses', each of which provides the same basic information categories.
📖 Landau 1984, Steele 1986, Atkins *et al.* 1988, Hausmann & Wiegand 1989, Roberts 1992, Svensén 1993.

entry database
⇨ DATABASE.

entry-form
⇨ CANONICAL FORM.

entry format
⇨ FORMAT.

entry-line
The initial line of an ENTRY in a dictionary or other reference work, highlighted by INDENTATION or protrusion ('hanging indentation') and containing the headword (usually in bold) and sometimes information on pronunciation and grammar.

entry-term
The form of a word or phrase which serves as the 'main entry', or HEADWORD, for a RECORD in a terminological dictionary, in contrast to a 'secondary entry' which lists alternative terms.
📖 ISO 1990.

entry-term list
⇨ TERM LIST.

entry-word
⇨ HEADWORD.

environment
⇨ CONTEXT (2).

epithet
A word or phrase used as a comment on, or brief description of, a person or object of attention, e.g. *E. K. 'Duke' Ellington*.

📖 *A Dictionary of Epithets and Terms of Address*
(L. Dunkling), London, 1990.

eponym
A word or phrase formed from a PERSONAL NAME,
e.g. *a Roget* (i.e. a kind of thesaurus) < Peter M.
Roget (1779–1869), the compiler of the *Thesaurus
of English Words and Phrases* (London, 1852).
📖 *Human Words; The Compleat Uncomputerized
Human Wordbook* (R. Hendrickson), Philadelphia
PA, 1972; *A Dictionary of Eponyms* (C. Beeching),
London, 1988.

equipollent opposition
⇨   OPPOSITION.

equivalence
The relationship between words or phrases, from
two or more languages, which share the same
MEANING. Because of the problem of ANISO-
MORPHISM, equivalence is 'partial' or 'relative'
rather than 'full' or 'exact' for most contexts.
Compilers of bilingual dictionaries often struggle
to find and codify such translation EQUIVALENTS,
taking into account the directionality of the
operation. In bilingual or multilingual TERMINO-
LOGICAL DICTIONARIES, equivalence implies
interlingual correspondence of DESIGNATIONS for
identical CONCEPTS.
⇨   CONVERGENCE, DIVERGENCE, TRANSLATION.
📖 Zgusta 1984, ISO 1990, Kromann *et al.* 1991.

equivalence discrimination
SENSE DISCRIMINATION in the bilingual dictionary. Words with multiple meaning ('polyequivalence') need to have translation EQUIVALENTS
specified for each of these meanings.
📖 Schnorr 1986, Kromann *et al.* 1991.

equivalent
A word or phrase in one language which corres-
ponds in MEANING to a word or phrase in another
language, e.g. English *mystery tour* and German
Fahrt ins Blaue. Because of linguistic and cultural
ANISOMORPHISM, translation equivalents are
typically partial, approximative, non-literal and
asymmetrical (rather than full, direct, word-for-
word and bidirectional). Their specification in the
BILINGUAL DICTIONARY is therefore fraught with
difficulties, and recourse must be had to surrogate
EXPLANATORY EQUIVALENTS.
⇨   CONVERGENCE, DIVERGENCE, TRANSLATION.
📖 Iannucci 1985.

error analysis
A practical field concerned with the study of lan-
guage learners' errors. A strong case has been
made for the use of error CORPORA to modify the
contents and presentation of the LEARNER'S DIC-
TIONARY, monolingual as well as bilingual.
⇨   INTERLANGUAGE.
📖 Granger *et al.* 1994, Milton & Chowdhury 1994,
Tono 1996.

-ese
A COMBINING FORM used in USAGE GUIDES and
similar genres to label particular text types as
'jargon', e.g. *commercialese, dictionarese, jour-
nalese*.

ESL
Abbreviation for ENGLISH AS A SECOND LAN-
GUAGE.

ESL dictionary
⇨   EFL DICTIONARY.

ESP
Abbreviation for English for Specific Purposes.
⇨   ESP DICTIONARY, LANGUAGE FOR SPECIFIC
PURPOSES.

ESP dictionary
A type of DICTIONARY intended to describe a
variety of English used by experts in a particular
subject field. Dictionaries of this kind are conceived as aids for users who are already specialists in the field, but want to practise or study it
further through the medium of English, e.g. for
preparing an academic paper at an international
conference.
⇨   LANGUAGE FOR SPECIFIC PURPOSES.
📖 Minaeva 1996.
📖 *Longman English–Chinese Dictionary of
Business English* (J. H. Adam), Hong Kong, 1995;
*Oxford Dictionary of Computing for Learners of
English* (S. Pyne & A. Tuck), Oxford, 1996.

ESP lexicography
A complex of activities concerned with the design,
compilation, use and evaluation of ESP DICTION-
ARIES.
📖 Diab 1989.

état de langue
⇨   PERIOD.

ethnic name

⇨ ETHNONYM.

ethnonym

A word or phrase used to refer to a particular
community. Ethnonyms range from affectionate
NICKNAMES to racial slurs.

⇨ BIAS-FREE VOCABULARY, RACISM.

📖 Winer 1991, McArthur 1992.

ethnophaulism

An international slur, e.g. *Dutch courage* 'bravery
under the influence of alcohol'.

📰 *A Dictionary of International Slurs (Ethno-
phaulisms)* (A. A. Roback), Waukesha WI, 1979.

etymological dictionary

A type of DICTIONARY in which words are traced
back to their earliest appropriate forms and meanings. Some etymological information is contained
in many general monolingual dictionaries, but
more detail can be found in specialised HISTORI-
CAL DICTIONARIES. The emphasis in such dictionaries is on the original form of the word (also
called its ROOT or ETYMON), but often its whole
history or 'curriculum vitae' is documented, supported by evidence from COGNATES.

⇨ DIACHRONIC DICTIONARY, ETYMOLOGICAL
INFORMATION.

📖 Collison 1982, Drysdale 1989, Hartmann 1990.

📰 *American Heritage Dictionary of Indo-
European Roots* (C. Watkins), Boston MA, 1985;
Dictionary of Word Origins (J. T. Shipley), Totowa NJ,
1985; *Concise Oxford Dictionary of English Etym-
ology* (T. F. Hoad), Oxford, 1986; *Merriam Webster's
Word Histories* (F. C. Mish), Springfield MA, 1989;
*The Henry Holt Encyclopedia of Word and Phrase
Origins* (R. Hendrickson), New York NY, 1990.

etymological information

One of the INFORMATION CATEGORIES presented
by the compiler and consulted by the user of a
dictionary, based on ETYMOLOGY. Dictionaries
differ according to how much material they offer
and how they present it: both decisions are influenced by assumptions about the needs of the
user. Although there is some doubt about how
much a knowledge of the early origins of words
can help elucidate their meanings, many general
dictionaries and all HISTORICAL DICTIONARIES
make an effort to trace the forms and meanings
of vocabulary items as far back as possible.
Sometimes information is provided about COG-

NATES and even hypothetical, reconstructed 'proto
forms'. Etymological information may be located
at the beginning or end of entries, in full or abbreviated form, and is often omitted from derivatives
(such as adjectives and participles) which are
treated as RUN-ON ENTRIES.

⇨ BASIC SENSE, ETYMOLOGICAL DICTIONARY,
ETYMOLOGY.

📖 Drysdale 1989, Svensén 1993, Considine 1996.

etymological lexicography

A complex of activities concerned with the design,
compilation, use and evaluation of ETYMOLOGI-
CAL DICTIONARIES.

etymology

The origin and history of the elements in the
VOCABULARY of a language. Etymological studies have a long tradition (Isidore of Seville's
seventh-century treatise, *Etymologiae*, contained
a one-volume alphabetical dictionary of Latin
etymology), but there are inherent limitations to
factual evidence when there are no texts available
for ancient periods of the language. It is therefore
very difficult, and sometimes impossible, to
determine the precise ETYMON of a particular
word, and modern lexicographers often use vague
labels such as 'of uncertain origin' rather than
definite but unverifiable dates. For example, the
English word *lexicography* derives from Greek
lexis 'word' < *legein* 'gather, speak' and *graphia*
'writing' (via Latin and French). The origin of the
Greek words in turn, however, can be determined
only by speculation or linguistic reconstruction
using COGNATES, e.g. the hypothesised Indo-
European 'proto form' **bhrater* is the reconstructed ROOT of Latin *frater*, Greek *p^hrater* and
Sanskrit *bhrata* as well as of English *brother*.

⇨ ETYMOLOGICAL DICTIONARY, FOLK ETYMOL-
OGY.

📖 Bivens 1982, Malkiel 1987, Jackson 1988,
Drysdale 1989, McArthur 1992.

etymon

The form from which a word in a subsequent
period of the language is derived. Thus, the etymon of the English word *glossary* is Latin *glossa*
'word (requiring explanation)' which in turn can
be traced back to Greek *glossa* 'tongue, language'.

⇨ ETYMOLOGY, ROOT (1).

euphemism

A word or phrase used as a substitute for a vulgar,
profane, blasphemous or otherwise disturbing

expression.The label 'euphem(istic)' is sometimes used in general dictionaries to mark such substitutes, especially for TABOO WORDS.

⇨ DOUBLESPEAK, DYSPHEMISM.

▤ *A Dictionary of American and British Euphemisms* (R. W. Holder), Bath, 1987; *Kind Words. A Thesaurus of Euphemisms* (J. S. Neaman & C. G. Silver), New York NY & Oxford, 1990.

EURALEX

Acronym for EUROPEAN ASSOCIATION FOR LEXICOGRAPHY.

EURODICAUTOM

The multilingual and interdisciplinary computerised TERMINOLOGICAL DATABASE operated on-line (last updated in 1995) by the language and computer services of the European Union in Brussels, Luxembourg and Strasbourg.

🖥 Website: www2.echo.lu/echo/databases/ eurodictum/en/eu92home.html

European Association for Lexicography

A professional society, founded at the University of Exeter in 1983. It holds international congresses every two years (with published proceedings), publishes a newsletter and co-sponsors, with the DICTIONARY SOCIETY OF NORTH AMERICA, the *INTERNATIONAL JOURNAL OF LEXICOGRAPHY* and the double series *LEXICOGRAPHICA* (*Series Maior* and *International Annual*).

🖥 Website: www.ims.uni-stuttgart.de/euralex

European Association for Terminology

A professional society, founded in 1996 in Kolding (Denmark) to represent TERMINOLOGISTS.

Europeanism

⇨ INTERNATIONALISM.

European Language Council

An association concerned with the state of language and culture in Europe. Supported by a European Union grant, it has initiated a Thematic Network Project in the Area of Languages, for investigating and improving language teaching in higher education. One of the ten policy groups is surveying DICTIONARY CULTURE in various European countries.

🖥 Website: userpage.fu-berlin.de/~elc

evaluation

The process or result of assessing a dictionary or other reference work, often in comparison with others. A systematic framework for formulating criteria with respect to COVERAGE, FORMAT, SCOPE, SIZE, TITLE etc. has yet to be developed.

⇨ ACCEPTABILITY RATING, BUYING GUIDE, COMPARISON OF DICTIONARIES, CRITICISM, STANDARD (2).

evidence

The DATA used to prove the authenticity of a particular USAGE or its description in the compilation of a reference work. Techniques for gathering evidence range from personal introspection by the compiler via FIELDWORK to the collection of CORPORA of texts. Even evidence in the form of ERROR ANALYSIS can produce valuable source material for the reference professional.

⇨ AUTHENTICATION, CITATION FILE, DATABASES, EDITORIAL EXAMPLE.

▤ Sinclair 1987, Rundell & Stock 1992, Schmid 1996, Tono 1996.

exact equivalence

⇨ EQUIVALENCE.

example

A word or phrase used in a REFERENCE WORK to illustrate a particular form or meaning in a wider context, such as a sentence. Examples can either be based on objective evidence (e.g. from a CITATION FILE or CORPUS) or be invented by the compiler (EDITORIAL EXAMPLE).

▤ Landau 1984, Fox 1987, Cowie 1989b, Rosenkilde Jacobsen *et al.* 1991, Ahmad *et al.* 1992, Laufer 1992, Svensén 1993, Béjoint 1994.

excerption

The selection of suitable material from a set of DATA, for the purpose of compiling a REFERENCE WORK.

⇨ CITATION FILE, EXAMPLE, READING PROGRAMME.

▤ Schäfer 1980, Landau 1984, Warburton 1986, ISO 1990, Svensén 1993.

exclusion list

A list of TERMS not (to be) processed in a TERMINOLOGICAL DICTIONARY.

⇨ INCLUSION LIST, SELECTION.

▤ ISO 1990.

exegesis
The interpretation of texts, especially as part of a canon.
⇨ AUTHOR'S DICTIONARY.
▤ *Theological Dictionary of the Old Testament* (G. J. Butterweck & H. Ringgren), Grand Rapids MI, 1974– [incomplete].

exemplification
The use of EXAMPLES to explain and/or illustrate the USAGE of a word or phrase in a reference work.
▢ Ilson 1990, Williams 1996.

exoglossic language
A language spoken as a NATIVE LANGUAGE by the minority of people, but sometimes used as an AUXILIARY LANGUAGE, in a given geographic region, e.g. English in India.
⇨ BRIDGE DICTIONARY, ENDOGLOSSIC LANGUAGE.

expansion
A technique by which the meaning of an ABBREVIATION can be explained, e.g. *AA* 'abbrev. 1 Automobile Association, 2 Alcoholics Anonymous, 3 anti-aircraft . . .'.

expert system
A knowledge-based electronic system used to study and automate DATA-PROCESSING in specific fields. Experts in a technical subject are observed in action so that their decision routines can be copied and, if possible, improved upon. The application of this technique to the design of integrated WORK-STATIONS may bring advances to DICTIONARY-MAKING in terms of the transparency of the process.
▢ Knowles 1990, Picchi *et al*. 1992.

explanation
The totality of techniques available to the compiler to clarify the MEANING of a word or phrase to be included in a REFERENCE WORK. The type of explanation most widely known, because of its long tradition, is the DEFINITION, but there are several others, from the use of verbal EXEMPLIFICATION and pictorial ILLUSTRATION to DISCUSSION, PARAPHRASE and TRANSLATION.
▢ Hanks 1987, Ilson 1990.

explanatory chart
A diagram in a USER'S GUIDE to explain the layout of, and conventions in, ENTRIES, e.g. for head-word marking, phonetic symbols ('pronunciation key') and grammatical codes, cross-references and examples.

explanatory dictionary
A type of REFERENCE WORK which gives detailed explanations of the meanings of the vocabulary covered. The prototype of this dictionary is the monolingual GENERAL DICTIONARY, but the term has also been applied to a BILINGUAL DICTIONARY which is intended to help with decoding (but not necessarily translating) foreign-language texts.
⇨ COLLOCATION, MEANING, TEXT.
▢ Steele 1986, 1990, Mel'čuk 1988, Apresjan 1992, Mel'čuk & Wanner 1994.
▤ *Tolkovo-kombinatornyj slovar'* . . . [*Explanatory-Combinatorial Dictionary of Modern Russian*] (I. Mel'čuk & A. K. Zholkovskij), Vienna, 1984.

explanatory equivalent
In the translation of CULTURE-SPECIFIC VOCABULARY, the explanation of a word or phrase by means of a surrogate PARAPHRASE in the target language rather than a one-to-one EQUIVALENT, e.g. German *Dolchstoßlegende* – English 'myth of the "stab in the back" (betrayal of Germany after the First World War by its own politicians)'.
▢ Zgusta 1984, Schnorr 1986.

explanatory word
A word or phrase which clarifies the meaning of a term, e.g. *ulna* ('a bone in the arm').

expletive
A mild SWEAR WORD.

expression
⇨ FIXED EXPRESSION.

extension
1 The totality of all objects (or specific concepts) covered by a word or phrase (or generic concept).
⇨ EXTENSIONAL DEFINITION, HYPERONYMY, INTENSION.
2 A widening in the semantic scope of a word or phrase to cover more CONCEPTS, e.g. *head* 'top of human anatomy', 'leader of a group', 'highest part of an elevation', 'froth at the top of a glass of beer' etc.
⇨ SEMANTIC CHANGE.

extensional definition

A DEFINITION which explains a concept by reference to its HYPONYMS, e.g. *academic staff member*: 'professor, lecturer, instructor, demonstrator . . .'.

⇨   INTENSIONAL DEFINITION.

📖   ISO 1990, Svensén 1993.

external access structure

⇨   ACCESS STRUCTURE.

external search path

⇨   SEARCH PATH.

extra column

An additional column of text by the side of the one containing the ENTRY proper, in which supplementary information is provided. In the *Collins COBUILD English Language Dictionary* (London & Glasgow, 1987) the extra column gives grammatical and semantic details, reducing the usual degree of TEXT COMPRESSION inside the entry and making it more transparent.

extra-linguistic information

⇨   ENCYCLOPEDIC INFORMATION.

F

facet

A feature of the subdivisions in the CLASSIFICA-TION of a technical subject, such as 'personality', 'matter', 'energy', 'space' or 'time'.
⇨ CATEGORY (2), CLASS.

facsimile edition

The identical reproduction of a DOCUMENT, with or without ANNOTATIONS. Facsimile editions of early dictionaries in manuscript or printed form allow their comparative-historical study.
⇨ COPYING IN DICTIONARIES, REPRINT.

factual information
⇨ ENCYCLOPEDIC INFORMATION.

false cognate
⇨ FALSE FRIEND.

false friend

One of two or more words or phrases from different languages, which are similar in form but not in meaning, e.g. English *sympathetic* 'understanding' and French *sympathique* 'pleasant'. A distinction can be made between 'interlingual homographs', e.g. English *gift* 'present' and German *Gift* 'poison', and 'interlingual homophones', e.g. English *man* 'male' and Persian /mæn/ 'I'. Such pairs may confuse foreign-language learners, and they are often collected in special dictionaries of false friends.
📖 van Roey 1988, Gorbahn-Orme & Hausmann 1991, Veisbergs 1996.
📔 *Faux Amis and Key Words: A Dictionary-Guide to French Language, Culture and Society through Lookalikes and Confusables* (P. Thody & H. Evans), London, 1985; *NTC's Dictionary of Spanish False Cognates* (M. Prado), Lincolnwood IL, 1993.

family

1 With reference to dictionary typology, ⇨ DIC-TIONARY FAMILY.
2 With reference to morphology, ⇨ WORD FAMILY.

family name
⇨ PERSONAL NAME.

family of dictionaries
⇨ DICTIONARY FAMILY.

fascicle

One of several instalments of a REFERENCE WORK published at more or less regular intervals. Many large-scale HISTORICAL DICTIONARIES have been issued in sections over a long period, making consultation difficult, particularly when they have to be (re-)bound in the libraries where they are held.

faux ami
⇨ FALSE FRIEND.

Fédération internationale d'information et de documentation

A professional society, based in the Hague, founded in 1895 to represent information professionals and users. It publishes a *News Bulletin*, the *FID Directory* as well as the journal *International Forum on Information and Documentation*, and holds biennial conferences. There are a number of special committees, e.g. on classification research, and special interest groups, e.g. on archives and records management.
💻 fid.conicyt.cl.8000

FID

Abbreviation for FÉDÉRATION INTERNATIONALE D'INFORMATION ET DE DOCUMENTATION.

field

1 In lexicology and semantics, a SEMANTIC FIELD.
2 In database design, one of several slots in which INFORMATION CATEGORIES are presented, e.g. headword, definition, example.
3 In the marking of SENSES in the dictionary, the FIELD LABEL.
4 In the specification of disciplines, a SUBJECT FIELD.

field dictionary

A type of DICTIONARY which is the result of FIELDWORK. Because of the limited ranges of the languages investigated and the informal nature of such compilations, they do not always get published.
⇨ ROOT DICTIONARY (1).
📖 Bartholomew & Schoenhals 1983.

field label

The SUBJECT LABEL used to indicate the technical discipline with which a word or phrase is associated.
⇨ DIATECHNICAL INFORMATION.

fieldwork

The collection of DATA by interview with speakers of a language or language variety. The gathering and documentation of such material, although difficult and labour-intensive, is a defining feature of many dictionaries, particularly FIELD DICTIONARIES of previously unrecorded languages and dictionaries of dialect, slang and other special-purpose languages.
⇨ ELICITATION, TRANSCRIPTION (1).
📖 Bartholomew & Schoenhals 1983, Béjoint 1983.

fifteener

⇨ INCUNABULA.

figurative meaning

A non-literal sense of a word or phrase which is the result of metaphorical EXTENSION, e.g. *head* 'top of human anatomy' > 'top of elevation', 'leader of organisation' etc., or a transfer of sense, e.g. *pig* 'porcine animal' > 'dirty person'. In dictionaries, such meanings are sometimes marked with special USAGE LABELS ironically termed 'fig. leaves' by critics, because they can be said to hide the underlying BASIC SENSE.
📖 Ayto 1988, McArthur 1992, Osselton 1995, van der Meer 1996b.

file

A system for classifying records, such as the data collected for a DICTIONARY or entries in a library CATALOGUE. Formats (alphabetic or thematic) and house rules may vary from one organisation to another.
⇨ CITATION FILE, DIRECT ENTRY.

film

Motion pictures to display information visually, which have become a powerful aid to education, science and the media. The storage, transmission and presentation of film by electronic means have opened up new possibilities for MULTIMEDIA reference works, which have not yet been fully exploited.
⇨ CD-ROM.
📖 *International Dictionary of Film and Film-makers* (N. Thomas), London, 1984–91; *International Dictionary of Broadcasting and Film* (D. K. Bognar), Boston MA, 1995.

first language

⇨ NATIVE LANGUAGE.

first name

⇨ PERSONAL NAME.

fixed expression

A phrase whose constituent elements cannot be moved randomly or substituted without distorting the overall meaning or allowing a literal interpretation. Fixed (or set) phrases range from COMPOUNDS (e.g. adjective–noun phrases used as technical terms, as in *etymological dictionary*) through COLLOCATIONS (*nice surprise* versus *good surprise*) to IDIOMS (*red herring*). Their treatment and labelling in general and specialised dictionaries varies considerably.
⇨ COMBINING FORM, MULTI-WORD EXPRESSION.
📖 Jackson 1988, Alexander 1992, Botha 1992, Moon 1992.

flyleaf

A (double) page bound in with the book cover of a REFERENCE WORK containing additional information, e.g. an EXPLANATORY CHART, table of phonetic symbols or summary of grammatical codes.

folk classification system

⇨ FOLK TAXONOMY.

folk definition

A popular, non-scholarly explanation of the meaning of a word or phrase, e.g. '*inherit* is when you get some money after somebody has died'.

⇨ DEFINITION.

📖 Stock 1988.

folk etymology

A popular, non-scholarly or hypothetical interpretation of the origin of a word or phrase by morphological and/or phonological adaptation, e.g. *bankrupt* < '*bank-robbed*'.

⇨ ETYMOLOGY.

📖 Svensén 1993.

folk taxonomy

A popular, non-scholarly classification system applied to words or phrases, e.g. animal and plant names.

⇨ PROTOTYPE, TAXONOMY.

📖 Wierzbicka 1985, Bartholomew 1991, Rajendran 1995.

foreignism

A word or phrase which has been copied and transferred from one language to another, but is not yet fully 'assimilated', and is often presented (in English texts) in italics. Sometimes purists deprecate foreignisms as unhealthy contamination, e.g. *franglais* expressions in French or *Fremdwörter* 'foreign words' in German. Dictionaries record and LABEL foreignisms in a number of ways.

⇨ BORROWING, DIAINTEGRATIVE INFORMATION, FALSE FRIEND, LOAN-WORD, NATIVE VOCABULARY, REGIONALISM.

📖 Filipović 1984, Berg 1993.

📖 *Loanwords Dictionary* (L. Urdang & F. Abate), Detroit MI, 1988.

foreign language

The language used by learners for whom it is not the NATIVE LANGUAGE, usually outside a country where it is the dominant language.

⇨ SECOND LANGUAGE.

foreign learner's dictionary

⇨ EFL DICTIONARY, LEARNER'S DICTIONARY.

foreign word

⇨ FOREIGNISM.

fore-matter

⇨ FRONT MATTER.

forename

⇨ PERSONAL NAME.

form

1 The phonic or graphic shape in which words appear in spoken or written discourse, in contrast to their content or meaning. This is the basis for a distinction, inside dictionary entries, between two types of COMMENT on the topic introduced by the HEADWORD: the 'formal' comment (with information on spelling, pronunciation and grammar) and the 'semantic' comment (with information on meaning, usage and etymology).

⇨ BASE STRUCTURE.

2 The STRUCTURE of a published text such as a REFERENCE WORK, which may be a criterion for its classification into one of several types or genres.

formal

⇨ STYLE LABEL.

formal comment

⇨ COMMENT.

formal definition

⇨ DEFINITION.

formality label

⇨ STYLE LABEL.

format

A general term for the arrangement of the contents in a particular REFERENCE WORK.

⇨ DESIGN, ORGANISATION, TYPOLOGY (1).

form of address

A word or phrase used to designate a person in formal or informal interaction. This includes a range of devices from pronouns and personal NAMES to professional, honorific and social titles as well as NICKNAMES, all of which may be codified in general or specialised dictionaries.

⇨ APTRONYM, EPITHET.

📖 McArthur 1992.

formulaic definition

A DEFINITION STYLE which relies on a standardised, often truncated explanation. An example from this *Dictionary of Lexicography* is the routine formula for defining *X* (e.g. *bilingual*) *lexicography* as 'a complex of activities concerned with the design, compilation, use and evaluation of *X* (e.g. *Bilingual*) *Dictionaries*'.

form word
⇨ FUNCTION WORD.

four-letter word
An OBSCENITY, so called because in English some of the words considered most taboo happen to consist of four letters. Those GENERAL DICTION-ARIES that include four-letter words tend to mark them with appropriate labels and paraphrase them with more or less euphemistic synonyms.
⇨ EUPHEMISM, PROSCRIPTION, TABOO WORD.
 Gates 1992.
 The Fucktionary/Slownik wyrazen z Fuck (M. Widawski), Gdansk, 1994.

frame theory
An approach to DEFINITION which uses ARTIFI-CIAL INTELLIGENCE techniques to elicit and sim-ulate semantic knowledge in terms of situational scenes. Thus a characteristic frame such as 'eat-ing in a restaurant' which determines the typical actions and relationships of the persons and objects involved is claimed to be a more realistic basis for explaining the various meanings than abstract appeal to formal properties such as semantic features in hierarchical trees or grid-like fields.
⇨ SEMANTICS.
 Makkai 1980, Fillmore & Atkins 1992.

free morpheme
⇨ MORPHEME.

free translation
⇨ TRANSLATION.

frequency
The number of occurrences of a word or other linguistic unit in a (written or spoken) TEXT or collection of texts. Word frequencies are estab-lished by means of FREQUENCY COUNTS, often by reference to a CORPUS, using computational and statistical techniques. In lexicography, evidence of this kind can help in the selection of the WORD-LIST, in decisions on the ordering of senses within dictionary entries, and in controlling the DEFIN-ING VOCABULARY, particularly in the LEARNER'S DICTIONARY.
⇨ CORE WORD, FREQUENCY DICTIONARY, LEM-MATISATION, TOKEN.

 Sinclair 1987, Bogaards 1992, McArthur 1992, James *et al*. 1994, 1996, 1997.

frequency count
The process or result of establishing the FRE-QUENCY of words or other linguistic units in a TEXT or text CORPUS.
⇨ FREQUENCY DICTIONARY, TOKEN, TYPE.

frequency dictionary
A type of REFERENCE WORK which provides information about the FREQUENCY of linguistic units, especially of the BASIC VOCABULARY. Work on frequency dictionaries has been motivated by, and beneficial to, various fields such as the design of shorthand systems (e.g. J. W. Kaeding's *Häufig-keitswörterbuch der deutschen Sprache* [Steglitz, 1897–8]), the teaching of reading to children (e.g. E. L. Thorndike's *Teacher's Word Book* [New York NY, 1921]), the selection of basic vocabularies for foreign-language teaching (e.g. M. West's *General Service List of English Words* [London, 1953]). One particularly fruitful application of the fre-quency approach is the design and improvement of the LEARNER'S DICTIONARY.
⇨ BASIC VOCABULARY, COBUILD, CONCOR-DANCE, DEFINING VOCABULARY.
 Martin 1990.
 The Cambridge English Lexicon (R. X. Hind-marsh), Cambridge, 1980.

frequency information
One of the INFORMATION CATEGORIES presented by the compiler and consulted by the user of a REFERENCE WORK, based on FREQUENCY. In general dictionaries frequency may be indicated by USAGE LABELS such as 'mostly', 'occasionally' or 'rarely', but this approach has been criticised as too vague, especially since the availability of usage data from large-scale corpora. In specialised dictionaries, such as the LEARNER'S DICTIONARY, frequency can be indicated by various means such as numbers and other symbols, or even specific figures and tables indicating absolute and relative occurrences, distribution, dispersion and the like.
⇨ DIAFREQUENTIAL INFORMATION.

frequency label
Traditionally, an indication in a dictionary of the relative rarity of a word or phrase. The modern LEARNER'S DICTIONARY, by contrast, often marks the relative commonness of occurrence.
⇨ FREQUENCY INFORMATION.

frequency lexicography

A complex of activities concerned with the design, compilation, use and evaluation of FREQUENCY DICTIONARIES. As the contexts which lead to (and apply the results of) such work are very diverse and the methodology is interdisciplinary, requiring elements of statistics, computing, education, linguistics and LSP terminology, there is as yet no coherent framework.

frequency list

1 With reference to basic vocabulary, ⇨ FRE-QUENCY COUNT.
2 With reference to dictionary typology, ⇨ FRE-QUENCY DICTIONARY.

front matter

Those component parts of a dictionary's MACRO-STRUCTURE which precede the central WORD-LIST section. Examples of such 'preliminaries' in general dictionaries may include: title page, copyright page and imprint, acknowledgements and dedication, foreword or preface, table of contents, list of contributors, list of abbreviations and/or illustrations used, pronunciation key, USER'S GUIDE, notes on the nature, history and structure of the language, dictionary grammar.
⇨ OUTSIDE MATTER
📖 Hausmann & Wiegand 1989, Svensén 1993.

full equivalence
⇨ EQUIVALENCE.

function

The purpose(s) for which a REFERENCE WORK is designed or used. Research into dictionary use has revealed that there can be a discrepancy between the functions intended by the compiler and the actual look-up practices in specific situations of use, or indeed the IMAGE users have of the dictionary.

Thus, this *Dictionary of Lexicography* may have been designed to explain the terminology of the field to students, but at the very moment of you (the reader) consulting it (in this particular entry),

it may fulfil one of several functions: to help with this concept, to illustrate usage, to clarify a distinction or to assist in a writing task. It may be advisable, therefore, to distinguish between 'macro-functions' (such as 'general dictionary for laymen', 'special dictionary for linguists', 'bilingual dictionary for language learners', 'technical dictionary for translators') and 'micro-functions' related to a user's REFERENCE NEEDS in a particular context. Examples of such micro-functions would be checking the spelling of a word to solve a crossword clue, checking the pronunciation of a word for preparing a speech, selecting a synonym for writing an essay, finding a foreign-language equivalent in a translation exercise or verifying a fact for settling an argument.
⇨ FUNCTIONALITY, LANGUAGE FOR SPECIFIC PURPOSES, TYPOLOGY (1).
📖 Mufwene 1984, Hartmann 1989, Tono 1989, Béjoint 1994.

functionality

The USER PERSPECTIVE of a dictionary according to the purpose of the look-up operation. Most general monolingual dictionaries fulfil several different functions, such as providing information on spelling to assist the writing task. In the bilingual dictionary, DIRECTIONALITY is an additional factor.
⇨ BIFUNCTIONAL DICTIONARY, CONSULTATION, MULTIFUNCTIONAL DICTIONARY.

functional shift
⇨ CONVERSION (1).

functional typology
⇨ TYPOLOGY (1).

function word

A word that plays a grammatical role in the sentence, such as an article, a conjunction or a preposition, in contrast with a CONTENT WORD which has semantic value (meaning or sense), such as a noun, a verb or an adjective.

G

gazetteer

A type of REFERENCE WORK with descriptions of geographical locations and other ONOMASTIC and ENCYCLOPEDIC INFORMATION, sometimes with maps and other illustrations.

 A Gazetteer of the World: or, dictionary of geographical knowledge (Royal Geographical Society), Edinburgh, 1850–6; *World Gazetteer of Tram, Trolleybus, and Rapid Transit Systems* (R. Peschkes), Exeter, 1986.

gem dictionary

A relatively small-format reference work.

⇨ DICTIONARY FAMILY.

Collins Gem English–Hindi Dictionary (D. P. Pandey & V. P. Sharma), New Delhi, 1993.

gender bias

⇨ GENDERLECT.

genderlect

The varieties of a language associated with maleness or femaleness. The extent of this difference varies considerably from culture to culture, and in some societies is highly codified. In modern industrial societies, the argument as to how far biological and social differentiation is reflected in language ('gender bias') has affected DICTIONARY-MAKING in at least two ways: there is now a more conscious attempt to make definitions and examples gender-neutral, and there are specialised dictionaries documenting aspects of 'female' rather than 'male' language.

⇨ DIALECT, BIAS-FREE VOCABULARY.

McArthur 1992.

The Nonsexist Word Finder: A Dictionary of Gender-Free Usage (R. Maggio), Phoenix AZ, 1987.

general dictionary

A type of REFERENCE WORK intended to provide a comprehensive description of the whole language, with special attention to VOCABULARY. The general (or 'general-purpose') dictionary fulfils a number of different FUNCTIONS (information on meaning, spelling, idiomatic use etc.) and thus satisfies various reference needs of the user, or many diverse needs of different user groups. It is typically MONOLINGUAL, although it shares many features with the BILINGUAL DICTIONARY, where translation EQUIVALENTS replace definitions.

⇨ CULTURAL DICTIONARY, DEFINING DICTIONARY, ENCYCLOPEDIC DICTIONARY, EXPLANATORY DICTIONARY, LANGUAGE DICTIONARY, SPECIALISED DICTIONARY, SYNCHRONIC DICTIONARY, USAGE DICTIONARY.

Landau 1984, Jackson 1988, Svensén 1993, Béjoint 1994.

The Concise Oxford Dictionary of Current English (R. E. Allen), Oxford, 1990; *The American Heritage Dictionary of the English Language* [3rd edition] (A. H. Soukhanov), Boston MA, 1992; *Collins English Dictionary* [3rd edition] (M. Makins), London & Glasgow, 1991.

generalized mark-up language

⇨ STANDARD GENERALIZED MARK-UP LANGUAGE.

general lexicography

1 The discipline concerned with the theoretical foundations and principles of LEXICOGRAPHY, independent of language or dictionary type.

⇨ COMPARATIVE LEXICOGRAPHY, GENERAL THEORY OF TERMINOLOGY, REFERENCE SCIENCE, SPECIAL LEXICOGRAPHY.

Hartmann 1993.

2 The complex of activities concerned with the design, compilation, use and evaluation of GENERAL DICTIONARIES.

⇨ SPECIALISED LEXICOGRAPHY.

general linguistics
⇨ LINGUISTICS.

general-purpose dictionary
⇨ GENERAL DICTIONARY.

general terminology
⇨ GENERAL THEORY OF TERMINOLOGY.

general theory of terminology
The discipline concerned with the theoretical foundations and principles of TERMINOLOGY, independent of language or technical subject field.
⇨ GENERAL LEXICOGRAPHY (1), REFERENCE SCIENCE, SPECIAL THEORY OF TERMINOLOGY.
📖 ISO 1990.

generic concept
A superordinate concept in a hierarchical generic relationship, e.g. 'reference work' in respect of the subordinates 'dictionary', 'thesaurus' and 'atlas'.
⇨ GENERIC TERM.
📖 ISO 1990.

generic relation
⇨ HIERARCHICAL RELATION.

generic term
In a hierarchy of sense-related words, the one which covers a greater conceptual space than the SPECIFIC TERM. The relationship between 'genus' and 'species' can be explained in a number of ways. Taxonomically, the genus term is superordinate to the species term; semantically, it covers a wider area (the genus is a HYPERONYM, the species is a HYPONYM); logically, the genus is equivalent to a class of which the species is a member. The debate as to whether the generic term 'includes' or 'is included in' the species term can only be settled by reference to particular examples: linguistically, the word *tree* is less precise than *fir*, therefore its general meaning is included in the more specialised word *fir*. Terminologically, on the other hand, *tree* can be applied to more concepts than *fir*, which is therefore one of several included in *tree*. In lexicography, the traditional ANALYTICAL DEFINITION formula 'X is a kind of Y which . . .' makes use of these sense relations: 'a *fir* is a kind of *tree* which has evergreen needles', the first part being the GENUS PROXIMUM, the second the DIFFERENTIA SPECIFICA.
⇨ BINOMIAL COMPOUND, GENERIC CONCEPT.
📖 ISO 1990.

genre
The prototypical TEXT format associated with a particular field or context of human activity, e.g. novel, letter, report, or telephone conversation. In lexicography, the term 'dictionary genre' is used as a synonym of 'dictionary type'.
⇨ DIATEXTUAL INFORMATION, HYBRID, TYPE (1).
📖 Swales 1990, Bhatia 1993.

genteelism
A word or phrase associated with the USAGE of polite society, often contrasted with SLANG.
⇨ EUPHEMISM.

genus
1 In the classical definition formula, ⇨ GENUS PROXIMUM.
2 In a hierarchical sense relation, ⇨ GENERIC TERM.

genus proximum
In the classical DEFINITION, the first part, of which the word to be explained is considered to be a specific instance. Semantically, the genus proximum is a superordinate word (HYPERONYM) to which the word to be defined is subordinate (HYPONYM). For example, the word *fir* can be defined as 'a kind of *tree* [genus proximum] *with evergreen needles* [DIFFERENTIA SPECIFICA]'.
⇨ GENERIC TERM.
📖 Svensén 1993.

genus term
⇨ GENERIC TERM.

geographical filing
The arrangement of material within an INDEX or CATALOGUE by place or country.

geographical information
One of the INFORMATION CATEGORIES presented by the compiler and consulted by the user of a reference work, based on geography. Material of this kind is provided in encyclopedic or specialised dictionaries (such as ATLASES and GAZETTEERS) rather than general dictionaries, although the latter occasionally provide such detail in the BACK MATTER.
📖 *Webster's New Geographical Dictionary*, Springfield MA, 1988.

geographical register label
⇨ REGIONAL LABEL.

geonym
⇨ TOPONYM.

gesture
Hand, facial and other body movements which accompany and sometimes replace verbal communication.
⇨ SIGN LANGUAGE.
▤ *A Dictionary of Gestures* (B. J. Bäuml & F. H. Bäuml), Metuchen NJ, 1975.

ghost word
A word or phrase which has been included in a dictionary, by error or design, although there is no EVIDENCE for its existence.
▢ Landau 1984, Iannucci 1986, Svensén 1993.

given name
⇨ PERSONAL NAME.

gloss
1 In the early history of European lexicography, a marginal or interlinear note inserted in the text of a medieval manuscript to explain a (Latin) word or phrase. These glosses were then gathered together to create vocabulary lists, or GLOSSARIES, with paraphrases or translation equivalents, arranged in thematic or alphabetic order.
  ⇨ GLOSSOGRAPHY.
  ▢ Hüllen 1989.
2 A PARAPHRASE or SYNONYM used within a dictionary entry to provide an explanation of the sense of a word or phrase related to the HEADWORD. In the monolingual dictionary, this can happen when a brief DEFINITION of a word is given within an example or an idiom within a sub-entry (producing a HIDDEN ENTRY). In the bilingual dictionary, glossing is used as a means of discriminating the various senses of a headword which may have different translation equivalents. While glosses are part of the definition, they must be distinguished from LABELS which are used to mark the headword as belonging to a particular context or language variety.
  ▢ Hausmann & Wiegand 1989.

glossarian
One who engages in the compilation of a GLOSS or GLOSSARY.

glossarist
One who engages in the compilation of a GLOSS or GLOSSARY.

glossary
A type of REFERENCE WORK which lists a selection of words or phrases, or the terms in a specialised field, usually in alphabetical order, together with minimal definitions or translation equivalents.
  Glossaries, which range widely in scope, technicality and treatment, derive from the medieval vocabulary lists of students of Latin, informal manuscript compilations of regionalisms, and collections of the vocabulary used in specific books and workshops. Some developed into bilingual and multilingual specialised dictionaries (TERMINOLOGICAL DICTIONARY), but most have remained limited in size, sometimes forming part of another publication, e.g. as an appendix or INDEX in a book.
▢ Stein 1985.
▤ *Civil Service. An English–Chinese Glossary of Terms Commonly Used in Government Departments* (Chinese Language Division, Hong Kong Government), Hong Kong, 1995.

glossator (*also* glosser, glossist)
One who engages in the compilation of GLOSSES or GLOSSARIES.

glossographer
One who engages in the compilation of GLOSSES or GLOSSARIES.
⇨ GLOSSOGRAPHY.

glossography
A complex of activities concerned with the compilation of GLOSSARIES from the Middle Ages to the Renaissance. Starting with GLOSSES or notes on hard words in Latin texts, VOCABULARY lists gradually developed into context-independent compilations, laying the foundations for LEXICOGRAPHY, monolingual as well as bilingual and multilingual, alphabetic as well as thematic, lexical as well as encyclopedic.
▢ Hüllen 1989.

gradable antonymy
⇨ ANTONYMY.

graded antonymy
⇨ ANTONYMY.

graded vocabulary

A list of words and phrases correlated with school-grade levels, and based on assumptions of simplicity or notions of frequency.
⇨ SCHOOL DICTIONARY.

gradus

The short form of *Gradus ad Parnassum* (Paris, 1666), formerly used as a general term for 'primer' or 'dictionary'.

grammar

A branch of LINGUISTICS concerned with the structure of words and their constituents (MORPHOLOGY) and their compatibility within sentences and texts (SYNTAX). Sometimes the term 'grammar' is used to refer to the overall system of a language or language variety, including PHONOLOGY and SEMANTICS, which the linguist is charged to describe and which may or may not reflect the native speaker's intuition. Such 'descriptive' grammar, based on evidence of observed USAGE, is often contrasted with 'prescriptive' grammar, based on rules of CORRECTNESS, which is the conventional notion of grammar that underlies much of traditional DICTIONARY-MAKING.
⇨ DICTIONARY GRAMMAR, GRAMMAR DICTIONARY, GRAMMATICAL INFORMATION, NORM, USAGE GUIDE.
📖 Lemmens & Wekker 1986, Sinclair 1987, Greenbaum 1988, Herbst 1989, Sherwood 1990, Milroy & Milroy 1991, Svensén 1993.
📖 *NTC's Dictionary of Grammar Terminology* (R. A. Spears), Lincolnwood IL, 1991; *Introducing English Grammar* (G. Leech), London, 1992.
💻 Grammar checker: *Microsoft Word 6 [Office 4]*, Redmond WA, 1994.

grammar dictionary

A type of REFERENCE WORK containing GRAMMATICAL INFORMATION, such as PARTS OF SPEECH, in alphabetical or thematic order.
⇨ DICTIONARY GRAMMAR, MORPHOLOGICAL DICTIONARY, USAGE GUIDE, VALENCY DICTIONARY.
📖 Noël *et al.* 1996.
📖 *Dictionary of English Grammar Based on Common Errors* (W. J. Ball & F. T. Wood), London, 1987; *The BBI Combinatory Dictionary of English* (M. Benson *et al.*), Amsterdam, 1986; *Bloomsbury Grammar Guide* (G. Jarvie), London, 1993; *The Oxford Dictionary of English Grammar* (S. Chalker & E. Weiner), Oxford, 1994.

grammatical category

⇨ WORD CLASS.

grammatical code

The system of (usually abbreviated) terms and symbols used to designate various types of syntactic information, e.g. *vt* for 'transitive verb'.
⇨ GRAMMATICAL INFORMATION, GRAMMATICAL LABEL.

grammatical construction

⇨ CONSTRUCTION.

grammatical content

⇨ GRAMMATICAL INFORMATION.

grammatical dictionary

⇨ GRAMMAR DICTIONARY.

grammatical information

One of the INFORMATION CATEGORIES presented by the compiler and consulted by the user of a DICTIONARY, based on GRAMMAR. Material codified in dictionaries may consist of word-class indication (PART OF SPEECH) and some word-formation, collocation and clause patterns. Regrettably, this is often incomplete and lagging behind the reported results of grammatical research, such as the refinement of the simplistic distinction between 'transitive' and 'intransitive' verbs to recognise various kinds of relations between verbs and their objects, goals, complements etc. In the GENERAL DICTIONARY such information tends to be limited to (abbreviated) inflectional details and part-of-speech labelling placed between the headword and the definition, occasionally amplified by illustrative sentences inside entries, essays in the FRONT MATTER, or lists of irregularities in the BACK MATTER. Specialised dictionaries such as USAGE GUIDES, GRAMMAR DICTIONARIES and LEARNER'S DICTIONARIES provide more detail, e.g. on phraseological combinations, word-formation patterns and complementation patterns, based on observed encoding difficulties.
⇨ CONSTRUCTION, DICTIONARY GRAMMAR, LEXICAL INFORMATION, MORPHOLOGICAL INFORMATION.
📖 Jackson 1985, Lemmens & Wekker 1986, Sinclair 1987, Cowie 1989a, Kromann *et al.* 1991, McCorduck 1993, Svensén 1993, Mitchell 1994, Wachal 1994.

grammatical item
⇨   FUNCTION WORD.

grammaticality
An aspect of USAGE by which members of a given speech community characterise a word or phrase as conforming to the rules of GRAMMAR. A contrast is often made between grammaticality and APPROPRIATENESS, the suitability of an expression in a particular context. Individual speakers do not always agree on issues of grammaticality, and in contentious cases may consult dictionaries, such as USAGE GUIDES, for authoritative judgements.
⇨   ACCEPTABILITY, CORRECTNESS, STANDARD (1).
    Greenbaum 1988.

grammatical label
A symbol, code or abbreviated term used to mark GRAMMATICAL INFORMATION on a particular word or phrase in a dictionary. Many lexicographers reserve the term 'label' for the marking of USAGE features rather than for part-of-speech indication.
⇨   GRAMMATICAL CODE, TAG.
    Hausmann & Wiegand 1989, Berg 1993.

grammatical supplement
A DICTIONARY GRAMMAR included in the BACK MATTER of a dictionary or other reference work.

grammatical word
⇨   FUNCTION WORD.

grammatography
⇨   CODIFICATION.

graph
An illustration of numerical data in pictorial form, e.g. in a table or pie chart.

grapheme
The minimal distinct unit in the WRITING SYSTEM of a language.
⇨   CHARACTER, GRAPHEMICS, LETTER.

graphemics
A branch of LINGUISTICS concerned with the study of WRITING SYSTEMS. Graphemics deals with the graphic units (GRAPHEMES) within a written code (SCRIPT) and their relations with speech sounds (PHONEMES), in contrast to GRAPHETICS, the study of individual handwritten or printed shapes.
⇨   ALPHABET, ORTHOGRAPHIC INFORMATION.

graphetics
A branch of LINGUISTICS concerned with the study of the WRITING process. Graphetics concentrates on the shapes of the graphic signs used, e.g. in handwriting or printing, rather than their systematic relations within a script (GRAPHEMICS).
⇨   GRAPHOLOGY.

graphics
Non-verbal artwork such as drawings, graphs, maps and photographs used to illustrate TEXT.
⇨   DESIGN, ILLUSTRATION (1), PICTURE DICTIONARY.

graphology
The study of handwriting.
⇨   GRAPHEMICS, GRAPHETICS.
    Encyclopedia of the Written Word. A Lexicon for Graphology and Other Aspects of Writing (K. G. Roman/R. Wolfson & M. Edwards), New York NY, 1968.

-graphy
⇨   -OGRAPHY.

grouping
The arrangement of SUB-ENTRIES within entries, either on subsequent new lines ('listing') or in run-on form (CLUSTERING).
⇨   NESTING, NICHING.
    Hausmann & Wiegand 1989.

guide
A type of REFERENCE WORK which presents information on a place (such as country, city, library, museum or gallery) or on a subject field for beginners in relatively easy-to-follow steps, usually supported by diagrams and illustrations. Users of reference works are given help in this way either inside the same publication (e.g. in the form of a dictionary USER'S GUIDE) or in a separate text (WORKBOOK).
⇨   COMPANION, TYPOLOGY (1), PHRASEBOOK, USAGE GUIDE, VADE-MECUM.
    A Reference Guide for English Studies (M. J. Marcusi), Berkeley CA, 1990; *APA Guide Deutschland* (B. Schümann), Munich, 1996; *Cambridge Paperback Guide to Literature in English* (I. Ousby), Cambridge 1996.

guidebook
⇨   GUIDE.

guideword
A word or part of a word which helps the user of a reference work to find required INFORMATION easily and quickly, e.g. the catchwords printed at the top ('running title' or 'running head') and/or bottom ('running foot') of a dictionary column or page to assist recognition of the alphabetical order of entries, or the indicators used to separate senses of polysemous headwords in such dictionaries as the *Cambridge International Dictionary of English* (Cambridge, 1995).
⇨   ORDERING DEVICE, SENSE DISCRIMINATION.

H

half-title
The page preceding the TITLE PAGE, usually containing only the title of the publication.

handbook
A type of REFERENCE WORK which is intended as a professional-standard text for a technical skill or field.
⇨ TYPOLOGY (1).
▤ *The Seaspeak Reference Manual* (F. Weeks *et al*.), Oxford, 1984; *Merriam Webster's Secretarial Handbook* [3rd edition] (M. A. Stevens), Springfield MA, 1993; *The Writer's Handbook 1997* (B. Turner), London, 1996.

hanging indentation
⇨ INDENTATION.

hànyǔ pīnyīn
⇨ ROMANISATION.

hapax legomenon
A word or phrase (< Greek 'said once') which occurs only once in a CORPUS and which may therefore not be included in a dictionary.
⇨ NONCE WORD.

hard copy
The printed version of a machine-readable TEXT, in contrast to the version stored electronically ('soft copy').

hard word
A word associated with the formal style of written text, and which is therefore relatively unfamiliar. Hard words are the ones that prompt users to consult, and compilers to supply, dictionaries. It was the hard-word tradition which motivated the first English dictionaries. Today's GENERAL DICTIONARY attempts to cover the bulk of the vocabulary, but there are also specialised dictionaries of difficulties.
▢ Starnes & Noyes 1946/91, Whitcut 1989, Brown 1996.
▤ *An English Expositor* (J. Bullokar), London, 1616; *Glossographia; or a Dictionary, Interpreting all such Hard Words . . . as are now Used in our Refined English Tongue* (T. Blount), London, 1656; *The Everyday Dictionary of Misunderstood, Misused, Mispronounced Words* (L. Urdang), London, 1972.

head form
⇨ CANONICAL FORM.

headword
The form of a word or phrase which is chosen for the LEMMA, the position in the dictionary structure where the ENTRY starts. Practices vary as to how headwords are marked typographically (e.g. by bold letters on indented or protruding lines), or how multiple and variant forms are distinguished (e.g. subscripts/superscripts for homonymous words or sub-entries for words with multiple senses), but most recognise a CANONICAL FORM. The headword constitutes an important link between the MACROSTRUCTURE and MICROSTRUCTURE.
▢ Jackson 1988, Zgusta 1989b, Svensén 1993.

hidden entry
A GLOSS for a word or phrase which is contained inside the entry for a related word or phrase rather than marked by a separate headword. Thus *common gnat* does not have an entry in the *Collins English Dictionary* [2nd edition] (London & Glasgow, 1986), but appears in the entry **gnat** as part of the definition: 'any of various small fragile biting dipterous insects of the suborder *Nematocera*, esp. *Culex pipiens* (**common gnat**), which abounds near stagnant water.'
▢ Landau 1984.

hidden glossary

A list of words or phrases or technical terms, usually in alphabetical order, published not as a separate REFERENCE WORK, but as part of another, relatively inaccessible text, such as book or journal article.

⇨ DICTIONARY JOURNAL.

📖 Robinson 1984.

📄 'A glossary of contemporary English lexicographic terminology', in *Dictionaries* 5 (1983): 76–114.

hierarchical classification

⇨ HIERARCHICAL RELATION.

hierarchical concept system

⇨ HIERARCHICAL RELATION.

hierarchical relation

An ordered system of conceptual links in a technical subject field, which can be either 'generic' (based on the dependent relationship between SPECIFIC CONCEPTS and GENERIC CONCEPTS) or a PARTITIVE RELATION (based on a part–whole hierarchy). By contrast, non-hierarchical relations include those which are 'sequential' (based on linear progression in space or time) or 'pragmatic' (based on thematic connections).

⇨ CO-ORDINATION.

📖 ISO 1990.

hierarchical structure

The ranking of the component parts of a dictionary or other reference work in hierarchical order, e.g. the information categories in relation to the headword inside entries (BASE STRUCTURE) or the entries in relation to the overall word-list (MACROSTRUCTURE).

⇨ ACCESS STRUCTURE.

high variety

⇨ DIGLOSSIA.

historical dictionary

A type of REFERENCE WORK in which the vocabulary of a language is traced through time. General dictionaries provide information on the derivation of words (ETYMOLOGY), but under the influence of the historical-comparative perspective in LINGUISTICS, dictionaries 'on historical principles' have developed which document the changes in form and meaning of words (the 'curriculum vitae of vocabulary'), often in large-scale multi-volume projects or by means of more specialised CHRONOLOGICAL DICTIONARIES or PERIOD DICTIONARIES.

⇨ HISTORICAL LEXICOGRAPHY.

📖 Murray 1977, Bailey 1987, Zgusta 1992, Berg 1993.

📄 *Deutsches Wörterbuch* (J. Grimm & W. Grimm), Leipzig, 1854–1961; *A Chronological English Dictionary* (T. Finkenstaedt *et al.*), Heidelberg, 1970; *Concise Oxford Dictionary of English Etymology* (T. F. Hoad), Oxford, 1986; *The Oxford English Dictionary* (J. Murray *et al.*), Oxford, 1928/89; *A Dictionary of South African English on Historical Principles* (P. Silva), Oxford, 1996.

historical information

One of the INFORMATION CATEGORIES presented by the compiler and consulted by the user of a reference work, based on history. General dictionaries contain material on the derivation of words (ETYMOLOGICAL INFORMATION), HISTORICAL DICTIONARIES trace the formal and semantic changes in the vocabulary of a language throughout its history or in a particular period. Factual information about historical events is codified in encyclopedias or specialised reference works such as ALMANACKS or BIOGRAPHICAL DICTIONARIES.

⇨ PHILOLOGY.

📖 Bailey 1990, Zgusta 1992.

historical lexicography

A complex of activities concerned with the design, compilation, use and evaluation of HISTORICAL DICTIONARIES.

📖 Merkin 1986, Zgusta 1986b, Burchfield 1987b.

historical linguistics

⇨ PHILOLOGY.

historic dictionary

An early DICTIONARY or other reference work which has significance within a lexicographic tradition, e.g. INCUNABULA. Such works, because of their relative rarity or value, often become part of specialised COLLECTIONS. Occasionally FACSIMILE EDITIONS are published as reprints.

📖 Learmouth & Macwilliam 1986, Vancil 1993.

historiolect

⇨ PERIOD.

homograph

⇨ HOMONYMY.

homologue
⇨ HOMONYMY.

homonym
A member of a set of words or phrases characterised by HOMONYMY.

homonymy
The relationship between two or more words which are identical in form but not in meaning. The identity may be in pronunciation ('homophones', e.g. *fair* and *fare*), in spelling ('homographs', e.g. *minute* 'division of time' and *minute* 'tiny') or both ('homologues', e.g. *band* 'ribbon' and *band* 'group of musicians'). Dictionaries tend to treat homonyms in separate entries on the grounds that native speakers regard them as different words, but the decision as to whether two words are homonymous or different senses of the same word (POLYSEMY) may not be easy to make. Criteria include, in addition to spelling, pronunciation and meaning, the etymology of the word(s), their grammatical status, and the scope and user convenience intended. Sometimes homonyms and other 'confusible' pairs (PARONYMS) are listed separately in the BACK MATTER of the dictionary.
⇨ SYNONYMY (1).
📖 Malakhovski 1987, Ilson 1988, Svensén 1993, Gouws 1996.
📑 *A Dictionary of Homonyms: New Word Patterns* (L. Ellyson), Sherman Oaks CA, 1977; *The Dictionary of British and American Homophones* (S. N. Williams), London, 1987; *Homophones and Homographs: An American Dictionary* (J. R. Hobbs), Jefferson NC, 1993; *Collins COBUILD English Guides 6: Homophones* (H. Bruce & M. Stocks), London, 1995.

homophone
⇨ HOMONYMY.

honorific
⇨ FORM OF ADDRESS.

host
A central computer system through which a number of terminals are linked in a network, providing access to a range of databases, data files and facilities for on-line processing.

house style
Typesetting and other conventions used by a particular publisher.

⇨ STYLE MANUAL.
📖 McArthur 1992.
📑 *Hart's Rules* [39th edition] (H. Hart), Oxford, 1989.

HTML
⇨ HYPERTEXT

humorous definition
A DEFINITION presented in a light-hearted or entertaining style, often appropriate to particular types of REFERENCE WORK, such as CHILDREN'S DICTIONARIES or dictionaries of 'levities'.
⇨ ALTERNATIVE LEXICOGRAPHY, ANTIDICTIONARY.
📑 *Another Almanac of Words at Play* (W. R. Espy), London, 1981; *The Official Liar's Handbook* (D. Dale), North Ryde NSW, 1986.

hybrid
The combination of one or more types of REFERENCE WORK in a single product. Often there are no distinct designations for these compromise genres, which include 'dictionary-cum-atlas', 'dictionary-cum-encyclopedia', 'dictionary-cum-grammar', 'dictionary-cum-thesaurus', 'dictionary-cum-usage guide', and 'monolingual-cum-bilingual dictionary'. It is also possible to combine different formats, e.g. a mixture of alphabetical and thematic ARRANGEMENT in a thesaurus or terminological dictionary, or a Chinese dictionary with a sequence of entries by characters and romanised transcriptions.
⇨ BILINGUALISED DICTIONARY, ENCYCLOPEDIC DICTIONARY, REFERENCE SET, REFERENCE SHELF.
📖 Mair 1991.
📑 *Collins Dictionary and Thesaurus in One Volume* (W. T. McLeod), London & Glasgow, 1987; *New Webster's Dictionary and Roget's Thesaurus* [with world atlas and medical dictionary], New York NY, 1992.
💻 *The American Heritage Electronic Dictionary* [with] *Roget's II: Electronic Thesaurus*, Boston MA & Monterey CA, 1991; *Diciopedia. Grande dicionário enciclopédico multimédia*, Oporto, 1996.

hydronym
The name of a river, waterway, lake, bay etc.
📑 *Hydronymia Europaea* (W. P. Schmid), Stuttgart 1985– [incomplete].

hypercorrection
The process or result of overgeneralising a STANDARD form (or what is considered standard) by a

DIALECT speaker, or a target form (or what is assumed to be the target form) by a learner. USAGE GUIDES may be consulted in such situations of linguistic insecurity.

hypermedia

The technology which provides on-screen INFORMATION with multiple links to other documents, even material using pictures and sound.
⇨   ILLUSTRATION (1), WORLD WIDE WEB.

hyperonym

A member of a set of words or phrases characterised by HYPERONYMY.

hyperonymy

The SENSE RELATION obtaining between the members of a set of words or phrases, one of whose meaning is more general than, or super-ordinate to, that of its hyponyms. The sense of the hyperonym or GENERIC TERM can be said to 'include' that of the hyponyms or SPECIFIC TERMS, e.g. *plant* covers *flower*, *vegetable* etc. As the hyponym is more specific than the hyperonym, it can be said to have more defining features. This relationship is exploited in DEFINITIONS and in TERMINOLOGY where technical terms can be ranked in conceptual hierarchies.
⇨   HYPONYMY, WORDNET.

hypertext

The combination of TEXT material from different sources, using specially formatted 'mark-up languages' for transmission.
📖   Davis 1993.

⇨   HYPERMEDIA, KNOWLEDGE BASE, STANDARD GENERALIZED MARK-UP LANGUAGE.

hyphenation

The indication in a dictionary of the conventional points at which words may be divided when they occur at the ends of lines. Many languages have strict conventions governing hyphenation, based on syllable structure or morphology, but for English there is no universal agreement, and the major publishing houses and the quality press have evolved their own standards (e.g. *ex-amin-ation* versus *ex-amina-tion*).
📗   *Oxford Spelling Dictionary* (R. E. Allen), Oxford, 1986.

hyponym

A member of a set of words or phrases characterised by HYPONYMY.

hyponymy

The SENSE RELATION obtaining between the members of a set of words or phrases and their hyperonym. The sense of the hyponym or SPECIFIC TERM can be said to be 'included' in that of the hyperonym or GENERIC TERM, e.g. *flower* or *vegetable* covered by *plant*. This relationship is exploited in DEFINITIONS (e.g. 'a *flower* is a *plant* which . . .' or 'a *vegetable* is a *plant* which . . .') and in TERMINOLOGY where technical terms can be arranged in conceptual chains or hierarchies, e.g. *etymological dictionary* / (kind of) *historical dictionary* / (kind of) *dictionary* / (kind of) *reference work*.
⇨   CO-HYPONYM, HYPERONYMY.
📖   Lyons 1968, Jackson 1988.

I

ICAME
Acronym for INTERNATIONAL COMPUTER ARCHIVE OF MODERN AND MEDIEVAL ENGLISH.

-icon
A COMBINING FORM used in lexicography for dictionary titles, e.g. R.-H. Zuidinga's *Eroticon* (The Hague, 1990).

ideological dictionary
⇨ ONOMASIOLOGICAL DICTIONARY.

idiolect
The language of a single speaker. Such personal dialects are not normally investigated to any degree except in the study of famous individuals such as politicians or literary authors, in which case their vocabulary may be collected and codified in specialised dictionaries.
⇨ AUTHOR'S DICTIONARY, LANGUAGE VARIETY.

idiom
A FIXED EXPRESSION whose overall meaning is not always transparent from the combination of the meanings of its constituent words, e.g. *go to the country* 'announce a general election' versus its literal counterpart *go to the country* 'travel to the countryside'.
⇨ COLLOCATION, MULTI-WORD EXPRESSION, PHRASEOLOGY.
📖 Fernando 1996, Moon 1996.
📄 *Oxford Dictionary of English Idioms* (A. P. Cowie *et al.*), Oxford, 1983/93; *A Chinese–English Dictionary of Idioms and Proverbs* (X. J. Heng & X. Z. Zhang), Tübingen, 1988; *NTC's American Idioms Dictionary* [2nd edition] (R. A. Spears), Lincolnwood IL, 1994.

idioticography
An archaic term for DIALECT LEXICOGRAPHY.

idiotography
An archaic term for DIALECT LEXICOGRAPHY.

illustrated dictionary
A DICTIONARY which contains some ILLUSTRATIONS for selected words or phrases, in contrast to a PICTURE DICTIONARY which depicts all objects treated systematically. Although the use of illustrations, especially in pedagogically oriented dictionaries, dates back to the fifteenth century, printed reference works did not generally contain many illustrations until the nineteenth century. Today, the ELECTRONIC DICTIONARY can offer the possibility of film and sound recordings as well.
⇨ VISUAL DICTIONARY.
📄 *Orbis sensualium pictus* (J. A. Komenský), Nürnberg, 1658; *Reader's Digest Great Illustrated Dictionary* (R. Ilson), London, 1984.

illustration
1 A drawing, diagram or photograph which is intended to clarify the DEFINITION of a concept. Illustrations may take the form of representations of single items or groups of related items in diagrams, tables, charts or maps. The relationship between a labelled part of an illustration and the corresponding part of an entry in a reference work is not always clearly established.
⇨ ATLAS, CHILDREN'S DICTIONARY, FILM, ILLUSTRATED DICTIONARY, PICTURE DICTIONARY.
📖 Hancher 1988, Nesi 1989, Ilson 1990, ISO 1990, Stein 1991, Svensén 1993.
2 A verbal EXAMPLE.

image of the dictionary
The public perception of DICTIONARIES and other reference works. Very little is known about this subject except that they evoke mixed feelings,

from an appreciation of their value as cultural tools, which is associated with their AUTHORITY on etymology, spelling, pronunciation and definition, to a complete ignorance of their benefits and limitations.

⇨ DICTIONARY CULTURE, STANDARD (2), USER PERSPECTIVE.

▢ Greenbaum *et al.* 1984, Algeo 1989a, 1989b.

implicit definition

A contextual EXAMPLE used to elaborate on a DEFINITION.

impression

⇨ EDITION.

imprint

An indication, usually on the TITLE PAGE of a book or other published document, of the name of the printer and/or publisher.

incipit

⇨ STRUCTURAL INDICATOR.

inclusion

⇨ SENSE RELATION.

inclusion list

A list of items (to be) included, e.g. TERMS in a TERMINOLOGICAL DICTIONARY.

⇨ COVERAGE, EXCLUSION LIST, SELECTION.

▢ ISO 1990.

incompatibility

A SENSE RELATION between two or more HYPONYMS in relation to their HYPERONYM, either serially (e.g. *word*, *phrase*, *clause*, *sentence* in relation to *syntax*) or cyclically (e.g. *poodle*, *dachshund* and *spaniel* in relation to *dog*).

⇨ ANTONYMY.

incunable dictionaries

⇨ INCUNABULA.

incunabula

Books published before 1501. Early 'incunable dictionaries' and other reference works, also known as 'fifteeners', can be very valuable and are the subject of specialised collections.

⇨ COLLECTION (1), DICTIONARY HISTORY, Panel 'A Selection of European Dictionary Titles' (page 144).

▢ Vancil 1994.

indentation

A shortening of one or more lines of text from the margin to highlight a section, e.g. the start of a paragraph. In dictionaries and other reference works, reverse (or 'hanging') indentation is used to mark the text of an entry following the ENTRY-LINE. Progressive indentation is sometimes used to indicate SUBORDINATION of concepts in an index of hierarchically related words in a thesaurus.

index

A systematic LIST, usually of words or symbols occurring in a TEXT. In contrast with the CONCORDANCE which provides information on the context of each of the cited words, the index usually gives only references to their positions, e.g. line numbers. In practice, indexes can range from simple lists of selected terms contained in a textbook or reference work, allowing the user access to each by means of page numbers, to complex AUTHOR'S DICTIONARIES providing full information on the vocabulary of a writer by location numbers in the works documented. Some reference works have in addition to the main (alphabetically or thematically arranged) WORD-LIST one or more separate indexes for access to particular information categories such as personal or place names. An index to all variant forms of a lemmatised word is called an 'inverted index'; an alphabetic index in which items are arranged in reverse order of their constituent letters is called a 'reverse index', 'index a tergo' or REVERSE-ORDER DICTIONARY.

⇨ CATALOGUE.

▤ *Index to Science Fiction Anthologies and Collections* (W. Contento), Boston MA, 1984; *An Index of Icons in Emblem Books 1500–1700* (H. Diehl), Norman OK, 1986; *The Omnicon Index of Standards for Distributed Information and Telecommunication Systems*, Vienna & New York NY, 1989.

index a tergo

⇨ REVERSE-ORDER DICTIONARY.

indexer

One who engages in the compilation of an INDEX.

⇨ AMERICAN SOCIETY OF INDEXERS, SOCIETY OF INDEXERS.

indices

The Latin plural form of INDEX, interchangeable in English with *indexes*.

indigenous language

A local language, usually contrasted with a colonial 'world language', e.g. the 'vernacular' languages in medieval Europe in relation to Latin, or the South American Indian languages in relation to Spanish or Portuguese.

⇨ FIELD DICTIONARY.

📖 Bartholomew & Schoenhals 1983.

infix

⇨ AFFIX.

inflection

The marking of grammatical function by means of MORPHOLOGY, e.g. to show case or number.

⇨ DERIVATION, INFLECTIONAL INFORMATION.

inflectional information

One of the INFORMATION CATEGORIES presented by the compiler and consulted by the user of a reference work, based on INFLECTION. LEMMATISATION is the process by which compilers of dictionaries establish the canonical forms of headwords either by removing or retaining inflections. In the GENERAL DICTIONARY, inflectional information is usually limited to an indication of part-of-speech information. There also may be cross-references to forms that deviate from a paradigm, such as irregular past tenses of English verbs. But, in general, only skilled users may be able to predict the appropriate inflected forms.

⇨ AFFIXATION, CONJUGATION, DECLENSION.

📖 Mugdan 1989.

inflectional morpheme

A MORPHEME added to a BASE or STEM to indicate grammatical function.

⇨ DERIVATIONAL MORPHEME.

inflectional morphology

⇨ MORPHOLOGY.

informal

⇨ STYLE LABEL.

informant

1 In FIELDWORK, one who provides linguistic or other DATA.

⇨ EVIDENCE.

2 In USER RESEARCH, one who provides information on the suitability or otherwise of dictionaries and other reference works in relation to certain needs or skills.

information

Knowledge acquired or required. The DICTIONARY and other REFERENCE WORKS attempt to satisfy the need for information, and INFORMATION TECHNOLOGY is used to develop or find ways and means of storing, presenting and interpreting the data of interest to various users. Two classes of INFORMATION CATEGORY can be sought or provided: (a) linguistic information about ORTHOGRAPHY, PHONOLOGY, MORPHOLOGY and SYNTAX, SEMANTICS, ETYMOLOGY, idiomatic and stylistic and other aspects of USAGE; (b) encyclopedic information about TERMINOLOGY, personal and other NAMES, geographical and historical and other facts, items of cultural-artistic and scientific knowledge. The trend recently has been to present more and more of these kinds of information in various types of reference works, and computers have improved ACCESS by making formats more flexible.

⇨ DATA.

📖 McArthur 1992, Svensén 1993.

information category

One of several types of INFORMATION presented by the compiler and consulted by the user of a REFERENCE WORK. Examples of such information provided in general dictionaries include the spoken and written form of words and phrases (PRONUNCIATION and SPELLING), their MEANINGS as explained in DEFINITIONS, and their structural, historical and stylistic properties (GRAMMAR, ETYMOLOGY, USAGE). In encyclopedically oriented reference works, knowledge from specialised fields may also be made available in the form of technical terms, biographical and geographical facts, historical data, artistic and scientific information, often put in a systematic context and pictorially illustrated.

The selection, treatment and utility of these information types depend on the dictionary in question and the FUNCTIONS which it is intended to fulfil. Thus the text layout and access FORMAT can vary considerably, e.g. between a general monolingual defining dictionary for lay users and a bilingual terminological database for experts. There is also a wide range of lexicographic styles and conventions used in different cultures. In all these respects, changes are frequent, e.g. through recent forms of computerisation.

⇨ DICTIONARIES AS DISCOURSE, DICTIONARY, ENCYCLOPEDIA, ILLUSTRATION (1), LEXICOGRAPHY, MICROSTRUCTURE, Panel 'Information Categories' (page 74).

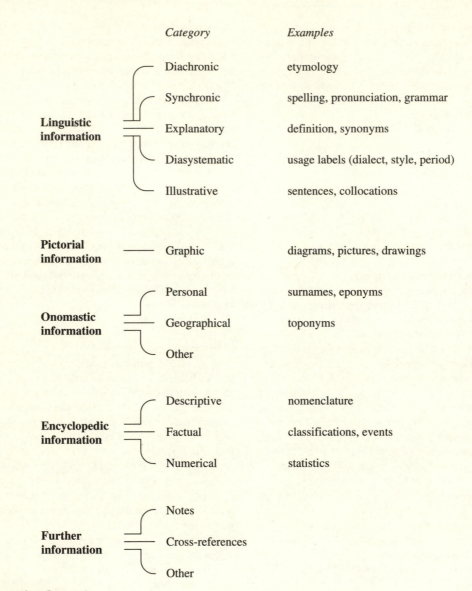

	Category	Examples
Linguistic information	Diachronic	etymology
	Synchronic	spelling, pronunciation, grammar
	Explanatory	definition, synonyms
	Diasystematic	usage labels (dialect, style, period)
	Illustrative	sentences, collocations
Pictorial information	Graphic	diagrams, pictures, drawings
Onomastic information	Personal	surnames, eponyms
	Geographical	toponyms
	Other	
Encyclopedic information	Descriptive	nomenclature
	Factual	classifications, events
	Numerical	statistics
Further information	Notes	
	Cross-references	
	Other	

Information Categories

📖 Collison 1982, Benson *et al.* 1986, Jackson 1988, Hausmann & Wiegand 1989, Svensén 1993, Béjoint 1994.

information retrieval
The successful conclusion of a SEARCH for relevant information.
⇨ CONSULTATION, DATA, INFORMATION CATEGORY.

information technology
The use of various tools and systems, especially computerisation, for the presentation of INFOR-MATION. In the widest sense, this includes writing (which enables the transmission of messages and its systematic storage on the basis of the script used), but more specifically it refers to the machinery (typing, printing, broadcasting etc.) that aids the spreading of knowledge of all kinds. In the production of REFERENCE WORKS, computers are used to collect data (FIELDWORK), process text (EDITING) and present the information for the benefit of users (PUBLISHING).

📓 *Concise Dictionary of Computing and Information Technology* (D. B. Lynch), Bromley, 1991;

Encyclopedic Dictionary of Information Technology and Systems (A. E. Cawkell), London, 1993.

information type
⇨ INFORMATION CATEGORY.

initialism
⇨ ABBREVIATION.

inkhorn term
A word or phrase coined to splendificate the writer's 'learnedness'.
⇨ HARD WORD.

inner access structure
⇨ ACCESS STRUCTURE.

inner search path
⇨ SEARCH PATH.

insert
1 With reference to dictionary structure, ⇨ MID-DLE MATTER.
2 A loose-leaf panel, e.g. of the grammar codes used in a dictionary.

insult
⇨ TERM OF ABUSE.

integrative concept
⇨ COMPREHENSIVE CONCEPT.

intension
The set of attributes which characterise a specific concept in relation to a superordinate generic concept.
⇨ EXTENSION, HYPONYMY, INTENSIONAL DEFIN-ITION.

intensional definition
A DEFINITION which specifies the attributes of a specific concept in relation to its HYPERONYM, e.g. *tulip* 'a kind of *flower* which . . .'.
⇨ EXTENSIONAL DEFINITION.
📖 ISO 1990.

interactive dictionary
An ELECTRONIC DICTIONARY which is not only capable of being integrated into a personal computer (e.g. text processing) system, but also allows the potential combination with other media, such as the INTERNET, film and sound, and – most crucially – an adaptation to the needs and preferences of the individual USER, in terms of frequently performed lexical, grammatical and textual SEARCHES. Only a small proportion of currently available software offers such facilities.
⇨ COMPUTATIONAL LEXICOGRAPHY, HYPER-TEXT, MULTIMEDIA, WORDNET.

interference
The process or result of interlingual transfer resulting in, for example, error in the target language.
⇨ BORROWING, ERROR ANALYSIS, FALSE FRIEND, INTERLANGUAGE, LEARNER'S DICTIONARY.

interlanguage
A learner's unique approximations of a target language, on a dynamic continuum. The study of INTERFERENCE shows the relative influence of the NATIVE LANGUAGE, while ERROR ANALYSIS measures the relative distance from the NORMS of the target language.
⇨ FALSE FRIEND, LEARNER'S DICTIONARY.
📖 Davies *et al.* 1984, Tarone 1988, Granger *et al.* 1994.

interlinear gloss
⇨ GLOSS.

interlingual dictionary
A type of REFERENCE WORK with information on more than one language. The term is used either when the contrast with MONOLINGUAL DICTION-ARY is stressed or when the distinction between BILINGUAL DICTIONARY and MULTILINGUAL DIC-TIONARY is considered irrelevant. Other inter-lingual sub-types include the QUASI-BILINGUAL DICTIONARY in which a more accessible language (e.g. English) is used for describing the words of a less accessible language (e.g. archaic Akkadian) and the BILINGUALISED DICTIONARY which is based on a monolingual (learner's) dictionary whose entries are translated wholly or in part. In spite of their long tradition and usefulness, inter-lingual dictionaries have not received a great deal of attention in DICTIONARY RESEARCH.

interlingual homograph
⇨ FALSE FRIEND.

interlingual homophone
⇨ FALSE FRIEND.

internal access structure
⇨ ACCESS STRUCTURE.

internal search path
⇨ SEARCH PATH.

International Association of Applied Linguistics
⇨ ASSOCIATION INTERNATIONALE DE LINGUISTIQUE APPLIQUÉE.

International Computer Archive of Modern and Medieval English
An academic organisation, based at the Norwegian Computing Centre for the Humanities in Bergen, and concerned with CORPORA of English. It hosts annual conferences, and publishes the *ICAME Journal*.
⌨ Website: www.hd.uib.no/icame.html

International Council of Onomastic Sciences
A academic organisation, based in Louvain (Belgium), which holds triennial conferences and published the journal *ONOMA*.

International Federation for Information and Documentation
⇨ FÉDÉRATION INTERNATIONALE D'INFORMATION ET DE DOCUMENTATION.

International Forum on Information and Documentation
⇨ FÉDÉRATION INTERNATIONALE D'INFORMATION ET DE DOCUMENTATION.

internationalism
A word or phrase shared across several languages, e.g. combining forms such as *CACO-*, *-ISM*, *LEXI-* and *ORTHO-*. Scientific internationalisms can be marked in dictionaries by labels, e.g. *ISV* for 'international scientific vocabulary' in *Webster's Third New International Dictionary* (Springfield MA, 1961).
📖 Kirkness 1984.

International Journal of Corpus Linguistics
The title of a journal established in 1996, and published in Amsterdam.

International Journal of Lexicography
The title of a journal established in 1988, and published in Oxford in association with the DICTIONARY SOCIETY OF NORTH AMERICA and the EUROPEAN ASSOCIATION FOR LEXICOGRAPHY.
⌨ Website: www.oup.co.uk/jnls/list/lexico/

international language
⇨ AUXILIARY LANGUAGE.

International Organization for Standardization
A world-wide federation of national standards institutions, founded in 1947, and based in Geneva. It has over 200 Technical Committees, one of which is concerned with the principles and standardisation of TERMINOLOGY.
⌨ Website: www.iso.ch

International Phonetic Alphabet
An internationally agreed PHONETIC ALPHABET, based on the Latin alphabet, developed by the International Phonetic Association in the late nineteenth century.
▤ *Introducing Phonetics* (P. Roach), London, 1992.

Internet
A system of interconnected computer networks allowing access to global INFORMATION, e.g. by electronic mail.
⇨ WORLD WIDE WEB.
📖 LaQuey 1993, Cumming 1995, Biagini & Picchi 1996, Carr 1997.
▤ *The Whole Internet: User's Guide and Catalog* (E. Krol), Sebastopol CA, 1992.

intertextuality
The similarities and cross-references among different texts. In METALEXICOGRAPHY, shared text features allow the classification of reference works. In DICTIONARY HISTORY, they permit the tracing of links amongst dictionaries over time.
⇨ COMPARISON OF DICTIONARIES, DICTIONARY ARCHAEOLOGY, GENRE, PARALLEL TEXTS.

intonation
⇨ PROSODIC FEATURE.

introspection
⇨ EVIDENCE.

inventory
A structured LIST of items or sets of items, e.g. of property or stock.
⇨ CATALOGUE.

inverted entry
The listing of a MULTI-WORD EXPRESSION under its last (rather than first) constituent.
⇨ DIRECT ENTRY.

inverted index
⇨ INDEX.

-(io)nary
A COMBINING FORM used in lexicography for dictionary titles, e.g. E. Naha's *The Science Fictionary* (New York NY, 1980), B. Kasravi's *Indexionary* (Santa Barbara CA, 1990) and M. McCutcheon's *Descriptionary* (New York NY, 1992).

IPA
Abbreviation for INTERNATIONAL PHONETIC ALPHABET.

irreversible idiom
A multi-word expression whose order cannot be changed, e.g. *through thick and thin*.

-ism
A COMBINING FORM used to refer to language styles (ARCHAISM, COLLOQUIALISM, NEOLO-GISM etc.) or varieties (Americanism, Anglicism, Briticism etc.), or to sets of prejudices (SEXISM, RACISM etc.)
📖 Filipović 1984, Görlach 1994.
📰 *Dictionary of Americanisms* (J. R. Bartlett), Boston MA, 1848.

ISO
A COMBINING FORM (< Greek 'equal') used alone to designate the INTERNATIONAL ORGANIZATION FOR STANDARDIZATION.
📰 *International Standard ISO 1087 Terminology – Vocabulary*, Geneva, 1990.

isogloss
⇨ LINGUISTIC ATLAS (1).

J

jargon

A word or phrase associated with a subject field which is clear to the experts using it, but not to outsiders. Jargon shares with other special-language varieties like SLANG an in-group orientation which outsiders often criticise. Jargon dictionaries attempt to explain specialised usage for the benefit of the non-initiated, sometimes in pseudo-humorous and/or critical fashion, while technical or TERMINOLOGICAL DICTIONARIES have less of a bridge-building function.

⇨ HARD WORD, LANGUAGE FOR SPECIFIC PURPOSES, TECHNICAL LANGUAGE.

📖 McArthur 1992.

📑 *Newspeak: A Dictionary of Jargon* (J. Green), London, 1984.

journals in lexicography

Regular publications devoted to lexicography and related fields.

⇨ *CAHIERS DE LEXICOLOGIE, CÍSHŪ YÁNJIÙ, DICTIONARIES, INTERNATIONAL JOURNAL OF CORPUS LINGUISTICS, INTERNATIONAL JOURNAL OF LEXICOGRAPHY, LEXICOGRAPHICA INTERNATIONAL ANNUAL, LEXICON, LEXICONORDICA, LEXIKOS, LEXIQUE, ONOMA, TERMINOLOGY.*

K

kanji
⇨ CHARACTER.

keyword
1 A word or phrase which has become representative of a field, movement or lifestyle, e.g.
communicative, green, postmodern.
 *Keywords: A Vocabulary of Culture and
Society* (R. Williams), New York NY, 1985;
Keywords in Language and Literacy (R. Carter),
London & New York NY, 1995.
2 A word or phrase used to index or catalogue a
document.
3 ⇨ KEYWORD IN CONTEXT.

keyword in context
A word or phrase extracted from a text and listed
in alphabetical, frequency or other order, together
with the words occurring in its immediate environment.
⇨ CONCORDANCE.

keyword out of context
A word or phrase extracted from a text and listed
with references to the sources in which it occurs.
⇨ INDEX.

knowledge base
A computer-based system where information is
linked by methods such as HYPERTEXT rather than
in structured fields as in conventional DATABASES.
⇨ EXPERT SYSTEM.
📖 Vossen 1992.

kośa
⇨ METRICAL DICTIONARY.

KWIC concordance
⇨ KEYWORD IN CONTEXT.

KWOC index
⇨ KEYWORD OUT OF CONTEXT.

L

label

A special symbol or abbreviated term used in REF-ERENCE WORKS to mark a word or phrase as being associated with a particular USAGE or LANGUAGE VARIETY. Dictionaries differ widely in the way they do this. As the INFORMATION necessary to support a particular decision is not always available and boundary lines between different usage features are fluid, consistency is rarely achieved.

There are several potential scales along which a word such as *cuss* can be placed, and each of these can be subdivided in different ways. Thus, on a scale of regionality, it could be labelled 'Am(erican) E(nglish)'. On a scale of formality, it may need the label 'inf(ormal)' or 'fam(iliar)', at least for one or two of its senses. But does it also have to be labelled, on a scale of chronology, as 'old-f(ashioned)', or even 'arch(aic)'? If attitude is considered relevant, what about 'derog(atory)'? And in a bilingual dictionary, do the translation equivalents for each sense of the word need to be separately marked with corresponding labels?

⇨ DIASYSTEMATIC LABELLING, FIELD LABEL, FREQUENCY LABEL, GLOSS (2), LANGUAGE CODE, REGIONAL LABEL, STYLE LABEL, SUBJECT LABEL, TEMPORAL LABEL, Panel 'Usage Labels' (page 151).
📕 Landau 1984, Ilson 1990, Berg 1993, Svensén 1993, Thomsen 1994.

ladder

An informal term for DICTIONARY FAMILY.

language

The most basic means of COMMUNICATION between human beings, studied in a number of disciplines, notably LINGUISTICS. Languages are never static (LANGUAGE CHANGE) nor uniform internally (LANGUAGE VARIETY) or in comparison or contrast with each other (LANGUAGE TYP-OLOGY). Knowledge about various aspects of language (LINGUISTIC INFORMATION) is codified in general and specialised dictionaries which also perform an important function in language learning and TRANSLATION.

⇨ ARTIFICIAL LANGUAGE, SEMIOTICS, USAGE.
📕 Benson *et al*. 1986.
📑 *The Cambridge Encyclopedia of Language* (D. Crystal), Cambridge, 1987; *An Encyclopedia of Language* (N. E. Collinge), London & New York NY, 1990; *Compendium of the World's Languages* (G. L. Campbell), London & New York NY, 1991; *Routledge Dictionary of Language and Linguistics* (H. Bussmann *et al*.), London & New York NY, 1996.

language acquisition

⇨ LANGUAGE LEARNING.

language arts

A collective term for a number of disciplines linked to the teaching of languages, particularly that of the NATIVE LANGUAGE.
📑 *Handbook of Research on Teaching the English Language Arts* [International Reading Association/ National Council for the Teaching of English] (J. Flood *et al*.), New York NY & Toronto, 1991.

language change

The process and result of variation in pronunciation, structure and vocabulary over time. Specialised DIACHRONIC DICTIONARIES make a feature of tracing chronological changes where evidence is available. The GENERAL DICTIONARY has never attempted to chronicle all such developments, but marks the poles of ARCHAISM and NEOLOGISM by means of labels. Modern technology allows the observation of change in the making through MONITOR CORPORA, so that the ELECTRONIC DICTIONARY of the future will be kept up to date.
📕 Bauer 1994, Labov 1994, Trask 1994.

language code

An abbreviation or symbol used to LABEL the language associated with a particular word, phrase or term.
📖 ISO 1990.

language dictionary

A type of REFERENCE WORK which provides linguistic information about the total vocabulary covered. The prototype of this dictionary is the monolingual GENERAL DICTIONARY, which may be viewed in contrast with the ENCYCLOPEDIC DICTIONARY or the TERMINOLOGICAL DICTIONARY.

language engineering

The harnessing of technology to the development of language-related activities, products and services.
📃 *The Language Engineering Directory* (P. M. Hearn), Madrid, 1996; *Language Engineering: Progress and Prospects* (C. Watson, LINGLINK), Luxembourg, 1997.

language for special purposes

⇨ LANGUAGE FOR SPECIFIC PURPOSES.

language for specific purposes

In language teaching and LSP LEXICOGRAPHY, the variety of the language ('special language') used by experts in a particular subject field. Textbooks for teaching and reference books for explaining the 'registers' of such TECHNICAL LANGUAGES or 'sub-languages' take into account the specialist knowledge (e.g. active and passive VOCABULARY) of the target learner–user and make a deliberate effort to select the HEADWORDS and couch the definitions according to the criteria of familiarity and frequency.
⇨ CORPUS LINGUISTICS, ESP DICTIONARY, LSP DICTIONARY.
📖 Robinson 1980, Sager *et al*. 1980, Diab 1989, ISO 1990, James *et al*. 1994, 1997, James & Purchase 1996, Minaeva 1996.

language information

⇨ LINGUISTIC INFORMATION.

language learning

The process of mastering a language, either the mother tongue or a second/foreign language. A distinction can be made between 'learning' (in a formal environment, e.g. a school) and 'acquisition' (in an informal setting). There is a lack of awareness of the needs of different learners for different types of reference works, e.g. monolingual versus bilingual, alphabetical versus thematic, general versus specialised.
⇨ INTERLANGUAGE, LEARNER'S DICTIONARY, PEDAGOGICAL LEXICOGRAPHY.
📖 Nation 1989, Johnson 1995.

language maintenance

The totality of activities aimed at preserving a minority language, e.g. an INDIGENOUS LANGUAGE vis-à-vis a colonial language. Dictionaries, monolingual or bilingual, may have a role to play in codifying the minority language and giving it cultural status.
⇨ CULTURAL DICTIONARY, EXOGLOSSIC LANGUAGE.

language planning

The totality of activities aimed at regulating the use of a language, often linked to national policies. Such control is usually imposed centrally by governmental or quasi-governmental agencies, such as ACADEMIES or language policy bureaux. Measures may include banning FOREIGNISMS, coining NEOLOGISMS and technical TERMINOLOGY, controlling the media and redirecting education policies.
⇨ CENSORSHIP, CULTURAL DICTIONARY, LANGUAGE RIGHTS, STANDARDISATION.
📖 Kurtböke 1996, Raadik 1996, Kaplan & Baldauf 1997.

language policy

A set of governmental decisions on the relative priorities of the use of languages in a state, for the purposes of employment, education etc., which can influence the number and types of REFERENCE WORKS produced and used.
⇨ LANGUAGE RIGHTS.

language purification

The deliberate attempt to achieve PURISM in a language.

language purism

⇨ PURISM.

language reform

The totality of activities aimed at improving the conditions in which a language can develop and be taught, e.g. through SPELLING REFORM.
⇨ STANDARDISATION.

language resource database

⇨ DATABASE.

language rights

The exercise and protection of the fundamental right to use the language of one's choice.
⇨ LANGUAGE MAINTENANCE, LANGUAGE POLICY.
📖 Tollefson 1991, Phillipson & Skutnabb-Kangas 1995.

language standardisation

⇨ STANDARDISATION.

language teaching

The practice of creating an environment conducive to LANGUAGE LEARNING by the use of appropriate instructional methodologies.
⇨ APPLIED LINGUISTICS, INTERLANGUAGE, LANGUAGE ARTS, LEARNER'S DICTIONARY, PEDAGOGICAL LEXICOGRAPHY.
📖 Hartmann 1992a, Johnson 1995.

language typology

A branch of LINGUISTICS concerned with the classification of languages, based on structural similarities rather than genetic affiliation. The nature and types of reference works reflect the diversity of language types, e.g. by taking morphology into account in determining CANONICAL FORMS.
📖 Zgusta 1989b.
📖 *The Atlas of Languages* (B. Comrie *et al.*), New York NY, 1996.

language variety

The presence in a language of several distinctive systems, conditioned by such factors as regionality (DIALECT), personality (IDIOLECT), gender (GENDERLECT), social class (SOCIOLECT), subject field (TECHNOLECT) or historical stage (PERIOD).
⇨ REGISTER (1), SOCIOLINGUISTICS, STYLE.
📖 Jackson 1988, Chambers 1994.

last name

⇨ PERSONAL NAME.

latent word

A word which according to the rules of phonology and morphology is possible, but whose use has not been documented in a TEXT, e.g. a DERIVATIVE generated as a RUN-ON ENTRY in a dictionary entry.
📖 Landau 1984, Svensén 1993.

Latin alphabet

The conventional set of graphic symbols used for the representation of the sounds of Latin, and retained, with some modifications through the centuries, for writing, and subsequently printing, the languages of western Europe (with the exception of Greek). Through colonisation, missionary activities and other historical events, the Latin alphabet has now been adopted as the writing system of many of the world's languages.
⇨ ALPHABET.

layout

The way the page of a reference work is displayed. Recently more attention has been paid to the user-friendliness of the presentation, taking into consideration such criteria as the legibility and effectiveness of variable typography, the use of ILLUSTRATIONS, the limitation of TEXT COMPRESSION and other graphic support.
⇨ DESIGN, EXTRA COLUMN, GUIDEWORD.
📖 Simpson 1989.

LDC

Abbreviation for LINGUISTIC DATA CONSORTIUM.

learner corpus

⇨ ERROR ANALYSIS.

learner language

⇨ INTERLANGUAGE.

learner lexicography

⇨ PEDAGOGICAL LEXICOGRAPHY.

learner's dictionary

A PEDAGOGICAL DICTIONARY aimed primarily at non-native learners of a language. The degree to which dictionaries have been integrated into the learning process varies from culture to culture. The true dictionary as a learning tool ('learning dictionary') is still in its infancy.
⇨ ACTIVE DICTIONARY, BILINGUAL LEARNER'S DICTIONARY.
📖 Strevens 1978, 1987, Cowie 1987a, Jackson 1988, Rundell 1988, Tickoo 1989, Battenburg 1991, Zöfgen 1991, Hartmann 1992a, Allen 1996, Kernerman 1996, Stark 1996.
📖 *Cambridge International Dictionary of English* (P. Procter), Cambridge, 1995; *Longman Dictionary of Contemporary English* [3rd edition] (D. Summers), Harlow, 1995; *Oxford Advanced Learner's Dictionary* [5th edition] (J. Crowther), Oxford, 1995; *Collins COBUILD Learner's Dictionary* (J. Sinclair), London, 1996; *Random House Webster's Dictionary of American English* (G. M. Dalgish), New York, 1997;

Australian Learners Dictionary (D. Blair & C. N. Candlin), Sydney NSW, 1997.

learning dictionary
⇨   LEARNER'S DICTIONARY.

-lect
A COMBINING FORM used in LINGUISTICS to refer to a number of distinct language varieties, e.g. DIALECT, GENDERLECT, IDIOLECT, SOCIOLECT, TECHNOLECT.
⇨   CREOLE.

left-core structure
⇨   CORE STRUCTURE.

legal lexicography
A complex of activities concerned with the design, compilation, use and evaluation of reference works in the field of law.
◻   Šarćević 1988, 1989.
▤   *Campus florum* (T. Wallensis), *c.* 1335; *The International Law Dictionary* (R. L. Bledsoe & B. A. Boczek), Santa Barbara CA, 1987.

lemma
The position at which an entry can be located and found in the structure of a REFERENCE WORK. The relationships of the lemma in the reference work are two-way: within the overall (e.g. alphabetical) MACROSTRUCTURE it constitutes the point of ACCESS where the compiler can place and the user can find the information listed; within the MICRO-STRUCTURE it establishes the 'topic' on which the rest of the entry is a 'comment', e.g. the definition of the HEADWORD.

   Some authorities favour including all information preceding the definition within the notion of the lemma, i.e. all 'formal' items such as spelling, pronunciation and grammar, while others use the term as a synonym for 'headword' or even the whole ENTRY.
⇨   SUB-LEMMA.
◻   Ilson 1988, Hausmann & Wiegand 1989, Osselton 1995.

lemma clustering
⇨   CLUSTERING.

lemma sign
⇨   SIGN.

lemmata
The Greek plural form of LEMMA, interchangeable in English with *lemmas*.

lemmatic form
⇨   LEMMATISATION.

lemmatisation
The reduction of a paradigm of variant word forms to a CANONICAL FORM, e.g. the inflected forms (*-s*, *-ed*, *-ing* etc.) of English verbs to the infinitive. Lemmatisation is a problem awaiting a comprehensive solution (attempted by computational approaches) in connection with wider tasks such as how to choose a suitable HEADWORD from the constituents of a FIXED EXPRESSION, and how to list BINOMIAL COMPOUNDS (under the last or first constituent).
⇨   DIRECT ENTRY, TAGGING.
◻   ISO 1990, Schnorr 1991, Botha 1992, Lorentzen 1996, Mills 1996.
▣   *LEXICO* (R. Venezky), 1969; *LEXA* (R. Hickey), 1993.

lemmatised word index
An ordered list of CANONICAL FORMS.
⇨   LEMMATISATION.

letter
A graphic symbol used in an alphabetic writing system to represent one or more speech sounds.
⇨   GRAPHEME, SPELLING, WRITING.

letter-by-letter alphabetisation
A principle of ALPHABETICAL ORGANISATION in which words or phrases are listed in order of their letters, ignoring word boundaries. Thus in this *Dictionary of Lexicography*, *lexicalisation* comes between *lexical information* and *lexical item*.
⇨   WORD-BY-WORD ALPHABETISATION.
◻   Svensén 1993.

lexeme
A basic unit in the linguistic study of VOCABULARY. Lexemes are usually interpreted as a combination of a FORM (graphic/phonic substance) with a MEANING (semantic value) in a particular grammatical context. As such they occur as simple words (e.g. *face*), complex words (*preface*), phrasal and compound words (*face up to*, *face-lift*), 'multi-word expressions' (*fly-by-night*, *face the music*), and shortened forms which can stand by themselves (*prefab*). Lexemes are studied paradigmatically in SEMANTIC FIELDS, and syntagmatically in COLLOCATIONS.

   When lexemes are used in dictionaries as HEADWORDS, they are cited in their CANONICAL

FORMS (e.g. in English, verbs in the bare infinitive [*face*] shorn of all grammatical inflections [*face|d, face|s, fac|ing*]). The meanings of lexemes are explained in the general dictionary by DEFINITIONS or in specialised reference works such as THESAURUSES or SYNONYM DICTIONARIES (in thematically grouped conceptual lists).

⇨ AFFIX, HOMONYMY, LEMMATISATION, LEXICOLOGY, POLYSEMY, WORD FORMATION.

📖 Jackson 1988, Sinclair 1991, Svensén 1993, Gouws 1996.

lex(i)-

A COMBINING FORM used to coin terms associated with 'words' and 'lexicography', e.g. *lexicomputing*.

lexica

The Greek plural form of LEXICON, interchangeable in English with *lexicons*.

lexical ambiguity
⇨ AMBIGUITY.

lexical collocation
⇨ COLLOCATION.

lexical database
⇨ DATABASE.

lexical definition
⇨ DEFINITION.

lexical domain
⇨ SEMANTIC FIELD.

lexical equivalent
⇨ EQUIVALENT.

lexical field
⇨ SEMANTIC FIELD.

lexical gap

The absence of a word to express a particular meaning, e.g. lack of translation equivalents for CULTURE-SPECIFIC VOCABULARY terms across languages.

lexical information

One of the INFORMATION CATEGORIES presented by the compiler and consulted by the user of the dictionary, based on VOCABULARY. Lexical information, sometimes contrasted either with GRAMMATICAL INFORMATION or ENCYCLOPEDIC INFORMATION, may contain e.g. word origins (ETYMOLOGY), forms (MORPHOLOGY) or meanings (SEMANTICS).

📖 Thelen 1992.

lexicalisation

The process or result of assigning to a word or phrase the status of a LEXEME.

⇨ WORD FORMATION.

lexical item
⇨ WORD.

lexical knowledge base
⇨ KNOWLEDGE BASE.

lexical meaning
⇨ MEANING.

lexical relation
⇨ SENSE RELATION.

lexical resources

A collective term for language DATA available primarily by electronic means.

📖 Vossen 1996.

lexical semantics
⇨ SEMANTICS.

lexical set
⇨ SEMANTIC FIELD.

lexical unit
⇨ WORD.

lexical word
⇨ CONTENT WORD.

lexicographer

One who engages in LEXICOGRAPHY, either as a COMPILER or as a METALEXICOGRAPHER.

⇨ COMPILER PERSPECTIVE, REFERENCE PROFESSIONAL, WHO'S WHO.

📖 Kipfer 1985, Lombard 1994, Zgusta 1996.

lexicographese
⇨ DICTIONARESE.

Lexicographica

A double series of publications co-sponsored by the EUROPEAN ASSOCIATION FOR LEXICOGRAPHY and the DICTIONARY SOCIETY OF NORTH

AMERICA, consisting of a monograph series (*Lexicographica Series Maior*) established in 1984, and a yearbook (*Lexicographica. International Annual for Lexicography*) established in 1985.

Lexicographical Society of China

A professional society established in Beijing in 1992. It holds biennial conferences, and awards the CHINESE LEXICOGRAPHY PRIZE.
⇨ *CÍSHŪ YÁNJIÙ*.

Lexicographical Society of India

A professional society established in Hyderabad in 1975. It issues a newsletter, the *LxSI News Bulletin*.

lexicographic(al) archaeology
⇨ DICTIONARY ARCHAEOLOGY.

lexicographic(al) archive
⇨ ARCHIVE (1).

lexicographic(al) computing
⇨ COMPUTATIONAL LEXICOGRAPHY.

lexicographic(al) corpus
⇨ CORPUS.

lexicographic(al) coverage
⇨ COVERAGE.

lexicographic(al) definition
⇨ DEFINITION.

lexicographic(al) evidence
⇨ EVIDENCE.

lexicographic(al) information
1 With reference to information presented in a dictionary, ⇨ DICTIONARY INFORMATION.
2 With reference to information on vocabulary, ⇨ LEXICAL INFORMATION.

lexicographic(al) label
⇨ LABEL.

Lexicographic Research Centre
⇨ DICTIONARY RESEARCH CENTRE.

lexicographic(al) style
⇨ DICTIONARY STYLE.

lexicographist

An archaic term for one who engages in LEXICOGRAPHY.

lexicography

The professional activity and academic field concerned with DICTIONARIES and other REFERENCE WORKS. It has two basic divisions: lexicographic practice, or DICTIONARY-MAKING, and lexicographic theory, or DICTIONARY RESEARCH. The former is often associated with commercial book publishing, the latter with scholarly studies in such disciplines as LINGUISTICS (especially LEXICOLOGY), but strict boundaries are difficult to maintain and, in any case, are being bridged by such means as professional training, societies, conferences and publications. There are as yet no internationally agreed standards of what constitutes a good dictionary, but human ingenuity (and computer technology) produces new types every day against the background of various historical traditions, to meet people's insatiable need for rapid access to INFORMATION, linguistic as well as encyclopedic.

Depending on the orientation and purpose of such reference works, several branches of lexicography can be distinguished, each with its own practices and theories:

AUTHOR LEXICOGRAPHY
BILINGUAL LEXICOGRAPHY
BIOGRAPHICAL LEXICOGRAPHY
COMPUTATIONAL LEXICOGRAPHY
CULTURAL LEXICOGRAPHY
DIALECT LEXICOGRAPHY
ENCYCLOPEDIC LEXICOGRAPHY
ETYMOLOGICAL LEXICOGRAPHY
FREQUENCY LEXICOGRAPHY
HISTORICAL LEXICOGRAPHY
LEGAL LEXICOGRAPHY
LSP LEXICOGRAPHY
MEDICAL LEXICOGRAPHY
MONOLINGUAL LEXICOGRAPHY
MULTILINGUAL LEXICOGRAPHY
MUSICAL LEXICOGRAPHY
ONOMASIOLOGICAL LEXICOGRAPHY
ONOMASTIC LEXICOGRAPHY
PEDAGOGICAL LEXICOGRAPHY
PERIOD LEXICOGRAPHY
REGIONAL LEXICOGRAPHY
RHYME LEXICOGRAPHY
SLANG LEXICOGRAPHY
SPECIALISED LEXICOGRAPHY

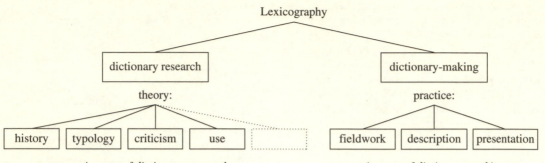

Aspects of dictionary research   *Aspects of dictionary-making*

Lexicography: Theory and Practice

TECHNICAL LEXICOGRAPHY
TERMINOLOGICAL LEXICOGRAPHY
TEXT-SPECIFIC LEXICOGRAPHY
THESAURUS LEXICOGRAPHY
USAGE LEXICOGRAPHY.

⇨ COMPARATIVE LEXICOGRAPHY, GENERAL LEXICOGRAPHY, METALEXICOGRAPHY, PRESCRIPTIVE LEXICOGRAPHY, PROFESSIONAL RESOURCES, REFERENCE SCIENCE, THEORY OF LEXICOGRAPHY, TRAINING, TYPOLOGY (1), Panel 'Lexicography: Theory and Practice' (above).
📖 Zgusta 1971, 1991, Hartmann 1983, 1993, Landau 1984, Ilson 1986a, 1990, Jackson 1988, Geeraerts 1989, Cowie 1990, Frawley 1992–3, Svensén 1993, Béjoint 1994.
📓 *Wörterbücher/Dictionaries/Dictionnaires* (F. J. Hausmann *et al.*), Berlin, 1989–91; *Císhūxué cídiǎn* (Z. X. Yang & Q. K. Xu), Shanghai, 1992; *Diccionario de lexicografía práctica* (J. M. de Sousa), Barcelona, 1995; *Nordisk leksikografisk ordbok* (H. Bergenholtz *et al.*), Oslo, 1997.

lexicologist
One who engages in LEXICOLOGY.

lexicology
A branch of LINGUISTICS concerned with the study of the basic units of vocabulary (LEXEMES), their formation, structure and meaning. Lexicology is relevant to DICTIONARY-MAKING in a number of respects as it can clarify how words and phrases are created, combined, modified and defined, and how USAGE varies within a language according to such parameters as dialect, formality and technicality. However, the relationship between lexicology and LEXICOGRAPHY cannot be reduced to theory versus practice: lexicography is not merely 'applied lexicology', but an auton-

omous field with its own premises (DICTIONARY RESEARCH), utilising and adapting the findings of other disciplines to its own ends. Conversely, lexicology has incorporated many of the facts accumulated in dictionaries throughout their history, such as 'common core words' and 'hard words', 'colloquialisms' and 'technical terms', 'simple words' and 'multi-word expressions', 'archaic words' and 'neologisms', 'regionalisms' and 'internationalisms'.
⇨ ETYMOLOGY, MORPHOLOGY, SEMANTICS, TERMINOLOGY.
📖 Jackson 1988.

lexicomputing
⇨ COMPUTATIONAL LEXICOGRAPHY.

lexicon
1 The totality of a language's VOCABULARY, seen either as a list or as a structured whole. The view of vocabulary as a LIST of words has led to the development of glossaries, dictionaries and other works of reference, while the structural view has encouraged such linguistic disciplines as GRAMMAR, LEXICOLOGY and SEMANTICS.
📖 Jackson 1988, Svartvik 1992b, Pemberton & Tsang 1993.
2 A type of REFERENCE WORK in which the words of a language, language variety, speaker or text are listed and explained, either in alphabetical or in thematic order. In English, this term is associated not with the GENERAL DICTIONARY, but with more specialised works of a classical, literary or technical orientation. In the Renaissance, *lexicon* was one of several competing titles for (often multilingual) specialised dictionaries.

⇨ GLOSSARY.

📖 Stein 1985, Green 1996.

📄 *Lexicon* [Latin–Spanish] (E. A. de Nebrija), Salamanca, 1492; *Lexicon tetraglotton* [English–French–Italian–Spanish] (J. Howell), 1660; *Lexicon technicum* (J. Harris), 1704; *Lexicon Grammaticorum* (H. Stammerjohann), Tübingen, 1996.

3 The mental vocabulary stored in the (native) speaker's mind. Some issues studied (in PSYCHOLINGUISTICS and related disciplines such as ARTIFICIAL INTELLIGENCE) include: how and where words are stored, in what order they are learned and remembered, whether bilinguals have separate or joint lexicons, etc.

⇨ ACTIVE VOCABULARY, PASSIVE VOCABULARY.

📖 Aitchison 1987.

Lexicon
The title of the journal of the Iwasaki Linguistic Circle (Tokyo), published since 1972.

LexicoNordica
The title of the journal of the NORDISK FORENING FOR LEKSIKOGRAFI, established in 1994.

lexicophile
A lover or collector of DICTIONARIES and other works of reference.

lexicostatistics
⇨ FREQUENCY.

lexigraphy
The art of constructing and expressing DEFINITIONS of words.

Lexikos
The title of a journal published annually by the Buro van die Woordeboek van die Afrikaanse Taal in Stellenbosch, South Africa since 1991, now also the journal of the AFRICAN ASSOCIATION FOR LEXICOGRAPHY.

Lexique
The title of a journal published annually since 1982 by the Presses universitaires de Lille, Villeneuve d'Ascq, France.

lexis
⇨ LEXICON (1).

librarian
One who engages in library work. This may include the indexing and cataloguing of REFERENCE WORKS, and advice to users on their content and consultation.

⇨ LIBRARY SCIENCE.

librarianship
⇨ LIBRARY SCIENCE.

Library Association
A professional society, based in London, founded in 1877 to represent LIBRARIANS. There are 23 subject groups, including one for (Reference and) Information Services and one for Information Technology.

⇨ AMERICAN LIBRARY ASSOCIATION, McCOLVIN MEDAL, WALFORD AWARD, WHEATLEY MEDAL.

📄 *World Guide to Libraries, Archives and Information Science Associations* (J. R. Fang & A. H. Songe), London, 1990.

💻 www.la-hq.org.uk

library of deposit
⇨ DEPOSITORY LIBRARY.

library science
A field with close ties to LEXICOGRAPHY, concerned with the organisation of libraries as systematic collections of books and other DOCUMENTS. This involves archiving and classification of manuscripts and printed materials, including REFERENCE WORKS of all kinds, and providing access to them, e.g. by means of CATALOGUES, BIBLIOGRAPHIES, INDEXES and INFORMATION TECHNOLOGY.

📄 *Harrod's Librarians' Glossary* (R. Prytherch), Aldershot, 1995.

library union database
An electronic UNION LIST.

💻 *Worldcat* [incorporating 15,000 library catalogues] website: bart.prod.oclc.org:3050

ligature
⇨ DIGRAPH.

lingua franca
A link language used by speakers of different languages as a common medium of communication.

⇨ AUXILIARY LANGUAGE, CONTACT VERNACULAR.

linguist
One who engages in activities involving (foreign) languages and/or LINGUISTICS.

linguistic atlas

1 A type of REFERENCE WORK consisting of maps illustrating the features of one of more regional varieties of a language. The maps which plot, by the use of 'isoglosses', the regional distribution of aspects of pronunciation, grammar and vocabulary are based on FIELDWORK surveys by means of personal interviews. This technique was pioneered by Jules Gilliéron in France at the beginning of the twentieth century and has since been refined by dialectologists in other parts of the world. For English, several linguistic atlases are available for areas of Britain and the USA. Linguistic information of this kind has also been published in the form of DIALECT DICTIONARIES and REGIONAL DICTIONARIES.

⇨ DIALECT.

  📖 McArthur 1992.

  ▤ *The Linguistic Atlas of England* (H. Orton *et al.*), London, 1978; *The Linguistic Atlas of Scotland* (J. Y. Mather & H. H. Speitel), London, 1975–86; *The Linguistic Atlas of New England* (H. Kurath), Providence RI, 1939–43; *An Atlas of English Dialects* (C. Upton & J. D. A. Widdowson), Oxford, 1996.

2 A type of reference work with information on the distribution of the world's languages.

  ▤ *Atlas of the World's Languages* (C. Moseley & R. E. Asher), London & New York, 1993; *The Atlas of Languages* (B. Comrie *et al.*), New York NY, 1996.

linguistic change

⇨ LANGUAGE CHANGE.

linguistic content

⇨ LINGUISTIC INFORMATION.

Linguistic Data Consortium

A research-based organisation specialising in projects on text CORPORA and similar fields.

  🖥 Website: www.ldc.upenn.edu/

linguistic dictionary

⇨ LANGUAGE DICTIONARY.

linguistic geography

⇨ DIALECT GEOGRAPHY.

linguistician

An informal term for LINGUIST.

linguistic information

A collective term for the INFORMATION CATEGORIES presented by the compiler and consulted by the user of a dictionary, based on LANGUAGE. Information types in entries may be diachronic, e.g. etymology; orthographic, e.g. spelling; phonological, e.g. pronunciation; grammatical, e.g. part of speech; semantic, e.g. definitions or translation equivalents; and pragmatic, e.g. usage labels. These can be supplemented and complemented by other means, e.g. pictorial, onomastic and encyclopedic, either within the entry or in the OUTSIDE MATTER. There are also SPECIALISED DICTIONARIES available for each of these information categories, e.g. GRAMMAR DICTIONARIES, PRONOUNCING DICTIONARIES, SPELLING DICTIONARIES and SYNONYM DICTIONARIES.

There are numerous formats and conventions for presenting these details on the dictionary page. The distribution, range, status and quality of linguistic information included in reference works vary widely across different speech communities and cultures.

⇨ LEXICAL INFORMATION, STRUCTURE.

  📖 Landau 1984, Ilson 1985, Swanepoel 1992, Svensén 1993.

linguistic insecurity

The feeling of inadequacy that a language user may experience in the choice of a linguistic form appropriate to a specific situation, e.g. meaning, spelling, pronunciation, usage. One solution to the problem may be to consult a reference work.

⇨ FUNCTION.

linguistic mark-up

⇨ TAGGING.

linguistic norm

⇨ NORM.

linguistic purism

⇨ PURISM.

linguistics

An academic discipline concerned with the study of LANGUAGE in all its manifestations. LINGUISTIC INFORMATION, the result of research in several branches of linguistics, is codified in general dictionaries (e.g. PRONUNCIATION, GRAMMAR, MEANING) or in specialised dictionaries, e.g. in ETYMOLOGICAL DICTIONARIES or USAGE GUIDES. Progress in LEXICOGRAPHY often depends on the findings of linguistic analysis, but DICTIONARY-MAKING is an autonomous professional field.

⇨ APPLIED LINGUISTICS, CORPUS LINGUISTICS, LEXICOLOGY, PHILOLOGY, SEMIOTICS, SOCIOLINGUISTICS.

📖 Béjoint 1994, Lombard 1994, Hudson 1995, Hartmann 1996a, O'Grady *et al.* 1997.

📔 *The Encyclopedia of Language and Linguistics* (R. E. Asher & J. M. Y. Simpson), Oxford, 1994; *Routledge Dictionary of Language and Linguistics* (H. Bussmann *et al.*), London & New York NY, 1996.

linguistic science(s)
⇨ LINGUISTICS.

linguistic sign
⇨ SIGN.

linguistic standard
⇨ STANDARD.

link word
A word or phrase used to connect sentences or parts of sentences, e.g. *but*, *however*.

📔 *Dictionary of Link Words in English Discourse* (W. J. Ball), London, 1986; *Collins COBUILD English Guides 9: Linking Words* (S. Chalker), London, 1996.

list
A basic tool for structuring INFORMATION. In REFERENCE WORKS such as dictionaries, lists are fundamental tools in the organisation of information and in the way this is structured so it can be presented, searched and found. Much of the terminology of lexicography is an elaboration of the list-of-words metaphor, from the traditional card-box to the computerised database, from the MICROSTRUCTURE (e.g. the ordering of the senses of the HEADWORD) of the entry and its subdivisions to the MACROSTRUCTURE (e.g. the alphabetical arrangement of the WORD-LIST) of the whole reference work.

Lists of items, such as words or phrases, normally follow the top-to-bottom order of writing (left-to-right in scripts based on the Latin alphabet), but more complex groupings (NICHING, NESTING) may make access more difficult for users. The information items listed can range from letters (ALPHABET) and words (INDEX, CONCORDANCE) to complex structures (BIBLIOGRAPHY, DICTIONARY, DIRECTORY, ENCYCLOPEDIA, THESAURUS, etc.).

⇨ EXCLUSION LIST.

📖 Hüllen 1994.

listing
⇨ CLUSTERING, GROUPING.

literacy
The skill of reading and writing. It is often assumed that literacy is a basic REFERENCE SKILL, but there are many examples from oral cultures, e.g. in ancient India, of the compilation and use of memorised reference works.

⇨ ORACY, READING, WRITING.

📖 James 1991, 1995a, Barton 1994.

📔 *Keywords in Language and Literacy* (R. Carter), London & New York NY, 1995.

literal meaning
A basic non-metaphorical meaning of a word or phrase.

⇨ BASIC SENSE, FIGURATIVE MEANING.

literal translation
⇨ TRANSLATION.

loan translation
The process of BORROWING a word or phrase from another language, retaining the meaning but replacing the constituents by native morphological elements, resulting in a 'calque', e.g. Cantonese *yiht* 'hot' *gáu* 'dog' = 'hot dog'.

loan-word
A word or phrase which is the result of BORROWING, and which has not been fully assimilated into the NATIVE VOCABULARY, e.g. *cídiǎn* 'Chinese character dictionary'.

⇨ FOREIGNISM, LOAN TRANSLATION.

📖 Pratt 1992.

📔 *German Loanwords in English: An Historical Dictionary* (J. A. Pfeffer & G. Cannon), Cambridge, 1994.

local ordering
The listing of items in the order in which they occur in a text, e.g. new words occurring in chapters of a textbook.

⇨ ORGANISATION.

logical definition
⇨ DEFINITION.

logical sense ordering
⇨ SENSE ORDERING.

-logy
⇨ -(O)LOGY.

lookalike
An informal term for PARONYM.

look up
⇨ CONSULTATION.

look-up form
⇨ CANONICAL FORM.

look-up strategies
⇨ USER STRATEGIES.

loose synonym
⇨ SYNONYMY (1).

loose synonymy
⇨ SYNONYMY (1).

low variety
⇨ DIGLOSSIA.

LSP
Abbreviation for LANGUAGE FOR SPECIFIC PURPOSES.

LSP dictionary
A type of REFERENCE WORK intended to describe a variety of a language used by experts in a particular subject field. Dictionaries of this kind are conceived as aids for users who are already specialists in the field, but want to practise or further study it through the medium of the target LANGUAGE FOR SPECIFIC PURPOSES, e.g. for preparing an academic paper for delivery at a conference.
▤ *Oxford Dictionary of Computing for Learners of English* (S. Pyne & A. Tuck), Oxford, 1996.

LSP lexicography
A complex of activities concerned with the design, compilation, use and evaluation of LSP DICTIONARIES.

M

machine-aided lexicography
⇨ COMPUTATIONAL LEXICOGRAPHY.

machine indexing
The compilation of an INDEX by computer.

machine lexicography
⇨ COMPUTATIONAL LEXICOGRAPHY.

machine-readable dictionary
A version of a dictionary which can be processed by or in a computer. Such dictionaries are used, e.g. in natural language processing, for purposes of semantic analysis and disambiguation, machine translation or the representation of knowledge.
⇨ ELECTRONIC DICTIONARY.
📖 Boguraev 1991, Ide *et al*. 1992, Fontenelle 1996, Sobkowiak 1996.

machine translation
⇨ TRANSLATION.

macrofunction
⇨ FUNCTION.

macrostructure
The overall LIST structure which allows the compiler and the user to locate information in a REFERENCE WORK. The most common format in Western dictionaries is the alphabetical WORD-LIST (although there are other ways of ordering the HEADWORDS, e.g. thematically, chronologically or by frequency), which constitutes the central component. This can be supplemented by OUT-SIDE MATTER in the front, middle or back of the work.
⇨ MEGASTRUCTURE, MICROSTRUCTURE, Panel 'Megastructure' (page 92).
📖 Hausmann & Wiegand 1989, ISO 1990, Svensén 1993.

macrothesaurus
⇨ THESAURUS (2).

main-entry
⇨ ENTRY TERM.

main source
⇨ SOURCE.

manual
⇨ HANDBOOK.

manual language
⇨ SIGN LANGUAGE.

manuscript dictionary
A DICTIONARY copied in handwriting. Before the advent of printing, manuscript dictionaries were the norm. Many of the early dictionaries of European languages and the languages of e.g. China and India, some very extensive, produced by the first European missionaries to those lands, have never been published.
⇨ COMPARATIVE DICTIONARY, OLA DICTIONARY.

map
The presentation of geographical and cultural information in cartographic form.
⇨ ATLAS, CULTURAL ATLAS.

marginal gloss
⇨ GLOSS (1).

markedness
The feature that distinguishes a 'marked' from an 'unmarked' member of a pair or set of linguistic items, e.g. *dog* (unmarked) versus *bitch* (marked). In lexicography marking is used in systems of USAGE LABELS which classify words or phrases in particular language contexts, e.g. dialect, register, technicality, genre and attitude.
⇨ DIASYSTEMATIC LABELLING.

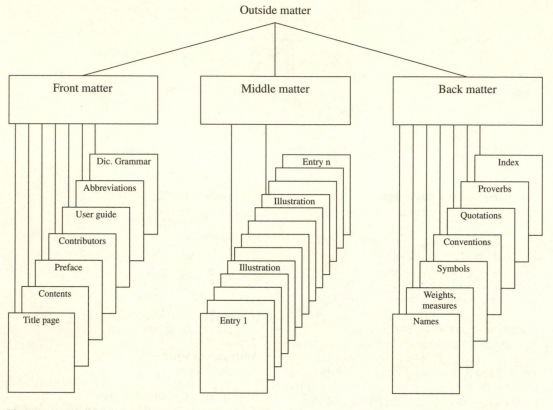

Megastructure (Macrostructure and outside matter)

mark-up language
⇨ STANDARD GENERALIZED MARK-UP LANGUAGE.

mass media
⇨ MEDIA STUDIES.

McColvin Medal
An annual award by the LIBRARY ASSOCIATION for the most outstanding reference work published.

meanalike
An informal term for PARONYM.

meaning
The relationship between words or phrases and the objects or ideas which they designate. Several different aspects of this complex relationship have been studied in SEMANTICS, producing a range of theories and models according to how they approach the connection either between 'words and things' or between 'words and words'. REF-ERENCE is the meaning relation between a linguistic unit and its referent(s) in the extralinguistic world; this can be objective (DENOTATION) or subjective (CONNOTATION), but rarely is it one-to-one because of SENSE RELATIONS of polysemy, synonymy, antonymy, hyponymy and hyperonomy. SEMANTIC INFORMATION of various kinds is covered in the general dictionary by means of DEF-INITION and EXAMPLE, and specialised reference works (such as THESAURUSES, WORD-FINDING DICTIONARIES and SYNONYM DICTIONARIES) address particular aspects of meaning.
⇨ CONCEPT, ETYMOLOGY, ONOMASIOLOGY, SENSE.
📖 Wierzbicka 1985, Allen 1986, Cruse 1986, Moon 1987, Jackson 1988, Swanepoel 1994, Considine 1996, Gouws 1996.

meaning discrimination
⇨ SENSE DISCRIMINATION.

meaning distinction
⇨ SENSE DISCRIMINATION.

meaning shift
⇨   SEMANTIC CHANGE.

meaning specialisation
⇨   SEMANTIC CHANGE.

mechanical dictionary
⇨   ELECTRONIC DICTIONARY.

media studies
A field concerned with the nature and social impact of newspapers, radio and television, often together with the technologies on which these 'mass media' are based, such as the motion picture, telecommunications and computing.
⇨   FILM, INFORMATION TECHNOLOGY, MULTIMEDIA, TELEMATICS.
▤   *The Complete A–Z Media & Communication Studies Handbook* (S. Price), London, 1997.

medical lexicography
A complex of activities concerned with the design, compilation, use and evaluation of reference works in the field of medicine.
▥   Manuila 1981, McConchie 1983, Landau 1984, Jost & Crocker 1987, Mackenzie & Mel'čuk 1988.
▤   *Aggregator Paduanus de medicinis simplicibus* (J. Dondi dall'Orologia), *c.* 1470; *Dictionary of Pharmaceutical Medicine* (G. Nahler), Vienna & New York NY, 1994; *The Merck Index. An Encyclopedia of Chemicals, Drugs, and Biologicals* [12th edition] (S. Budavari), Whitehouse Station NJ, 1996; *Encyclopedia of Molecular Biology and Molecular Medicine* (R. A. Myers), Weinheim NY, 1996.

mediostructure
⇨   CROSS-REFERENCE STRUCTURE.

megastructure
The totality of the component parts of a reference work, including the MACROSTRUCTURE and the OUTSIDE MATTER.
⇨   Panel 'Megastructure', page 92
▥   Hausmann & Wiegand 1989.

melioration
⇨   SEMANTIC CHANGE.

mental lexicon
⇨   LEXICON (3).

menu
A metaphor adopted in computing and further adapted to the construction of ENTRIES in reference works, e.g. in the form of a table of contents at the head of an entry, referring to numbered sections.

meronymy
⇨   PARTITIVE RELATION.

mesolect
⇨   CREOLE.

metalanguage
The language used to present and comment on a subject field. In linguistics, metalanguage is the terminology used to describe the 'object language' (human language). In lexicography, metalanguage includes such conventions as grammatical codes, labelling of usage and the formulation of definitions. In this *Dictionary of Lexicography*, an attempt is made to use a neutral metalanguage to describe the metalanguage of lexicography.
⇨   METALEXICOGRAPHY.
▥   Svensén 1993.

metalexicographer
One who engages in the THEORY OF LEXICOGRAPHY.

metalexicography
A complex of activities concerned with the status of the field of LEXICOGRAPHY.
▥   Huang 1994.

metaphor
The use of a word or phrase usually designating a concept of one domain or semantic field (the source domain) used to designate an aspect of another domain or semantic field (the target domain). Metaphors are usually established on the basis of perceived similarity between the two concepts, e.g. *virus* 'destructive computer code' from *virus* 'microscopic agent causing infection'. This process has often been used to designate TITLES of reference books, e.g. THESAURUS ('treasure chest'), ENCYCLOPEDIA ('circle of knowledge').
▥   Frawley 1982, Regan 1989, McArthur 1992, Svensén 1993.
▤   *Collins COBUILD English Guide 7: Metaphor* (A. Deignan), London, 1995.

metatext
A section of a dictionary used to present and comment on the body of the work, e.g. an explanatory chart in the FRONT MATTER which illustrates the structure of entries.

metonymy

A word or phrase designating a concept of a specific domain or semantic field used to designate another aspect of the same domain on the basis of contiguity. Metonomy is based on a semantic link established by association, e.g. *Fleet Street* for 'the British press' (the place, for the institution located there).

metrical dictionary

A DICTIONARY compiled according to a conventional rhyme scheme, often for the purpose of ease of memorisation. Such a format is typical of classical Sanskrit 'kośa' or 'nighaṇṭu' dictionaries of sacred texts.
📖 Vogel 1979, James 1991.

micro-function

⇨ FUNCTION

microstructure

The internal design of a REFERENCE UNIT. In contrast to the overall word-list (MACROSTRUCTURE), the microstructure provides detailed information about the HEADWORD, with comments on its formal and semantic properties (spelling, pronunciation, grammar, definition, usage, etymology). If the headword has more than one SENSE, the information is given for each of these (SUB-LEMMA). Dictionaries vary according to the amount of information they provide, and how they present it in the text of the ENTRY. Users may not have sufficient reference skills to follow the intricacies of the microstructure, and may need explicit guidance and/or instruction to find and extract the details required.

⇨ ADDRESS, BASE STRUCTURE, USER'S GUIDE, Panel 'Microstructure' (below).
📖 Hausmann & Wiegand 1989, ISO 1990, Svensén 1993.

microthesaurus

⇨ THESAURUS (2).

middle matter

Those components of a dictionary's MACROSTRUCTURE which may be inserted into the central WORD-LIST section without forming a constituent part of it. Examples from general dictionaries include plates of illustrations, maps or diagrams, lists of grammatical terms or semantic fields, encyclopedic information; in two-way bilingual dictionaries examples include lists of phrases or idiomatic expressions inserted between the two parts.

⇨ OUTSIDE MATTER.
📖 Cop 1989.

minimum vocabulary

⇨ BASIC VOCABULARY.

minority language

⇨ EXOGLOSSIC LANGUAGE.

mixed arrangement

⇨ ARRANGEMENT.

modernising dictionary

A dictionary which makes a feature of the selection and treatment of CONTEMPORARY USAGE.
⇨ ARCHAISING DICTIONARY.
📖 Zgusta 1989a.

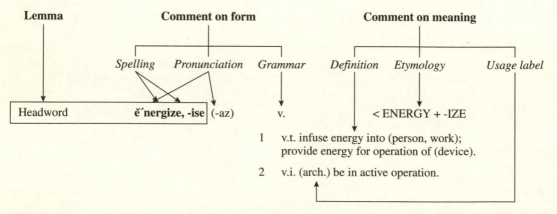

Microstructure

monitor corpus

A CORPUS of texts which is open-ended, allowing for the addition and subtraction of material, to take account of the progress of language change.

⇨ NEOLOGISM.

📖 Clear 1988.

monoaccessible dictionary

⇨ ACCESS STRUCTURE.

monodirectional dictionary

A type of BILINGUAL DICTIONARY in which the translation equivalents can be accessed only from one of the two languages. Thus if a French–English dictionary had only this one side, it could only be consulted by an English-speaking user for decoding, i.e. reading a French text, rather than for encoding, i.e. translating an English text into French. A French speaker, on the other hand, could not easily use such a monodirectional dictionary for understanding English texts. Compilers and publishers therefore strive to satisfy these two-way needs by providing BIDIRECTIONAL DICTIONARIES, to suit speakers of both languages, ideally for both encoding and decoding functions.

monofunctional dictionary

A type of REFERENCE WORK designed to help a user perform one particular task. Thus a bilingual dictionary for translating from the foreign into the native language (decoding function only) contrasts with a BIFUNCTIONAL DICTIONARY which is aimed at aiding translation from and into the foreign language (both decoding and encoding functions).

monoglot dictionary

⇨ MONOLINGUAL DICTIONARY.

monolingual-cum-bilingual dictionary

⇨ HYBRID.

monolingual dictionary

A type of REFERENCE WORK in which the words of a language are explained by means of that same language, in contrast to INTERLINGUAL DICTIONARIES. For most practical purposes and for most languages, the monolingual dictionary (also called 'general', 'explanatory' or 'usage' dictionary) is the prototypical work of reference for native speakers. For the same reason, it has also been the most popular and best studied dictionary genre.

Even so, many variants (alphabetic or thematic, commercial or scholarly, comprehensive or concise, general or specialised, etc.) have been recognised.

One relatively recent sub-type is the LEARNER'S DICTIONARY for foreign-language users, another is the ENCYCLOPEDIC DICTIONARY. The wider availability of text corpora and computer technology is likely to lead to new and better versions of all of these monolingual dictionaries.

⇨ METALANGUAGE, TYPOLOGY (1).

📖 Landau 1984, Bailey 1987, Rundell 1988, Béjoint 1994.

▤ *Collins English Dictionary and Thesaurus in One Volume* (W. T. McLeod), London & Glasgow, 1987; *The Random House Dictionary of the English Language* (S. B. Flexner), New York NY, 1987; *The Concise Oxford Dictionary of Current English* (R. E. Allen), Oxford, 1990; *Collins COBUILD English Dictionary* (J. Sinclair) London, 1995.

monolingual lexicography

A complex of activities concerned with the design, compilation, use and evaluation of MONOLINGUAL DICTIONARIES.

⇨ BILINGUAL LEXICOGRAPHY, DICTIONARY RESEARCH.

📖 Geeraerts 1989, Svensén 1993.

monolingual thesaurus

⇨ THESAURUS (2).

mononymy

A SENSE RELATION in which a concept is designated by only one term.

⇨ MONOSEMY.

📖 ISO 1990.

monosemy

The SENSE RELATION that obtains when a word or phrase has a single meaning. This is rather rare for ordinary general vocabulary items, but in technical TERMINOLOGY it is desirable that a term should designate only one concept.

⇨ MONONYMY, POLYSEMY.

📖 Béjoint 1990, ISO 1990.

morpheme

A grammatical unit which is used to constitute WORDS. Some can stand by themselves or form STEMS ('free morphemes', e.g. *black*, *bird* as well as *blackbird* – a lexicalised compound), whereas some can only combine with others ('bound morphemes', e.g. *con-stit-ution*). The totality of morphemes in a language and their word-formation potential are studied in MORPHOLOGY. The result of such studies (MORPHOLOGICAL INFORMATION) is codified in specialised reference works such as MORPHOLOGICAL DICTIONARIES.

⇨ AFFIX, BASE, LEXEME.

morphological dictionary

A type of REFERENCE WORK providing information on the structure and composition of WORDS. Such specialised dictionaries may contain details on usage and grammatical information (e.g. a GRAMMAR DICTIONARY or USAGE GUIDE), derivational morphology (e.g. a REVERSE-ORDER DICTIONARY or ROOT DICTIONARY), inflectional morphology and PART-OF-SPEECH specifics.

⇨ STEM DICTIONARY, WORD-CLASS DICTIONARY.

▤ *Bloomsbury Grammar Guide* (G. Jarvie), London, 1993; *Grammar Patterns 1: Verbs* (G. Francis), London & Glasgow, 1996.

morphological information

One of the INFORMATION CATEGORIES presented by the compiler and consulted by the user of the dictionary, based on MORPHOLOGY. Material on the structure (INFLECTION) and formation (DERIVATION) of words is provided in general and specialised dictionaries in a number of ways, e.g. as part of a DICTIONARY GRAMMAR in the front matter, a list of irregular forms in the back matter, or as part of the grammatical information given inside entries. PART-OF-SPEECH indication also supplements morphological details in the form of abbreviated word-class labels. Less information is given in general dictionaries about derivational AFFIXES and WORD-FORMATION elements. For these, specialised MORPHOLOGICAL DICTION-ARIES exist in some languages.

⇨ LEMMATISATION.

▭ Mugdan 1989, Zgusta 1989b.

morphology

A branch of GRAMMAR concerned with the structure and formation of WORDS. A distinction can be made between 'inflectional morphology' (the use of MORPHEMES as grammatical elements) and 'derivational morphology' (the use of morphemes as word-formation elements).

⇨ MORPHOLOGICAL INFORMATION.

▭ Katamba 1994.

mother tongue

⇨ NATIVE LANGUAGE.

multifunctional dictionary

A type of REFERENCE WORK designed to meet several needs of the user simultaneously. ELEC-TRONIC DICTIONARY systems allow the combination of information types so that several functions can be fulfilled, e.g. looking up definitions for decoding activities (reading), synonyms for encoding activities (writing), and factual knowledge for study and practice.

⇨ FUNCTION.

▭ Zimmermann 1983.

multi-language dictionary

⇨ MULTILINGUAL DICTIONARY.

multilingual dictionary

A type of REFERENCE WORK in which the vocabularies of several languages are related to each other, usually by means of translation equivalents. (The special case of two-language dictionaries is treated under BILINGUAL DICTIONARY.) In the history of Western lexicography, two prototypes can be highlighted: the sixteenth-century 'polyglot' tradition based on such models as Ambrosius Calepinus's *Dictionarium* (1502 Latin and some Greek, 1545 five languages, gradually increasing to ten languages by 1585), and the modern development of the TERMINOLOGICAL DICTIONARY of the technical vocabulary of various disciplines across languages, usually the result of some international standardisation of the terms and definitions covered. Numerous sub-types exist, from the polyglot travel phrasebook to the electronic terminological database such as EURODICAUTOM.

⇨ INTERLINGUAL DICTIONARY.

▭ Rosenstein 1985, Kabdebo 1992.

▤ *Wörterbuch der Landwirtschaft/Dictionary of Agriculture* [German/English/French/Spanish/Russian, 6th edition] (G. Haensch/rev. I. Alsing *et al.*), Munich, 1996; *Nordisk leksikografisk ordbok* [Norwegian (Bokmål and Nynorsk)/Danish/Finnish/Icelandic/Swedish/English/French/German] (H. Bergenholtz *et al.*), Oslo, 1997.

multilingual lexicography

A complex of activities concerned with the design, compilation, use and evaluation of MULTILINGUAL DICTIONARIES. As the numbers and types of such dictionaries are infinitely variable, owing to the many potential combinations of languages and information categories covered, generalisations are difficult to make. No overall framework has yet been developed for this field which nowadays tends to focus on specialised TERMINOLOGY.

multilingual thesaurus
⇨   THESAURUS (2).

multimedia
A combination of TEXT with (moving) pictures and/or sound by computer to form an (interactive) learning environment.
⇨   CD-ROM, FILM, HYBRID, HYPERMEDIA.
📖   Davis 1993.
💻   *The Multimedia CD-ROM Dictionary on CD-ROM* [15th edition], London & Washington DC, 1996.

multiple meaning
An informal term for POLYSEMY.

multi-word combination
⇨   MULTI-WORD EXPRESSION.

multi-word expression
A phrase consisting of two or more words functioning as a single LEXEME. The constituents are relatively stable (FIXED EXPRESSION) and, if used idiomatically, their combined meaning is more or other than the sum of the parts, e.g. *fly-by-night*, *face the music*.
⇨   DIRECT ENTRY, INVERTED ENTRY, PERMUTATION.
📖   Gates 1988, Jackson 1988, Bogaards 1992.

multi-word lexical unit
⇨   MULTI-WORD EXPRESSION.

mumpsimus
An orthographically or phonologically incorrect word that, by dint of usage, has become accepted in a language, e.g. *Mount Kościuszko*.

musical lexicography
A complex of activities concerned with the design, compilation, use and evaluation of reference works in the field of music.
📘   *The New Grove Dictionary of Music and Musicians* (S. Sadie), London & Washington DC, 1995.

mutation
⇨   CANONICAL FORM.

N

name

A word or phrase used to designate a specific person, place, organisation, artistic creation or object. In English and in many other languages this is done by using capitalised words (e.g. *Abraham Lincoln, Hong Kong, British Broadcasting Corporation* [*the BBC*], *Gone with the Wind, Mazda*). Names (often called 'proper nouns' or 'proper names') are part of a language's cultural vocabulary, but many dictionaries do not provide this ONOMASTIC INFORMATION.

⇨ APTRONYM, EPONYM, ETHNONYM, FORM OF ADDRESS, NICKNAME, ONOMASTICS, PERSONAL NAME, PSEUDONYM, TOPONYM, TRADE NAME.

📖 Mufwene 1988, Rader 1989, ISO 1990, McArthur 1992, Svensén 1993, Urdang 1996.

📓 *A Collector's Compendium of Rare and Unusual, Bold and Beautiful, Odd and Whimsical Names* (P. Dickson), New York NY, 1986.

name dictionary

⇨ ONOMASTIC DICTIONARY.

name lexicography

⇨ ONOMASTIC LEXICOGRAPHY.

naming principle

A set of standards for the creation and standardisation of names in the terminologies of technical fields.

⇨ NOMENCLATURE.

narrow transcription

⇨ TRANSCRIPTION.

national archive

A public collection of records and government documents.

national dictionary

A cultural or historical dictionary of significance to the official language of a country, often financed by central government or an ACADEMY and compiled by a team of scholarly lexicographers.

⇨ ACADEMY DICTIONARY.

national language

A language used *de facto* for everyday purposes in a country or territory, e.g. English in Ireland.

⇨ OFFICIAL LANGUAGE.

national library

A library of major significance to a country, often centrally funded and located in the capital city, such as the Bibliothèque nationale in Paris, or the Library of Congress in Washington DC.

⇨ DEPOSITORY LIBRARY.

native language

A language acquired in early childhood, often called 'first language' or 'mother tongue', in contrast to a language learned later, either as a SECOND LANGUAGE or as a FOREIGN LANGUAGE. Throughout the world, in situations of intensive language contact, the co-existence of two native languages ('bilingualism') is common, but in practice in individual cases one language is usually dominant in specific functional contexts. Different dictionary types have been developed to cater for the needs of these different speakers, but their nature and coverage vary from one language and culture to another.

⇨ BILINGUAL DICTIONARY, ENDOGLOSSIC LANGUAGE, GENERAL DICTIONARY, LEARNER'S DICTIONARY, MONOLINGUAL DICTIONARY.

native vocabulary

The word-stock of a language which is felt by native speakers to be preserved from influences from other languages. The degree of assimilation of vocabulary varies over time, and FOREIGNISMS, while possibly at first resisted, can become integrated into the indigenous lexicon.

⇨ BORROWING, DIAINTEGRATIVE INFORMATION, ETYMOLOGICAL DICTIONARY, ROOT.

    Berg 1993.

nativisation

The assimilation of FOREIGNISMS.

⇨ NATIVE VOCABULARY.

natural language processing

The application of computer techniques to linguistic analysis, including DISAMBIGUATION, LEMMATISATION, parsing, machine TRANSLATION and speech synthesis.

    Boguraev & Briscoe 1989, Butler 1990, Macleod *et al.* 1996.

needs analysis

The investigation and assessment of the REFERENCE NEEDS of different groups of USERS.

⇨ USER PERSPECTIVE, USER RESEARCH.

neoclassical compound

⇨ CLASSICAL COMPOUND.

neologism

A word or phrase which has entered the language (as a BORROWING or a COINAGE or through SEMANTIC CHANGE) relatively recently, often commented on and collected in specialised dictionaries.

    Cannon 1982, Bradley & McTernan 1988, Simpson 1988, Barnhart & Barnhart 1990, ISO 1990, Thelen & Starren 1992, Svensén 1993, Algeo 1995.

    The Longman Register of New Words (J. Ayto), Harlow, 1990; *The Macquarie Dictionary of New Words* (S. Butler), Sydney NSW, 1990.

nested entry

A dictionary entry which is the result of NESTING.

nesting

The CLUSTERING of several related words and phrases inside one entry in non-alphabetical order, in contrast to 'niching', where such items are given alphabetically. Thus in the *Longman Dictionary of Contemporary English* [3rd edition] (Harlow, 1995), the bold sub-entries **informally** and **informality** are nested together at the end of the entry **informal**. By contrast, in the *Oxford*

Advanced Learner's Dictionary [5th edition] (Oxford, 1995), **informality** and **informally** are niched alphabetically at the end of the entry **informal**.

    Hausmann & Wiegand 1989, Svensén 1993, Béjoint 1994.

new edition

⇨ EDITION.

new word

⇨ NEOLOGISM.

niching

The CLUSTERING of several related words and phrases alphabetically inside one entry, in contrast to 'nesting', where such items are given non-alphabetical order.

⇨ NESTING.

nickname

A word or phrase used informally to designate a person, place or object.

⇨ APTRONYM, EPITHET, EPONYM, ONOMASTIC INFORMATION.

    The Dictionary of Historic Nicknames (C. Sifakis), Oxford, 1984; *Names & Nicknames of Places & Things* (L. Urdang), Boston MA, 1987; *Harrap's Book of Nicknames and their Origins* (B. Freestone), London, 1990.

nighaṇṭu

⇨ METRICAL DICTIONARY.

NLP

Abbreviation for NATURAL LANGUAGE PROCESSING.

nomenclature

1 The systematic TERMINOLOGY of a specialised technical field, e.g. plant and animal names in biology, often lexicalised in the form of BINOMIAL COMPOUNDS.

    ISO 1990.

    South African Code of Stratigraphic Terminology and Nomenclature [4th edition] (The South African Committee for Stratigraphy), Pretoria, 1996.

2 An alternative term for WORD-LIST.

nominative

⇨ DECLENSION.

non-alphabetic arrangement

A system of sequencing entries which does not follow an alphabet, either because a different script is used, or because a different ORGANISATION principle is chosen, e.g. thematic.

nonce word

A word or phrase coined for a particular occasion, deliberately or accidentally, and often not recorded.

⇨ HAPAX LEGOMENON, INKHORN TERM.

non-discriminatory vocabulary

⇨ BIAS-FREE VOCABULARY.

non-hierarchical relation

⇨ HIERARCHICAL RELATION.

non-lemmatic address

A component part of an entry which does not refer directly to the LEMMA or the HEADWORD. Non-lemmatic addressing is common with idiomatic phrases inserted at the end of the entry and given a sub-sense, but whose link with the headword is not always transparent, e.g. in the *Longman Dictionary of Contemporary English* [3rd edition] (Harlow, 1995) the multi-word expression **leave feet first** is sub-entry 23 under the headword **foot**, and defined as 'to die before you leave a place or job'.

📖 Hausmann & Wiegand 1989.

non-standard

⇨ STANDARD (1).

Nordisk Forening for Leksikografi

The Nordic Association for Lexicography, a professional society established at the University of Oslo in 1991. It holds biennial conferences and publishes proceedings and a journal, *LEXICONORDICA*. It has sponsored the multilingual *NORDISK LEKSIKOGRAFISK ORDBOK*.

Nordisk Leksikografisk Ordbok

The *Nordic Dictionary of Lexicography*, compiled and edited by Henning Bergenholtz, Ilse Cantell, Ruth Vatvedt Fjeld, Dag Gundersen, Jón Hilmar Jónsson and Bo Svensén, and published in 1997, with headwords and definitions in Norwegian (Bokmål) and equivalents in Danish, Finnish, Icelandic, Nynorsk, Swedish, English, French and German.

norm

A general term for the regular USAGE of a language or language variety. Depending on the context, it is possible to recognise observed, actual norms and posited, authoritative norms. The former are 'descriptive' (derived from e.g. linguistic FIELDWORK and CORPUS analysis), the latter are 'prescriptive' (e.g. recommended by language teachers and compilers of USAGE GUIDES). Both may, in the long run, contribute to the establishment of a STANDARD.

⇨ AUTHORITY, BARBARISM, CODIFICATION, CORRECTNESS, DESCRIPTIVE LEXICOGRAPHY, PRESCRIPTIVE LEXICOGRAPHY, PURISM.

📖 Zgusta 1989a, Milroy & Milroy 1991, Svensén 1993.

normative dictionary

⇨ PRESCRIPTIVE LEXICOGRAPHY.

normative lexicography

⇨ PRESCRIPTIVE LEXICOGRAPHY.

notation

⇨ TRANSCRIPTION.

note

⇨ USAGE NOTE.

notion

⇨ CONCEPT.

noun

A PART OF SPEECH which serves to name or designate entities.

⇨ DECLENSION, GRAMMATICAL INFORMATION.

numerical information

An INFORMATION CATEGORY based on figures and statistics.

-nym

⇨ *-(O)NYM*.

object language
⇨ METALANGUAGE.

obscenity
A word or phrase which is felt to be indecent because of its explicit reference to bodily functions, and therefore often taboo.
⇨ FOUR-LETTER WORD.

obsolescent
⇨ DIACHRONIC INFORMATION.

obsolete
⇨ ARCHAIC.

obsolete term
A TERM no longer used.
📖 ISO 1990.

obsolete word
⇨ ARCHAISM.

offensive word
⇨ TERM OF ABUSE.

official language
A language legally sanctioned for use in a particular country or organisation. Some countries have a LANGUAGE POLICY which prescribes one or more official languages, sometimes in contradistinction to the *de facto* NATIONAL LANGUAGE, for official government business or education, whereas others (such as Britain and the USA) have no official language. In organisations such as the European Union or the United Nations, certain languages are designated as official 'working' languages.

The establishment of, or change in, the status of official languages can promote the need for the creation of general monolingual and bilingual dictionaries as well as multilingual terminological reference works.

-(o)graphy
A COMBINING FORM used to designate a descriptive activity, as in *lexicography*, sometimes in contrast with a theoretical discipline, as in *terminography* versus *terminology*.
⇨ CODIFICATION.

ola dictionary
A dictionary written on palm leaves, a medium common in south and south-east Asia before the widespread availability of paper and printing.

-(o)logy
A COMBINING FORM used to designate a discipline, as in *lexicology*, sometimes in contrast with a descriptive activity, as in *terminology* versus *terminography*.

on-line dictionary
A dictionary or other reference work available via a computer network, such as the INTERNET.
⇨ ELECTRONIC DICTIONARY.

Onoma
The title of the journal published by the International Council of Onomastic Sciences at the International Centre of Onomastics, Louvain (Belgium).

onomasiological dictionary
A type of REFERENCE WORK which presents words or phrases as expressions of semantically linked CONCEPTS, which may be meanings, ideas, notions, word families and similar relationships. These can be designated in a number of different ways: by pictures, words, terms, definitions, synonyms or translation equivalents. The important

criterion is the direction from concept to word, rather than from word to explanation (as in the traditional SEMASIOLOGICAL DICTIONARY). Typical examples of onomasiological dictionaries are the THESAURUS, the SYNONYM DICTIONARY and the WORD-FINDING DICTIONARY. Because of this conceptual, systematic or ideological approach, THEMATIC ORDER is sometimes preferred to ALPHABETICAL ORDER.
⇨ ACTIVE DICTIONARY, PARADIGMATIC RELATION, REVERSE-ORDER DICTIONARY.
📖 Šarćević 1989, van Sterkenburg 1992, Svensén 1993, Hüllen 1994.
📄 *Thesaurus of English Words and Phrases* (P. M. Roget), London, 1852; *A Dictionary of Selected Synonyms in the Principal European Languages* (C. D. Buck), Chicago IL, 1949; *The Oxford Thesaurus. An A–Z Dictionary of Synonyms* (L. Urdang), Oxford, 1991.

onomasiological information
One of the INFORMATION CATEGORIES presented by the compiler and consulted by the user of a reference work, based on SENSE RELATIONS, or paradigmatic choices between semantically linked words or phrases.

onomasiological lexicography
A complex of activities concerned with the design, compilation, use and evaluation of ONOMASIOLOGICAL DICTIONARIES.

onomasiology
An approach in SEMANTICS which is concerned with the matching of the most appropriate word or phrase to a given CONCEPT. When its principles are applied to the 'tip-of-the-tongue' phenomenon, the result can be a reference work (an ONOMASIOLOGICAL DICTIONARY) which guides the user from relatively well-known concepts to relatively less familiar words, in contrast to the traditional SEMASIOLOGICAL DICTIONARY in which relatively unknown words are explained in terms of familiar ones. The onomasiological approach is associated with the solution of word-finding problems and the creation of TERMINOLOGY.
⇨ ACTIVE DICTIONARY, WORD-FINDING DICTIONARY.
📖 Kipfer 1986.

onomastic dictionary
A type of REFERENCE WORK which provides explanations about personal or other NAMES.

Specialised dictionaries containing such ONOMASTIC INFORMATION include dictionaries of surnames, pseudonyms and place-names, some with pronunciations and biographical and other details.
⇨ GAZETTEER, WHO'S WHO.
📄 *The Concise Oxford Dictionary of English Place-Names* (E. Ekwall), Oxford, 1936; *A Collector's Compendium of Rare and Unusual, Bold and Beautiful, Odd and Whimsical Names* (P. Dickson), New York NY, 1986.

onomastic information
One of the INFORMATION CATEGORIES presented by the compiler and consulted by the user of a reference work, based on NAMES. Names can refer to persons (PERSONAL NAMES and their derivatives, APTRONYMS, EPONYMS and PSEUDONYMS), places (TOPONYMS, specifically of settlements, mountains, rivers etc.), institutions, events and works of art. Some general dictionaries, especially those influenced by the American encyclopedic tradition, contain (some of) this information in entries or as appendices, but there are also many specialised ONOMASTIC DICTIONARIES such as GAZETTEERS and BIOGRAPHICAL DICTIONARIES.

onomastic lexicography
A complex of activities concerned with the design, compilation, use and evaluation of ONOMASTIC DICTIONARIES.

onomastics
An academic discipline concerned with the study of NAMES. This includes proper nouns used as names for persons (PERSONAL NAMES), domesticated animals, places (TOPONYMS), institutions, events, works of art (including fictional characters) and commercial products.
⇨ ONOMASTIC INFORMATION.

onomatopoeic expression
A word or phrase that seeks to suggest or imitate the sound of the designated object or action.
📖 Veldi 1994.

-(o)nym
A COMBINING FORM used to designate a term for a type of word (e.g. *antonym*) or name (e.g. *anthroponym*).

open-class word
⇨ CONTENT WORD.

open corpus
⇨ MONITOR CORPUS.

operational definition
A DEFINITION that specifies the conditions under which a TERM is used.

opposition
A term for a number of SENSE RELATIONS indicating degrees of ANTONYMY, e.g. 'equipollent opposition' with both members of a pair being positive: *male – female*; 'privative opposition' with one member of the pair being the negative of the other: *rational – irrational*.

oracy
The skill of speaking.
⇨ ORALITY, LITERACY.

orality
The ability to communicate through the medium of speech. This allows traditions to be passed on from generation to generation through the spoken word. Easily memorised, METRICAL DICTIONARIES evolved within oral cultures to codify and transmit knowledge.
📖 Ong 1982.

order
⇨ ARRANGEMENT.

ordering
⇨ ORGANISATION.

ordering device
One of several different ways of making dictionary text transparent and accessible, thus increasing the efficiency of CONSULTATION. Such devices, which may be included either inside the entry or across entries, include EXTRA COLUMNS, GUIDEWORDS, PICTOGRAPHIC SYMBOLS, SECTION MARKS, SENSE NUMBERS, STRUCTURAL INDICATORS, THUMB INDEXES.
⇨ ACCESS STRUCTURE, LAYOUT, SEARCH PATH, TEXT COMPRESSION.

ordo mnemonicus
A phrase (< Latin 'mnemonic order') used in the seventeenth and eighteenth centuries to refer to CLUSTERING of derivatives and compounds in one entry, as opposed their LISTING in alphabetical order as separate HEADWORDS.

organisation
The principle which governs the arrangement of HEADWORDS in the WORD-LIST of a reference work. Three main types can be distinguished: LOCAL ORDERING (in order of occurrence of words in source texts); thematic or conceptual ordering (association, as in ONOMASIOLOGICAL DICTIONARIES); or ordering by phonic and/or graphic forms (e.g. ALPHABETICAL ORGANISATION, RHYME).
⇨ ARRANGEMENT, CHRONOLOGICAL ORDER, HIERARCHICAL STRUCTURE, PHONETICAL-ANAGRAMMATICAL ARRANGEMENT, SYSTEMATIC ORDER.
📖 Zgusta 1989b, Béjoint 1994.

orismology
An archaic term for TERMINOLOGY.

ortho-
A COMBINING FORM (< Greek 'correct') used in terms such as *orthography*, to suggest correct or appropriate usage.

orthoepic dictionary
⇨ PRONOUNCING DICTIONARY.

orthoepy
A collective term for a number of approaches to develop a standard PRONUNCIATION. For English, these are associated with several PRONOUNCING DICTIONARIES published since the eighteenth century and parallel similar efforts to regularise spelling (ORTHOGRAPHY).
⇨ STANDARD

orthographic dictionary
⇨ SPELLING DICTIONARY.

orthographic information
One of the INFORMATION CATEGORIES presented by the compiler and consulted by the user of the dictionary, based on SPELLING. This includes the principles on which the writing system is based (e.g. LETTERS or CHARACTERS) and how it is used to organise the macrostructure of the reference work. Although the relation between speech and writing (phoneme–grapheme correspondence) is rarely one-to-one, lexicographers make an effort to document such regularities, e.g. in the RESPELLING or TRANSCRIPTION systems used to represent features of PRONUNCIATION, PROSODIC FEATURES, PUNCTUATION, HYPHENATION etc.

⇨ SPELLING DICTIONARY.

📖 Zgusta 1989b.

orthography

The set of norms that regulate SPELLING conventions in a particular language, and the basis for codifying linguistic units at the level of WRITING. Languages differ as to the extent to which a writing system has been developed for representing speech.

⇨ SPELLING DICTIONARY, STANDARD (1).

📖 Ayto 1992, Murphy 1996.

ostensive definition

A definition in which a word or phrase is explained either by pointing directly at an object, or indirectly by association with an object (e.g. '*blue*: the colour of the sky'). In dictionaries, the limits of this DEFINITION STYLE can be overcome by the use of pictorial illustrations, film, hypertext, sound cards etc.

📖 Landau 1984.

outer access structure

⇨ ACCESS STRUCTURE.

outer search path

⇨ SEARCH PATH.

outside matter

A cover term for all those components of the MACROSTRUCTURE of a reference work which do not form part of the central WORD-LIST. Outside matter is usually subdivided into FRONT MATTER (such as preface and user's guide), MIDDLE MATTER (such as panels and plates of illustrations) and BACK MATTER (such as lists of names and weights and measures).

⇨ MEGASTRUCTURE, Panel 'Megastructure' (page 92).

📖 Cop 1989.

Oxford Studies in Lexicography and Lexicology

A specialist monograph series established in 1994.

P

palindrome
⇨ ANAGRAM.

panel of advisers
⇨ ADVISORY PANEL.

paper dictionary
The traditional printed dictionary, in contrast with the ELECTRONIC DICTIONARY or MACHINE-READABLE DICTIONARY.
⇨ MANUSCRIPT DICTIONARY, OLA DICTIONARY.

paradigm
A representation of the set of variant inflectional forms of a LEXEME, one of which is conventionalised as a CANONICAL FORM for HEADWORD status in a dictionary. Sometimes a defective paradigm is completed by 'suppletive' forms from another, e.g. *went*, in the paradigm of *go*.
⇨ CONJUGATION, DECLENSION.
📖 Zgusta 1989b.

paradigmatic dictionary
⇨ ONOMASIOLOGICAL DICTIONARY.

paradigmatic information
⇨ ONOMASIOLOGICAL INFORMATION.

paradigmatic relation
The relationship between words or phrases which is based on substitution rather than grammatical sequencing, e.g. sense relations such as ANTONYMY, HYPONYMY, SYNONYMY. This relationship is one of three dimensions in SEMIOTICS.
⇨ ONOMASIOLOGICAL DICTIONARY, PRAGMATIC RELATION (2), SYNTAGMATIC RELATION.

paradigmatics
⇨ PARADIGMATIC RELATION.

paralinguistics
The study of non-verbal communication which accompanies speech, e.g. PROSODIC FEATURES or GESTURE.

parallel edition
A version of a published work using PARALLEL TEXTS in columns or on facing pages, e.g. a polyglot Bible.

parallel publishing
The simultaneous publication of a DOCUMENT in print and electronic format.

parallel texts
Two or more TEXTS in different languages which convey the same message either because they are the result of a translation from one language to another ('bi-texts') or because they are independently formulated in a similar context ('comparable texts'). Some recognise intralingual parallel texts, which may be the result of paraphrase, parody etc. Parallel text CORPORA are a useful aid in bilingual lexicography, especially for identifying translation EQUIVALENTS. In the electronic processing of such corpora, the matching and extraction of corresponding words and phrases is termed 'alignment'.
⇨ INTERTEXTUALITY.
📖 Hartmann 1991, Dickens & Salkie 1996, Peters & Picchi 1996, Roberts & Montgomery 1996, Teubert 1996.

paraphrase
The process or result of reformulating a phrase or text to explain or translate its meaning.
⇨ GLOSS (2).
📖 Svensén 1993.

parasynthesis
A word-formation process resulting in a COMPLEX TERM or COMPLEX WORD.

paroemiography
A complex of activities concerned with the design, compilation, use and evaluation of dictionaries of PROVERBS.

paroemiology
The study of PROVERBS.

paronym
A member of a pair of words or phrases characterised by PARONYMY.

paronymy
The relationship between two or more words partly identical in form and/or meaning, which may cause confusion in reception or production. In the narrow sense the term *paronymy* refers to 'soundalikes' (cognate near-HOMOPHONES such as *affect/effect* or *feminine/feminist*), but in the wider sense it covers any 'lookalike' or 'mean-alike' CONFUSIBLE WORDS.
⇨ DERIVATIVE.

parser
A computer program for automatic PARSING.

parsing
1 The structural analysis of sentences in terms of their grammatical categories and functions. Parsing constitutes an important stage in the preparation of a text CORPUS for linguistic processing.
   ⇨ TAGGING.
   📖 Martin 1992.
2 In TERMINOLOGY, the scanning of texts to determine terms for the INCLUSION LIST.
   📖 ISO 1990.

partial equivalence
⇨ EQUIVALENCE.

partial synonym
⇨ SYNONYMY (1).

partial synonymy
⇨ SYNONYMY (1).

partitive concept
⇨ PARTITIVE RELATION.

partitive relation
A hierarchical SENSE RELATION between concepts, linking one or more (subordinate) parts to a (superordinate) whole, e.g. *Scandinavia*: 'Denmark, Norway, Sweden'.
⇨ COMPREHENSIVE CONCEPT.
📖 ISO 1990, Svensén 1993.

part of speech
A traditional term for 'word class', or the grammatical role words or phrases play in sentences. Minimal part-of-speech information is given in the GENERAL DICTIONARY, usually in abbreviated or coded form. More detail is provided in specialised dictionaries such as GRAMMAR DICTIONARIES and USAGE GUIDES.
⇨ GRAMMATICAL CODE, GRAMMATICAL INFORMATION, GRAMMATICAL LABEL, SYNTAX.
📖 Svensén 1993, Wachal 1994.

part-of-speech dictionary
⇨ GRAMMAR DICTIONARY.

partonymy
⇨ PARTITIVE RELATION.

passive dictionary
A type of REFERENCE WORK designed to help with decoding tasks, such as the comprehension of a text. In monolingual lexicography, most dictionaries fulfil this function as their aim is to explain the meaning of words or phrases the user may have come across in reading. In bilingual lexicography, passive dictionaries are those that address the needs of receptive tasks such as reading a foreign-language text or translating it into the native language. The ACTIVE DICTIONARY, by contrast, is aimed primarily at encoding tasks such as writing.
⇨ PASSIVE VOCABULARY.
📖 Kromann *et al*. 1991, Svensén 1993, Berkov 1996.

passive vocabulary
The VOCABULARY available to a native speaker or a learner for decoding purposes such as listening, reading or translating from a foreign language into the native language. Estimates suggest that this is considerably greater than the ACTIVE VOCABULARY associated with encoding tasks such as speaking and writing.
⇨ PASSIVE DICTIONARY.
📖 Goulden *et al*. 1990.

pattern code
⇨ GRAMMATICAL CODE.

pedagogical dictionary

A REFERENCE WORK specifically designed for the practical didactic needs of teachers and learners of a language. The distinction usually made between a dictionary for native speakers (SCHOOL DICTIONARY) and one for non-native learners (LEARNER'S DICTIONARY) is not helpful.

⇨ BILINGUAL LEARNER'S DICTIONARY, COLLEGE DICTIONARY.

pedagogical lexicography

A complex of activities concerned with the design, compilation, use and evaluation of PEDAGOGICAL DICTIONARIES.

📖 Ilson 1985, Cowie 1987a, Diab 1990, Zöfgen 1991.

pejoration

⇨ SEMANTIC CHANGE.

pen name

⇨ PSEUDONYM.

period

A distinct stage in the historical development of a language. The variety thus isolated may also be called 'chronolect', 'historiolect' or 'état de langue'. Because of the difficulties in dividing the diachronic continuum of a language, there is a tension between those who favour the holistic approach to HISTORICAL DICTIONARIES and those who stress the value of separate PERIOD DICTIONARIES.

📖 Bailey 1990.

period dictionary

A type of REFERENCE WORK which documents a particular PERIOD of a language. Period dictionaries are sub-types of the HISTORICAL DICTIONARY in which the formal and semantic changes of the vocabulary are illustrated in terms of word formation, etymology and other information categories. Such dictionaries are usually compiled by scholars trained in historical-comparative LINGUISTICS.

⇨ REGIONAL DICTIONARY.

📖 Aitken 1987, Bailey 1990, McArthur 1992.

📑 *Dictionary of the Older Scottish Tongue* (W. A. Craigie *et al.*), Chicago IL/Oxford/Aberdeen, 1925– [incomplete]; *The Middle English Dictionary* (H. Kurath *et al.*), London/Oxford, 1952– [incomplete]; *A Comprehensive Old English Dictionary* (A. R. Borden), Washington DC, 1992.

period lexicography

A branch of HISTORICAL LEXICOGRAPHY concerned with the design, compilation, use and evaluation of PERIOD DICTIONARIES. The historical development of languages can be divided into more or less distinct stages (PERIODS) correlated with cultural and political events, e.g. Middle English (1150–1500) and Early Modern English (1500–1700); linguists and lexicographers study and document the features, especially of vocabulary, that characterise and differentiate them.

📖 Goebel 1990.

periodicals in lexicography

⇨ JOURNALS IN LEXICOGRAPHY.

permutation

The rearrangement of a multi-word expression in order to list each of its main constituents in their alphabetical sequence, either as cross-references or as separate entries.

⇨ BINOMIAL COMPOUND, DIRECT ENTRY, INVERTED ENTRY.

📖 ISO 1990.

personal name

The NAME given to an individual, often a combination of one or more 'forenames' ('Christian names' or 'given names') and a 'surname' (or 'family name'). Naming conventions, including the ordering of first and last names, differ from one language or culture to another.

📖 Mufwene 1988, Urdang 1996.

📑 *A Dictionary of Surnames* (P. Hanks & F. Hodges), Oxford, 1988.

phantonym

⇨ GHOST WORD.

phenomenological typology

⇨ TYPOLOGY (1).

philology

A branch of LINGUISTICS concerned with the comparative-historical perspective in language study. The principles of philology have led to the development of HISTORICAL LEXICOGRAPHY and COMPARATIVE LEXICOGRAPHY.

⇨ LANGUAGE CHANGE.

📖 Collison 1982.

phoneme

The minimal distinct unit in the sound system of a language.

⇨ PHONOLOGY.

phonemics

⇨   PHONOLOGY.

phonemic transcription

⇨   TRANSCRIPTION (1).

phonetical-anagrammatical arrangement

An ORGANISATION principle in which the HEAD-WORDS of a dictionary are arranged according to the articulatory characteristics of their initial consonants, e.g. in Arabic from guttural to labial.
📖   Haywood 1991.

phonetic alphabet

A notation system used for the TRANSCRIPTION of speech and the representation of PRONUNCIATION in dictionaries. The most widely used system is that of the INTERNATIONAL PHONETIC ALPHABET.

phonetic dictionary

⇨   PRONOUNCING DICTIONARY.

phonetic information

⇨   PHONOLOGICAL INFORMATION.

phonetic transcription

⇨   TRANSCRIPTION (1).

phonetics

A branch of LINGUISTICS concerned with the study of SPEECH as transmitted sound. Phonetics concentrates on the production and nature of the sounds, e.g. in articulatory-biological or acoustic-physical terms, rather than their relationships with units at other linguistic levels such as syllables and words (PHONOLOGY).
⇨   PRONUNCIATION.
📖   Clark & Yallop 1995, Hardcastle & Laver 1996.
▤   *Dictionary of Phonetics and Phonology* (R. L. Trask), London & New York NY, 1995.

phonological information

One of the INFORMATION CATEGORIES presented by the compiler and consulted by the user of the dictionary, based on PRONUNCIATION. Sometimes erroneously called 'phonetic information', this is the result of studies in PHONETICS and PHONOLOGY as interpreted by lexicographers and displayed in general dictionaries in the form of phonetic TRANSCRIPTION or RESPELLING of the headword, usually at the beginning of entries. In

specialised PRONOUNCING DICTIONARIES and some USAGE GUIDES additional information may be provided about alternative pronunciations and PROSODIC FEATURES such as stress and intonation. Modern multimedia technology allows the inclusion of the reproduction of sound in electronic dictionaries.
📖   Abercrombie 1978, Read 1982, Bronstein 1994.
▤   *English Pronouncing Dictionary* (D. Jones/rev. P. Roach & J. Hartmann), London, 1917/Cambridge, 1996; *Longman Pronunciation Dictionary* (J. C. Wells), Harlow, 1990.

phonology

A branch of LINGUISTICS concerned with the study of SPEECH as a system of sounds. Phonology (or 'phonemics') deals with the units of sound (PHONEMES) within the whole language and their relations with units at other levels (GRAPHEMES, SYLLABLES, MORPHEMES, LEXEMES etc.) rather than the conditions of their production (PHONETICS). The totality of phonological units and PROSODIC FEATURES (such as stress and intonation) constitutes PHONOLOGICAL INFORMATION which is included in various forms in general and specialised dictionaries, usually under the heading of PRONUNCIATION.
📖   Clark & Yallop 1995, Spencer 1996.
▤   *Introducing Phonetics* (P. Roach), London, 1992.

photo dictionary

A PEDAGOGICAL DICTIONARY which includes illustrations in the form of photographs.
▤   *Longman English–Chinese–Japanese Photo Dictionary* (M. S. Rosenthal & D. B. Freeman), Hong Kong, 1987; *Oxford Photo Dictionary* (J. Taylor), Oxford, 1991.

phrasal dictionary

⇨   PHRASEOLOGICAL DICTIONARY.

phrasal entry

A MULTI-WORD EXPRESSION appearing as a HEADWORD or as a SUB-LEMMA.
📖   Landau 1984.

phrasal verb

A MULTI-WORD EXPRESSION comprising a verb and one or more particles, e.g. *put up with* 'tolerate'.
📖   Svensén 1993, Pye 1996.
▤   *Longman Dictionary of Phrasal Verbs* (R. Courtney), Harlow, 1983; *Collins COBUILD Diction-*

ary of Phrasal Verbs (J. Sinclair & R. Moon), London & Glasgow, 1989.

phrase
Two or more words combined into a unit which performs a syntactic function.
⇨   PHRASEOLOGICAL DICTIONARY.

phrasebook
A type of reference work containing useful phrases and sentences for practical communication in foreign-language settings such as polite conversation, travel, commercial correspondence etc.
⇨   ACTIVE DICTIONARY.
▤   *Irish–English/English–Irish Dictionary and Phrasebook*, New York NY, 1992.

phraseography
⇨   PHRASEOLOGICAL LEXICOGRAPHY.

phraseological dictionary
A type of reference work which lists FIXED EXPRESSIONS, PHRASES or SENTENCES.
⇨   IDIOM.
▥   Spears 1990.
▤   *NTC's Dictionary of American English Phrases* (R. A. Spears), Lincolnwood IL, 1995; *Phrases and Sayings* (N. Rees), London, 1997.

phraseological information
One of the INFORMATION CATEGORIES presented by the compiler and consulted by the user of a dictionary, based on PHRASEOLOGY, or words and phrases in syntactic context. Dictionaries differ as to how much material they offer and how they present it. Because of their complexity, PHRASES and IDIOMS are often dealt with together in the GENERAL DICTIONARY towards the end of the entry, or in separate paragraphs.

phraseological lexicography
A complex of activities concerned with the design, compilation, use and evaluation of PHRASE-OLOGICAL DICTIONARIES.
⇨   CODIFICATION.

phraseological unit
⇨   PHRASE.

phraseology
The study of PHRASES, IDIOMS and MULTI-WORD EXPRESSIONS. PHRASEOLOGICAL LEXICOGRA-

PHY ('phraseography') deals with their codification in dictionaries.
⇨   PHRASEOLOGICAL DICTIONARY.
▥   Meyer & Mackintosh 1994, Howarth 1996.

pictographic symbol
A graphic mark used as an ORDERING DEVICE or as a label (e.g. ⇨ for cross-references, ◆ for phrasal verbs). In this *Dictionary of Lexicography*, three such symbols are used for bibliographical references: ▥ for related literature, ▤ for selected relevant reference works, and ▣ for electronic information.

pictorial dictionary
⇨   PICTURE DICTIONARY.

pictorial illustration
⇨   ILLUSTRATION (1).

picture dictionary
A type of reference work in which the information treated is exclusively depicted by ILLUSTRATIONS, in contrast to an ILLUSTRATED DICTIONARY where pictorial material is only supplementary. The ARRANGEMENT in picture dictionaries is typically onomasiological or thematic. Illustrations can be in the form of line drawings, pictures, photographs etc. and, in electronic dictionaries, also FILM.
⇨   ATLAS, CHILDREN'S DICTIONARY, PHOTO DIC-TIONARY, VISUAL DICTIONARY.
▤   *Oxford Duden Pictorial English–Japanese Dictionary* (J. Pheby & A. Miyamoto), Oxford, 1983.

pidgin
A CONTACT VERNACULAR which, in contrast to a CREOLE, is not the native language of those who use it, typically in informal, limited contexts.
▥   McArthur 1992.

pīnyīn
⇨   ROMANISATION.

place-name
An informal term for TOPONYM.

plagiarism
The illegal COPYING IN DICTIONARIES from other sources.
⇨   CRIMINALITY.
▥   Burchfield 1984, Williams 1992.

planned language
⇨   AUXILIARY LANGUAGE (1).

plurilingual dictionary
⇨ MULTILINGUAL DICTIONARY.

pocket dictionary
An easily portable small-sized dictionary.
▤ *The Reticule and Pocket Companion* (L. Cobb), New York NY, 1834; *Dicionário de algibeira português–chinês*, Macao, 1969.

pocket electronic dictionary
A small hand-held calculator-type reference work, containing basic vocabulary in one or more languages.
▢ Taylor & Chan 1994.

politically correct vocabulary
⇨ BIAS-FREE VOCABULARY.

political vocabulary
⇨ VOCABULARY (1).

polyaccessible dictionary
⇨ ACCESS STRUCTURE.

polyequivalence
⇨ EQUIVALENCE DISCRIMINATION.

polyfunctional dictionary
⇨ MULTIFUNCTIONAL DICTIONARY.

polyglot dictionary
⇨ MULTILINGUAL DICTIONARY.

polyinformative dictionary
A dictionary which provides multiple INFORMATION CATEGORIES, to meet the reference needs of different users.
⇨ GENERAL DICTIONARY.

polylingual dictionary
⇨ MULTILINGUAL DICTIONARY.

polyseme
A word or phrase with more than one related MEANING. Multiple meaning (POLYSEMY) is one of the most central problems in and justification for dictionaries, since most common-core items in the basic vocabulary of any language have several senses which need to be distinguished, e.g. *band* 'ribbon', 'belt', '(radio) wavelength', '(disk) track' etc. Is *band* in the sense of 'group of musicians' another instance of the same word or an accidentally similar but different word (HOMONYM)?

polysemous word
⇨ POLYSEME.

polysemy
The relation obtaining between the different SENSES of a word or phrase. Most items of the vocabulary are polysemous, and it is one of the chief functions of the GENERAL DICTIONARY to distinguish between them, by means of definitions, synonyms or examples. A distinction can be made between multiple meaning of one and the same word (POLYSEME) and words which may accidentally have the same graphic or phonic form (HOMONYM). Polysemous items are assigned distinct (and often numbered) senses within an entry, while homonyms are treated in different entries, but sometimes the boundary between polysemy and homonymy is not clearly drawn, with grammatical status, etymology and native speakers' semantic judgements being used as criteria.
   In TERMINOLOGICAL LEXICOGRAPHY both polysemy and homonymy are deliberately minimised in the interest of creating unambiguous TERMS in one-to-one relation with the CONCEPTS they designate.
⇨ MONOSEMY, SENSE ORDERING.
▢ Robins 1987, ISO 1990, Sager 1990, Nunberg & Zaenen 1992, Svensén 1993, Gouws 1996.

polysyllabic word
A word comprising two or more syllables.
⇨ HYPHENATION.

polytechnic dictionary
An ENCYCLOPEDIC DICTIONARY which covers information from a wide range of technical SUBJECT FIELDS.
▤ *Academic Press Dictionary of Science and Technology*, New York NY, 1991.

portmanteau word
⇨ BLEND.

possible word
⇨ LATENT WORD.

postposition
A PART OF SPEECH typically governing a preceding word or phrase, and expressing relationships of time, place, cause, modality etc.
⇨ GRAMMATICAL INFORMATION, PREPOSITION.

pragmatic information

Information on the sociocultural rules of speaking. Exponents include paralinguistic features such as tone and intonation, gesture, pitch etc., as well as choice of vocabulary in terms of politeness and formality conventions, which can reinforce or contradict the speaker's intended meaning. In the past, dictionary compilers have paid little attention to this aspect of communication, merely giving unsystematic indications via USAGE LABELS such as 'informal', 'derogatory', 'sarcastic'.

⇨   APPROPRIATENESS, DIASYSTEMATIC LABELLING, DISCOURSE ANALYSIS, PRAGMATICS, SEMIOTICS, SOCIOLINGUISTICS.

📖   Sharpe 1989, Hurley 1992.

▤   *Common Social English Errors in Hong Kong* (D. Bunton), Hong Kong, 1994.

pragmatic relation

1   In TERMINOLOGY, a type of HIERARCHICAL RELATION between concepts.
2   In PRAGMATICS, the relationship between the participants in an interaction.
       ⇨   PARADIGMATIC RELATION, SEMIOTICS, SYNTAGMATIC RELATION.

pragmatics

One of the semiotic dimensions of communication, related to a setting.

⇨   PRAGMATIC INFORMATION.

📖   Thomas 1995.

preface

The place in the FRONT MATTER of a reference work where publishers and/or editors state their aims and the intended functions of the work.

preferred term

A technical TERM selected by the practitioners in a subject field as the most suitable of several synonyms for designating a particular CONCEPT.

⇨   ACCEPTABILITY RATING.

📖   ISO 1990.

prefix

⇨   AFFIX.

preliminaries

⇨   FRONT MATTER.

prelims

Abbreviation for 'preliminaries'.

⇨   FRONT MATTER.

preposition

A PART OF SPEECH typically governing a following word or phrase, and expressing relationships of time, place, cause, modality etc.

⇨   GRAMMATICAL INFORMATION, POSTPOSITION.

▤   *Collins COBUILD English Guides 1: Prepositions* (E. Manning), London, 1991.

prescriptive dictionary

⇨   PRESCRIPTIVE LEXICOGRAPHY.

prescriptive grammar

⇨   GRAMMAR.

prescriptive lexicography

An approach to DICTIONARY-MAKING which is based on normative attitudes as to how a language or language variety should be used rather than the facts observed about its USAGE.

⇨   DESCRIPTIVE LEXICOGRAPHY.

📖   Svensén 1993, Béjoint 1994.

presentation

A stage in the DICTIONARY-MAKING process concerned with the publication of the work in a format appropriate to the needs and skills of the USER.

⇨   DESIGN, LAYOUT.

presentation language

⇨   METALANGUAGE.

prestige dialect

⇨   DIALECT.

primary source

⇨   SOURCE.

principal parts

The traditional citation of regular and irregular forms as exemplars of the CONJUGATION pattern of a verb, e.g. in Latin, the first person singular present and perfect indicative active, the infinitive, and the supine.

print dictionary

⇨   PAPER DICTIONARY.

printing

The result of the third major COMMUNICATIVE SHIFT.

privative opposition

⇨   OPPOSITION.

procedural mark-up
⇨ STANDARD GENERALIZED MARK-UP LAN-GUAGE.

production
⇨ ACTIVE DICTIONARY.

productive dictionary
⇨ ACTIVE DICTIONARY.

productive morpheme
A derivational affix which contributes to the formation of new words, e.g. *un-*, *-ness*.

productive vocabulary
⇨ ACTIVE VOCABULARY.

professional resources
The totality of aids and services that contribute to the training of lexicographers and other reference professionals.
⇨ ASSOCIATIONS, BIBLIOGRAPHY (1), DIRECTORY, JOURNALS IN LEXICOGRAPHY, LEXICOGRAPHY, TEXTBOOKS, TRAINING.
📖 Ilson 1986a.
📰 *Wörterbücher/Dictionaries/Dictionnaires* (F. J. Hausmann *et al.*), Berlin, 1989–91.

pronoun
A PART OF SPEECH which can stand for a noun or noun phrase.
⇨ GRAMMATICAL INFORMATION.

pronouncing dictionary
A type of REFERENCE WORK which presents information on the PRONUNCIATION of words, phrases or names, usually in alphabetical order of their orthographic forms. Because of the complex and sometimes arbitrary relationship between speech and writing in many languages, the SPELLING of a word does not always allow the reader to deduce its phonology (compare the final syllables in *bayonet* and *beret*, or the initial syllables in *exact* and *Exeter*). This is why general and specialised dictionaries have given guidance on the standard – and sometimes dialect variant – pronunciations at least since the eighteenth-century 'orthoepic' English dictionaries, a development which parallels that of orthography.
⇨ RECEIVED PRONUNCIATION.
📖 Bronstein 1984, Pointon 1989.
📰 *Critical Pronouncing Dictionary* (J. Walker), London, 1791; *English Pronouncing Dictionary*

(D. Jones/rev. P. Roach & J. Hartmann), London, 1917/Cambridge, 1996; *A Pronouncing Dictionary of American English* (J. S. Kenyon & T. A. Knott), Springfield MA, 1944; *BBC Pronouncing Dictionary of British Names* (E. Miller/rev. G. Pointon), London & Oxford, 1971/90; *Longman Pronunciation Dictionary* (J. C. Wells), Harlow, 1990.

pronunciation
The form, production and representation of speech. The phenomenon is studied in PHONETICS and PHONOLOGY, and the results are codified in general dictionaries or specialised PRONOUNCING DICTIONARIES by means of one of two basic systems of graphic notation: phonetic TRANSCRIPTION or RESPELLING, the former by special symbols (e.g. those of the INTERNATIONAL PHONETIC ALPHABET), the latter by conventional letters or characters. PROSODIC FEATURES such as stress are also marked, but (sentence) intonation less often.
📖 Wells 1985, Bronstein 1986, 1994, Benson *et al.* 1986, Brazil 1987, Lee 1989, Svensén 1993.

pronunciation dictionary
⇨ PRONOUNCING DICTIONARY.

pronunciation information
⇨ PHONOLOGICAL INFORMATION.

pronunciation key
⇨ EXPLANATORY CHART.

proper name
⇨ NAME.

proper noun
⇨ NAME.

proprietary name
⇨ TRADE NAME.

proscription
The banning of words, phrases, styles or even languages. In dictionaries and USAGE GUIDES, words or phrases may be branded as incorrect or inappropriate by labels, or excluded altogether.
⇨ FOUR-LETTER WORD, TABOO WORD.

prosodic feature
An aspect of PRONUNCIATION, such as 'accent', 'stress', 'tone' and 'rhythm', which tends to be associated with the flow of syllables, words and

phrases rather than individual segmental phonemes. Some prosodic features, notably word-stress or tone, may be indicated in the pronunciations given in dictionaries.

⇨ PHONOLOGICAL INFORMATION, PRONOUNCING DICTIONARY, TRANSCRIPTION (1).

prosody
⇨ PROSODIC FEATURE.

proto form
⇨ ETYMOLOGY.

prototype
An exemplar felt to exhibit the essential MEANING of a word, which ignores all non-salient features. Thus, the prototypical dictionary is more likely to be regarded as a monolingual, lexical defining book in printed form than as a multilingual, encyclopedic thesaurus in electronic form.

⇨ BASIC SENSE, FOLK TAXONOMY.
📖 Geeraerts 1989, Barsalou 1992.

prototype semantics
An approach to the study of MEANING which seeks to determine what speakers regard as inherently typical or essential qualities of REFERENTS of words.

📖 Ungerer & Schmid 1996.

proverb
A culturally significant pithy saying with a moral or practical message.

⇨ PAROEMIOGRAPHY, PAROEMIOLOGY.
📖 Grauberg 1989, Svensén 1993.
📑 *The Prentice-Hall Encyclopedia of World Proverbs* (W. Mieder), Englewood Cliffs NJ, 1986; *A Chinese–English Dictionary of Idioms and Proverbs* (X. J. Heng & X. Z. Zhang), Tübingen, 1988.

provincialism
⇨ REGIONALISM.

pseudonym
A made-up name ('pen name') used by an author to disguise his or her true identity.

📑 *Pseudonyms and Nicknames Dictionary* (J. Mossman), Detroit MI, 1980.

pseudo-synonym
⇨ SYNONYMY (1).

pseudo-synonymy
⇨ SYNONYMY (1).

publication date
⇨ DATE.

publisher
One who engages in the production, distribution and sale of books and other materials and assumes the legal responsibility and commercial risk for any such undertaking.

publishing
The complex of activities concerned with the commissioning, design, production, editing, distribution and marketing of books and related products. Computer technology has revolutionised the publishing industry, and has encouraged 'alternative' (or 'desktop') book production.

⇨ AUTHORSHIP, COPYRIGHT, DICTIONARY-MAKING, HOUSE STYLE, REFERENCE WORK.
📖 Whitcut 1989.
📑 *A Pocket Dictionary of Publishing Terms* (H. Jacob), London, 1976.

punctuation
A system of graphic marks used to link or separate words and phrases in writing. Dictionaries use conventional punctuation marks in a variety of ways, e.g. as STRUCTURAL INDICATORS or LABELS or for CROSS-REFERENCES.

⇨ DIACRITIC, HYPHENATION.

purism
A prescriptive approach to language which favours native over foreign words, standard over non-standard forms, literary over colloquial USAGE, and traditional dictionary definitions over popular meanings.

⇨ CORRECTNESS.
📖 Thomas, G. 1992.

Q

quasi-bilingual dictionary

A type of REFERENCE WORK in which the words of a less accessible language (such as archaic Akkadian) are explained by means of a more accessible language (such as English). Its structure follows that of the MONOLINGUAL DICTIONARY, the headwords being vocabulary items from the language which is the object of the description, but the language used for providing the lexicographic information in the entries is a language familiar to the scholar–user.

📖 Zgusta 1989b.

quasi-synonym

⇨ SYNONYMY (1).

quasi-synonymy

⇨ SYNONYMY (1).

quick reference

⇨ READY REFERENCE.

quotation

1 In a dictionary entry or citation file, a CITATION.

2 A saying from a literary or other text and recorded for posterity because of its content and/or style.

📖 Jackson 1988, Al-Kasimi 1992.

📕 *The Oxford Dictionary of Modern Quotations* (T. Augarde), Oxford, 1991.

R

racism
The disparaging use of a word or phrase referring to the ethnic origins of groups or individuals.
⇨ ETHNOPHAULISM, TERM OF ABUSE, USAGE LABEL.
📖 Murphy 1991, Hauptfleisch 1993.

radical
A semantic part of a Chinese CHARACTER, which is used by the compiler to locate and the user to find the entry within the overall word-list, which itself may be arranged in a variety of ways.

rare
⇨ DIAFREQUENTIAL INFORMATION.

readability
The degree to which a text of a reference or other work is comprehensible to the USER. Means to enhance readability in a reference work include control of the DEFINING VOCABULARY, the use of ORDERING DEVICES and the LAYOUT of the page.

reader
One engaged in reading, e.g. of a literary or reference work.
⇨ USER.

reading
1 The act of decoding a TEXT.
   ⇨ READABILITY.
   📖 Neubach & Cohen 1988, Tono 1989.
2 ⇨ READING PROGRAMME.

reading programme
The systematic EXCERPTION process in a dictionary-making project.
📖 Jost 1985.

ready reckoner
A type of reference work with information on weights, measures etc. in the form of tables.
📑 *The Carpenter's Metric Roofing Ready Reckoner* (W. E. Gray), London, 1972.

ready reference
The process or result of rapid CONSULTATION of a reference work.
📑 *The Chemist's Ready Reference Handbook* (G. J. Shugar), New York NY, 1990.

received pronunciation
A relatively region-free British English accent, originally based on a southern standard usually associated with the usage of middle- and upper-class speakers. This is often used as the norm for indicating PRONUNCIATION in British dictionaries.
⇨ PRONOUNCING DICTIONARY.

recension
The process or result of continuous revision of a published work.
📖 Steiner 1986a.

reception
⇨ PASSIVE DICTIONARY.

receptive dictionary
⇨ PASSIVE DICTIONARY.

receptive vocabulary
⇨ PASSIVE VOCABULARY.

reciprocal word
⇨ ANTONYMY.

record
The basic REFERENCE UNIT in a terminological dictionary, catalogue or database. The typical

MICROSTRUCTURE of such reference works may include: the ENTRY-TERM; the CONCEPT designated by the term, and its first documented use, usually with a definition; relations of concept and term with others in the hierarchical system of the subject field; translation equivalent(s) in other languages; bibliographical details.

📖 ISO 1990, Sager 1990.

recto
⇨ TITLE PAGE.

recursive definition
A definition which is dependent on one or more other definitions of related concepts, either within or between entries, e.g. in E. L. Thorndike & C. L. Barnhart's *Primary Dictionary of the English Language with Chinese Translation* (Tienjin, 1992): '**roof** [. . .] 1 the top covering of a building. 2 something like it: *the roof of a cave . . .*'

reduction
⇨ TRANSCRIPTION (1).

redundancy
⇨ TEXT COMPRESSION.

reference
1 The process by which INFORMATION is classified, stored and retrieved. It is the basic human need for all kinds of information, linguistic as well as encyclopedic, that motivates writers, librarians and lexicographers to provide it, e.g. in the form of REFERENCE WORKS, which are structured in such a way that they can be consulted easily. There have been great advances in the understanding of various ACCESS systems and how their efficiency can be increased, e.g. by improving the transparency of the text structure of entries in reference works, and computers now allow greater flexibility in presenting and locating information for the benefit of users.
    ⇨ REFERENCE SCIENCE.
    📖 McArthur 1986a, Hausmann & Wiegand 1989, Zgusta 1989b.
2 In dictionaries and other reference works, a CROSS-REFERENCE.
3 In dictionary typology, a REFERENCE WORK.
4 In academic textbooks and papers, the bibliographical details of a cited publication.
    ⇨ BIBLIOGRAPHY.
5 In semantics, the relationship between words and the objects which they denote.

⇨ DENOTATION, DESIGNATION, REFERENT, SENSE RELATION.

reference act
⇨ CONSULTATION.

reference book
⇨ REFERENCE WORK.

reference circularity
⇨ CIRCULAR REFERENCE.

reference department
A section in a library, bookshop or publishing house, concerned with REFERENCE WORKS.

reference dictionary
⇨ ENCYCLOPEDIC DICTIONARY.

reference division
⇨ REFERENCE DEPARTMENT.

reference mark
A graphic symbol, such as an asterisk (*), used to refer from a portion of a text to e.g. a footnote or other associated text.

reference material
A collective term for all types of REFERENCE WORKS and similar systems.

reference needs
The circumstances that drive individuals to seek INFORMATION in REFERENCE WORKS such as DICTIONARIES, e.g. a scholar looking up the ETYMOLOGY of a word, an editor checking a spelling, or a foreign-language learner searching for a TRANSLATION EQUIVALENT. The detailed study of dictionary use can provide useful information not only about REFERENCE SKILLS of users, but also about the nature and qualities of the dictionary consulted.
⇨ FUNCTION, USER PERSPECTIVE.
📖 Mufwene 1984, Hartmann 1989.

reference professional
One who engages in the design, compilation, use and evaluation of all types of REFERENCE WORKS. If LEXICOGRAPHY is viewed within the wider perspective of a REFERENCE SCIENCE, its practitioner, the LEXICOGRAPHER, may be considered to be a reference professional, i.e. a person who knows why and how users consult reference works

and how these should be designed. The terminology is still unsettled, with terms such as AUTHOR, EDITOR, COMPILER, TERMINOGRAPHER, TERMINOLOGIST, lexicographer etc. often being used indiscriminately.

⇨ COMPILER PERSPECTIVE, COMPUTATIONAL LEXICOGRAPHY, DICTIONARY-MAKING, PROFESSIONAL RESOURCES, TRAINING.

◫ Kipfer 1985, Ilson 1986a, James 1989, Osselton 1995, Green 1996.

reference science

A cover term for the complex of activities concerned with the design, compilation, use and evaluation of all types of REFERENCE WORKS. There is as yet no unified framework for such an interdisciplinary field, but a strong case can be made for broadening the perspectives of LEXICOGRAPHY and TERMINOLOGY, and considering works other than dictionaries (such as ATLASES, CATALOGUES, DIRECTORIES, ENCYCLOPEDIAS and TERMINOLOGICAL DATABASES) together. What unites them is the basic human reference need for INFORMATION, linguistic as well as factual, and the possibilities of INFORMATION TECHNOLOGY, above all the computer, which are likely to produce new MULTIMEDIA reference formats in future.

⇨ INTERNET.

◫ McArthur 1986a, Calzolari 1996.

▤ *The Language Engineering Directory* (P. M. Hearn), Madrid, 1996.

reference section

⇨ REFERENCE DEPARTMENT.

reference set

A collection of related reference works in book or electronic format, usually issued by the same publisher, packaged and sold as one unit.

⇨ COMPENDIUM.

▤ *The Merriam-Webster Compact Reference Set* [*Webster's Compact Dictionary*, *Webster's Compact Dictionary of Synonyms*, *Webster's Compact Writer's Guide*, *Webster's Compact Dictionary of Quotations*], Springfield MA, [various dates].

reference shelf

A collection of related reference works in electronic format, packaged and sold as one unit.

▣ *Microsoft Bookshelf* [*American Heritage Dictionary*, *Roget's II Electronic Thesaurus*, *World Almanac and Book of Facts*, *Bartlett's Familiar Quotations*, *The Concise Columbia Dictionary of Quotations*, *The Concise Columbia Encyclopedia*, *The Hammond Atlas*], Redmont WA, 1993; *Oxford Reference Shelf on CD-ROM* [*The Oxford Writer's Shelf*, *The Oxford Business Shelf*, *The Oxford Language Shelf*, *The Oxford Science Shelf*], Oxford, 1994; *Oxford Compendium* [*The Concise Oxford Dictionary*, *The Oxford Thesaurus*, *The Oxford Dictionary of Quotations and Modern Quotations*], Oxford, 1996.

reference skills

The abilities required on the part of the dictionary user to find the INFORMATION being sought. Very little is known about the behaviour and preferences of dictionary users, except that a knowledge of the ACCESS STRUCTURE employed in the REFERENCE WORK, e.g. ALPHABETICAL ORDER, is essential for locating the particular entry in which the information is likely to be found. Not until relatively recently has there been any systematic attempt to relate such notational conventions as abbreviations, codes, labels etc. in dictionary entries to the complex operations involved in dictionary consultation, but more attention is now being paid to deliberate instruction, with or without the use of such teaching aids as WORKBOOKS.

⇨ CONSULTATION.

◫ O'Brien & Jordan 1985, Béjoint 1989, Hartmann 1989, Stark 1990.

reference technology

The use of electronic and other media to compile, produce and use REFERENCE WORKS.

⇨ COMMUNICATIVE SHIFT.

reference unit

The basic device for storing information in a reference work. In the dictionary, this is usually called the ENTRY, in the encyclopedia the ARTICLE, and in terminological and computer-based dictionaries, the RECORD. The head of the reference unit is the LEMMA.

⇨ ADDRESS, BASE STRUCTURE, MICROSTRUCTURE.

reference work

Any product, such as a published book or a computer software, that allows humans to store and retrieve INFORMATION relatively easily and rapidly. The DICTIONARY is the prototypical 'reference book', as it provides structural linguistic and/or encyclopedic information by means of a generally known access system (such as an ALPHABET).

⇨ TYPOLOGY (1).

📖 Calzolari 1996, Hartmann 1996a.

📰 *Walford's Guide to Reference Material*, London, 1989; *Dictionary of Dictionaries* (T. Kabdebo), London, 1992.

referent

The object referred to by a word or phrase. Since the relationship is not direct or one-to-one, e.g. one object can be denoted by several words (SYNONYMY), or one word can denote several objects (POLYSEMY), it is necessary to call upon the notion of the mental images we have of the referent (MEANING). One variant of this is the terminological approach which concentrates on the relations between TERMS as words of designation, and CONCEPTS as representations of meaning.

⇨ DENOTATUM, DESIGNATUM, SEMANTICS, SENSE RELATION.

📖 Jackson 1988, Svensén 1993.

referential meaning

⇨ DENOTATION.

regional dictionary

A type of REFERENCE WORK which describes a particular (provincial or metropolitan) variety of a language. Such dictionaries vary greatly according to when and where they have been compiled, from early lists of words and phrases used in different localities through the late nineteenth-century glossaries of colonial vocabulary, to the contemporary 'national' dictionaries codifying usage separately for each regional variant of the language. Since historical considerations play a part, overlaps with HISTORICAL DICTIONARIES, PERIOD DICTIONARIES and ETYMOLOGICAL DICTIONARIES are sometimes unavoidable.

⇨ DIALECT DICTIONARY.

📖 McArthur 1992, Pakir 1992.

📰 *Dictionary of American Regional English* (F. G. Cassidy), Cambridge MA, 1985– [incomplete]; *A Dictionary of South African English on Historical Principles* (P. Silva), Oxford, 1996.

regionalism

A word or phrase associated with a particular locality where a language is used. The term may refer to features typical of a geographical DIALECT or TOPOLECT, e.g. the French of Paris or Québec, or of a national variety, e.g. Americanisms or Briticisms. Such regionalisms may be marked in general dictionaries by USAGE LABELS or become the subject of specialised REGIONAL DICTIONARIES.

regionality label

⇨ REGIONAL LABEL.

regional label

A LABEL used to mark the dialect or regional variety with which a word or phrase is associated. Dictionaries record such features in different and sometimes inconsistent ways, e.g. by associating dialect vocabulary with 'sub-standard' usage, and have been criticised for relying on incomplete and out-of-date EVIDENCE. General dictionaries of English today tend to concentrate on 'metropolitan' regional varieties rather than 'provincial' local dialects, e.g. Am(erican) or U.S., Br(itish) and Austral(ian) English.

⇨ DIALECT DICTIONARY, DIATOPICAL INFORMATION, REGIONAL DICTIONARY, REGIONALISM, STANDARD (1).

📖 Landau 1984, Berg 1993, Norri 1996.

regional lexicography

A complex of activities concerned with the design, compilation, use and evaluation of REGIONAL DICTIONARIES.

register

1 A variety of language associated with a particular situational context, such as an occupation or social activity. Such DIAPHASIC INFORMATION is indicated in dictionaries by formality or style LABELS.

📖 Jackson 1988.

2 An official list or INDEX.

register label

A general term for a LABEL used to mark a feature of usage such as formality, style or variation in place and time.

⇨ STYLE LABEL, TEMPORAL LABEL.

📖 Svensén 1993.

register marking

⇨ DIASYSTEMATIC LABELLING.

register range

The extent of varieties within a language available for different communicative contexts.

⇨ LANGUAGE VARIETY, REPERTOIRE.

rejected term
⇨   DEPRECATED TERM.

relational database
⇨   DATABASE.

relative equivalence
⇨   EQUIVALENCE.

relative synonym
⇨   SYNONYMY (1).

relative synonymy
⇨   SYNONYMY (1).

religious vocabulary
⇨   VOCABULARY (1).

repertoire
The range of varieties of a language that an individual speaker has available for different communicative contexts.
⇨   IDIOLECT, LANGUAGE VARIETY, REGISTER RANGE.

repertory
An alternative term for REPERTOIRE.

repetition symbol
A graphic mark, such as the tilde (~) or hyphen (-), used in place of a HEADWORD within an entry, e.g. 'give [. . .] 6 ~ sth to sb/sth to devote time . . .'.

reprint
A reissue of a book or other document, sometimes with minor modifications to the title page and/or corrections.
⇨   FACSIMILE EDITION.

research
⇨   DICTIONARY RESEARCH.

respelling
A method of representing PRONUNCIATION by using a combination of traditional alphabetic letters and diacritic marks.
⇨   TRANSCRIPTION (1).

restricted collocation
⇨   COLLOCATION.

restricted defining vocabulary
⇨   DEFINING VOCABULARY.

restricted dictionary
⇨   SPECIALISED DICTIONARY.

restriction of meaning
⇨   SEMANTIC CHANGE.

retrograde dictionary
⇨   REVERSE-ORDER DICTIONARY.

retronym
A modification of an existing term to distinguish it from a NEOLOGISM denoting a recent innovation, e.g. *white pages* 'residential telephone directory' in contrast with *yellow pages* 'classified telephone directory'.
📖   Ahmad & Collingham 1996.

reverse alphabetisation
The alphabetical sorting of words by last-to-first rather than first-to-last letter order.
⇨   REVERSE-ORDER DICTIONARY.
📖   Svensén 1993.

reverse dictionary
1   With reference to format, ⇨ REVERSE-ORDER DICTIONARY.
2   With reference to function, ⇨ WORD-FINDING DICTIONARY.

reverse index
⇨   REVERSE-ORDER DICTIONARY.

reverse-order dictionary
A type of REFERENCE WORK which lists the vocabulary alphabetically by last-to-first rather than first-to-last letter order. Because of the back-to-front arrangement of items, it may also be called 'a tergo' dictionary or 'reverse index'.
⇨   MORPHOLOGICAL DICTIONARY, RHYMING DICTIONARY.
📖   ISO 1990.
🗏   *Rückläufiges Wörterbuch der englischen Gegenwartssprache/Reverse Dictionary of Present-day English* (M. Lehnert), Leipzig, 1971; *Back-Words for Crosswords. A Reverse-sorted Word List* (J. C. P. Schwarz), Edinburgh, 1995.

reversibility
The capability of using a reference work or database bidirectionally or multidirectionally.
⇨   CONVERSION, DIRECTIONALITY.
📖   Martin & Tamm 1996.

review

A critique of one or more reference or other works, usually published in a periodical.

📖 Steiner 1984, 1993, Tomaszczyk 1988.

revision

⇨ EDITION.

rhyme

The use of parallel graphic or phonic forms for special effect. Rhyming has a long history as one of the principles of ARRANGEMENT in reference works.

⇨ RHYMING DICTIONARY.

rhyme dictionary

⇨ RHYMING DICTIONARY.

rhyme lexicography

A complex of activities concerned with the design, compilation, use and evaluation of RHYMING DICTIONARIES.

rhyming dictionary

1 A type of REFERENCE WORK which contains information on RHYMES in alphabetical order of their orthographic forms. English RHYME LEXICOGRAPHY has a relatively long tradition, going back to the English–Latin *Manipulus vocabulorum* by Peter Levins (London, 1570) which predates the publication of the first monolingual general English dictionary.

⇨ REVERSE-ORDER DICTIONARY.

📘 *The Penguin Rhyming Dictionary* (R. Fergusson), Harmondsworth, 1985; *Words to Rhyme with: A Rhyming Dictionary* (W. Espy), London, 1986.

2 A reference work which uses rhyme as a principle of ORGANISATION. In oral cultures, rhyme is a powerful memory aid, and was used in e.g. early Arabic and Indian dictionaries.

⇨ METRICAL DICTIONARY.

rhyming slang

An informal ARGOT based on rhyme.

📘 *A Dictionary of Rhyming Slang* (J. Franklyn), London, 1975.

rhythm

⇨ PROSODIC FEATURE.

right-core structure

⇨ CORE STRUCTURE.

romaji

⇨ ROMANISATION.

Roman alphabet

⇨ LATIN ALPHABET.

romanisation

The representation of words written in a non-Latin script by means of the LATIN ALPHABET, either through TRANSLITERATION, e.g. from Cyrillic, or TRANSCRIPTION, e.g. from Chinese ('(hànyǔ) pīnyīn') or Japanese ('romaji').

⇨ HYBRID, SCRIPT REFORM.

📖 ISO 1990.

root

1 In ETYMOLOGY, the part of the word which is common to a WORD FAMILY and may have COGNATES in genetically related languages. The historical derivation may not always be obvious even to native speakers, e.g. *sal-* in *salary* < Latin *salarium* 'salt allowance' < the ETYMON *sal* 'salt'.

It is often held that a knowledge of roots can help in understanding meaning relations and word-formation processes, which are especially relevant to the creation of technical TERMS. However, such knowledge can also be (mis-) used by protagonists of PURISM to make claims for 'true meanings' and 'correct forms'.

⇨ ROOT-CREATION, ROOT DICTIONARY (1).

📖 ISO 1990.

📘 *Roots. Family Histories of Familiar Words* (P. Davies), New York NY, 1981; *The American Heritage Dictionary of Indo-European Roots* (C. Watkins), Boston MA, 1985; *A First Handbook of the Roots of English* (N. Bird), St Helier, 1990; *Grow Your Vocabulary by Learning the Roots of English Words* (R. Schleifer), New York NY, 1995.

2 In MORPHOLOGY, the BASE of a word.

root-creation

A WORD-FORMATION process in which a word or phrase is deliberately coined according to the phonotactic rules of the language, but not on the basis of any other morphological constituents, e.g. the trade name *Kodak* or the number *googol*.

root dictionary

1 A type of REFERENCE WORK developed during FIELDWORK, e.g. on indigenous American Indian languages, which uses BASES rather than full words to list the morphological elements of the vocabulary.

⇨ STEM DICTIONARY.

📖 Bartholomew 1991.

2 A dictionary or database which serves as a source for the compilation of other reference works, e.g. for bilingual versions of a monolingual THESAURUS, or for terminological dictionaries based on a common conceptual index.

⇨   CONVERSION, DERIVATIVE DICTIONARY.

▤   *Root Thesaurus* (British Standards Institution), Milton Keynes, 1988; *Cambridge Word Routes Anglais–Français* (M. McCarthy), Cambridge, 1994.

routing
⇨   SEARCH PATH.

royalty
The fee paid to a COPYRIGHT holder for permission to reproduce all or part of a given text.

RP
Abbreviation for RECEIVED PRONUNCIATION.

rule
A statement of observed regularity in language use, e.g. grammar, style, vocabulary, pronunciation. Descriptive rules are based on linguistic EVIDENCE, but in pedagogical contexts they tend to be formulated prescriptively. Information of this type is presented in general dictionaries by GRAMMATICAL CODES or USAGE LABELS. Specialised reference works such as USAGE GUIDES, in addition, seek to offer guidance, which can include PROSCRIPTION.

⇨   GRAMMATICAL   INFORMATION,   LEXICAL INFORMATION,   PHONOLOGICAL   INFORMATION, PRAGMATIC INFORMATION.

running foot
⇨   GUIDEWORD.

running head
⇨   GUIDEWORD.

running title
⇨   GUIDEWORD.

run-on entry
A word or phrase which is not given separate HEADWORD status but is cited as a sub-entry under a related word or phrase. The typical example is the treatment of DERIVATIVES, whose selection is often arbitrary, thus making CONSULTATION of run-on entries difficult.

▢   Landau 1984.

S

sacred vocabulary
⇨ VOCABULARY (1).

sampling
Statistical and other techniques to ensure that the words or phrases selected for inclusion in a reference work are representative of the language documented.

sandhi
⇨ CANONICAL FORM.

saying
A short phrase or sentence, reflecting folk wisdom, passed on through the generations.
⇨ PHRASEOLOGICAL DICTIONARY.

scanning
1 The act of reading a text quickly in order to locate a piece of required information.
   ⇨ CONSULTATION.
2 The electronic recognition and processing of text and graphics.
   ⇨ DATA-CAPTURE.

scholarly dictionary
A type of REFERENCE WORK compiled by a team of academics as part of a (usually long-term) research project, e.g. linguists working on a HISTORICAL DICTIONARY or DIALECT DICTIONARY.
⇨ ACADEMY DICTIONARY, CULTURAL DICTIONARY.
📖 Algeo 1990.

school dictionary
A dictionary written for school-children, common features of which are a controlled DEFINING VOCABULARY, a clear design and the incorporation of illustrations. The boundaries between the school dictionary on the one hand, and CHILDREN'S DICTIONARIES, COLLEGE DICTIONARIES and DESK DICTIONARIES on the other, are not clearly demarcated.
⇨ GRADED VOCABULARY, LEARNER'S DICTIONARY.
📖 Algeo 1990, Svensén 1993.
📑 *The School Etymological Dictionary and Workbook* (J. Stormonth), Edinburgh & London, 1876; *Macmillan School Dictionary* (W. D. Halsey), New York NY, 1981.

scientific and technical vocabulary
⇨ VOCABULARY (1).

scientific dictionary
A type of reference work with information on one or more disciplines of science.
⇨ LSP DICTIONARY, POLYTECHNIC DICTIONARY.
📑 *Longman Illustrated Science Dictionary* (A. Goodman), London, 1981; *Chambers Science and Technology Dictionary* (P. M. B. Walker), Cambridge, 1988; *Longman English–Chinese Science & Technology Dictionary*, Hong Kong, 1994.

scope
The relative specialisation of a reference work, e.g. the range of topics treated, the technicality of details included and the time-scale covered.
⇨ COVERAGE, SIZE.

Scrabble®
⇨ CROSSWORD.

script
⇨ WRITING.

scriptorium
A room for preparing manuscripts.

script reform
The process or result of change in the WRITING SYSTEM of a particular language, e.g. the change from the Perso-Arabic script to the Latin alphabet

for Turkish in 1928, or the introduction of simplified characters in Chinese from 1955.
📖 James 1985.

search
The process of seeking INFORMATION in response to a reference need. The choice of reference source precedes the act of CONSULTATION which leads the user along a SEARCH PATH.
⇨ ACCESS, INFORMATION RETRIEVAL, LEMMATISATION, REFERENCE SKILLS.

search area
The notional subdivision of a dictionary entry, often indicated by SECTION MARKS, where particular types of information (e.g. idioms, compounds, derivatives) are located.

search engine
Software for locating sites on the World Wide Web.
💻 *Altavista Search*: altavista.digital.com

search path
The route along which a user is led in a REFERENCE WORK in order to retrieve information, via the 'outer' or 'external' search path (e.g. the information on the spine), GUIDEWORDS, and the 'inner' or 'internal' search path (e.g. SEARCH AREAS indicated by SECTION MARKS).
⇨ ACCESS STRUCTURE.
📖 Hausmann & Wiegand 1989, Spears 1990.

search strategy
⇨ USER STRATEGIES.

secondary entry
⇨ ENTRY-TERM.

secondary source
⇨ SOURCE.

second language
A language used by speakers for whom it is not the NATIVE LANGUAGE, usually in a country where it is endoglossic or dominant, or in countries where it has an acknowledged function.
⇨ LEARNER'S DICTIONARY.

secret language
⇨ ARGOT.

section mark
An ORDERING DEVICE which delimits the SEARCH AREA. Examples include sense numbers,

labels (e.g. id(iom), hum(orous)) and symbols (◆, ■, ⇨ etc.).
📖 Svensén 1993.

segmental dictionary
⇨ SPECIALISED DICTIONARY.

select(ed) bibliography
A list of references of the essential literature on a topic or subject.
⇨ BIBLIOGRAPHY (1).

selection
The EXCERPTION and subsequent sifting of DATA for treatment in entries in a reference work.
⇨ INCLUSION LIST, WORD-LIST.
📖 Svensén 1993.

selection restriction
⇨ COLLOCATION.

semantic change
The loss or acquisition of meanings in words or phrases, motivated by a number of factors. A variety of processes may be at work, e.g. the narrowing of senses ('reduction' or 'specialisation'), the widening of senses ('generalisation'), the shift to a positive ('(a)melioration') or negative ('pejoration') connotation. Semantic extension is a powerful way of increasing the scope and function of the vocabulary of a language, but dictionaries do not always reflect this either in their sense-discrimination techniques or in their ability to document lexical innovations.
⇨ ARCHAISM, DIACHRONIC INFORMATION, HISTORICAL DICTIONARY, MEANING, NEOLOGISM, SENSE DISCRIMINATION, WORD FORMATION.
📖 Béjoint 1990.
📑 *NTC's Dictionary of Changes in Meaning* (A. Room), Lincolnwood IL, 1991.

semantic comment
⇨ COMMENT.

semantic dictionary
⇨ ONOMASIOLOGICAL DICTIONARY.

semantic domain
⇨ SEMANTIC FIELD.

semantic extension
⇨ SEMANTIC CHANGE.

semantic field

A lexical set with related meanings, which form a conceptual network or mosaic, e.g. in the domain of kinship vocabulary or colour terminology, which can be analysed in terms of COMPONENTIAL ANALYSIS into distinctive features.

📖 Walter 1992, Wierzbicka 1992.

semantic information

One of the INFORMATION CATEGORIES presented by the compiler and consulted by the user of the dictionary, based on SEMANTICS. Material of this kind can be in many different forms, e.g. words or phrases with similar meaning (SYNONYMS), explanations of one or more senses of a word or phrase in the form of DEFINITIONS, commentaries on the semantic extension of a word or phrase (a GLOSS on a 'figurative' use), TRANSLATION EQUIVALENTS in a bilingual dictionary, or EXAMPLES. In THESAURUSES and conceptually organised TERMINOLOGICAL DICTIONARIES, words and phrases are related to each other within SEMANTIC FIELDS.

📖 Ayto 1983, Svensén 1993.

semantic label

A symbol or abbreviated term used to mark the semantic role that a word or phrase plays to achieve a particular effect. Many lexicographers reserve the term LABEL for the marking of USAGE features, and consider 'figurative', 'transferred' and other metaphorical uses as part of the explanation of meaning.

⇨ GLOSS (2), DEFINITION.

📖 Hausmann & Wiegand 1989, Berg 1993, Osselton 1996.

semantic prototype

⇨ PROTOTYPE.

semantic reduction

⇨ SEMANTIC CHANGE.

semantic relation

⇨ SENSE RELATION.

semantics

A branch of LINGUISTICS concerned with the study of MEANING. Traditionally, the focus of attention was the WORD ('lexical semantics'), and this is still its main relevance to lexicography. Increasingly, however, semantic studies have turned to other levels of linguistic structure, such as sentences (SYNTAX) and texts (DISCOURSE ANALYSIS). A range of approaches and models is available, from SEMANTIC FIELD theory to COMPONENTIAL ANALYSIS and PROTOTYPE SEMANTICS, to throw light on SENSE RELATIONS between LEXEMES. SEMANTIC INFORMATION of this kind is codified in general and specialised dictionaries, typically in the form of meaning explanations (DEFINITIONS).

⇨ FRAME THEORY, ONOMASIOLOGY, REFERENT, SEMASIOLOGY, SYNONYMY (1), THESAURUS.

📖 Wierzbicka 1985, Allen 1986, Cruse 1986, Jackson 1988, Lehrer & Kittay 1992, Swanepoel 1994, Gouws 1996.

semantic set

⇨ SEMANTIC FIELD.

semantic specialisation

⇨ SEMANTIC CHANGE.

semantic sub-comment

⇨ COMMENT.

semantic subdivision

⇨ SUB-SENSE.

semasiological dictionary

A type of REFERENCE WORK which presents and explains the meanings of a given word or phrase, in contrast to the ONOMASIOLOGICAL DICTIONARY which shows the various words that can be used to express a given meaning.

📖 Svensén 1993.

semasiology

An approach in SEMANTICS concerned with the explanation of the meaning of given words or phrases. Traditional monolingual and bilingual dictionaries supply such semasiological information (e.g. in terms of DEFINITIONS and TRANSLATION EQUIVALENTS), while thesauruses, synonym dictionaries and specialist terminologies follow the opposite route (ONOMASIOLOGY) and guide the user to a choice of words appropriate for the expression of particular meanings or concepts.

📖 Svensén 1993.

semi-bilingual dictionary

A BILINGUAL DICTIONARY which contains headwords and definitions in one language and translation equivalents in the other language.

⇨ BILINGUALISED DICTIONARY.

semiology

The linguistic study of SIGNS.

semiotics

A general theory of communication in terms of what (INFORMATION) is transmitted by whom and to whom and by what channels (visual, verbal, graphic etc.). Three dimensions are usually distinguished: the semantic or paradigmatic (MEANING), the syntagmatic (GRAMMAR) and the pragmatic (CONTEXT). Semiotics is relevant to lexicography since the dictionary is a communicative tool which relies on the highly developed code of human verbal language to transmit information to the user, but efficiency is sometimes compromised through a lack of transparency in one or more dimensions.

⇨ DICTIONARIES AS DISCOURSE, SEMIOLOGY, SIGN, TEXT.

sense

One of several MEANINGS that can be established for a word or phrase and covered by a DEFINITION in a reference work. Because of the multiple meanings of words, particularly core items in the basic vocabulary, compilers of dictionaries have for centuries tried to rationalise, discriminate and display these senses for the benefit of users, but there has not always been consistency even within one dictionary. The problem of SENSE DISCRIMINATION which is difficult enough in monolingual general dictionaries (how many meanings are there in *band*?) is compounded in bilingual dictionaries by that of uneven translation equivalents (each of the separate senses of *band* may be expressed by a different word in the other language).

The number and nature of variable senses of a word may be due to POLYSEMY (related by extension from an 'original' meaning or BASIC SENSE: *band* 'ribbon' > 'belt' > 'range' > 'track') or HOMONYMY (accidental similarity: *band* 1 'ribbon' (etc.) versus *band* 2 'group of musicians'), but these sometimes shade into one another. Distinct senses are used to subdivide dictionary entries into sections (SUB-LEMMA), but the ordering of these sub-senses (by etymology? by semantic 'logic'? by frequency?) is not always clear.

⇨ SEMANTICS, SENSE RELATION.

📖 Landau 1984, Moon 1987, McArthur 1992, Svensén 1993, Considine 1996.

sense discrimination

The division inside a dictionary entry of distinct SENSES of a word or phrase. Each sub-sense may be marked not only with a SENSE NUMBER, but by additional means. Thus, the lexeme *band* may be treated in two different entries separated by the criteria of homonymy and etymology: *band* 1 'ribbon' and *band* 2 'group'. Each of these may be subdivided into sub-senses marked not only with a sense number and/or punctuation marks, but by a range of additional devices ('sense discriminators') such as GLOSSES (*band* 'strip (of material)'), DEFINITIONS (*band* 'strip of material used as a distinguishing mark on clothes'), LABELS (*band* (Radio) 'range for broadcasting') or grammatical codes (*band* vb. 'to fasten'). In the bilingual dictionary, each of these senses may have a different translation EQUIVALENT, so clear meaning distinction is essential.

⇨ SENSE ORDERING, SUB-LEMMA.

📖 Iannucci 1985, Foxley & Gwei 1989, Kromann *et al.* 1991, Svensén 1993, Montemagni *et al.* 1996.

sense distinction

⇨ SENSE DISCRIMINATION.

sense discriminator

⇨ SENSE DISCRIMINATION.

sense history

The SEMANTIC CHANGE a word or phrase has undergone throughout the history of the language. HISTORICAL DICTIONARIES display this information from the earliest documented occurrence of the item to the present, and some GENERAL DICTIONARIES use this principle for ordering the distinct senses of the headword within entries.

⇨ ETYMOLOGY, SENSE DISCRIMINATION.

sense number

An ORDERING DEVICE used to divide dictionary entries into sections according to the different senses of the HEADWORD.

sense ordering

The principles by which the SENSES of a word or phrase are arranged within a dictionary entry. The order may be historical (according to the semantic changes the word has undergone since its first occurrence in the language), logical (according to the perceived 'core' meaning from which others have developed, e.g. by metaphorical extension), or by frequency (according to how often it occurs in a text CORPUS). In practice these different principles are not always made explicit, or are used in unexplained combinations.

📖 Kipfer 1984.

sense relation

The semantic link between two or more words. Two basic types of semantic relation can be distinguished: those between word shapes and the meanings of their extralinguistic referents ('conceptual' or 'reference' relations) and those between different words and the meanings they share (semantic 'inclusion' and 'opposition'). Among the former the most important are HOMONYMY (words with the same form but different meanings) and POLYSEMY (one word with at least two different meanings). Among the latter sense relations are the inclusive ones of SYNONYMY and HYPONYMY and various kinds of opposition (ANTONYMY). Such sense relations are specified in ONOMASIOLOGICAL DICTIONARIES such as the synonym dictionary and the thesaurus. In the general dictionary the hyponymy relation in particular is exploited in one type of DEFINITION which explains words as a specific instance of something more generic ('X is a kind of Y which . . .').

⇨ INCOMPATIBILITY, PARTITIVE RELATION.
📖 Cruse 1986, Jackson 1988, Swanepoel 1994, Gouws 1996.

sentence

A basic unit of SYNTAX. Sentences occur in the raw material for dictionary compilation (e.g. CITATIONS, QUOTATIONS). In the dictionary itself, they are used as verbal EXAMPLES, or in full-sentence definitions as in e.g. the COBUILD dictionaries.

⇨ GRAMMAR.
📖 Sinclair 1987, McArthur 1992.

sentential dictionary

⇨ PHRASEOLOGICAL DICTIONARY.

sequential relation

⇨ HIERARCHICAL RELATION.

serial incompatibility

⇨ INCOMPATIBILITY.

set expression

⇨ FIXED EXPRESSION.

set phrase

⇨ FIXED EXPRESSION.

sexism

The disparaging use of a word or phrase referring to the gender of groups or individuals.

⇨ GENDERLECT, TERM OF ABUSE.

sexual vocabulary

⇨ VOCABULARY (1).

SGML

Abbreviation for STANDARD GENERALIZED MARK-UP LANGUAGE.

shift

1 With reference to communication technology, ⇨ COMMUNICATIVE SHIFT.
2 With reference to meaning, ⇨ SEMANTIC CHANGE.

shorter dictionary

⇨ ABRIDGED (DICTIONARY).

shorthand

A system of recording speech in writing without transcribing the words in full. There are many varieties of shorthand writing, from conventionalised abbreviations to phonetic and orthographic adaptations.

📘 *The Pitman Dictionary of English and Shorthand*, London, 1988.

SIGLEX

⇨ ASSOCIATION FOR COMPUTATIONAL LINGUISTICS.

sign

The basic unit of communication, usually interpreted as a symbolic combination of meaning ('signifié') and its formal realisation in phonic or graphic substance ('signifiant'). At the word level, this is the linguistic notion of the LEXEME. In metalexicography, the sign has been further abstracted towards the LEMMA, which is the notional position at which an entry can be located in the structure of a REFERENCE WORK.

⇨ SYMBOL.

sign dictionary

A reference work with information on SIGN LANGUAGE.

signifiant

⇨ SIGN.

signifié

⇨ SIGN.

sign language

In the widest sense, any non-verbal system of communication. In a narrow sense, sign language refers to systems, based on manual, facial and gestural movements, used for communication amongst the deaf.

📖 Schein 1991.

📑 *American Sign Language. A Comprehensive Dictionary* (M. L. A. Sternberg), New York NY, 1981; *Dictionary of British Sign Language/English* (D. Brien), London, 1992.

simple term

A term comprising a BASE with or without affixes, e.g. *a head* 'top of the anatomy', *a heading* 'title at the top of a page'.

⇨ COMPLEX TERM, COMPOUND TERM.

📖 ISO 1990.

simple word

A word comprising a BASE with or without derivational affixes, e.g. *book*, *happy*.

⇨ COMPLEX WORD, COMPOUND WORD.

simplex

⇨ SIMPLE WORD.

single indexing

A system of cataloguing references in a library or bibliography by combining authors, subjects and titles, as opposed to 'divided' or 'split' indexing in which these are filed in separate lists.

situational context

⇨ CONTEXT (2).

size

The physical dimensions of a reference work, e.g. in terms of numbers of words, pages, volumes etc.

⇨ COMPARISON OF DICTIONARIES, COVERAGE, SCOPE.

📖 Svensén 1993.

slang

A word or phrase associated with the informal language of a particular social group. Interest in such USAGE has produced a range of studies and specialised reference works variously referred to as dictionaries of slang, cant or argot, such as Eric Partridge's on soldiers' vocabulary, but there are severe limitations on collecting evidence in an area where relative obscurity may be a feature of the discourse.

slang dictionary

A type of REFERENCE WORK which documents and interprets SLANG, sometimes in a light-hearted manner. Dictionaries of slang are concerned with a kind of USAGE that may be obscure because of its 'in-group' quality (a feature slang shares with JARGON and ARGOT), but it remains difficult to define and to differentiate from other LANGUAGES FOR SPECIFIC PURPOSES, a problem compounded in the design and use of bilingual slang dictionaries. Although there is a long tradition going back to sixteenth-century dictionaries of beggars' slang, and including J. S. Farmer and W. E. Henley's seven-volume historical-comparative dictionary *Slang and its Analogues Past and Present* (New York NY, 1890–1904), the inherent limitation of collecting CORPUS data among relatively isolated social groups impedes progress.

📖 Lovatt 1984, McArthur 1992.

📑 *A Dictionary of Slang and Unconventional English* (E. Partridge), London, 1937/84; *The Thesaurus of Slang* (E. Lewin & A. Lewin), New York NY/Oxford, 1988; *Bloomsbury Dictionary of Contemporary Slang* (T. Thorne), London, 1990.

slang lexicography

A complex of activities concerned with the design, compilation, use and evaluation of SLANG DICTIONARIES.

📖 Crystal 1980, Green 1996.

slip

A card with information on the use of a word or phrase, submitted as part of a READING PROGRAMME in a dictionary project, and subsequently incorporated in a CITATION FILE.

📖 Berg 1993.

slogan

A CATCH-PHRASE adopted by a cause, in politics or advertising.

Society of American Archivists

A professional society, based in Chicago IL, founded in 1936 to represent ARCHIVISTS.

🖥 www.archivists.org/

Society of Archivists

A professional society, based in London, founded in 1947 to represent ARCHIVISTS and records managers.

🖥 www.hmc.gov.uk/archon/6/arch6.htm

Society of Authors

A professional society, based in London, founded in 1884 to represent AUTHORS.

🖥 www.writers.org.uk/society/

Society of Indexers

A professional society, based in London, founded in 1957 to represent INDEXERS.
⇨   AMERICAN SOCIETY OF INDEXERS, WHEATLEY MEDAL.

sociolect

A social DIALECT.

sociolinguistics

A branch of LINGUISTICS concerned with the study of LANGUAGE VARIETY along such dimensions as age, sex, social class, context and location. Individuals unconsciously and consciously adapt their communicative styles to group norms; linguists describe them (as 'dialect', 'genderlect', 'sociolect', 'register' etc.); and lexicographers mark them, with or without USAGE LABELS, as 'regionalisms', 'slang', 'foreignisms', 'formal', 'literary' etc. What underlies most of these efforts is the notion of a STANDARD language which, however, is rarely made explicit even in specialised dictionaries.
📖   Chambers 1994, Coulmas 1996.

soft copy

⇨   HARD COPY.

software

Computer applications for the compilation, editing and presentation of reference works.
📖   DANLEX Group 1987, Svensén 1993.
📰   *Oriental* [Languages] *Software List* (J. Krzywicki), Warsaw, 1993.

solidarity relation

⇨   COLLOCATION.

sound

The audible effect of vibrations in the air, which allow the transmission of human SPEECH. Individual 'speech sounds' (PHONEMES) combine to form higher-level units, from syllables to words, and in most languages they are represented by graphic symbols (LETTERS, CHARACTERS). As the correspondence between speech and writing is not always direct, general dictionaries and USAGE GUIDES may be designed and consulted for guidance on both PRONUNCIATION and SPELLING.

soundalike

An informal term for PARONYM.

sound system

An informal term for PHONOLOGY.

source

The raw material from which DATA can be gathered. In many modern dictionaries, a CORPUS of text is used as a 'main' informing source, 'supplementary' sources being sought in cases of need (e.g. to cover aspects such as specialised vocabulary or novel senses). A distinction can also be made between 'primary' sources, or original material (e.g. FIELDWORK), and 'secondary' sources, or derivative material (e.g. other dictionaries).
📖   ISO 1990, Thompson 1992b, Svensén 1993.

source code

An abbreviation or symbol used to LABEL the texts associated with a particular word, phrase or term.
📖   ISO 1990.

source language

1   In TRANSLATION, the language of a text which is to be translated into another (the 'target') language.
    ⇨   ACTIVE DICTIONARY, BIDIRECTIONAL DICTIONARY.
2   In language teaching, the native language ('L1'), as opposed to the 'target language' ('L2'), of the learner.
    ⇨   BILINGUAL DICTIONARY, INTERLANGUAGE.
3   In BORROWING, the donor language from which a word or phrase has been transferred.
    ⇨   FOREIGNISM.

-speak

A COMBINING FORM used to construct a word or phrase descriptive of a particular form of speech, e.g. *Airspeak* (the language of air traffic control) or *Seaspeak* (the language of maritime communications).
📰   *The Seaspeak Reference Manual* (F. Weeks *et al.*), Oxford, 1984.

special dictionary

⇨   SPECIALISED DICTIONARY.

special field

⇨   SUBJECT FIELD (1).

special-field dictionary

⇨   SPECIALISED DICTIONARY.

specialised dictionary

The collective term for a range of REFERENCE WORKS devoted to a relatively restricted set of phenomena. In contrast to the GENERAL DICTIONARY which is aimed at covering the whole vocabulary for the 'general' user, specialised (or 'segmental') dictionaries concentrate either on more restricted information, such as idioms or names, or on the language of a particular subject field, such as the jargon of the drug scene or the technical terms of mechanical engineering.
⇨ LSP DICTIONARY, TECHNICAL DICTIONARY, TERMINOLOGICAL DICTIONARY.
    Jackson 1988, Svensén 1993.
Dictionary of Printing Terms (I. Foster), London, 1976; *Dictionary of Glass-making* [English–Spanish–Portuguese] (International Commission on Glass), Amsterdam, 1992.

specialised lexicography

A complex of activities concerned with the design, compilation, use and evaluation of SPECIALISED DICTIONARIES. There is no uniform framework for this as the nature and scope of such reference works can range widely, from a brief GLOSSARY without definitions, through TECHNICAL DICTIONARIES aimed at lay persons, to large-scale and standardised TERMINOLOGICAL DATABASES for subject experts and translators.
⇨ SPECIAL LEXICOGRAPHY.
    Bergenholtz & Tarp 1995.

specialised meaning
⇨ SEMANTIC CHANGE.

specialised sense
⇨ SEMANTIC CHANGE.

specialist dictionary
⇨ SPECIALISED DICTIONARY.

special language
⇨ LANGUAGE FOR SPECIFIC PURPOSES.

special lexicography

A branch of LEXICOGRAPHY concerned with a particular language, tradition, culture, subject field or type of reference work.
⇨ COMPARATIVE LEXICOGRAPHY, GENERAL LEXICOGRAPHY (1).

special library

A library, information centre or collection of material in a specialised field.

special-purpose dictionary
⇨ SPECIALISED DICTIONARY.

special-purpose lexicography
⇨ SPECIALISED LEXICOGRAPHY.

special theory of terminology

The discipline concerned with the theoretical foundations and principles of TERMINOLOGY, in relation to one technical subject field in one language.
⇨ GENERAL THEORY OF TERMINOLOGY, REFERENCE SCIENCE, SPECIAL LEXICOGRAPHY.
    ISO 1990.

species
⇨ SPECIFIC TERM.

specific concept

A subordinate concept in a hierarchical generic relationship.
⇨ GENERIC CONCEPT.
    ISO 1990.

specific term

In a hierarchy of sense-related words, the one which covers a smaller conceptual space than the GENERIC TERM. The relationship between 'genus' and 'species' can be explained in a number of ways. Taxonomically, the specific term is subordinate to the superordinate generic term; semantically, it is said to cover a more restricted area (the species is a HYPONYM, the genus a HYPERONYM); logically, the species is a member of a class which is equivalent to the genus.
⇨ BINOMIAL COMPOUND, DEFINITION.

specimen entry

1 During the initial stages of a dictionary project, a sample to typify the intended format and content of the work.
2 A sample of an ENTRY included in the EXPLANATORY CHART, to illustrate the various information categories presented in a reference work.

speech

The result of the first major COMMUNICATIVE SHIFT, from non-verbal communication to spoken language.

speech community

A group of people sharing a LANGUAGE or language variety.

⇨ CULTURAL DICTIONARY, DIALECT, LANGUAGE
POLICY.

speech sound
⇨ SOUND.

speller
⇨ SPELLING DICTIONARY.

spelling
The conventionalised system of representing
speech by writing in a particular language. In alphabetic scripts the graphic signs stand for one or more
speech sounds, and languages vary in their correspondence between GRAPHEMES and PHONEMES.
Hence, SPELLING REFORMS are periodically
advocated and/or carried out to regularise these
relationships. Spelling, together with capitalisation,
hyphenation and punctuation, forms the basis of
ORTHOGRAPHIC INFORMATION in dictionaries and,
through the ordered sequence of graphic signs (e.g.
alphabetic LETTERS or logographic CHARACTERS),
provides a system for arranging entries overall.
⇨ LITERACY, REFERENCE SKILLS, STANDARD (1).
📖 Jackson 1988, McArthur 1992, Svensén 1993,
Mitton 1996.
▤ *Collins COBUILD English Guides 8: Spelling*
(J. Payne), London, 1995.

spell(ing) checker
An application in a text-processing system which
highlights the deviations in ORTHOGRAPHY and
suggests appropriate standard forms.
⇨ SPELLING DICTIONARY.

spelling dictionary
A type of REFERENCE WORK which presents
ORTHOGRAPHIC INFORMATION, usually in alpha-
betical order. As the relationships between speech
and writing are complex in many languages,
SPELLING can be a difficult skill to acquire, and
general and specialised dictionaries cater for this
reference need.
⇨ USAGE GUIDE.
📖 Hatherall 1986.
▤ *Orthographic Dictionary* (N. Bailey), London,
1727; *Webster's New World Mis(s)peller's Diction(a)ry*
(P. Norback & C. Norback), New York NY, 1974/83.

spelling reform
The process or result of change in the orthography of a particular language, to reduce inconsis-
tencies and to harmonise the correspondence
between PHONEMES and GRAPHEMES.

⇨ SCRIPT REFORM, SPELLING, SPELLING DICTIO-
NARY.

split indexing
⇨ SINGLE INDEXING.

spoken corpus
A systematic collection of transcribed recordings
of samples of natural speech, which documents the
USAGE features of a language or language variety.
Advances in digital technology allow the simultaneous phonic and graphic display of spoken language, a facility which, in the future, will provide
the dictionary-maker and user with features not
previously available.
⇨ BRITISH NATIONAL CORPUS, PHONOLOGICAL
INFORMATION.

sponge word
An informal term for CLICHÉ.

standard
1 The relatively uniform variety of a LANGUAGE
   used for interregional communication. Standard language forms are the result of long-term
   effects of linguistic and other NORMS promoted
   by cultural institutions, such as ACADEMIES,
   and publications such as textbooks, grammars
   and DICTIONARIES, which tend to favour liter-
   ary/written rather than colloquial/dialectal
   USAGE. Rules for standard forms can be codified at various levels: spelling ('orthography'),
   pronunciation ('orthoepy'), grammar and
   vocabulary. In the field of technical terminology, official agreements among experts in
   different subjects can lead to national or international STANDARDISATION.
   ⇨ AUTHORITY, CODIFICATION, PRESCRIPTION,
   USAGE GUIDE.
   📖 Woods 1985, Zgusta 1989a, Milroy &
   Milroy 1991, McArthur 1992, Bauer 1994.
2 A nationally or internationally agreed bench-
   mark, e.g. in TERMINOLOGY. Whilst standards
   have been accepted for a wide variety of products and services (including book sizes, book
   and series numbers, even for the notion of
   'quality' itself), none is as yet generally available for the different types of reference works.
   ⇨ EVALUATION.

standard (desk) dictionary
A type of general dictionary for business or college use.

🗡 Landau 1984.

🗐 *Funk & Wagnalls Standard Desk Dictionary* (S. I. Landau), New York NY, 1966; *Larousse Standard Dictionary French–English, English–French* (F. Carney), London, 1994.

Standard Generalized Mark-up Language

The ISO standard for document description, specifically for the codes used to indicate document structure. It is primarily intended for publishing purposes, to enable various software programs (and humans) to interpret text consistently. Subsets of SGML include HTML (hypertext mark-up language), used to publish documents on the INTERNET so that WORLD WIDE WEB browsers display text as intended. Although meant primarily as a formatting tool, subsets of SGML have also been used by linguists to indicate syntactic, stylistic and other textual information.

🗡 Heidecke 1996.

standardisation

A collective term for those processes which bring about uniformity in LANGUAGE by reducing diversity of USAGE. In addition to such agents as national ACADEMIES, education and the print media, reference works such as GENERAL DICTIONARIES and more specialised USAGE GUIDES have made a contribution to the development of a STANDARD (or several standards) for English and many other languages, at the levels of pronunciation ('orthoepy'), spelling ('orthography'), grammar, vocabulary and discourse. Given widespread agreement, standardisation can be particularly effective in TERMINOLOGY.

⇨ CODIFICATION, PRESCRIPTION.

🗡 Landau 1984, ISO 1990, Sager 1990.

standardised term

A technical TERM which has been agreed by experts as being the most suitable for designating a particular concept in a subject field.

⇨ ACCEPTABILITY RATING.

🗡 ISO 1990.

standardised vocabulary

A list of technical TERMS in a specific subject field.

🗡 ISO 1990.

standard language

⇨ STANDARD (1).

status label

A LABEL used to mark the currency, frequency or degree of acceptability of a word or phrase in a dictionary. Practices vary widely, and critics have remarked that labels such as 'obsolete', 'rare', 'non-naturalised' and 'erroneous' are vague and in need of AUTHENTICATION by means of citation files and text corpora.

⇨ DIACHRONIC INFORMATION, DIAFREQUENTIAL INFORMATION, DIAINTEGRATIVE INFORMATION.

🗡 Landau 1984, Berg 1993.

status symbol

⇨ STATUS LABEL.

stem

That form of a word to which derivational and/or inflectional affixes can be added, e.g. *hand* + inflectional affix *-s*, *hand* + derivational affix *-ful*, or *handful* + inflectional affix *-s*.

⇨ BASE, WORD FORMATION.

🗡 ISO 1990.

stem dictionary

A type of reference work with information on the stems and/or roots of words.

⇨ MORPHOLOGICAL DICTIONARY, ROOT DICTIONARY (1).

🗐 *Roots. Family Histories of Familiar Words* (P. Davies), New York NY, 1981; *Grow Your Vocabulary by Learning the Roots of English Words* (R. Schleifer), New York NY, 1995.

stereotype

A word or phrase reflecting the image which the speaker has of the REFERENT, based on either fact or belief.

⇨ BIAS-FREE VOCABULARY.

stop word list

A list of words not (to be) included in an electronic reference work.

stress

⇨ PROSODIC FEATURE.

strict synonym

⇨ SYNONYMY (1).

strict synonymy

⇨ SYNONYMY (1).

structural indicator

A device which signals links and divisions within the text of a reference work, e.g. the capitalised incipits at the start of each section of the word-list, or punctuation marks (e.g. colons, semi-colons, brackets) and typographical devices (e.g. **bold**, *italic*) inside entries.

structure

The component parts of a DICTIONARY or other reference work in terms of its overall design (MACROSTRUCTURE) and contents of individual entries (MICROSTRUCTURE).
⇨   HIERARCHICAL STRUCTURE, LIST.
📖 Hausmann & Wiegand 1989.

structure word

⇨   FUNCTION WORD.

style

A variety of language associated with different texts, authors, genres, oeuvres, or periods, e.g. the compressed text of a dictionary entry (DICTION-ARESE).
⇨   DEFINITION STYLE, STYLE LABEL.
📖 Delbridge 1989.

style checker

An application in a text-processing system which highlights features of grammar, text cohesion and lexical choice, and may suggest appropriate alter-native forms.

Style Council

A conference first held at Macquarie University in 1986. Each Style Council is convened by Macquarie's Dictionary Research Centre, and supported by Language Australia (the National Languages and Literacy Institute of Australia) to produce a twice-yearly bulletin, *Australian Style*, and to carry out research on Australian English.

style guide

⇨   STYLE MANUAL.

style label

A LABEL used to mark the STYLE level of a word or phrase in a dictionary. 'Style' is notoriously difficult to define, and lexicographers have had problems marking aspects of USAGE with a unitary style label. (Is 'colloquial' a feature of style, or formality, or even social status?) The modern approach is to separate out several dimensions of variation within the DIASYSTEMATIC LABELLING scheme employed in any one dictionary. A 'collo-quial' word or phrase would then be classified along a scale of DIAPHASIC INFORMATION (from 'formal' to 'informal'), DIAMEDIAL INFORMATION (contrasting 'written' and 'spoken') or DIASTRATIC INFORMATION (from 'high' to 'demotic').
⇨   REGISTER.
📖 Landau 1984, Sharpe 1988, Berg 1993.

style manual

Instructions to authors and editorial staff for the use of a consistent HOUSE STYLE.
📖 Landau 1984, Svensén 1993.
📑 *The Oxford Dictionary for Writers and Editors* [11th edition] (R. E. Allen *et al.*), Oxford, 1981.

stylistics

An interdisciplinary field between LINGUISTICS and literary studies, concerned with the study of STYLE.
⇨   DISCOURSE ANALYSIS, SOCIOLINGUISTICS.
📑 *A Dictionary of Stylistics* (K. Wales), Harlow, 1990.

sub-culture

⇨   ARGOT.

sub-entry

A subdivision of the REFERENCE UNIT, e.g. the numbered senses of a HEADWORD within a dic-tionary entry.

subject

1 With reference to technical domains, ⇨ SUB-JECT FIELD (1).
2 With reference to the content of a text, ⇨ TOPIC.
3 With reference to user studies, ⇨ INFORMANT.

subject arrangement

A thematic or conceptual system of ordering items in a reference work or catalogue.

subject dictionary

A SPECIALISED DICTIONARY in a particular SUB-JECT FIELD.

subject field

1 A technical specialisation or discipline.
    📖 ISO 1990, Svensén 1993.
2 The TOPIC of a text.

subject-field dictionary

A SPECIALISED DICTIONARY in a particular SUBJECT FIELD.

subject label

A LABEL used to mark the field of specialisation with which a particular word or phrase is associated. Dictionaries differ as to the extent and the manner in which they cover and label technical terms. In general, vocabulary from the arts, humanities and social sciences, e.g. *Ling*(*uistics*), is better represented (but less well labelled) than that from the sciences and technology. In SUBJECT-FIELD DICTIONARIES the need to label is reduced because the technical context is given. Thus, the word *lemma* is unlabelled (for all three senses given) in the *New Shorter Oxford English Dictionary* (Oxford, 1993), while the first two senses of *lentil* are unlabelled and the third ('mass of rock') is labelled *Geol*. This *Dictionary of Lexicography* does not mark even terms borrowed from neighbouring disciplines since they are all considered relevant.

⇨   DIATECHNICAL INFORMATION.

📖   Landau 1984, ISO 1990, Berg 1993, Svensén 1993.

subject-specific dictionary

⇨   SUBJECT-FIELD DICTIONARY.

sub-language

⇨   LANGUAGE FOR SPECIFIC PURPOSES.

sub-lemma

The position at which a SUB-ENTRY can be located within an entry. Typically, this is either one of several numbered senses of a HEADWORD, or one of several associated derivative words or phrases, which can be clustered by means of NESTING or NICHING.

⇨   LEMMA.

sub-meaning

⇨   SUB-SENSE.

subordinate concept

⇨   SPECIFIC CONCEPT.

subordinate term

⇨   SPECIFIC TERM.

subordination

The SENSE RELATION obtaining between two or more CONCEPTS at different ranks of a hierarchy.

The subordinate concepts can be called HYPONYMS with respect to their superordinate concept or HYPERONYM, e.g. 'guideword' and 'thumb index' with respect to 'ordering device'.

📖   ISO 1990.

sub-sense

One of the distinct meanings of a polysemous word, often marked in dictionaries by means of numbered SUB-ENTRIES.

⇨   SENSE.

subsidiaries

⇨   BACK MATTER.

sub-standard

A word or phrase considered not to conform to the NORMS of the STANDARD language variety, and often labelled as such in dictionaries or usage guides.

substitutability

The principle by which a word or phrase in a text can be replaced by its dictionary definition. Such a rule cannot be applied to all categories of word, particularly FUNCTION WORDS.

📖   Landau 1984, Jackson 1988, Svensén 1993.

sub-technical vocabulary

A word or phrase from the BASIC VOCABULARY, used in technical contexts with a specialised sense, e.g. *window*, *mouse* or *to cut and paste* in the literature of computing.

⇨   TECHNICAL LANGUAGE.

suffix

⇨   AFFIX.

superordinate concept

⇨   GENERIC CONCEPT.

superordinate term

⇨   GENERIC TERM.

superordination

The SENSE RELATION obtaining between two or more CONCEPTS at different ranks of a hierarchy. The superordinate concept can be called a HYPERONYM with respect to its subordinate concepts or HYPONYMS, e.g. 'clustering' with respect to 'nesting' and 'niching'.

📖   ISO 1990.

supplement

An update to a dictionary, either bound in as an 'addendum' with a revised edition, or issued as a separate publication.

📖 Warburton 1986, Burchfield 1987a.

📄 *The Oxford English Dictionary Supplement* [4 volumes] (R. Burchfield), Oxford, 1957–86; *Webster's Third New International Dictionary* [Addenda section, pp. 55a–120a], Springfield MA, 1993.

supplementary source

⇨ SOURCE.

suppletive form

⇨ PARADIGM.

suprasegmental feature

⇨ PROSODIC FEATURE.

surname

⇨ PERSONAL NAME.

surrogate equivalent

⇨ EXPLANATORY EQUIVALENT.

swear word

A word or phrase often associated with a profane oath or an obscenity.

⇨ EUPHEMISM, TERM OF ABUSE.

📄 *Slang and Euphemism* (R. A. Spears), Middle Village NY, 1981.

syllabary

A system of graphic characters in a conventional sequence, used for the written representation of speech. Each character in a syllabic system, e.g. Japanese kana or Sanskrit Devanāgarī, normally represents one syllable.

syllabication

⇨ SYLLABIFICATION.

syllabification

The division of words into phonic SYLLABLES and their written representation in (or by) graphic syllables, for the purposes of memorisation or HYPHENATION.

syllable

A unit of PHONOLOGY consisting of one vowel sound or a combination of a vowel with one or more consonants. In syllabic scripts such as Korean, each grapheme represents a syllable (SYLLABOGRAPHY). These graphemes also form the basis for arranging information in the dictionary.

📄 *Phonetic Lexicon of Monosyllabic and some Disyllabic Words with Homophones, Arranged According to their Phonetic Structure* (D. Rockey), London & New York NY, 1973.

syllabography

A writing system using SYLLABLE-based graphic signs.

symbol

A visual or verbal SIGN used to represent a meaning or a sound. Examples include a picture representing an event, a term representing a concept, a grapheme representing a phoneme. In reference works, graphic symbols are used to abbreviate content (e.g. as grammar codes) and to guide the user (e.g. ordering devices).

⇨ PICTOGRAPHIC SYMBOL, SEMIOTICS.

📖 Svensén 1993.

synchronic dictionary

A dictionary which concentrates on the contemporary language, in contrast to a DIACHRONIC DICTIONARY which traces the origins and developments of words through one or more periods in the history of the language.

📖 Landau 1984, Svensén 1993, Béjoint 1994.

synonym

One of two or more words or phrases characterised by SYNONYMY (1).

synonym dictionary

A type of REFERENCE WORK which contains information on words or phrases grouped by semantic similarity. Such dictionaries fulfil a need for those engaged in encoding tasks by offering lexical choices for expressing a certain meaning. The synonyms may be arranged in alphabetical or thematic order, the latter usually with an alphabetical index (THESAURUS); they may be simply listed (CUMULATIVE SYNONYMY) or have meaning discrimination (DISTINCTIVE SYNONYMY).

📖 Landau 1984, van Sterkenburg 1992, Svensén 1993.

📄 *A Dictionary of Selected Synonyms in the Principal European Languages* (C. D. Buck), Chicago IL, 1949; *The Penguin Dictionary of English Synonyms and Antonyms* (R. Fergusson), Harmondsworth, 1986; *The Oxford Thesaurus. An A–Z Dictionary of Synonyms* (L. Urdang), Oxford, 1991.

synonym essay
⇨ SYNONYMY (2).

synonym finder
An informal term for SYNONYM DICTIONARY.
📃 *The Synonym Finder* (J. I. Rodale), New York NY, 1978.

synonymic definition
An explanation of a word or phrase by means of a SYNONYM.
⇨ DEFINITION STYLE.

synonymy
1 The SENSE RELATION obtaining between the members of a pair or group of words or phrases whose meanings are similar. This definition leaves out of account the degree and nature of the meaning similarity. 'Complete' ('absolute', 'strict' or 'total') synonymy is impossible as no two words ever have exactly the same sense in terms of denotation, connotation, formality or currency, but 'partial' ('relative', 'loose', 'quasi-' or 'pseudo-') synonyms can be substituted for each other in some contexts, e.g. *able, capable, competent, qualified.* Synonyms are said to be more common in the BASIC VOCABULARY than in technical terminology, but in the latter pairs, or even multiples, of words with (almost) identical denotation can be found, e.g. the terms *meaning discrimination, meaning differentiation, meaning distinction, sense discrimination* and *sense distinction* in semantics and lexicography.

General dictionaries provide information on synonymous expressions, either in entries (as a space-saving alternative to an explanatory DEFINITION) or in the form of supplementary essays on synonym groups (see 2 below). Specialised dictionaries offer additional guidance, e.g. through the SYNONYM DICTIONARY or the thematic THESAURUS.
📖 Jackson 1988, Hartmann 1990, ISO 1990, Svensén 1993, Gouws 1996.
📃 *The Synonym Finder* (J. I. Rodale), New York NY, 1978.
2 A display of synonym relations, in the form of essays in the general dictionary in the style of a DISTINCTIVE SYNONYMY.
📖 Hausmann 1990.

synset
⇨ WORDNET

syntactic code
⇨ GRAMMATICAL CODE.

syntactic construction
⇨ CONSTRUCTION.

syntactic information
⇨ GRAMMATICAL INFORMATION.

syntactic valency
⇨ VALENCY.

syntagmatic dictionary
A cover term for dictionaries with information on COLLOCATIONS, CONSTRUCTIONS, FIXED EXPRESSIONS, PHRASES etc.
⇨ PHRASEOLOGICAL DICTIONARY.

syntagmatic information
⇨ PHRASEOLOGICAL INFORMATION.

syntagmatic relation
The relationship between words or phrases which is based on grammatical sequencing rather than semantic choice, e.g. syntactic relations such as COLLOCATIONS, CONSTRUCTIONS, FIXED EXPRESSIONS, IDIOMS, PHRASES or SENTENCES. This relationship is one of three dimensions in SEMIOTICS.
⇨ PARADIGMATIC RELATION, PHRASEOLOGICAL DICTIONARY, PRAGMATIC RELATION (2).
📖 DeStadler 1992, Svensén 1993.

syntagmatics
⇨ SYNTAGMATIC RELATION (2).

syntax
A branch of GRAMMAR concerned with the compatibility of WORDS within sentences and texts.
⇨ GRAMMATICAL INFORMATION.
📖 Cowie 1987b.

systematic arrangement
⇨ SYSTEMATIC ORDER.

systematic dictionary
⇨ ONOMASIOLOGICAL DICTIONARY.

systematic order
The principle of arranging items thematically within a CONCEPTUAL SYSTEM of a subject field.

⇨   ORGANISATION.

📖 ISO 1990.

systemic lexicography

An approach to lexicography based on a coherent linguistic model.

⇨   EXPLANATORY DICTIONARY.

📖 Apresjan 1992.

system of concepts

⇨   CONCEPTUAL SYSTEM.

T

table
A device for presenting INFORMATION, e.g. statistics, in LISTS or grids.

table of contents
A LIST of the headings of the component parts of a printed publication. In reference books, this is usually placed in the FRONT MATTER or BACK MATTER, and indicates part of the external SEARCH PATH.
⇨ INDEX, MENU.

taboo word
A word, phrase or name the use of which is considered unacceptable for social reasons, e.g. sacred or sexual expressions. Avoidance strategies include ABBREVIATION, EUPHEMISM and PARAPHRASE.
⇨ FOUR-LETTER WORD.
📖 Gates 1992.

tag
A symbol, code or abbreviated term used to mark the part of speech or other syntactic or semantic information of a particular word or phrase in a CORPUS.

tagger
A computer program for automatic TAGGING.

tagging
The analysis of words and phrases in terms of their grammatical or semantic characteristics. Tagging constitutes an important stage in the preparation of a text CORPUS for concordancing, lemmatisation etc.
⇨ PARSING.
📖 Kiefer *et al.* 1992, Milton & Chowdhury 1994.

target group
The intended readership of a reference work.
⇨ USER.

target language
1 In TRANSLATION, the language into which a SOURCE LANGUAGE text is to be translated.
⇨ ACTIVE DICTIONARY, BIDIRECTIONAL DICTIONARY.
2 In language teaching, the language which the learner is aiming to master ('L2'), as opposed to the native or 'source' language ('L1').
⇨ BILINGUAL DICTIONARY, INTERLANGUAGE.

target user
⇨ USER.

taxonomy
The creation and use of principles for the CLASSIFICATION of terms and concepts.
⇨ FOLK TAXONOMY, NOMENCLATURE, TYPOLOGY.
📖 Barrière & Popowich 1996.

technical dictionary
A type of REFERENCE WORK devoted to the description of the TECHNICAL LANGUAGE of a specialised subject discipline. As the 'technicality' of a field varies according to the expert knowledge of the user, such dictionaries can display a wide range of formats. In the GENERAL DICTIONARY or the LEARNER'S DICTIONARY, technical information may be included in the form of simplified explanations, with or without a controlled DEFINING VOCABULARY. In so-called LSP DICTIONARIES a semi-technical vocabulary caters to relative neophytes or advanced learners, while in the TERMINOLOGICAL DICTIONARY for experts, relatively standardised terms are treated in their systematic conceptual contexts. Often, however, dictionaries (like this *Dictionary of Lexicography*) must compromise for mixed user groups.
⇨ SPECIALISED DICTIONARY.
📖 Béjoint 1988, Heltai 1988, ISO 1990, Opitz 1990, Bergenholtz & Tarp 1995.

▤ *Routledge German Technical Dictionary/
Universal-Wörterbuch der Technik Englisch*, London, 1995.

technicality label
⇨ SUBJECT LABEL.

technical language
A language variety, especially its VOCABULARY, as used in a specialised field of activity such as a scientific or applied discipline. In popular parlance, technical words are often considered unnecessary JARGON, but in the pursuit of ever-increasing specialisation, experts develop (and sometimes standardise) a TERMINOLOGY to reflect the conceptual distinctions they make. When the emphasis is on the teaching of the lexical and stylistic features of such registers, the term LANGUAGE FOR SPECIFIC PURPOSES is also used, and LSP LEXICOGRAPHY for the complex of activities concerned with the reference works that codify them.
⇨ TECHNICAL LEXICOGRAPHY.
�<book> Sager *et al.* 1980, Svensén 1993.

technical lexicography
A complex of activities concerned with the design, compilation, use and evaluation of TECHNICAL DICTIONARIES. Depending on the target users of such reference works, i.e. the general reader or language learner or subject specialist, the compilation is carried out from the perspectives of JARGON, LANGUAGE FOR SPECIFIC PURPOSES or TERMINOLOGY.

technical term
⇨ TERM.

technical vocabulary
1 The words or phrases used as TERMS in a subject field.
2 A specialised GLOSSARY.
    ⇨ TERMINOLOGY (3).

technolect
The TECHNICAL LANGUAGE of a particular subject field.

TEI
Abbreviation for TEXT ENCODING INITIATIVE.

telematics
A combination of television, broadcasting, information technology and other means of telecommunication. This technology can be harnessed for both the making and consultation of REFERENCE WORKS.

telephone book
⇨ TELEPHONE DIRECTORY.

telephone directory
A type of REFERENCE WORK which gives information on telephone numbers, with or without postal addresses, in order of personal or institutional subscribers' names. Classified telephone books are often called YELLOW PAGES.

telescoping
⇨ BLENDING.

teletext
A system which allows access to textual information broadcast by means of television.

television
A result of the fourth major COMMUNICATIVE SHIFT, which provides access to broadcast pictures and sound. Advances in technology allow choices for multi-channel programming and reception, promising an explosion in the number of MULTIMEDIA reference environments.
�<book> Thompson 1992b.
▤ *The Television Industry: A Historical Dictionary* (A. Slide), New York NY, 1991.

temporal information
⇨ DIACHRONIC INFORMATION.

temporal label
A REGISTER LABEL used to mark a word or phrase as belonging to a particular PERIOD.
�<book> Landau 1984.

term
A word, phrase or alphanumeric symbol used by the practitioners of a specialised technical subject to designate a CONCEPT. Within the TERMINOLOGY of the whole field, the unity between term and concept is claimed to be an essential requirement of unambiguous communication, strengthened by agreed definitions and the avoidance of synonymous expressions. Sometimes international, and even interlingual, STANDARDISATION

is possible, and the results are recorded in TER-MINOLOGICAL DICTIONARIES and TERMINOLOGICAL DATABASES.

⇨ COMPLEX TERM, COMPOUND TERM, SIMPLE TERM.

📖 Cluver 1989a, ISO 1990, Sager 1990, Varantola 1992.

term bank

⇨ TERMINOLOGICAL DATABASE.

term identification

The determination of the ACCEPTABILITY RATING of technical vocabulary excerpted from a CORPUS.

📖 ISO 1990.

terminographer

One who engages in TERMINOGRAPHY.

⇨ COMPILER PERSPECTIVE, REFERENCE PROFESSIONAL.

terminography

A complex of activities concerned with the design, compilation, use and evaluation of TERMINOLOGICAL DICTIONARIES. The term 'terminography', coined on the analogy of *lexicology:lexicography* :: *terminology:terminography*, is tending to replace the older term 'terminological lexicography'.

⇨ CODIFICATION, GENERAL THEORY OF TERMINOLOGY, TERMINOLOGY, Panel 'Terminological versus General Lexicography' (below).

📖 Knowles 1988, 1990, Cluver 1989a, ISO 1990, Bergenholtz & Tarp 1995.

📖 *Dictionary of Terminography/Terminografiewoordeboek* (A. D. de V. Cluver), Pretoria, 1989.

terminological analysis

The study of conceptual and terminological networks in TERMINOLOGY.

📖 ISO 1990.

terminological bank

⇨ TERMINOLOGICAL DATABASE.

terminological concordance

A CONCORDANCE of technical terms from one or more subject fields.

terminological data

DATA used as a basis for selecting and codifying information categories in TERMINOLOGICAL DICTIONARIES.

📖 ISO 1990.

terminological database

A computerised database, often multilingual, of the technical TERMS of one or more subject fields. Examples of nationally based term banks are TERMIUM in Canada, LEXIS in Germany and NORMATERM in France; international databases include the European Union's EURODICAUTOM.

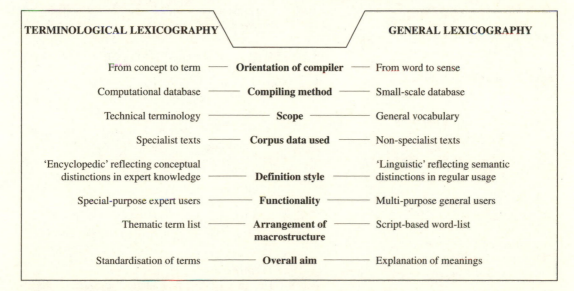

TERMINOLOGICAL LEXICOGRAPHY		GENERAL LEXICOGRAPHY
From concept to term	Orientation of compiler	From word to sense
Computational database	Compiling method	Small-scale database
Technical terminology	Scope	General vocabulary
Specialist texts	Corpus data used	Non-specialist texts
'Encyclopedic' reflecting conceptual distinctions in expert knowledge	Definition style	'Linguistic' reflecting semantic distinctions in regular usage
Special-purpose expert users	Functionality	Multi-purpose general users
Thematic term list	Arrangement of macrostructure	Script-based word-list
Standardisation of terms	Overall aim	Explanation of meanings

Terminological versus General Lexicography

terminological dictionary

A type of REFERENCE WORK which provides information about the language (especially the VOCABULARY) of a specialist field as defined by its practitioners. In addition to the usual problems of DICTIONARY-MAKING, several questions need to be addressed (here answered with special reference to this *Dictionary of Lexicography*):

> Is the dictionary monolingual or interlingual? *Monolingual (English).*
> Is it subject- or text-specific?
> *Based on the literature of the whole field, with glimpses of relevant neighbouring disciplines.*
> What is the format and readership?
> *Relatively independent entries, with encyclopedic definitions, examples and cross-references, as determined by a limited survey of potential specialist and non-expert users.*
> Is standardisation of the TERMINOLOGY an explicit aim?
> *There are few precedents to draw on, but decisions on preferred or less acceptable alternative terms had to be made, based on the personal judgements of the two authors.*

⇨ ACCEPTABILITY RATING, LEXICOGRAPHY, THESAURUS (2).

📖 Cluver 1989a, ISO 1990, Bergenholtz & Tarp 1995.

📑 *Bekleidungswörterbuch/Dictionary of Garment Terminology/Dictionnaire de l'habillement/ Dizionario della terminologia dell'abbigliamento* (G. Rebmann), Berlin, 1990.

terminological entry
⇨ RECORD.

terminological format

The microstructure of the terminological RECORD.

terminological glossary
⇨ GLOSSARY.

terminological lexicography
⇨ TERMINOGRAPHY.

terminological record
⇨ RECORD.

terminological standardisation

The process and result of the STANDARDISATION of terms and the principles governing their codification.

📖 ISO 1990.

terminologist

One who engages in the theory and/or practice of TERMINOLOGY.

⇨ COMPILER PERSPECTIVE, REFERENCE PROFESSIONAL.

terminology

1 A field concerned with the theory and practice of coining, documenting and explaining technical TERMS in general and their use in particular fields of specialisation. Since the 1930s, terminologists have focused on the improvement of interdisciplinary and interlingual communication by means of systematic CONCEPT formation and agreed definitions of the vocabulary of various TECHNICAL LANGUAGES. Interestingly, these efforts have been associated more often with engineers, translators and computer specialists than, say, linguists and lexicographers, and there is no unanimity concerning the underlying principles.

Terminologists have sometimes claimed a rigid division between 'technical' discourse and non-technical or 'general' language, deprecated the use of synonymous expressions, and stipulated that the creation of TERMS (and their translation equivalents) can be regulated prescriptively. With the support of information technology, international organisations (e.g. EURODICAUTOM) and multinational companies have built up large-scale TERMINOLOGICAL DATABASES which codify terminological systems across a range of disciplines and languages.

⇨ GENERAL THEORY OF TERMINOLOGY, GENERAL LEXICOGRAPHY (1).

📖 Riggs 1989, ISO 1990, Knowles 1990, Nedobity 1990, Sager 1990, Bergenholtz & Tarp 1995.

📑 *Dictionary of Terminology/Terminografie-woordeboek* (A. Cluver), Pretoria, 1989.

2 The principles governing the design, compilation, use and evaluation of TERMINOLOGICAL DICTIONARIES.

⇨ TERMINOGRAPHY.

3 A structured list of the vocabulary of a technical subject field, e.g. in the form of a GLOSSARY.

Terminology

The title of an international journal, published since 1994.

terminology extraction

The EXCERPTION of terminological data from a CORPUS.

📖 Bourigault *et al.* 1996.

terminology science

A cover term for GENERAL THEORY OF TERMI-NOLOGY and SPECIAL THEORY OF TERMINOLOGY.

terminology standard

⇨ STANDARD (2).

terminology work

⇨ TERMINOLOGY.

term list

In systems of TERMINOLOGY, the list of technical words and phrases from a specific field, which serves as a basis for collecting and locating the information in entries or RECORDS.

⇨ WORD-LIST.

📖 ISO 1990.

term of abuse

A word or phrase intended to insult or cause offence, often in the form of a VULGARISM, OBSCENITY or SWEAR WORD.

⇨ ETHNOPHAULISM, RACISM.

📖 McCluskey 1989, Hauptfleisch 1993, Harteveld & van Niekerk 1996.

📑 *Dictionary of Insults*, London, 1995.

term of address

⇨ FORM OF ADDRESS.

tertium comparationis

In CONTRASTIVE LINGUISTICS, a common dimension used as a basis for comparing equivalent items across languages.

📖 Hartmann 1991.

text

A relatively complete and self-contained unit of written or spoken language, such as a conversation, a poem or a report. Texts may also themselves be composed of constituent texts, e.g. a book of poetry or a film. Collections of texts in the form of CORPORA document language by bringing together representative samples from different text types or GENRES.

By considering dictionaries and other reference works as textual discourse, such issues as 'authorship', 'functionality', internal 'cohesion', and 'readership' can be addressed, which in turn may help to raise standards of CRITICISM, COMPILA-TION and use.

⇨ DICTIONARIES AS DISCOURSE, DISCOURSE ANALYSIS, HYPERTEXT, TELETEXT, TEXT COMPRES-SION.

📖 Dolezal 1989, Steele 1990, Wiegand 1990, Webster 1992, Biber *et al.* 1994, Flowerdew & Tong 1994, Stubbs 1996.

textbook

An introductory or advanced source book for TRAINING. There is still a relative shortage of such materials for lexicography and related fields.

⇨ PROFESSIONAL RESOURCES.

📖 Zgusta 1971, Hartmann 1983, Landau 1984, Ilson 1985, 1986a, Cluver 1989a, Sager 1990, Svensén 1993.

📑 *Wörterbücher/Dictionaries/Dictionnaires* (F. J. Hausmann *et al.*), Berlin, 1989–91.

text compression

The condensation of the text material presented in reference works, often motivated by the need to save space. Features include the use of CROSS-REFERENCES, a lack of repetition or redundancy, the use of abbreviations and symbols, and a telegraphic style of discourse.

The user needs to develop appropriate REFER-ENCE SKILLS to cope with these complexities, and an awareness of the various ACCESS STRUCTURES used and SEARCH PATHS provided.

⇨ DICTIONARESE, DICTIONARIES AS DISCOURSE, READABILITY.

📖 Wiegand 1996.

text condensation

⇨ TEXT COMPRESSION.

text corpus

⇨ CORPUS.

Text Encoding Initiative

Internationally agreed guidelines for the creation and interchange of machine-readable text.

⇨ STANDARD GENERALIZED MARK-UP LAN-GUAGE, TAGGING.

text lexicography

⇨ TEXT-SPECIFIC LEXICOGRAPHY.

text linguistics

A branch of LINGUISTICS concerned with the study of language as TEXT.

⇨ CORPUS LINGUISTICS, DISCOURSE ANALYSIS.

textography
⇨ CODIFICATION.

text processing
The electronic collection, manipulation, storage and presentation of texts.
⇨ CORPUS, PARSING, TAGGING.
📖 DANLEX Group 1987, Kiefer *et al*. 1992.

text-specific dictionary
A type of reference work based on a single TEXT (e.g. Homer's *Iliad*) or a collection of texts within a field of specialisation (e.g. venery, heraldry).
⇨ AUTHOR'S DICTIONARY, GENRE.
📄 *Lexicon of the Medieval German Hunt* (D. Dalby), Berlin, 1965.

text-specific lexicography
A complex of activities concerned with the design, compilation, use and evaluation of TEXT-SPECIFIC DICTIONARIES.

text type
⇨ GENRE.

textual book structure
⇨ MEGASTRUCTURE.

textuality label
⇨ DIATEXTUAL INFORMATION.

textual segmentation
The division of a dictionary or other reference work into its functional components, e.g. FRONT MATTER, WORD-LIST, BACK MATTER.
📖 Hausmann & Wiegand 1989.

theatre lexicography
A complex of activities concerned with the design, compilation, use and evaluation of dictionaries of dramatic art.
📖 Trapido 1980–1.
📄 *The Dictionary of Performing Arts in Australia* (A. Atkinson *et al*.) St Leonard's, 1996.

thematic arrangement
⇨ THEMATIC ORDER.

thematic dictionary
A type of REFERENCE WORK which uses THEMATIC ORDER as an organising principle, e.g. a THESAURUS or an ENCYCLOPEDIC DICTIONARY.
⇨ ONOMASIOLOGICAL DICTIONARY.

thematic lexicography
A complex of activities concerned with the design, compilation, use and evaluation of THEMATIC DICTIONARIES.
📖 McArthur 1986b, Jackson 1988.

thematic order
The systematic ARRANGEMENT of information in a reference work according to classes of topics.
⇨ ONOMASIOLOGICAL DICTIONARY, ORGANISATION, THESAURUS.

theoretical lexicography
⇨ THEORY OF LEXICOGRAPHY.

theoretical linguistics
⇨ LINGUISTICS.

theoretical terminology
⇨ THEORY OF TERMINOLOGY.

theory of lexicography
The academic study of LEXICOGRAPHY, its principles and research methods.
⇨ GENERAL LEXICOGRAPHY (1), SPECIAL LEXICOGRAPHY, Panel 'Lexicography: Theory and Practice' (page 86).
📖 Geeraerts 1989.

theory of terminology
A cover term for GENERAL THEORY OF TERMINOLOGY and SPECIAL THEORY OF TERMINOLOGY.
📖 ISO 1990.

thesauri
The Latin plural form of THESAURUS, interchangeable in English with *thesauruses*.

thesaurus
1 A type of REFERENCE WORK which presents the vocabulary of a language, language variety or subject discipline by systematically tracing synonym networks between words within semantic domains. The title *thesaurus* signifying a 'lexical storehouse' has been in use for a long time for large (sometimes polyglot) dictionaries. The earliest dictionaries of this type were rooted in Latin, e.g. Robert Estienne's *Dictionarium, seu Latinae linguae thesaurus* (Paris, 1531) and Thomas Cooper's Latin–English *Thesaurus linguae Romanae et Britannicae* (with an appendix of proper names and proverbs, London, 1565). In its modern

sense, the term is associated with Peter Roget's thematically arranged *Thesaurus of English Words and Phrases*, a synonym list first published in London in 1852, which was influenced by the classifications of the universalist philosopher John Wilkins. This work was a CUMULATIVE SYNONYMY rather than a DISTINCTIVE SYNONYMY: it merely listed and classified (rather than defined and discriminated) words of similar sense. It was designed as a system of grouped synonyms to assist writers' 'word-finding' and thus laid the foundations for modern THESAURUS LEXICOGRAPHY.

Access to the word-list in such systematic compilations is via an INDEX (Roget's *Thesaurus* did not have an alphabetical index in its first edition). Alternatively, the whole thesaurus can be designed as a SYNONYM DICTIONARY in A–Z format, each entry containing a set of discriminated or undefined words related in meaning, such as L. Urdang's *Oxford Thesaurus* (Oxford, 1991) or J. I. Rodale's *Synonym Finder* (New York NY, 1978). There are also HYBRID forms in combination with general dictionaries (such as W. T. McLeod's *Collins Dictionary and Thesaurus in One Volume* (London & Glasgow, 1987) which splits each page into a traditional dictionary section and a thesaurus section from the corresponding part of the alphabet). Thesauruses also exist for particular PERIODS of a language or for the written work of a particular author.
⇨ WORD-FINDING DICTIONARY.
   📖 McArthur 1986a, 1986b, Marello 1990, Hüllen 1994, Piotrowski 1994b.
   📄 *Longman Lexicon of Contemporary English* (T. McArthur), Harlow, 1981; *Dickson's Word Treasury: A Connoisseur's Collection of Old and New, Weird and Wonderful, Useful and Outlandish Words* (P. Dickson), New York NY, 1992; *Cambridge Word Routes Anglais–Français* (M. McCarthy), Cambridge, 1994.

2 In TERMINOLOGICAL LEXICOGRAPHY, a monolingual or multilingual alphabetical and/or systematic index of standardised key terms in a specialised field to facilitate access to a DATABASE. Depending on the range of specialisation, a distinction can be made between 'macrothesaurus' and 'microthesaurus'.
   📖 Cluver 1989a, Sager 1990.
   📄 *Root Thesaurus* [3rd edition] (British Standards Institution), Milton Keynes, 1988; *The Musaurus: A Music Thesaurus: A New Approach to Organising Music Information* (A. Harold & G. Lea), London, 1991; *Thesaurus of Psychological Index Terms* (A. Walker), Arlington VA, 1991.

thesaurus-cum-dictionary
⇨ HYBRID.

thesaurus lexicography
A complex of activities concerned with the design, compilation, use and evaluation of THESAURUSES. There is no unified framework except the intention to help users with encoding tasks, which involves the grouping of words and phrases into sets of (near-)synonyms so that the most appropriate items can be chosen to express a particular concept.
⇨ ONOMASIOLOGY.
   📖 Ravin *et al.* 1990, Hüllen 1994.

thinking-aloud protocol
In USER RESEARCH, a technique of tracing the mental processes at work during the act of CONSULTATION. This involves the user verbalising and recording the decisions taken during the search for required information in performing a task such as translating or reading a text with the aid of a dictionary.
⇨ DIARY (2), USER STRATEGIES.
   📖 Lam 1994.

threshold level
A minimal proficiency in language for performing basic communicative tasks, particularly associated with Council of Europe initiatives in developing graded objectives for LANGUAGE TEACHING.
⇨ BASIC VOCABULARY.
   📖 van Ek 1988.

thumb index
A series of notches in the fore-edges of the pages of a reference work, which act as STRUCTURAL INDICATORS to assist the user in finding the required section of the word-list.

tilde
⇨ REPETITION SYMBOL.

time register label
⇨ TEMPORAL LABEL.

title
A word or phrase used as an identifying NAME for a dictionary or other reference work. Terms such as 'dictionary', 'thesaurus' and 'encyclopedia' and

Language	Title	Translation	Author	Year
Greek	*Onomasticon*	name book	Julius Pollux	3rd c.
Greek	*Lexicon*	word book	?	4th c.
Latin	*Catholicon*	universal	Giovanni Balbi	13th c.
Latin	*Campus florum*	field of flowers	Thomas Wallensis	1335
Latin	*(H)ortus*	garden	?	15th c.
Eng/Lat.	*Promptorium*	storehouse	Galfridus Anglicus	1440
Latin	*Elegantiae*	fine words	Lorenzo de Valla	1444
Latin	*Aggregator*	increaser	Jacobus Dondi	1470
Ger./It.	*Porta*	gateway	Adam von Rottweil	1477
Latin	*Elucidarius*	enlightener	Hermannus Torrentinus	1498
Fr./Eng.	*Esclarcissement*	enlightener	John Palsgrave	1530
Latin	*Thesaurus*	treasurehouse	Robert Estienne	1531
Lat./Fr.	*Dictionarium*	book of words	Robert Estienne	1538
Lat./Gre. Fr.	*Nomenclator*	classifier	Adrianus Junius	1567
Lat./Eng.	*Manipulus vocabulorum*	bundle of words	Peter Levins	1570
Eng./Lat./Fr.	*Alvearie*	beehive	John Baret	1573
Eng./Lat.	*Sylva*	wood	Simon Pelegromius	1580
Lat./Eng.	*Bibliotheca*	library	John Rider	1589
Eng./It.	*Worlde of Words*		John Florio	1598
Lat./Eng.	*Medulla*	marrow	?	15th c.
Lat./Eng.	*Calliepeia*	Calliope (the muse)	Thomas Draxe	1612
English	*Expositor*	explainer	John Bullokar	1616
English	*Dictionary*		Henry Cockeram	1623
Latin	*Encyclopedia*	circle	Joannes Alstedius	1629
English	*Glossographia*	glossary	Thomas Blount	1656
Latin	*Etymologicon*	book of etymology	Gerhard Vossius	1662
Lat./Eng.	*Abecedary*	ABC	Thomas Hunt	1671
Latin	*Antibarbarus*	anti-barbarism	Johann Seybold	1676
English	*Parnassus*	Parnassus (the mountain of the gods)	Joshua Poole	1677
Pers./It./Lat./Fr.	*Gazophylacium*	treasure-chest	Angelus a Sancto Josepho	1684
English	*Cyclopaedia*	circle	Ephraim Chambers	1728
English	*Word bank*		Sophie Basescu	1949
English	*Reversicon*		Jacob Schmidt	1965
Hawis/Eng.	*Finderlist*		James Tharp	1976
Inupiaq	*Pictionary*		Martha Aiken	1977
English	*Descriptionary*		Mark McCutcheon	1992
English	*Language activator*		Michael Rundell	1993
English	*Factopedia*		Anna Kruger	1995
English	*Cyberpedia*		?	1997

A Selection of European Dictionary Titles

their equivalents in many other languages derive from metaphorical expressions suggesting such notions as 'bundle', 'storehouse', 'ocean', 'garden', 'key to enlightenment' etc.

⇨ Panel 'A Selection of European Dictionary Titles' (page 144).

title page
The initial part of the FRONT MATTER designating the topic or theme of the work. The right-hand page ('recto') typically includes the title itself, the sub-title, author(s) or editor(s) etc., name of publisher and place of publication; the reverse page ('verso') typically includes the name of the printer and publisher, the book number, the date of publication and history of the edition, and copyright and cataloguing details. Sometimes the information given on the title page does not correspond to that on the outer cover.

⇨ IMPRINT.

token
An instance of a graphic word occurring in a given CORPUS. FREQUENCY COUNTS are typically cited in numbers of tokens, e.g. one million word forms (tokens) in running English text will represent only about 27,000 different words ('types'), as many words (e.g. *the*, *of*, *a*, *to*, *is*, *and*) occur with very high frequency.

⇨ HAPAX LEGOMENON, TYPE (2).

📖 ISO 1990.

tone
⇨ PROSODIC FEATURE.

topic
The subject matter of a text, often summarised in the form of a title, e.g. of a book. In the ENTRY of a reference work, the topic is typically indicated by the HEADWORD, and the information provided may be considered a COMMENT on it.

⇨ BASE STRUCTURE, DEFINITION, FORM (1), LEMMA.

📖 Hausmann & Wiegand 1989.

topical arrangement
⇨ THEMATIC ORDER.

topical order
⇨ THEMATIC ORDER.

topographic(al) dictionary
A type of reference work which provides encyclopedic information on a particular place or region.

⇨ CULTURAL ATLAS, GEOGRAPHICAL INFORMATION.

topographic(al) filing
⇨ GEOGRAPHICAL FILING.

topolect
The variety of a language, specifically its VOCABULARY, associated with a particular geographical location.

⇨ REGIONALISM.

toponym
The NAME of a geographical location such as a village, town, port or district.

⇨ HYDRONYM.

📖 *Modern Place-Names in Great Britain and Ireland* (A. Room), Oxford, 1983.

toponymy
The study of TOPONYMS.

total synonym
⇨ SYNONYMY (1).

total synonymy
⇨ SYNONYMY (1).

trade directory
⇨ DIRECTORY.

trademark
⇨ TRADE NAME.

trademark term
⇨ TRADE NAME.

trade name
A proprietary symbol or name of a company or product officially registered and thus legally protected. Some trademark terms achieve generic status, and become part of everyday language, e.g. in English *biro*, *hoover*, *xerox*, and there is some debate as to whether such items still enjoy COPYRIGHT protection or can be freely cited in reference works.

📖 Landau 1984, Read 1984.

training
The academic and/or practical instruction of lexicographers and other REFERENCE PROFESSIONALS. Until recently, formal training programmes have largely been confined to publishers' in-house

apprenticeship schemes. Some universities and DICTIONARY RESEARCH CENTRES have begun to provide professionally oriented short courses and degrees, e.g. the Master of Arts in LEXICOGRAPHY at the University of Exeter and comparable programmes at Amsterdam, Barcelona, Lille, Stellenbosch and elsewhere.

⇨ DICTIONARY CULTURE, EUROPEAN LANGUAGE COUNCIL, PROFESSIONAL RESOURCES, USER EDUCATION.

📖 Kipfer 1985, Ilson 1986a, Atkins 1992, Hartmann 1992b.

transcription

1 The process and result of representing spoken language by means of a specific notation system, e.g. the INTERNATIONAL PHONETIC ALPHABET. Phonetic transcription, in which the symbols represent articulatory values, is used in linguistic fieldwork in the collection of evidence on speech features. Phonemic transcription (sometimes also erroneously called 'phonetic transcription'), in which the symbols represent distinct units of the sound system of a particular language, are used in dictionaries to indicate the PRONUNCIATION of words and phrases.

Depending on the degree of PHONOLOGICAL INFORMATION provided, a distinction is sometimes made between 'narrow' (more detailed) and 'broad' (less detailed) transcription.

⇨ RESPELLING, TRANSLITERATION.

📖 Roach 1992, Sobkowiak 1996.

📰 *Phonetic Symbol Guide* (G. K. Pullum & W. A. Ladusaw), Chicago IL, 1986.

2 The representation of words written in one script by means of another, e.g. the Korean or Devanagari scripts represented by the LATIN ALPHABET.

⇨ ROMANISATION, TRANSLITERATION.

📖 ISO 1990.

transfer dictionary

A bilingual ELECTRONIC DICTIONARY used in machine translation.

transferred sense

⇨ FIGURATIVE MEANING.

translated dictionary

A dictionary which is the result of a translation of another dictionary.

⇨ BILINGUALISED DICTIONARY, BRIDGE DICTIONARY, ROOT DICTIONARY (2).

translation

A practical field concerned with the restatement of the written or spoken forms of one language by those of another. Translation is relevant to lexicography in two major respects. Firstly, it is the process by which lexical EQUIVALENTS are codified in bilingual dictionaries. Secondly, in the process of translation, reference needs arise, both factual and linguistic, which the translator attempts to meet *inter alia* by consulting dictionaries and other reference works.

Depending on the degree of cultural and linguistic diversity between the source and target languages, and the communicative purposes of the activity, a distinction can be made between 'literal' translation (based on 'word-for-word' or phrase-by-phrase correspondence) and 'free' translation (or textual adaptation). These purposes may include foreign-language learning, professional interpreting, literary activity or technical publishing. Advances in information technology allow a degree of automation in translation, but machine translation has not yet reached perfection.

⇨ ACTIVE DICTIONARY, PARALLEL TEXTS, PASSIVE DICTIONARY.

📖 Snell-Hornby & Pöhl 1989, Starren & Thelen 1990, Larson 1991, Leemets 1992.

📰 *The Routledge Encyclopedia of Translation Studies* (M. Baker), London, 1998.

translation dictionary

⇨ BILINGUAL DICTIONARY.

translation equivalent

⇨ EQUIVALENT.

translation studies

An academic field concerned with the theory of TRANSLATION and the training of TRANSLATORS.

📖 Varantola 1992.

📰 *An Encyclopedia of Translation Studies, Chinese–English, English–Chinese* (S. W. Chan & D. E. Pollard), Hong Kong, 1995.

translation theory

⇨ TRANSLATION STUDIES.

translator

One who engages in TRANSLATION. Translators are among the most avid users and critics of monolingual as well as bilingual, general as well as specialised dictionaries and other reference works.

▣ *International Who's Who in Translation and Terminology* (Union Latine *et al.*), Nottingham, 1995.

transliteration
The representation of words written in an alphabetic script by means of another, e.g. the Greek alphabet represented by the LATIN ALPHABET.
⇨   ROMANISATION, TRANSCRIPTION.
▢   ISO 1990.

travel guide
⇨   GUIDE.

tree structure
The basic metaphor for displaying hierarchical structures and genetic relationships, e.g. conceptual relations, phrase structures or language families.
⇨   BASE STRUCTURE, ROOT (1).

trilingual dictionary
A type of DICTIONARY which relates the vocabularies of three languages together by translation EQUIVALENTS or other means.
⇨   BILINGUAL DICTIONARY, REVERSIBILITY.
▢   Kernerman 1994.
▣   *Alvearie or Triple Dictionarie* (J. Baret), London, 1573; *Longman English–Chinese–Japanese Photo Dictionary* (M. S. Rosenthal & D. B. Freeman), Hong Kong, 1987.

truncated definition
⇨   FORMULAIC DEFINITION.

two-way dictionary
⇨   BIDIRECTIONAL DICTIONARY.

type
1   A category or genre of REFERENCE WORK which usually, but not necessarily, has a distinct title, e.g. 'general dictionary', 'etymological dictionary', 'terminological dictionary', 'dictionary of personal names', 'thesaurus' etc.
⇨   TYPOLOGY (1), Panel 'Types of Reference Works' (page 148).
2   The individual examples of different words or combinations of words occurring in a given CORPUS.
⇨   HAPAX LEGOMENON, TOKEN.
▢   ISO 1990.
3   A category label for a group of CHARACTERISTICS, e.g. with respect to dictionaries, 'size'

for 'gem', 'compact', 'concise', 'comprehensive' etc.
▢   ISO 1990.

typeface
The design of an inventory of graphic characters in printed form, e.g. Helvetica 10 or Times New Roman 9.

typographic(al) device
⇨   STRUCTURAL INDICATOR.

typographic(al) display
The LAYOUT of the printed page in terms of lines, columns, grids, margins, headings etc.
⇨   TYPOGRAPHY.

typography
A practical field concerned with presenting texts in the form of printed pages. The LAYOUT of the material on the page of a reference work, including the use of different TYPEFACES and styles (e.g. bold or italic) is an important consideration in READABILITY and to help the USER locate required information.
▢   Svensén 1993.
▣   *The Bookman's Glossary* [3rd edition], New York NY, 1951.

typology
1   The classification of dictionaries and other REFERENCE WORKS. A typology based on formal features is termed 'phenomenological', one based on uses in context is termed 'functional'. More specifically, it is possible to distinguish dictionary types (sometimes called 'genres') by size (from 'unabridged' to 'gem'), by coverage ('general' versus 'specialised'), by format ('alphabetical' versus 'thematic'), by medium ('print' versus 'electronic'), by functionality ('active' versus 'passive'), by predominance of INFORMATION CATEGORIES provided (DICTIONARY, THESAURUS, ENCYCLOPEDIA, CATALOGUE etc.), by languages ('monolingual', 'bilingual', 'multilingual'), and by user type ('scholarly', 'learner's', 'translator's' etc.).
   The terminology used to distinguish reference works is extremely fluid; compare for instance the use of GUIDE, HANDBOOK and manual.
⇨   Panel 'Types of Reference Works' (page 148).

Shcherba 1940/95, Landau 1984, Svensén 1993, Béjoint 1994, James 1994a.
Dictionary of Dictionaries (T. Kabdebo), London, 1992.

2 In the context of linguistics, ⇨ LANGUAGE TYPOLOGY.

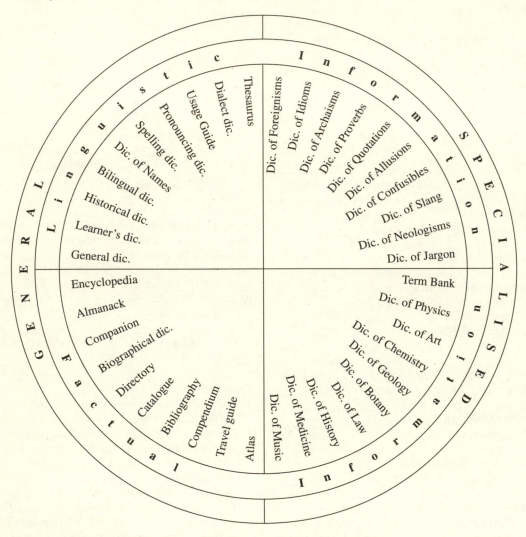

Types of Reference Works

U

unabridged (dictionary)
The largest size in a DICTIONARY FAMILY.
🗐 *Webster's Third New International Dictionary* (P. B. Gove), Springfield MA, 1961 (with Addenda, 1993).

unidirectional dictionary
⇨ MONODIRECTIONAL DICTIONARY.

Uniform Resource Locator
An address for accessing information on the INTERNET.

unilingual dictionary
⇨ MONOLINGUAL DICTIONARY.

union list
An alphabetically, thematically or chronologically arranged catalogue of publications held in a group of libraries.
⇨ LIBRARY UNION DATABASE.
🗐 *Historic English Dictionaries 1559–1899: A Union Catalogue of Holdings in Exeter Libraries* (T. Learmouth & S. Macwilliam), Exeter, 1986; *The South Asia and Burma Retrospective Bibliography* [*Stage 1: 1556–1800*] (G. Shaw), London, 1987.

unmarked
⇨ MARKEDNESS.

upward reference
A CROSS-REFERENCE from a specific (or less comprehensive) to a general heading in a CATALOGUE.

URL
Abbreviation for UNIFORM RESOURCE LOCATOR.

usage
A collective term for various judgements on aspects of language. To observe language in action objectively and without prejudice requires patience, and EVIDENCE which is often not available, e.g. because a comprehensive CORPUS of recorded utterances for a particular text type or situation has not been assembled. Meanwhile subjective linguistic intuition is invoked by those asked to judge a word or phrase as 'correct' or 'appropriate', supplemented by arguments about non-linguistic factors such as 'logic' or 'beauty'. USAGE INFORMATION is collected and presented in the general dictionary (also referred to as 'usage dictionary' because of this), often by using descriptive LABELS or USAGE NOTES and/or by giving example sentences. There are also specialised dictionaries (called USAGE GUIDES) codifying this information in various ways.
⇨ AUTHORITY, CORPUS LINGUISTICS, SOCIOLINGUISTICS, STANDARD (1), USAGE LABEL, USAGE PANEL.
📖 Creswell 1975, Landau 1984, Greenbaum 1988, Algeo 1989a, 1989b, Delbridge 1989, Wadsworth 1989, Gilman 1990, McArthur 1992.

usage dictionary
A type of REFERENCE WORK which describes and illustrates the (usually current) state of a language. The prototype of this dictionary is the popular monolingual GENERAL DICTIONARY. Depending on the compiler's view of, and the user's attitude to, the role of the dictionary in promoting forms which are considered regular, or 'correct', the term STANDARD DICTIONARY is sometimes used for the genre.
⇨ USAGE, USAGE GUIDE.

usage guide
A type of REFERENCE WORK intended to help USERS with encoding tasks such as speaking or writing. Entries are often mini-essays on (unresolved) issues rather than articles on particular

words or phrases. Examples include advice on spelling (e.g. *center* versus *centre*); hyphenation (e.g. *data base* versus *data-base* versus *database*); stress (e.g. *'controversy* versus *con'troversy*); regional usage (e.g. *agricultural show* versus *county fair*); grammar (e.g. split infinitive: *to boldly go* versus *boldly to go*).

⇨ GRAMMAR DICTIONARY, USAGE.

📖 McArthur 1992.

▤ *A Dictionary of Modern English Usage* (H. W. Fowler/rev. E. Gowers/rev. R. Burchfield), Oxford, 1926/65/96; *Oxford English. A Guide to the Language* (J. C. B. Dear), Oxford, 1986; *Longman Guide to English Usage* (S. Greenbaum & J. Whitcut), Harlow, 1988; *Webster's Dictionary of English Usage* (E. W. Gilman), Springfield MA, 1989; *Collins COBUILD English Guides: Reporting* (G. Thompson), London, 1994.

usage information

One of the INFORMATION CATEGORIES presented by the compiler and consulted by the user of the dictionary, based on USAGE. Although objective EVIDENCE on language in action is difficult to obtain, general and specialised dictionaries offer guidance on matters such as SPELLING, GRAMMATICALITY and APPROPRIATENESS in the form of USAGE LABELS, USAGE NOTES or illustrative sentences.

⇨ USAGE GUIDE, USAGE PANEL.

usage label

The marking of a word or phrase as typical or appropriate in a particular context or language variety. General and specialised dictionaries use a range of symbols and abbreviations for some or all of the following: currency or period, e.g. *arch*(*aic*); formality or register, e.g. *inf*(*ormal*); regionality or dialect, e.g. *Am*(*erican*), *York*(*shire*); technicality or subject field, e.g. *bot*(*anical*); textuality or genre, e.g. *poet*(*ic*).

This list is not exhaustive, and some of these distinctions do not have clear boundary lines. Consequently, dictionaries differ widely in the scope and consistency of their labelling practices. Native speakers have an 'intuitive' grasp of these sociolinguistic facts, but they do not always agree. Non-native learners are deemed to need explicit guidance, even warnings, about marginal, e.g. taboo, usages.

⇨ DIASYSTEMATIC LABELLING, USAGE PANEL, Panel 'Usage Labels' (page 151).

📖 Hartmann 1983, Landau 1984, Svensén 1993, Osselton 1995.

usage lexicography

A complex of activities concerned with the design, compilation, use and evaluation of USAGE DICTIONARIES and USAGE GUIDES. There is no unified framework except the intention to help speakers and writers in cases of LINGUISTIC INSECURITY.

usage note

A discursive paragraph providing additional information on a word or phrase, and inserted close to the respective dictionary entry. In GENERAL DICTIONARIES or LEARNER'S DICTIONARIES, usage notes, sometimes specially marked out on the page in boxed panels, draw the reader's attention to synonymous and related words or phrases, explanations of idiomatic expressions, stylistic or other restrictions on USAGE.

📖 Hausmann & Wiegand 1989, Herbst 1990.

usage panel

A group of advisers consulted by compilers or publishers of a dictionary on controversial issues of USAGE. The negative popular reviews of the third edition of *Webster's New International Dictionary of the English Language* (Springfield MA, 1961) prompted the editors of the *American Heritage Dictionary of the English Language* (Boston, 1969) to assemble a panel of 105 experts, whose composition and judgements were in turn criticised, leading to further changes.

⇨ IMAGE OF THE DICTIONARY.

📖 Creswell 1975, Read 1986, Algeo 1990.

Usenet

A network of INTERNET discussion groups.

use of reference works

The totality of activities involved in the CONSULTATION of a dictionary or other reference work.

⇨ FUNCTION, USER PERSPECTIVE, USER RESEARCH.

user

One who engages in the CONSULTATION of a dictionary or other reference work. Research into users' REFERENCE NEEDS and REFERENCE SKILLS (the so-called USER PERSPECTIVE) promises to bring new insights into the various strategies and patterns of use observed, and the DESIGN and FORMAT of reference works appropriate to each.

⇨ USER EDUCATION.

Type of markedness	Dimension of usage	Examples of scales	Popular term for marked vocabulary
DIACHRONIC	currency (period)	archaic/obsolescent (contemporary) new/in vogue	ARCHAISM / NEOLOGISM
DIAEVALUATIVE	emotionality (attitude)	appreciative (neutral) derogatory	EUPHEMISM / VULGARISM
DIAFREQUENTIAL	frequency of occurrence	basic (frequent) rare	CORE WORD / NONCE WORD
DIAINTEGRATIVE	assimilation (contact)	borrowing (national) vernacular	FOREIGNISM / NATIVE WORDS
DIAMEDIAL	mediality (channel)	written (neutral) spoken	WRITING / SPEECH
DIANORMATIVE	normativity (standard)	... (correct) incorrect	HYPERCORRECTION / BARBARISM
DIAPHASIC	formality (register)	elevated/formal (neutral) informal/intimate	CLASSICISM / COLLOQUIALISM
DIASTRATIC	style (social status)	high (neutral) demotic	GENTEELISM / SLANG
DIATECHNICAL	technicality (subject)	... e.g. Botany	JARGON
DIATEXTUAL	textuality (genre)	poetic (neutral) conversational	?
DIATOPIC	regionality (dialect)	... e.g. American	REGIONALISM (Americanism, Briticism, etc.)

Usage Labels

📖 Mufwene 1984, Hartmann 1989, Varantola 1994.

user education

The training of USERS in the development of REFERENCE SKILLS in response to REFERENCE NEEDS. Limited instruction is provided at secondary-school and university level in some syllabuses and coursebooks. The need for greater dictionary awareness is partly catered for by WORKBOOKS, and occasional local workshops for teachers, often sponsored by publishers.

⇨ USER'S GUIDE.

📖 Béjoint 1989.

user needs analysis

⇨ NEEDS ANALYSIS.

user orientation

⇨ USER PERSPECTIVE.

user perspective

An approach that considers LEXICOGRAPHY from the point of view of the USER. Issues to be considered include the status of users, their previous background and experience, their familiarity with available reference works and the look-up strategies required to consult these successfully, and whether deliberate instruction can develop and improve REFERENCE SKILLS.

⇨ COMPILER PERSPECTIVE, TYPOLOGY (1), USER EDUCATION, USER RESEARCH, Panel 'Compiler and User Perspectives' (page 25).

📖 Béjoint 1989, Hartmann 1989, Martin & Al 1990, Starren & Thelen 1990, Battenburg 1991, Bogaards 1992, Nuccorini 1992, 1994, Svensén 1993.

user research

A collective term for a number of methods employed to investigate the REFERENCE NEEDS and REFERENCE SKILLS of users of reference works. The USER PERSPECTIVE is still a relatively underdeveloped specialisation in lexicography, requiring an interdisciplinary approach and a combination of techniques ranging from relatively large-scale (but indirect) opinion polls and questionnaire surveys to more objective (but small-scale) tests and thinking-aloud protocols. Relevant findings are likely to influence DICTIONARY-MAKING and USER EDUCATION.

⇨ USE OF REFERENCE WORKS.

📖 Hartmann 1989, Atkins & Knowles 1990, Stark 1990.

💻 *Bibliography of user studies* (Y. Tono) website: www.u-gakugei.ac.jp/~tefldpt/tonolab/userstudy/index.html

user's guide

Help given to the USER of a particular reference work, either in the FRONT MATTER or as a separate publication (WORKBOOK).

user strategies

A collective term for those mental operations and decisions made by USERS in the process of CONSULTATION, from the selection of the relevant reference work, through appropriate search and retrieval acts, to integration of the information obtained with the original REFERENCE NEEDS.

⇨ SEARCH PATH, USER RESEARCH.

📖 Neubach & Cohen 1988, Laufer & Melamed 1994.

user studies

⇨ USER RESEARCH.

V

vade-mecum
A GUIDE to a subject field.

valency
The bonding potential of words and phrases in sentences, usually in relation to the verb as a syntactic nucleus.
⇨ CONSTRUCTION.
◻ Svensén 1993, Noël *et al.* 1996.

valency dictionary
A specialised GRAMMAR DICTIONARY devoted to information on VALENCY relations.
▤ *Wörterbuch zur Valenz und Distribution deutscher Verben* [5th edition] (G. Helbig & W. Schenkel), Leipzig, 1980.

variant
A form of a word which differs from other forms in SPELLING, PRONUNCIATION or GRAMMAR, e.g. *colour/color*, *'controversy/con'troversy*, *got/gotten*. CANONICAL FORMS are chosen from among several variants of a word or phrase to be cited as HEADWORDS in a dictionary entry, e.g. *open* from *opens*, *opening*, *opened*. Dictionaries and USAGE GUIDES often present variants, explain their existence, and comment on their use.
⇨ LANGUAGE VARIETY, LEMMATISATION.
◻ ISO 1990.

variation
⇨ LANGUAGE VARIETY.

variety
⇨ LANGUAGE VARIETY.

verb
A PART OF SPEECH which serves to express an action or state.

⇨ CONJUGATION, GRAMMATICAL INFORMATION, VALENCY.
◻ McArthur 1992, Svensén 1993.

verbal context
⇨ CONTEXT (1).

verbal illustration
⇨ EXAMPLE.

verification
⇨ AUTHENTICATION.

vernacular
⇨ INDIGENOUS LANGUAGE.

verso
⇨ TITLE PAGE.

visual design
⇨ VISUAL LANGUAGE.

visual dictionary
A type of PICTURE DICTIONARY with vivid illustrations in full colour.
▤ *Facts on File Visual Dictionary* (J.-C. Corbeil & M. Manser), New York NY & Oxford 1988; *Dorling–Kindersley Ultimate Visual Dictionary* (J. Evans), London & New York NY, 1996.

visual language
The totality of systems of communication which rely for their effect on the symbolism and variations in colour, shape, motion etc., exploited in e.g. the DESIGN, LAYOUT and presentation of reference works.
⇨ FILM, ILLUSTRATED DICTIONARY, MULTIMEDIA, PHOTO DICTIONARY, PICTURE DICTIONARY, TYPEFACE, VISUAL DICTIONARY.
◻ Kress & van Leeuwen 1996.

vocabulary

1 The sum total of the words used in a language, by a speaker, or for dictionary-making. Estimates vary as to the size of a language's word-stock (for English alone, it is estimated to be in excess of a billion items); the ACTIVE VOCABULARY or PASSIVE VOCABULARY of individual speakers; or the number of words codified in reference works.

A 'core', or BASIC VOCABULARY is often distinguished from more specialised words and phrases. All languages are ever-changing and variable in different communicative contexts, thus it is convenient to subdivide their vocabularies along such dimensions as DIALECT, IDIOLECT or SUBJECT FIELD, and compile reference works for these varieties. The specialisation of vocabulary for different uses is potentially infinite, but science and technology (TERMINOLOGY), and certain areas of popular social interest, e.g. politics, religion, or sex, are often singled out for lexical treatment in reference works.

⇨ CORE WORD, DEFINING VOCABULARY, LEXEME, LEXICON (1), STANDARD (1) TYPOLOGY, WORD, WORD-LIST.

📖 Béjoint 1988, Jackson 1988, McArthur 1992, Dodd 1993.

📓 *Hierolexicon linguarum orientalium, Hebraicae, Chaldaicae, et Syriacae* (I. Weitenauer), Freiburg, 1759; *Safire's Political Dictionary* (W. Safire), New York NY, 1978; *Eroticon* (R.-H. Zuidinga), The Hague, 1990.

2 A list of words or phrases, with or without definitions. The term 'vocabulary' is often used to refer to early forerunners of the dictionary, such as the GLOSSARY.

📖 Collison 1982, Stein 1985, ISO 1990, Green 1996.

vocabulary control

The deliberate restriction of the type and number of words for pedagogical or lexicographic purposes. Based on the technology of FREQUENCY COUNTS, attempts have been made to determine a basic common core vocabulary that would help children and foreign-language learners to read and acquire words. In LEARNER'S DICTIONARIES this principle has been applied to both the selection and the definition of lexical items.

⇨ CORE WORD, DEFINING VOCABULARY.

📖 Neubauer 1989.

vocabulary selection

⇨ VOCABULARY CONTROL.

vogue word

A NEOLOGISM in fashion for the time being.

⇨ CATCH-PHRASE.

voice synthesis

Electronically generated sound to simulate human speech. This is being used experimentally in helping the visually-impaired to consult reference works.

📖 Law & Sandness 1985.

vulgarism

An obscene or profane word or phrase which provokes shock or embarrassment in polite society.

⇨ FOUR-LETTER WORD.

W

Walford Award
An annual award by the LIBRARY ASSOCIATION for outstanding services to BIBLIOGRAPHY.

war of the dictionaries
⇨ DICTIONARY WAR.

website
⇨ WORLD WIDE WEB.

Wheatley Medal
An annual award by the LIBRARY ASSOCIATION and the SOCIETY OF INDEXERS for an outstanding index.

who's who
A type of REFERENCE WORK which presents information on selected individuals in order of their names.
⇨ BIOGRAPHICAL DICTIONARY, DIRECTORY.
📖 *Who's Who 1997*, London, 1996; *Lexicon Grammaticorum. Who's Who in the History of World Linguistics* (H. Stammerjohann), Tübingen, 1996; *Who's Who in Lexicography* (S. McGill), Exeter, 1996.

word
The basic unit of VOCABULARY. The word can be considered an entity of phonology (speech sounds united by a stress/intonation pattern), orthography (letters united by a spelling/punctuation pattern), grammar (morphemes united by a phrase/sentence pattern) or semantics (senses united by a conceptual pattern). The linguistic approach regards words as 'lexicological' units (LEXEMES), the result of a combination of graphic/phonic 'form' in grammatical 'context' with a semantic 'meaning'. In this lexical guise words are used in reference works to head entries (HEADWORDS) and to explain other words by means of DEFINITIONS. Words have varied origins (ETYMOLOGY), constituent structure (WORD FORMATION, PART OF SPEECH), stylistic associations (e.g. as ARCHAISMS, REGIONALISMS and FOREIGNISMS) and uses (e.g. as technical TERMS).
⇨ BASE, COMPLEX WORD, COMPOUND WORD, ROOT, WORD-LIST.
📖 Jackson 1988, ISO 1990, McArthur 1992, Katamba 1994.

wordbook
An informal term used as a popular alternative for DICTIONARY.
📰 *Human Words: The Compleat Uncomputerized Human Wordbook* (R. Hendrickson), Philadelphia PA, 1972.

word-by-word alphabetisation
A principle of ALPHABETICAL ORGANISATION in which words or phrases are listed in order of their letters, by taking account of word boundaries, in contrast to LETTER-BY-LETTER ALPHABETISATION, which is used in this *Dictionary of Lexicography*. In word-by-word alphabetisation, *lexicalisation* would follow *lexical word*.
📖 Svensén 1993.

word class
⇨ PART OF SPEECH.

word-class dictionary
A type of dictionary which contains GRAMMATICAL INFORMATION on a specific PART OF SPEECH, e.g. adjectives or verbs.
⇨ MORPHOLOGICAL DICTIONARY.
📰 *Cassell Dictionary of Appropriate Adjectives* (E. H. Mikhail), London, 1994; *Grammar Patterns 1: Verbs* (G. Francis), London & Glasgow, 1996.

word-class label
⇨ GRAMMATICAL LABEL.

word count

⇨ FREQUENCY COUNT.

word derivation

⇨ DERIVATION.

word division

⇨ HYPHENATION.

word entry

⇨ ENTRY.

word family

A group of words related by derivational history and/or morphological structure.

📖 Bauer & Nation 1993.

📄 *A German Word Family Dictionary. Together with English Equivalents* (H. H. Keller), Berkeley CA, 1978.

wordfinder

⇨ WORD-FINDING DICTIONARY.

word-finding dictionary

A type of REFERENCE WORK which supplies words for meanings. This is done by inverting the traditional order which explains the meaning of relatively unknown words by easy words (SEMA-SIOLOGY), providing instead access to the more unusual words via easy ones.

⇨ ONOMASIOLOGICAL DICTIONARY.

📄 *Reader's Digest Reverse Dictionary* (J. E. Kahn), London, 1989; *Sisson's Word and Expression Locator* (A. F. Sisson/rev. B. A. Kipfer), Englewood Cliffs NJ, 1994; *Oxford Learner's Wordfinder Dictionary* (H. Trappes-Lomax), Oxford, 1997.

word-finding list

⇨ WORD-FINDING DICTIONARY.

word form

⇨ VARIANT.

word formation

The creation of new words in a language. In English, the following derivational processes can be used: coining a new word (ROOT-CREATION), e.g. *googol*; combining a base with one or more AFFIXES or other morphological elements, e.g. *postmodern*; various forms of ABBREVIATION, e.g. *yuppie*; fusing words (BLENDING), e.g. *brunch*; changing word class (CONVERSION (1)), e.g. *tape* (noun) 'recording' > *to tape* (denominal verb) 'to

record'; BORROWING from another language, e.g. *perestroika* < Russian 'restructuring'; SEMANTIC CHANGE, e.g. the figurative extension from *window* 'fenestral opening' to 'part of computer screen' or 'gap in timetable'.

The results of some of these processes are documented in the general dictionary, and there are specialised reference works such as dictionaries of word-formation elements that cover them in detail.

⇨ LEXEME.

📖 Bauer 1983, Stein 1984, McArthur 1992, Denning & Leben 1995.

📄 *Collins COBUILD English Guides 2: Word Formation* (J. Bradbury), London, 1991.

word-for-word equivalent

⇨ EQUIVALENT.

word frequency

⇨ FREQUENCY.

word game

A form of entertaining competitive activity in which players are involved in the construction, definition, manipulation, selection or use of words. Dictionaries are often turned to for judgements as to the acceptability of solutions, and for some word games (e.g. CROSSWORDS), special dictionaries are available to assist players in their endeavours.

📄 *Vocabulon* [Board game based on dictionary definitions], Paris.

word geography

A specialisation within DIALECT GEOGRAPHY, concerned with the regional distribution of words.

word-list

The basic order in which entries in dictionaries and other reference works are sequenced. The conventional arrangement in English dictionaries is the ALPHABETICAL ORDER of entries, each headed by an appropriate HEADWORD.

⇨ MACROSTRUCTURE.

📖 Landau 1984, Béjoint 1994.

WordNet

An on-line lexical reference system in which English nouns, verbs, adjectives and adverbs are organised into SYNONYM sets ('synsets'), each representing one underlying lexical concept.

📖 Miller 1990, Vossen 1996.

Website: www.cogsci.princeton.edu/~wn/index

word origin
An informal term for ETYMOLOGY.

word-processing
An informal term for TEXT PROCESSING.

word-stock
An informal term for VOCABULARY (1).

word token
⇨ TOKEN.

word type
⇨ TYPE.

workbook
A pedagogic manual developed to enhance users' REFERENCE SKILLS.
⇨ USER EDUCATION.
📖 O'Brien & Jordan 1985, Stark 1990, Berg 1993.
📰 *Making the Most of Dictionaries in the Classroom (A Free Guide for Teachers of English)*, Oxford, n.d.; *Longman Dictionary Skills Handbook* (J. McAlpin), Harlow, 1988.

working language
⇨ OFFICIAL LANGUAGE.

work of reference
⇨ REFERENCE WORK.

work-station
A powerful desk computer with access facilities to telecommunications and specialised reference tools, which can be used for work in dictionary-making and translation.
📖 Picchi *et al.* 1992.

world lexicography
The internationalisation of the reference profession.
⇨ ASSOCIATIONS, PROFESSIONAL RESOURCES.
📖 Ilson 1986a.

World Wide Web
The global electronic information retrieval system. Organisations and individuals can establish 'websites' or information displays. In this *Dictionary of Lexicography*, the website addresses of several relevant bodies are cited.
⇨ INTERNET.

Wörterbücher/Dictionaries/ Dictionnaires
The title of a trilingual three-volume encyclopedia, edited by Franz Josef Hausmann, Oskar Reichmann, Herbert Ernst Wiegand and Ladislav Zgusta (1989–91), containing 337 keynote articles on all aspects of LEXICOGRAPHY.

writer
⇨ AUTHOR.

writer's dictionary
⇨ AUTHOR'S DICTIONARY.

writers' dictionary
⇨ DICTIONARY OF AUTHORS.

writing
The result of the second major COMMUNICATIVE SHIFT, from spoken communication to the graphic representation of language, which allowed the storage and more accurate and widespread transmission of information. This technology helped develop the processing of information in LIST and glossary form, making use of scripts (e.g. alphabetic or logographic) as an organising principle.
⇨ GRAPHEMICS, GRAPHOLOGY.
📖 Gaur 1984, Zgusta 1989b.
📰 *Handbook of Scripts and Alphabets* (G. L. Campbell), London, 1996.

writing system
An inventory of graphic symbols and the rules for their combination, used to represent human language. The totality of these symbols (LETTERS or CHARACTERS) in a particular language is used for giving the user access to the INFORMATION contained in reference works, e.g. the ALPHABETICAL ORGANISATION of entries in a dictionary.
⇨ GRAPHEMICS.
📖 Zgusta 1989b.

written corpus
A systematic collection of samples of written TEXTS, which document the USAGE features of a language or language variety or idiolect.
⇨ BRITISH NATIONAL CORPUS, CORPUS, DISCOURSE ANALYSIS.

written language
⇨ WRITING.

WWW
Abbreviation for WORLD WIDE WEB.

X

XYZ

The last three letters of the LATIN ALPHABET, used to mean the whole alphabet. The term is sometimes found in the titles of primers or introductory works on any subject, as a synonym of 'introductory dictionary'.

⇨ ABC.

▤ *The XYZ of Love* (I. Hengeler & S. Hengeler), New York NY, 1970; *The XYZ of Psychoanalysis: Epilogue to a Great Beginning* (H. Feldman), New York NY, 1991.

Y

yearbook

A type of REFERENCE WORK published in annual editions.

 The Humanities Computing Yearbook 1989–90 (I. Lancashire), Oxford, 1991.

yellow pages®

A TELEPHONE DIRECTORY classified thematically by the industries, trades, occupations and services etc. of the subscribers listed.

Z

zìdiǎn
⇨   CHARACTER DICTIONARY.

Bibliography

Abercrombie, D. (1978) 'The indication of pronunciation in reference books', in P. Strevens (ed.) 119–26.

Ahmad, K. and Collingham, S. (1996) 'Renewable terminology', in M. Gellerstam *et al.* (eds) 759–69.

Ahmad, K., Fulford, H. and Rogers, M. (1992) 'The elaboration of special language terms: the role of contextual examples, representative samples and normative requirements', in H. Tommola *et al.* (eds) 139–49.

Aijmer, K. and Altenberg, B. (eds) (1991) *English Corpus Linguistics. Studies in Honour of Jan Svartvik*, London: Longman. [10 papers by 26 authors.]

Aitchison, J. (1987) *Words in the Mind. An Introduction to the Mental Lexicon*, Oxford: B. Blackwell. [3rd edition 1994.]

Aitken, A. J. (1987) 'The period dictionaries', in R. Burchfield (ed.) 94–116.

Alexander, R. J. (1992) 'Fixed expressions, idioms and phraseology in recent English learner's dictionaries', in H. Tommola *et al.* (eds) 35–42.

Algeo, J. (1989a) 'Dictionaries as seen by the educated public in Great Britain and the USA', in F. J. Hausmann *et al.* (eds) I: 28–34.

—— (1989b) 'The image of the dictionary in the mass media: USA', in F. J. Hausmann *et al.* (eds) I: 34–8.

—— (1990) 'American lexicography', in F. J. Hausmann *et al.* (eds) II: 1987–2009.

—— (ed.) (1995) *Neology Forum*, (thematic issue) *Dictionaries* 16: 1–108. [10 papers by 12 authors.]

Al-Kasimi, A. M. (1992) 'Is the dictionary of quotations a dictionary?', in H. Tommola *et al.* (eds) 573–80.

Allen, K. (1986) *Linguistic Meaning* [2 volumes], London: Routledge.

Allen, R. E. (1996) 'The year of the dictionaries', *English Today* 12, 2: 41–51.

Alvar Ezquerra, M. (ed.) (1992) *EURALEX '90. Proceedings of the 4th International Congress*, Barcelona: Biblograf/VOX. [44 papers by 57 authors.]

Apresjan, J. D. (1992) 'Systemic lexicography', in H. Tommola *et al.* (eds) 3–16.

Atkins, B. T. S. (1992) 'Putting lexicography on the professional map: Training needs and qualifications of career lexicographers', in M. Alvar Ezquerra (ed.) 519–26.

—— (1996) 'Bilingual dictionaries: Past, present and future', in M. Gellerstam *et al.* (eds) 515–46.

Atkins, B. T. S. and Knowles, F. E. (1990) 'Interview report on the EURALEX/AILA Research Project into Dictionary Use', in T. Magay & J. Zigány (eds) 381–92.

Atkins, B. T. S. and Zampolli, A. (eds) (1994) *Computational Approaches to the Lexicon*, Oxford: Oxford University Press. [14 papers by 23 authors.]

Atkins, B. T. S., Kegl, J. and Levin, B. (1988) 'Anatomy of a verb entry: From linguistic theory to lexicographic practice', *International Journal of Lexicography* 1, 2: 84–126.

Ayto, J. R. (1983) 'On specifying meaning. Semantic analysis and dictionary definitions', in R. R. K. Hartmann (ed.) 89–98.

—— (1988) 'Fig. leaves. Metaphor in dictionaries', in M. Snell-Hornby (ed.) 49–54.

—— (1992) 'A minuscule question: Orthography and authority in dictionaries', in H. Tommola *et al.* (eds) 459–64.

Bailey, R. (ed.) (1987) *Dictionaries of English. Prospects for the Record of our Language*, Ann Arbor MI: University of Michigan Press. [9 papers by 9 authors.]

—— (1990) 'The period dictionary III: English', in F. J. Hausmann *et al.* (eds) II: 1436–57.

Baker, M. and Kaplan, R. B. (1993) 'Translated! A new breed of bilingual dictionaries', *Babel* 40, 1: 1–11.

Barnhart, R. K. (1989) 'Dating in etymology', *Dictionaries* 11: 53–63.

Barnhart, R. K. and Barnhart, C. L. (1990) 'The dictionary of neologisms', in F. J. Hausmann *et al.* (eds) II: 1159–66.

Barrière, C. and Popowich, F. (1996) 'Building a noun taxonomy from a children's dictionary', in M. Gellerstam *et al.* (eds) 27–35.

Barsalou, L. W. (1992) 'Frames, concepts, and conceptual fields', in A. Lehrer & E. F. Kittay (eds) 21–74.

Bartholomew, D. (1991) 'Lexicography of the languages of the Mesoamerican Indians', in F. J. Hausmann *et al.* (eds) III: 2697–700.

Bartholomew, D. A. and Schoenhals, L. C. (1983) *Bilingual Dictionaries for Indigenous Languages*, Mexico: Summer Institute of Linguistics/Instituto Lingüístico de Verano.

Barton, D. (1994) *Literacy. An Introduction to the Ecology of Written Language*, Oxford: Blackwell.

Battenburg, J. D. (1991) *English Monolingual Learners' Dictionaries. A User-oriented Study* (Lexicographica Series Maior 39), Tübingen: M. Niemeyer.

Bauer, L. (1983) *English Word-Formation*, Cambridge: Cambridge University Press.

—— (1994) *Watching English Change. An Introduction to the Study of Linguistic Change in Standard Englishes in the Twentieth Century*, Harlow: Longman.

Bauer, L. and Nation, P. (1993) 'Word families', *International Journal of Lexicography* 6, 4: 253–79.

Béjoint, H. (1983) 'On field-work in lexicography: Field dictionaries', in R. R. K. Hartmann (ed.) 67–76.

—— (1988) 'Scientific and technical words in general dictionaries', *International Journal of Lexicography* 1, 4: 354–68.

—— (1989) 'The teaching of dictionary use: Present state and future tasks', in F. J. Hausmann *et al.* (eds) I: 208–15.

—— (1990) 'Monosemy and the dictionary', in T. Magay & J. Zigány (eds) 13–26.

—— (1994) *Tradition and Innovation in Modern English Dictionaries* (Oxford Studies in Lexicography and Lexicology 1), Oxford: Clarendon Press.

Benson, M. (1989) 'The collocational dictionary and the advanced learner', in M. L. Tickoo (ed.) 84–93.

—— (1990) 'Culture-specific items in bilingual dictionaries of English', *Dictionaries* 12: 43–54.

Benson, M., Benson, E. and Ilson, R. F. (1986) *The Lexicographic Description of English* (Studies in Language Companion Series 14), Amsterdam: J. Benjamins.

Berg, D. L. (1993) *A Guide to the Oxford English Dictionary* [*The Essential Companion and User's Guide*], Oxford: Oxford University Press.

Bergenholtz, H. and Tarp, S. (eds) (1995) *Manual of Specialised Lexicography* (Benjamins Translation Library 12), Amsterdam: J. Benjamins. [13 chapters by 7 authors.]

Berkov, V. (1996) 'Passive vs. active dictionary. A revision', in M. Gellerstam *et al.* (eds) 547–50.

Bhatia, V. K. (1993) *Analysing Genre: Language Use in Professional Settings*, Harlow: Longman.

Biagini, L. and Picchi, E. (1996) 'Internet and DBT', in M. Gellerstam *et al.* (eds) 47–53.

Biber, D., Conrad, S. and Reppen, R. (1994) 'Corpus-based approaches in applied linguistics', *Applied Linguistics* 15, 2: 169–89.

Bivens, L. (1982) 'Noah Webster's etymological principles', *Dictionaries* 4: 1–13.

Bogaards, P. (1992) 'French dictionary users and word frequency', in H. Tommola *et al.* (eds) 51–61.

Boguraev, B. K. (ed.) (1991) *Building a Lexicon*, (thematic issue) *International Journal of Lexicography* 4, 3: 163–260. [3 papers by 3 authors.]

Boguraev, B. K. and Briscoe, T. (eds) (1989) *Computational Lexicography for Natural Language Processing*, New York NY: Longman. [10 papers by 16 authors.]

Boguraev, B. K., Briscoe, T., Carroll, J. and Copestake, A. (1992) 'Database models for computational lexicography', in M. Alvar Ezquerra (ed.) 59–78.

Bolinger, D. (1975) *Aspects of Language* [2nd edition], New York NY: Harcourt Brace Jovanovich.

Bool, H. and Carter, R. (1989) 'Vocabulary, culture and the dictionary', in M. L. Tickoo (ed.) 172–83.

Botha, W. (1992) 'The lemmatisation of expressions in descriptive dictionaries', in H. Tommola *et al.* (eds) 465–72.

Bourigault, D., Gonzalez-Mullier, I. and Gros, C. (1996) 'LEXTER, a natural language processing tool for terminology extraction', in M. Gellerstam *et al.* (eds) 771–9.

Bowker, L. (1996) 'Learning from cognitive science: Developing a new approach to classification in terminology', in M. Gellerstam *et al.* (eds) 781–7.

Bradley, D. and McTernan, A. J. (1988) 'Using a computer database to develop and operate an on-line dictionary of neologisms', in M. Snell-Hornby (ed.) 391–400.

Bragina, N. (1996) 'Restricted collocations: Cultural boundness', in M. Gellerstam *et al.* (eds) 199–207.

Brazil, D. (1987) 'Representing pronunciation', in J. Sinclair (ed.) 160–6.

Brewer, A. M. (ed.) (1988) *Dictionaries, Encyclopedias, and other Word-related Books* [4th edition, 2 volumes], Detroit MI: Gale Research Co.

Britto, F. (1986) *Diglossia*: *A Study of the Theory with Application to Tamil*, Washington DC: Georgetown University Press.

Bronstein, A. J. (1984) 'Updating a dictionary of American English pronunciation', in R. R. K. Hartmann (ed.) 51–7.

—— (1986) 'The history of pronunciation in English language dictionaries', in R. R. K. Hartmann (ed.) 23–33.

—— (1994) 'Extending the treatment of pronunciation entries in general dictionaries', in W. Martin *et al.* (eds) 619–28.

Brown, S. (1996) 'Hard words for the ladies: The first English dictionaries and the question of readership', in M. Gellerstam *et al.* (eds) 355–63.

BSI [British Standards Institution] (1988) *Root Thesaurus*, Milton Keynes: BSI.

Burchfield, R. W. (1984) 'Dictionaries, new and old: Who plagiarises whom, why, and when?', *Encounter* 63, 3: 10–19.

—— (1987a) 'The Supplement to the *Oxford English Dictionary*: The end of the alphabet', in R. Bailey (ed.) 11–21.

—— (ed.) (1987b) *Studies in Lexicography*, Oxford: Clarendon Press. [10 papers by 10 authors.]

Burnett, L. S. (1988) 'Making it short: The Shorter Oxford English Dictionary', in M. Snell-Hornby (ed.) 229–33.

Butler, C. S. (1990) 'Language and computation', in N. E. Collinge (ed.) 611–67.

Butler, S. (1992) 'Achievable goals in English language dictionary publishing in Singapore and the region', in A. Pakir (ed.) 15–28.

Bwenge, C. (1989) 'Lexicographical treatment of affixational morphology: A case study of four Swahili dictionaries', in G. James (ed.) 5–17.

Byrd, R. J. (1995) 'Dictionary systems for office practice', in D. A. Walker *et al.* (eds) 207–19.

Calzolari, N. (1996) 'Lexicon and corpus: A multifaceted interaction', in M. Gellerstam *et al.* (eds) 3–16.

Cannon, G. (1982) 'Linguistic analysis of 4,520 new meanings and new words in English', *Dictionaries* 4: 97–109.

—— (1990) 'English abbreviations and acronyms in recent new-words dictionaries', in T. Magay & J. Zigány (eds) 169–75.

Carr, M. (1997) 'Internet dictionaries and lexicography', *International Journal of Lexicography* 10,3: 209–30.

Caton, H. (1991) 'Dictionaries in and of Braille', in F. J. Hausmann *et al.* (eds) III: 3145–8.

Chambers, J. K. (1994) *Sociolinguistic Theory. Linguistic Variation and its Social Significance*, Oxford: Blackwell.

Chayen, M. J. (1989) 'Automatic conversion of place names in English orthography to Hebrew phonetic representation. The Jerusalem Carta Atlas project', *International Journal of Lexicography* 2, 1: 24–9.

Cignoni, L., Lanzetta, E., Pecchia, L. and Turrini, G. (1996) 'Children's aid to a children's dictionary', in M. Gellerstam *et al.* (eds) 659–66.

Clark, J. and Yallop, C. (1995) *An Introduction to Phonetics and Phonology*, Oxford: B. Blackwell. [2nd edition]

Clear, J. (1988) 'Trawling the language: Monitor corpora', in M. Snell-Hornby (ed.) 383–9.

Cluver, A. D. de V. (1989a) *A Manual of Terminography*, Pretoria: Human Sciences Research Council.

—— (1989b) *Dictionary of Terminography/Terminografie-woordeboek*, Pretoria: Human Sciences Research Council/Raad vir Geesteswetenskaplike Navorsing.

Collinge, N. E. (ed.) (1990) *An Encyclopedia of Language*, London and New York NY: Routledge. [26 chapters by 29 authors.]

Collison, R. L. (1982) *A History of Foreign-Language Dictionaries* (The Language Library), Oxford: B. Blackwell.

Collison, R. L. and Preece, W. E. (1974/92) 'Encyclopaedias', in *Encyclopaedia Britannica*, 15th edition 258–77.

Congleton, J. E. and Congleton, E. C. (1984) *Johnson's Dictionary: Bibliographical Survey 1746–1984*, Terre Haute IN: Indiana State University & Dictionary Society of North America.

Considine, J. (1996) ' "The *Meanings*, deduced logically from the Etymology" ', in M. Gellerstam *et al.* (eds) 365–71.

Cop, M. (1989) 'Linguistic and encyclopedic information not included in the dictionary articles', in F. J. Hausmann *et al.* (eds) I: 761–7.

—— (1990) *Babel Unravelled. An Annotated World Bibliography of Dictionary Bibliographies, 1658–1988* (Lexicographica Series Maior 36), Tübingen: M. Niemeyer.

—— (1991) 'Collocations in the bilingual dictionary', in F. J. Hausmann *et al.* (eds) III: 2775–8.

Coulmas, F. (ed.) (1996) *The Handbook of Socio-*

linguistics, Oxford: Blackwell. [28 chapters by 28 authors.]

Cowie, A.P. (ed.) (1987a) *The Dictionary and the Language Learner. Papers from the EURALEX Seminar at the University of Leeds, 1–3 April 1985* (Lexicographica Series Maior 17), Tübingen: M. Niemeyer. [18 papers by 28 authors.]

—— (1987b) 'Syntax, the dictionary and the language learner', in A. P. Cowie (ed.) 183–92.

—— (1989a) 'Information on syntactic constructions in the general monolingual dictionary', in F. J. Hausmann *et al.* (eds) I: 588–92.

—— (1989b) 'The language of examples in English learners' dictionaries' in G. James (ed.) 55–65.

—— (1990) 'Language as words: Lexicography', in N. E. Collinge (ed.) 671–700.

Creamer, T. B. I. (1991) 'Chinese lexicography', in F. J. Hausmann *et al.* (eds) III: 2595–611.

Creswell, T. J. (1975) *Usage in Dictionaries and Dictionaries of Usage* (Publications of the American Dialect Society 63–64), University AL: University of Alabama.

Cruse, D. A. (1986) *Lexical Semantics*, Cambridge: Cambridge University Press.

Crystal, D. (ed.) (1980) *Eric Partridge in His Own Words*, London: A. Deutsch. [30 extracts from E. P.'s works and 5 tributes by other authors.]

—— (1986) 'The ideal dictionary, lexicographer and user', in R. Ilson (ed.) 72–81.

Cumming, J. D. (1995) 'The Internet and the English language', *English Today* 11, 1: 3–8.

DANLEX Group [E. Hjorth, B. Nistrup Madsen, O. Norling-Christensen, J. Rosenkilde Jacobsen and H. Ruus] (1987) *Descriptive Tools for Electronic Processing of Dictionary Data* (Lexicographica Series Maior 20), Tübingen: M. Niemeyer.

Davies, A., Criper, C. and Howatt, A. P. R. (1984) *Interlanguage*, Edinburgh: Edinburgh University Press.

Davis, S. B. (1993) 'Hypertext and multimedia', *English Today* 9, 1: 17–24.

Delbridge, A. (1989) 'Usage and style: implications for lexicography', in G. James (ed.) 66–73.

DeMaria, R. (1986) *Johnson's Dictionary and the Language of Learning*, Chapel Hill NC: University of North Carolina Press.

Denning, K. and Leben, W. R. (1995) *English Vocabulary Elements*, New York NY: Oxford University Press.

DeStadler, L. G. (1992) 'Syntagmatic lexical relations: A lexicographic perspective', in H. Tommola *et al.* (eds) 411–8.

Diab, T. (1989) 'The role of dictionaries in English for specific purposes: A case study of student nurses at the University of Jordan', in G. James (ed.) 74–82.

—— (1990) *Pedagogical Lexicography. A Case Study of Arab Nurses as Dictionary Users* (Lexicographica Series Maior 31), Tübingen: M. Niemeyer.

Dickens, A. and Salkie, R. (1996) 'Comparing bilingual dictionaries with a parallel corpus', in M. Gellerstam *et al.* (eds) 551–9.

Dodd, W. S. (1989) 'Lexicomputing and the dictionary of the future', in G. James (ed.) 83–93.

—— (1993) 'Lexis – an uncharted land', in R. Pemberton & E. S. C. Tsang (eds) 35–47.

Dolezal, F. (1985) *Forgotten but Important Lexicographers: John Wilkins and William Lloyd. A Modern Approach to Lexicography before Johnson* (Lexicographica Series Maior 4), Tübingen: M. Niemeyer.

—— (1986) 'How abstract is the English dictionary?', in R. R. K. Hartmann (ed.) 47–63.

—— (ed.) (1989) *The Dictionary as Text*, (thematic issue) *International Journal of Lexicography* 2: 167–276. [Introduction and 5 papers by 5 authors.]

—— (ed.) (1992) *The Meaning of Definition*, (thematic issue) *Lexicographica International Annual* 8: 1–289. [Introduction and 8 papers by 7 authors.]

Drysdale, P. D. (1989) 'Etymological information in the general monolingual dictionary', in F. J. Hausmann *et al.* (eds) I: 525–30.

Duval, A. (1992) 'From the printed dictionary to the CD-ROM', in M. Alvar Ezquerra (ed.) 79–88.

Fang, J. R. and Songe, A. H. (1990) *World Guide to Libraries, Archives and Information Science Associations*, London: K. G. Saur.

Fernando, C. (1996) *Idioms and Idiomaticity (Describing English Language)*, Oxford: Oxford University Press.

Filipović, R. (1984) 'Can a dictionary of -isms be an etymological dictionary?', in R. R. K. Hartmann (ed.) 73–9.

Fillmore, C. J. and Atkins, B. T. S. (1992) 'Toward a frame-based lexicon: The semantics of RISK and its neighbors', in A. Lehrer & E. F. Kittay (eds) 75–102.

Finkenstaedt, T. and Wolff, D. (1973) *Ordered Profusion. Studies in Dictionaries and the English Lexicon*, Heidelberg: C. Winter.

Fischer, A. and Ammann, D. (1991) *An Index to Dialect Maps of Great Britain*, Amsterdam: J. Benjamins.

Flowerdew, L. and Tong, A. K. K. (eds) (1994) *Entering Text*, Hong Kong: Language Centre,

Hong Kong University of Science and Technology. [20 papers by 28 authors.]

Fontenelle, T. (1996) 'Ergativity, collocations and lexical functions', in M. Gellerstam *et al.* (eds) 209–22.

Fox, G. (1987) 'The case for examples', in J. Sinclair (ed.) 137–49.

—— (1989) 'A vocabulary for writing dictionaries', in M. L. Tickoo (ed.) 153–71.

Foxley, E. and Gwei, G. (1989) 'Synonymy and contextual disambiguation of words', *International Journal of Lexicography* 2, 2: 111–34.

Frawley, W. (1982) 'Aspects of metaphorical definition in sciences', *Dictionaries* 4: 118–50.

—— (ed.) (1992–3) *Forum on the Theory and Practice of Lexicography*, (thematic issue) *Dictionaries* 14: 1–159. [9 papers by 8 authors.]

Friend, J. H. (1967) *The Development of American Lexicography 1798–1864*, The Hague: Mouton.

Gates, E. (1988) 'The treatment of multiword lexemes in some current dictionaries of English', in M. Snell-Hornby (ed.) 99–106.

—— (1992) 'Should a dictionary include only the "good" words?', in K. Hyldgaard-Jensen & A. Zettersten (eds) 265–80.

—— (1994) 'Review of Cordell Collection Catalog [1993]', *Dictionaries* 15: 198–208.

Gaur, A. (1984) *A History of Writing*, London: British Library.

Geeraerts, D. (1989) 'Principles of monolingual lexicography' in F. J. Hausmann *et al.* (eds) I: 287–96.

Gellerstam, M., Järborg, J., Malmgren S.-G., Norén, K., Rogström, L. and Papmehl, C. R. (eds) (1996) *Euralex '96 Proceedings I–II. Papers Submitted to the Seventh EURALEX International Congress in Göteborg, Sweden*, Gothenburg: Gothenburg University, Department of Swedish. [80 papers by 117 authors.]

Gilman, E. W. (1990) 'Dictionaries as a source of usage controversy', *Dictionaries* 12: 75–84.

Goebel, U. (1990) 'Methodological criteria for the preparation of a period dictionary', *Dictionaries* 12: 85–100.

Gorbahn-Orme, A. and Hausmann, F. J. (1991) 'The dictionary of false friends', in F. J. Hausmann *et al.* (eds) III: 2882–8.

Görlach, M. (1990) 'The dictionary of transplanted varieties of languages: English', in F. J. Hausmann *et al.* (eds) II: 1475–99.

—— (1994) 'A usage dictionary of Anglicisms in selected European languages', *International Journal of Lexicography* 7, 3: 223–46.

Goulden, R., Nation, P. and Read, J. (1990) 'How large can a receptive vocabulary be?', *Applied Linguistics* 11, 4: 341–63.

Gouws, R. H. (1987) 'Lexical meaning versus contextual evidence in dictionary articles', *Dictionaries* 9: 87–96.

—— (1996) 'Aspects of lexical semantics', in R. R. K. Hartmann (ed.) 98–131.

Granger, S., Meunier, F. and Tyson, S. (1994) 'New insights into the learner lexicon: A preliminary report from the International Corpus of Learner English', in L. Flowerdew & A. K. K. Tong (eds) 102–13.

Grauberg, W. (1989) 'Proverbs and idioms: mirrors of national experience?', in G. James (ed.) 94–9.

Green, J. (1996) *Chasing the Sun. Dictionary-makers and the Dictionaries they Made*, London: J. Cape.

Greenbaum, S. (1988) *Good English and the Grammarian*, Harlow: Longman.

Greenbaum, S., Meyer, C. F. and Taylor, J. (1984) 'The image of the dictionary for American college students', *Dictionaries* 6: 31–52.

Grefenstette, G., Heid, U., Schulze, B. M., Fontenelle, T. and Gerardy, C. (1996) 'The DECIDE Project: Multilingual collocation attraction', in M. Gellerstam *et al.* (eds) 93–107.

Haebler, T. (1989) 'The reception of the *Third New International Dictionary*', *Dictionaries* 11: 165–218.

Haiman, J. (1980) 'Dictionaries and encyclopedias', *Lingua* 50: 329–57.

Halpern, J. (1992) 'New Japanese–English character dictionary. A semantic approach to Kanji lexicography', in M. Alvar Ezquerra (ed.) 157–66.

Hancher, M. (1988) 'Bagpipe and distaff: Interpreting dictionary illustrations', *Dictionaries* 10: 93–109.

Hanks, P. (1987) 'Definitions and explanations', in J. Sinclair (ed.) 116–36.

Haraldsson, H. (1996) 'Problems of dictionary grammar. The Zaliznyak solution: a boon or a burden?', in M. Gellerstam *et al.* (eds) 561–72.

Hardcastle, W. J. and Laver, J. (eds) (1996) *The Handbook of Phonetic Sciences*, Oxford: Blackwell. [21 chapters by 31 contributors.]

Harteveld, P. and van Niekerk, A. E. (1996) 'Policy for the treatment of insulting and sensitive lexical items in the *Woordeboek van die Afrikaanse Taal*', in M. Gellerstam *et al.* (eds) 381–93.

Hartmann, R. R. K. (ed.) (1983) *Lexicography. Principles and Practice* (Applied Language Studies), London: Academic Press. [15 chapters by 14 authors.]

—— (ed.) (1984) *LEXeter '83 Proceedings* (Lexicographica Series Maior 1), Tübingen: M. Niemeyer. [55 papers by 63 authors.]

—— (ed.) (1986) *The History of Lexicography* (Amsterdam Studies in the Theory and History of Linguistic Science III, 40), Amsterdam: J. Benjamins. [23 papers by 24 authors.]

—— (1989) 'Sociology of the dictionary user: Hypotheses and empirical studies', in F. J. Hausmann *et al.* (eds) I: 102–11.

—— (1990) 'On some discrepancies in our German dictionaries. Apropos the new KLUGE and a new synonymy of German idioms', *International Journal of Lexicography* 3, 3: 218–29.

—— (1991) 'Contrastive linguistics and bilingual lexicography', in F. J. Hausmann *et al.* (eds) III: 2854–9.

—— (1992a) 'Lexicography, with particular reference to English learners' dictionaries', *Language Teaching* 25: 151–9.

—— (1992b) 'Training in lexicography: The Exeter ERASMUS initiative', in M. Alvar Ezquerra (ed.) 527–32.

—— (1993) 'General lexicography in Europe', *Lexikos* 3: 67–82.

—— (1994) 'Bilingualised versions of learner's dictionaries', *Fremdsprachen Lehren und Lernen* 23: 206–20.

—— (1996a) 'Lexicography as an applied linguistic discipline', in R. R. K. Hartmann (ed.) 230–44.

—— (ed.) (1996b) *Solving Language Problems. From General to Applied Linguistics* (Exeter Linguistic Studies 20), Exeter: University of Exeter Press. [10 chapters by 8 authors.]

Hatherall, G. (1986) 'The "Duden Rechtschreibung" 1880–1986: Development and function of a popular dictionary', in R. R. K. Hartmann (ed.) 85–97.

Hauptfleisch, D. C. (1993) 'Racist language in society and in dictionaries: A pragmatic perspective', *Lexikos* 3: 83–139.

Hausmann, F. J. (1989) 'Dictionary criminality', in F. J. Hausmann *et al.* (eds) I: 97–101.

—— (1990) 'The dictionary of synonyms: Discriminating synonymy', in F. J. Hausmann *et al.* (eds) II: 1067–75.

Hausmann, F. J. and Wiegand, H. E. (1989) 'Component parts and structures of general monolingual dictionaries: A survey', in F. J. Hausmann *et al.* (eds) I: 328–60.

Hausmann, F. J., Reichmann, O., Wiegand, H. E. and Zgusta, L. (eds) (1989–91) *Wörterbücher/ Dictionaries/Dictionnaires. An International Encyclopedia of Lexicography* (Handbücher zur Sprach- und Kommunikationswissenschaft 5.1, 5.2, 5.3), Berlin: W. de Gruyter. [Vol. I: 104 articles, II: 123 articles, III: 122 articles, by 248 authors.]

Haywood, J. A. (1991) 'Arabic lexicography', in F. J. Hausmann *et al.* III: 2438–48.

Healey, J. F. (1990) *Reading the Past. The Early Alphabet*, London: British Museum Publications.

Hearn, P. M. (1996) *The Language Engineering Directory*, Madrid: Language & Technology.

Hegyi, O. (1979) 'Minority and restricted uses of the Arabic alphabet: the *aljamiado* phenomenon', *Journal of the American Oriental Society* 99: 262–9.

Heid, U. (1992) 'Monolingual, bilingual, "interlingual" description. Some remarks on a new method for the production of bilingual dictionaries', in M. Alvar Ezquerra (ed.) 167–84.

—— (1994) 'On ways words work together – topics in lexical combinatorics', in W. Martin *et al.* (eds) 226–57.

Heidecke, S. (1996) 'SGML-tools in the dictionary-making process – experiences with a German–Polish/Polish–German dictionary', in M. Gellerstam *et al.* (eds) 395–403.

Heltai, P. (1988) 'Contrastive analysis of terminological systems and bilingual technical dictionaries', *International Journal of Lexicography* 1, 1: 32–40.

Herbst, T. (1989) 'Grammar in dictionaries', in M. L. Tickoo (ed.) 94–111.

—— (1990) 'Dictionaries for foreign language teaching: English', in F. J. Hausmann *et al.* (eds) II: 1379–85.

—— (1996) 'On the way to the perfect learner's dictionary: A first comparison of OALD5, LDOCE3, COBUILD2 and CIDE', *International Journal of Lexicography* 9, 4: 321–57.

Honselaar, W. and Elstrodt, M. (1992) 'The electronic conversion of a dictionary: from Dutch–Russian to Russian–Dutch', in H. Tommola *et al.* (eds) 229–37.

Howarth, P. A. (1996) *Phraseology in English Academic Writing. Some Implications for Language Learning and Dictionary Making* (Lexicographica Series Maior 75), Tübingen: M. Niemeyer.

Huang, J.-H. (1994) 'Chinese and Western metalexicography', in L. Flowerdew & A. K. K. Tong (eds) 228–38.

Hudson, R. (1995) 'Identifying the linguistic foundations for lexical research and dictionary design', in D. A. Walker *et al.* (eds) 21–51.

Hüllen, W. (1986) 'The paradigm of John Wilkins' Thesaurus', in R. R. K. Hartmann (ed.) 115–25.

—— (1989) 'In the beginning was the gloss. Remarks on the historical emergence of lexicographical paradigms', in G. James (ed.) 100–16.

—— (1990) 'Motives behind 17th century lexicography: A comparison between German and English dictionaries of that time', in T. Magay & J. Zigány (eds) 189–96.

—— (ed.) (1994) *The World in a List of Words* (Lexicographica Series Maior 58), Tübingen: M. Niemeyer. [21 papers by 21 authors.]

Hüllen, W. and Haas, R. (1992) 'Adrianus Junius on the order of his Nomenclator (1577)', in H. Tommola *et al*. (eds) 581–8.

Hurley, D. S. (1992) 'Issues in teaching pragmatics, prosody, and non-verbal communication', *Applied Linguistics* 13, 3: 259–81.

Hyldgaard-Jensen, K. and Zettersten, A. (eds) (1992) *Symposium on Lexicography V. Proceedings of the Fifth International Symposium on Lexicography, Copenhagen 1990* (Lexicographica Series Maior 43), Tübingen: M. Niemeyer. [23 papers by 24 authors.]

Iannucci, J. E. (1985) 'Sense discriminations and translation complements in bilingual dictionaries', *Dictionaries* 7: 57–65.

—— (1986) 'Ghost adjectives in dictionaries', *Dictionaries* 8: 164–8.

Ide, N., Veronis, J., Warwick-Armstrong, S. and Calzolari, N. (1992) 'Principles for encoding machine readable dictionaries', in H. Tommola *et al*. (eds) 239–46.

Ilson, R. F. (ed.) (1985) *Dictionaries, Lexicography and Language Learning* (ELT Documents 120), Oxford: Pergamon Press. [14 papers by 14 authors.]

—— (ed.) (1986a) *Lexicography as an Emerging International Profession*, Manchester University Press in association with the Fulbright Commission. [11 papers by 11 authors.]

—— (1986b) 'Lexicographic archaeology. Comparing dictionaries of the same family', in R. R. K. Hartmann (ed.) 127–36.

—— (1988) 'Contributions to the terminology of lexicography', in M. Snell-Hornby (ed.) 73–80.

—— (1990) 'Present-day British lexicography', in F. J. Hausmann *et al*. (eds) II: 1967–83.

ISO [International Organization for Standardization] (1990) *Terminology – Vocabulary. Terminologie – Vocabulaire*, Geneva: ISO.

Jackson, H. (1985) 'Grammar in the dictionary', in R. Ilson (ed.) 53–9.

—— (1988) *Words and their Meaning* (Learning about Language), London: Longman.

James, G. (1985) 'The Tamil script reform: A case study of folk linguistic standardisation', in D. Woods (ed.) 102–39.

—— (ed.) (1989) *Lexicographers and their Works*

(Exeter Linguistic Studies 14), Exeter: University of Exeter Press. [19 papers by 19 authors.]

—— (1991) *Tamil Lexicography* (Lexicographica Series Maior 40), Tübingen: M. Niemeyer.

—— (1994a) 'Towards a typology of bilingualised dictionaries', in G. James (ed.) 184–96.

—— (ed.) (1994b) *Meeting Points in Language Studies*, Hong Kong: Language Centre, Hong Kong University of Science and Technology. [13 papers by 17 authors.]

—— (1995a) 'From *nikaṇṭu* to *akarāti*', in G. James (ed.) 49–61.

—— (ed.) (1995b) *Tamil Lexicography*, (thematic issue) *South Asian Language Review* 5, 1: 1–121. [6 papers by 6 authors.]

James, G. with Davison, R., Cheung, A. H.-Y. and Deerwester, S. (1994) *English in Computer Science. A Corpus-Based Lexical Analysis*, Hong Kong: Longman Asia and Hong Kong University of Science and Technology.

James, G., Ho, P. W.-L. and Chu, A. C.-Y. (1997) *English in Biology, Biochemistry and Chemistry. A Corpus-Based Lexical Analysis*. Hong Kong: Language Centre, Hong Kong University of Science and Technology.

James, G. and Purchase, J. (1996) *English in Business Studies and Economics. A Corpus-Based Lexical Analysis*, Hong Kong: Language Centre, Hong Kong University of Science and Technology.

Johnson, K. (1995) *Language Teaching and Skill Learning*, Oxford: Blackwell.

Jost, D. A. (1985) 'Survey of the reading program of the Middle English Dictionary', *Dictionaries* 7: 201–13.

Jost, D. A. and Crocker, A. C. (1987) 'The handling of Down Syndrome and related terms in modern dictionaries', *Dictionaries* 9: 97–109.

Kabdebo, T. (1992) *Dictionary of Dictionaries*, London: Bowker-Saur.

Kachru, B. B. and Kahane, H. (eds) (1995) *Cultures, Ideologies, and the Dictionary. Studies in Honor of Ladislav Zgusta* (Lexicographica Series Maior 64), Tübingen: M. Niemeyer. [36 papers by 36 authors.]

Kaplan, R. B. and Baldauf, R. B. (1997) *Language Planning: From Theory to Practice*, Clevedon: Multilingual Matters.

Karpova, O. M. (1992) 'Shakespeare lexicography. Trends of development (XVIII–XX cc.)', in H. Tommola *et al*. (eds) 593–600.

Katamba, F. (1994) *English Words*, London: Routledge.

Kennedy, G. (1997) *An Introduction to Corpus Linguistics*, Harlow: Addison Wesley Longman.

Kernerman, L. (1994) 'A 3-part, fully trilingual tridirectional dictionary', in W. Martin *et al.* (eds) 472–78.

—— (1996) 'English learners' dictionaries: How much do we know about their use?', in M. Gellerstam *et al.* (eds) 405–14.

Key, M. R. (1991) 'Lexicography of the languages of the Andean Indians', in F. J. Hausmann *et al.* (eds) III: 2704–6.

Kiefer, F., Kiss, G. and Pajzs, J. (eds) (1992) *Papers in Computational Lexicography COMPLEX '92*, Budapest: Hungarian Academy of Sciences. [Introduction and 29 papers by 44 authors.]

Kipfer, B. A. (1984) 'Methods of ordering senses within entries', in R. R. K. Hartmann (ed.) 101–8.

—— (1985) 'The declining role of the in-house dictionary staff', *Dictionaries* 7: 237–45.

—— (1986) 'Investigating an onomasiological approach to dictionary material', *Dictionaries* 8: 55–64.

Kirk, J. M. (1994) 'Taking a byte at corpus linguistics', in L. Flowerdew & A. K. K. Tong (eds) 18–43.

Kirkness, A. (1984) 'The etymology of Europeanisms, or: lexicographers' difficulties with "lexicographer"', in R. R. K. Hartmann (ed.) 109–16.

—— (1994) 'Aero-lexicography: Observations on the treatment of combinemes and neo-classical combinations in historical and scholarly European dictionaries', in W. Martin *et al.* (eds) 530–5.

Kister, K. F. (1994) *Kister's Best Encyclopedias: A Comparative Guide to General and Specialized Encyclopedias*, Phoenix AZ: Oryx Press.

Knowles, F. E. (1988) 'Lexicography and terminography: A rapprochement?', in M. Snell-Hornby (ed.) 329–37.

—— (1990) 'The computer in lexicography', in F. J. Hausmann *et al.* (eds) II: 1645–72.

Kress, G. and van Leeuwen, T. (1996) *Reading Images: The Grammar of Visual Design*, London: Routledge.

Krishnamurthy, R. (1987) 'The process of compilation', in J. Sinclair (ed.) 62–85.

—— (1996) 'Exploiting the masses: the corpus-based study of language', in A. Zettersten & V. Hjørnager Pedersen (eds) 141–56.

Kromann, H.-P. (1991) 'Grammatical constructions in the bilingual dictionary', in F. J. Hausmann *et al.* (eds) III: 2770–5.

Kromann, H.-P., Riiber, T. and Rosbach, P. (1991) 'Principles of bilingual lexicography', in F. J. Hausmann *et al.* (eds) III: 2711–28.

Kuhn, H. (1988) 'Dialect dictionaries – a contradiction in itself?', in M. Snell-Hornby (ed.) 237–47.

Kurtböke, P. (1996) 'The impact of corpus planning on bilingual dictionaries', in M. Gellerstam *et al.* (eds) 591–96.

Labov, W. (1994) *Principles of Linguistic Change* [Vol. 1 Internal Factors], Oxford: Blackwell.

Lai, C.-Y. (1992) 'The influence of language reform in the People's Republic of China on character indexing in dictionaries', *Lexicographica International Annual* 8: 290–306.

Lam, J. K.-M. (1994) 'The thinking-aloud protocol in the investigation of the translation process', in G. James (ed.) 118–28.

Landau, S. I. (1984/9) *Dictionaries. The Art and Craft of Lexicography*, New York NY: S. Scribner & Cambridge: Cambridge University Press.

—— (1994) 'The American college dictionaries', *International Journal of Lexicography* 7, 4: 311–51.

LaQuey, T. (1993) *The Internet Companion*, Reading MA: Addison Wesley.

Lara, L. F. (1995) 'Towards a theory of the cultural dictionary', in B. B. Kachru & H. Kahane (eds) 41–51.

Large, A. (1985) *The Artificial Language Movement*, Oxford: B. Blackwell.

Larson, M. (ed.) (1991) *Translation: Theory and Practice, Tension and Interdependence*, Amsterdam & Philadelphia PA: J. Benjamins.

Laufer, B. (1992) 'Corpus-based versus lexicographer examples in comprehension and production of new words', in H. Tommola *et al.* (eds) 71–6.

Laufer, B. and Melamed, L. (1994) 'Monolingual, bilingual and "bilingualised" dictionaries: which are more effective, for what and for whom?', in W. Martin *et al.* (eds) 565–76.

Laufer, B. and Nation, P. (1995) 'Vocabulary size and use: Lexical richness in L2 written production', *Applied Linguistics* 16, 3: 307–22.

Law, A. G. and Sandness, G. D. (1985) 'A microcomputer-based electronic dictionary for blind persons', *Dictionaries* 7: 246–52.

Learmouth, T. and Macwilliam, S. (1986) *Historic English Dictionaries, 1595–1899: A Union Catalogue of Holdings in Exeter Libraries*, Exeter: University Library and Dictionary Research Centre.

Lee, W. R. (1989) 'The treatment of pronunciation in some (mainly British) monolingual general dictionaries used by learners of English', in M. L. Tickoo (ed.) 112–23.

Leemets, H. (1992) 'Translating the "untranslatable words"', in H. Tommola *et al.* (eds) 473–8.

Lehrer, A. and Kittay, E. F. (eds) (1992) *Frames, Fields and Contrasts. New Essays in Semantic and Lexical Organization*, Hillsdale NJ: L. Erlbaum. [Introduction and 17 papers by 18 authors.]

Lemmens, M. and Wekker, H. (1986) *Grammar in English Learners' Dictionaries* (Lexicographica Series Maior 16), Tübingen: M. Niemeyer.

Lemmens, M. and Wekker, H. (1990) 'Optical data storage and dictionaries', in T. Magay & J. Zigány (eds) 281–6.

Lombard, F. J. (1994) 'Lexicographer, linguist and dictionary user: an uneasy triangle?', *Lexikos* 4: 204–14.

Lorentzen, H. (1996) 'Lemmatization of multi-word lexical units: In which entry?', in M. Gellerstam *et al.* (eds) 415–21.

Lovatt, E. A. (1984) 'Illustrative examples in a bilingual colloquial dictionary', in R. R. K. Hartmann (ed.) 216–20.

Lyons, J. (1968) *Introduction to Theoretical Linguistics*, Cambridge: Cambridge University Press.

Mackenzie, I. and Mel'čuk, I. (1988) 'Crossroads of obstetrics and lexicography: A case study', *International Journal of Lexicography* 1, 2: 71–83.

Macleod, C., Grishman, R. and Meyers, A. (1996) 'COMLEX Syntax: An on-line dictionary for natural language processing', in M. Gellerstam *et al.* (eds) 131–9.

Magay, T. and Zigány, J. (eds) (1990) *BudaLEX '88 Proceedings. Papers from the EURALEX 3rd International Congress*, Budapest: Akadémiai Kiadó. [61 papers by 81 authors.]

Mair, V. H. (1991) 'Brief desiderata for an alphabetically ordered Mandarin–English dictionary', *International Journal of Lexicography* 4, 2: 79–98.

Makkai, A. (1980) 'Theoretical and practical aspects of an Associative Lexicon for 20th Century English', in L. Zgusta (ed.) 125–46.

Malakhovski, L. V. (1987) 'Homonyms in English dictionaries', in R. Burchfield (ed.) 36–51.

Malkiel, Y. (1987) 'How English dictionaries present the etymology of words of Romance origin', in R. Burchfield (ed.) 178–95.

Manuila, A. (ed.) (1981) *Progress in Medical Terminology*, Basel & New York NY: S. Karger. [3 prefaces and 5 papers by 8 authors and one international committee report.]

Marcuse, M. J. (1990) *Reference Guide for English Studies*, Los Angeles CA: University of California Press.

Marello, C. (1990) 'The thesaurus', in F. J. Hausmann *et al.* (eds) II: 1083–94.

Markowitz, J. and Franz, S. K. (1988) 'The develop-

ment of defining style', *International Journal of Lexicography* 1, 3: 253–67.

Martin, W. (1990) 'The frequency dictionary', in F. J. Hausmann *et al.* (eds) II: 1314–22.

—— (1992) 'On the parsing of definitions', in H. Tommola *et al.* (eds) 247–56.

Martin, W. and Al, B. P. F. (1990) 'User-orientation in dictionaries: 9 propositions', in T. Magay & J. Zigány (eds) 393–99.

Martin, W. and Tamm, A. (1996) 'OMBI: An editor for constructing reversible lexical databases', in M. Gellerstam *et al.* (eds) 675–87.

Martin, W., Meijs, W., Moerland, M., ten Pas, E., van Sterkenberg, P. and Vossen, P. (eds) (1994) *Euralex 1994 Proceedings. Papers Submitted to the 6th EURALEX Congress on Lexicography*, Amsterdam: Vrije Universiteit. [66 papers by 92 authors.]

McArthur, T. (1986a) *Worlds of Reference. Lexicography, Learning and Language from the Clay Tablet to the Computer*, Cambridge: Cambridge University Press.

—— (1986b) 'Thematic lexicography', in R. R. K. Hartmann (ed.) 157–66.

—— (1989a) 'Companionship: Notes and reflections on the making of *The Oxford Companion to the English Language*', in G. James (ed.) 160–4.

—— (1989b) 'The background and nature of ELT learners' dictionaries' in M. L. Tickoo (ed.) 52–64.

—— (ed.) (1992) *The Oxford Companion to the English Language*, Oxford: Oxford University Press. [Over 4,000 entries by 95 authors.]

McCalman, I. (ed.) (1996) *Dictionaries of National Biography and National Identity. A Critical Approach to Theory and Editorial Practice*, Canberra: Australian National University. [13 papers by 16 authors.]

McCluskey, J. (1989) 'Dictionaries and labeling of words offensive to groups, with particular attention to the Second Edition of the *OED*', *Dictionaries* 11: 111–23.

McConchie, R. W. (1983) '"Wise and learned cunctation": Medical terminology 1547–1612 and the *OED*', *Dictionaries* 5: 22–35.

McCorduck, E. S. (1993) *Grammatical Information in ESL Dictionaries* (Lexicographica Series Maior 48), Tübingen: M. Niemeyer.

McEnery, A. M. (1992) *Computational Linguistics*, Wilmslow: Sigma Press.

McEnery, T. and Wilson, A. (1996) *Corpus Linguistics*, Edinburgh: Edinburgh University Press.

McGregor, C. (1985) 'From first idea to finished artefact: The general editor as chief engineer', in R. Ilson (ed.) 123–32.

McNaught, J. (1988) 'Computational lexicography and computational linguistics', in L. Urdang (ed.) 19–33.

Meijs, W. (1992) 'Computers and dictionaries', in C. S. Butler (ed.) *Computers and Written Texts* (Applied Language Studies), Oxford: B. Blackwell 141–65.

—— (1996) 'Linguistic corpora and lexicography', *Annual Review of Applied Linguistics* 16: 99–114.

Mel'čuk, I. (1988) 'Semantic description of lexical units in an Explanatory Combinatorial Dictionary: Basic principles and heuristic criteria', *International Journal of Lexicography* 1, 3: 165–88.

Mel'čuk, I. and Wanner, L. (1994) 'Lexical co-occurrence and lexical inheritance. Emotion lexemes in German: A lexicographical case study', *Lexikos* 4: 86–161.

Merkin, R. (1986) 'Four remarks on the prehistory of historical lexicography', in R. R. K. Hartmann (ed.) 167–73.

Meyer, I. and Mackintosh, K. (1994) 'Phraseme analysis and concept analysis: Exploring a symbiotic relationship in the specialized lexicon', in W. Martin *et al.* (eds) 339–48.

Miller, G. A. (ed.) (1990) *WordNet: An On-line Lexical Database*, (thematic issue) *International Journal of Lexicography* 3, 4: 235–312. [5 papers by 5 authors.]

Mills, J. (1996) 'Computers in applied linguistics', in R. R. K. Hartmann (ed.) 245–69.

Milroy, J. and Milroy, L. (1991) *Authority in Language. Investigating Language Standardisation and Prescription*, London: Routledge.

Milton, J. and Chowdhury, N. (1994) 'Tagging the interlanguage of Chinese learners of English', in L. Flowerdew & A. K. K. Tong (eds) 127–43.

Minaeva, L. (1996) 'Words and word combinations in ESP', in M. Gellerstam *et al.* (eds) 237–44.

Mitchell, L. C. (1994) 'Inversion of grammar books and dictionaries in the seventeenth and eighteenth centuries', in W. Martin *et al.* (eds) 548–54.

Mitton, R. (1996) *English Spelling and the Computer*, Harlow: Addison Wesley Longman.

Montemagni, S., Federici, S. and Pirrelli, V. (1996) 'Example-based word sense disambiguation: A paradigm-driven approach', in M. Gellerstam *et al.* (eds) 151–9.

Moon, R. (1987) 'The analysis of meaning', in J. Sinclair (ed.) 86–103.

—— (1992) '"There is reason in the roasting of eggs": A consideration of fixed expressions in native-speaker dictionaries', in H. Tommola *et al.* (eds) 493–502.

—— (1996) 'Data, description, and idioms in corpus lexicography', in M. Gellerstam *et al.* (eds) 245–56.

Moore, C. L. (1994) 'Three dictionaries of international auxiliary languages', *Dictionaries* 15: 55–73.

Morkovkina, A. V. (1996) 'Russian agnonyms as an object of lexicographic treatment', in M. Gellerstam *et al.* (eds) 437–42.

Morton, H. C. (1994) *The Story of Webster's Third. Philip Gove's Controversial Dictionary and its Critics*, Cambridge: Cambridge University Press.

Mufwene, S. S. (1984) 'The manifold obligations of the dictionary to its users', *Dictionaries* 6: 1–30.

—— (1988) 'Dictionaries and proper names', *International Journal of Lexicography* 1, 3: 268–86.

Mugdan, J. (1989) 'Information on inflectional morphology in the general monolingual dictionary', in F. J. Hausmann *et al.* (eds) I: 518–25.

Murphy, L. (1991) 'Defining racial labels: problems and promise in American dictionaries', *Dictionaries* 13: 43–64.

—— (1996) 'Dictionaries and orthography in modern Africa', *Lexikos* 6: 44–70.

Murray, K. M. E. (1977) *Caught in the Web of Words. James A. H. Murray and the* Oxford English Dictionary, New Haven CT: Yale University Press & Oxford: Oxford University Press.

Naden, T. (1993) 'From wordlists to comparative lexicography: The lexinotes', *Lexikos* 3: 167–90.

Nakao, K. (1989) 'English–Japanese learners' dictionaries', *International Journal of Lexicography* 2, 4: 295–314.

Nation, P. (1989) 'Dictionaries and language learning', in M. L. Tickoo (ed.) 65–71.

Nedobity, W. (1990) 'New developments in terminology', in T. Magay & J. Zigány (eds) 421–8.

Neff, M. S. and Cantor, L. (1990) 'Computational tools for lexicographers', in T. Magay & J. Zigány (eds) 297–311.

Nesi, H. (1989) 'How many words is a picture worth?', in M. L. Tickoo (ed.) 124–34.

Neubach, A. and Cohen, A. D. (1988) 'Processing strategies and problems encountered in the use of dictionaries', *Dictionaries* 10: 1–19.

Neubauer, F. (1989) 'Vocabulary control in the definitions and examples of monolingual dictionaries', in F. J. Hausmann *et al.* (eds.) I: 899–905.

Neubert, A. (1992) 'Fact and fiction of the bilingual dictionary', in M. Alvar Ezquerra (ed.) 29–42.

Nguyen, D.-H. (1980–81) 'Teaching culture through bilingual dictionaries', *Dictionaries* 3: 57–68.

Noël, D., Devos, F. and Defrancq, B. (1996) 'Towards

a more grammatical bilingual dictionary', in M. Gellerstam *et al.* (eds) 597–607.

Norri, J. (1996) 'Regional labels in some British and American dictionaries', *International Journal of Lexicography* 9, 1: 1–29.

Nuccorini, S. (1992) 'Monitoring dictionary use', in H. Tommola *et al.* (eds) 89–102.

—— (1994) 'On dictionary misuse', in W. Martin *et al.* (eds) 586–97.

Nunberg, G. and Zaenen, A. (1992) 'Systematic polysemy in lexicology and lexicography', in H. Tommola *et al.* (eds) 387–96.

O'Brien, T. and Jordan, R. R. (1985) *Developing Reference Skills*, London: Collins ELT.

O'Grady, W., Dobrovolsky, M. and Katamba, F. (1997) *Contemporary Linguistics. An Introduction*, Harlow: Addison Wesley Longman.

O'Neill, M. and Palmer, C. (1992) 'Editing a bilingual dictionary entry within the framework of a bidirectional dictionary', in M. Alvar Ezquerra (ed.) 211–7.

Ong, W. A. (1982) *Orality and Literacy: The Technologizing of the Word*, London: Methuen.

Opitz, K. (1990) 'The technical dictionary for the expert', in F. J. Hausmann *et al.* (eds) II: 1505–12.

—— (1992) 'On the borders of semantic invariance: Connotation and the dictionary', in H. Tommola *et al.* (eds) 397–403.

Osselton, N. E. (1989a) 'Alphabetisation in monolingual English dictionaries to Johnson', in G. James (ed.) 165–73.

—— (1989b) 'The history of academic dictionary criticism with reference to major dictionaries', in F. J. Hausmann *et al.* (eds) I: 225–30.

—— (1990) 'English lexicography from the beginning up to and including Johnson', in F. J. Hausmann *et al.* (eds) II: 1943–53.

—— (1995) *Chosen Words. Past and Present Problems for Dictionary Makers* (Exeter Linguistic Studies 18), Exeter: University of Exeter Press.

—— (1996) 'Authenticating the vocabulary: a study in seventeenth-century lexicographical practice', *Lexikos* 6: 215–32.

Paikeday, T. M. (1992) 'O corpora!', *Lexicographica International Annual* 8: 307–17.

Pakir, A. (ed.) (1992) *Proceedings of the Lexicography Workshop 'Words in a Cultural Context'*, Singapore: UniPress. [19 papers by 16 authors.]

Pemberton, R. and Tsang, E. S. C. (eds) (1993) *Studies in Lexis. Working Papers from a Seminar*, Hong Kong: Language Centre, Hong Kong University of Science and Technology. [12 papers by 13 authors.]

Peters, C. and Picchi, E. (1996) 'From parallel to comparable text corpora', in M. Gellerstam *et al.* (eds) 173–80.

Phillipson, R. and Skutnabb-Kangas, T. (1995) 'Linguistic rights and wrongs', *Applied Linguistics* 16, 4: 483–504.

Picchi, E., Peters, C. and Marinai, E. (1992) 'The Pisa lexicographic workstation: the bilingual components', in H. Tommola *et al.* (eds) 277–85.

Piotrowski, T. (1994a) *Problems in Bilingual Lexicography*, Wrocław: Wydawnictwo Uniwersytetu Wrocławskiego.

—— (1994b) 'British and American Roget', in W. Hüllen (ed.) 123–36.

Pointon, G. (1989) 'The B.B.C. Pronouncing Dictionary of British Names', in G. James (ed.) 174–80.

Poirier, C. (1985) 'Coping with English borrowings in the *Dictionnaire du Français Québécois*', *Dictionaries* 7: 94–111.

Pratt, C. (1992) 'The status of loan-words in modern monolingual dictionaries', in M. Alvar Ezquerra (ed.) 509–16.

Prytherch, R. (1995) *Harrod's Librarians' Glossary*, Aldershot: Gower.

Pye, G. (1996) 'Don't give up, look it up! Defining phrasal verbs for the learner of English', in M. Gellerstam *et al.* (eds) 697–704.

Raadik, M. (1996) 'The treatment of compound words in a language planning dictionary', in M. Gellerstam *et al.* (eds) 451–6.

Rader, J. (1989) 'People and language names in Anglo-American dictionaries', *Dictionaries* 11: 125–38.

Rajendran, S. (1995) 'Towards the compilation of a thesaurus for Modern Tamil', in G. James (ed.) 62–99.

Ravin, Y., Chodrow, M. S. and Sachar, H. E. (1990) 'Tools for lexicographers revising an on-line thesaurus', in T. Magay & J. Zigány (eds) 331–45.

Read, A. W. (1982) 'Theoretical basis for determining pronunciations in dictionaries', *Dictionaries* 4: 87–96.

—— [with summary of Testimony by J. Stein] (1984) 'Dictionaries and proprietary names: the airshuttle case', *Dictionaries* 6: 53–65.

—— (1986) 'Competing lexicographical traditions in America', in R. R. K. Hartmann (ed.) 197–206.

Reddick, A. (1990) *The Making of Johnson's Dictionary, 1746–1773* (Cambridge Studies in Publishing and Printing History), Cambridge: Cambridge University Press.

Regan, V. D. (1989) 'Lexicographical metaphor', *Dictionaries* 11: 1–9.

Renouf, A. (1987) 'Corpus development', in J. Sinclair (ed.) 1–22.

Riggs, F. W. (1984) 'Lexicographical terminology: Some observations', in R. R. K. Hartmann (ed.) 401–12.

—— (1989) 'Terminology and lexicography: Their complementarity', *International Journal of Lexicography* 2, 2: 89–110.

Roach, P. (1992) *Introducing Phonetics*, Harmondsworth: Penguin English.

Roberts, R. P. (1992) 'Organization of information in a bilingual dictionary', in M. Alvar Ezquerra (ed.) 219–31.

Roberts, R. P. and Montgomery, C. (1996) 'The use of corpora in bilingual lexicography', in M. Gellerstam *et al.* (eds) 457–64.

Robins, R. H. (1987) 'Polysemy and the lexicographer', in R. Burchfield (ed.) 52–75.

Robinson, J. (1983) 'A glossary of contemporary English lexicographic terminology', *Dictionaries* 5: 76–114.

—— (1984) 'Glossary of English lexicographical terms, A–Z', in B. A. Kipfer *Workbook on Lexicography. A Course for Dictionary Users*, Exeter: University of Exeter Press 173–207.

Robinson, P. (1980) *ESP (English for Specific Purposes)*, Oxford: Pergamon Press.

Roe, K. (1978) 'A survey of the encyclopedic tradition in English dictionaries', in D. Hobar (ed.) *Papers of the Dictionary Society of North America 1977*, Terre Haute IN: Dictionary Society of North America & Indiana State University 16–23.

Romaine, S. (1988) *Pidgin and Creole Languages*, London: Longman.

Rosenkilde Jacobsen, J., Manley J. and Hjørnager Pedersen, V. (1991) 'Examples in the bilingual dictionary', in F. J. Hausmann *et al.* (eds) III: 2782–9.

Rosenstein, R. (1985) 'Jan Nicot's *Thresor* and Renaissance multilingual lexicography', *Dictionaries* 7: 32–56.

Rundell, M. (1988) 'Changing the rules: Why the monolingual learner's dictionary should move away from the native-speaker dictionary', in M. Snell-Hornby (ed.) 127–37.

Rundell, M. and Ham, N. (1994) 'A new conceptual map of English: [*The Longman Language Activator*]', in W. Martin *et al.* (eds) 172–80.

Rundell, M. and Stock, P. (1992) 'The corpus revolution', *English Today* 8, 2: 9–14; 8, 3: 21–32; 8, 4: 45–51.

Ryan, J. (1989) *First Stop: The Master Index to Subject Encyclopedias*, Phoenix AZ: Oryx Press.

Sager, J. (1990) *A Practical Course in Terminology Processing*, Amsterdam: J. Benjamins.

Sager, J., Dungworth, D. and McDonald, P. F. (1980) *English Special Languages*, Wiesbaden: Brandstetter.

Sands, D. B. (1980–1) 'Engaged lexicography: Comment on an East German dictionary', *Dictionaries* 3: 39–51.

Šarćević, S. (1988) 'The challenge of legal lexicography: Implications for bilingual and multilingual dictionaries', in M. Snell-Hornby (ed.) 307–14.

—— (1989) 'Conceptual dictionaries for translation in the field of law', *International Journal of Lexicography* 2, 4: 277–94.

Särkkä, H. (1984) 'Improving the usability of the Finnish comprehension dictionary', in R. R. K. Hartmann (ed.) 268–73.

Schäfer, J. (1980) *Documentation in the O.E.D.: Shakespeare and Nashe as Test Cases*, Oxford: Clarendon Press.

—— (1989) *Early Modern English Lexicography*, Oxford: Clarendon Press.

Schein, J. D. (1991) 'Dictionaries of deaf languages', in F. J. Hausmann *et al.* (eds) III: 3141–4.

Schmid, H.-J. (1996) 'Introspection and computer corpora: The meaning and complementation of *start* and *begin*', in A. Zettersten & V. Hjørnager Pedersen (eds) 223–39.

Schnorr, V. (1986) 'Translational equivalent and/or explanation? The perennial problem of equivalence', *Lexicographica International Annual* 2: 53–60.

—— (1991) 'Problems of lemmatization in the bilingual dictionary', in F. J. Hausmann *et al.* (eds) III: 2813–7.

Sciarone, A. G. and Ahmadi, M. R. (1996) 'Towards a universal dictionary', in M. Gellerstam *et al.* (eds) 465–72.

Sharpe, P. (1988) 'Japanese speech levels and how to indicate them in an English–Japanese dictionary', *Dictionaries* 10: 69–80.

—— (1989) 'Pragmatic considerations for an English–Japanese dictionary', *International Journal of Lexicography* 2, 4: 315–24.

Shcherba, V. (1940/95) 'Opyt obshchei teorii leksikografii' [Transl. 'A contribution to theoretical lexicography', ed. D. M. T. G. Farina], *International Journal of Lexicography* 8, 4: 304–50.

Sheehy, E. P. (1986) *Guide to Reference Books*, Chicago IL: American Library Association [10th edition].

Sherwood, P. (1990) 'Grammar in the bilingual dictionary, with special reference to English and Hungarian', in T. Magay & J. Zigány (eds) 129–40.

Simpson, J. A. (1988) 'Computers and the New OED's new words', in M. Snell-Hornby (ed.) 437–44.

—— (1989) 'Nathaniel Bailey and the search for a lexicographical style', in G. James (ed.) 181–91.

Sinclair, J. M. (ed.) (1987) *Looking Up. An Account of the COBUILD Project in Lexical Computing*, London & Glasgow: Collins. [10 chapters by 8 authors.]

—— (1991) *Corpus, Concordance, Collocation*, Oxford: Oxford University Press.

—— (1996) 'Prospects for automatic lexicography', in A. Zettersten & V. Hjørnager Pedersen (eds) 1–10.

—— (1997) *Reading Concordances: An Introduction*, Harlow: Addison Wesley Longman.

Sledd, J. H. and Ebbitt, W. R. (eds) (1962) *Dictionaries and THAT Dictionary: A Casebook on the Aims of Lexicographers and the Targets of Reviewers*, Chicago IL: Scott-Foresman. [Extracts from 7 authors/dictionaries and 62 reviews.]

Snell-Hornby, M. (ed.) (1988) *ZüriLEX '86 Proceedings. Papers Read at the EURALEX International Congress, Zürich 1986*, Tübingen: A. Francke. [45 papers by 51 authors.]

—— (1990) 'Bilingual dictionaries – visions and revisions', in T. Magay & J. Zigány (eds) 227–36.

Snell-Hornby, M. and Pöhl, E. (eds) (1989) *Translation and Lexicography*, Amsterdam: J. Benjamins. [19 papers by 20 authors.]

Sobkowiak, W. (1996) 'Phonetic transcription in machine-readable dictionaries', in M. Gellerstam *et al.* (eds) 181–8.

Spears, R. A. (1987) 'Piracy in argot dictionaries', *Dictionaries* 9: 124–32.

—— (1989) 'Historical principles in dictionaries of non-standardized vocabularies', *Dictionaries* 11: 97–109.

—— (1990) 'Computational approaches to alphabetization and routing in phrasal dictionaries', in T. Magay & J. Zigány (eds) 347–53.

Spencer, A. (1996) *Phonology: Theory and Description*, Oxford: Blackwell.

Stammerjohann, H. (ed.) (1996) *Lexicon Grammaticorum. Who's Who in the History of World Linguistics*, Tübingen: M. Niemeyer.

Stark, M. P. (1990) *Dictionary Workbooks. A Critical Evaluation of Dictionary Workbooks for the Foreign Learner* (Exeter Linguistic Studies 16), Exeter: University of Exeter Press.

—— (1996) 'Encyclopedic learners' dictionaries. A study of their design features from the user perspective', unpublished M.Phil. thesis, University of Exeter.

Starnes, D. T. and Noyes, G. E. (1946/91) *The English Dictionary from Cawdrey to Johnson* [new edition by G. Stein], Chapel Hill NC: University of North Carolina Press & Amsterdam: J. Benjamins.

Starren, P. and Thelen, M. (1990) 'General dictionaries and students of translation: A report on the use of dictionaries in the translation process', in T. Magay & J. Zigány (eds) 447–58.

Steele, J. (1986) 'A lexical entry for an Explanatory-combinatorial Dictionary of English (hope II.1)', *Dictionaries* 8: 1–54.

—— (ed.) (1990) *Meaning–Text Theory. Linguistics, Lexicography, and Implications*, Ottawa: Ottawa University Press. [13 chapters by 9 authors.]

Stein, G. (1979) 'The best of British and American lexicography', *Dictionaries* 1: 1–23.

—— (1984) 'Word-formation in Dr. Johnson's *Dictionary of the English Language*', *Dictionaries* 6: 66–112.

—— (1985) *The English Dictionary before Cawdrey* (Lexicographica Series Maior 9), Tübingen: M. Niemeyer.

—— (1989) 'Recent developments in EFL dictionaries', in M. L. Tickoo (ed.) 10–41.

—— (1991) 'Illustrations in dictionaries', *International Journal of Lexicography* 4, 2: 99–127.

Steiner, R. J. (1984) 'Guidelines for reviewers of bilingual dictionaries', *Dictionaries* 6: 166–81.

—— (1986a) 'The three-century recension in Spanish and English lexicography', in R. R. K. Hartmann (ed.) 229–39.

—— (1986b) 'How many languages should a "bilingual" dictionary offer?', *Lexicographica International Annual* 2: 85–92.

—— (1993) 'Reviews of dictionaries in learned journals in the United States', *Lexicographica International Annual* 9: 158–73.

—— (1995) 'The bilingual dictionary in cross-cultural contexts', in B. B. Kachru & H. Kahane (eds) 275–80.

Stock, P. (1988) 'The structure and function of definitions', in M. Snell-Hornby (ed.) 81–9.

—— (1992) 'The cultural dimension in defining', in H. Tommola *et al.* (eds) 113–20.

Strevens, P. (ed.) (1978) *In Honour of A. S. Hornby*, Oxford: Oxford University Press. [13 papers by 13 authors.]

—— (1987) 'The effectiveness of learners' dictionaries', in R. Burchfield (ed.) 76–93.

Stubbs, M. (1996) *Text and Corpus Analysis. Computer-Assisted Studies of Language and Culture*, Oxford: Blackwell.

Sundström, M.-P. (1992) 'Tackling lexicographical

anisomorphism in front matter comments', in H. Tommola *et al.* (eds) 527–32.

Svartvik, J. (ed.) (1992a) *Directions in Corpus Linguistics*, Berlin: Mouton/W. de Gruyter [15 papers by 18 authors.]

—— (1992b) 'Lexis in English language corpora', in H. Tommola *et al.* (eds) 17–31.

Svensén, B. (1993) *Practical Lexicography. Principles and Methods of Dictionary-making* [tr. J. Sykes & K. Schofield], Oxford: Oxford University Press.

Swales, J. (1990) *Genre Analysis: English in Academic and Research Settings*, Cambridge: Cambridge University Press.

Swanepoel, P. (1992) 'Linguistic motivation and its lexicographical application', in M. Alvar Ezquerra (ed.) 291–314.

—— (1994) 'Problems, theories and methodologies in current lexicographic semantic research', in W. Martin *et al.* (eds) 11–26.

Tarone, E. (1988) *Variation in Interlanguage*, London: E. Arnold.

Taylor, A. and Chan, A. (1994) 'Pocket electronic dictionaries and their use', in W. Martin *et al.* (eds) 598–605.

Taylor, A. and Poon, W. (1994) 'Cantonese–English and English–Cantonese dictionaries', in L. Flowerdew & A. K. K. Tong (eds) 251–71.

Ten Hacken, P. (1992) 'On the definition of compounding', in H. Tommola *et al.* (eds) 345–51.

Teubert, W. (1996) 'Comparable or parallel corpora?', *International Journal of Lexicography* 9, 3: 238–64.

Thelen, M. (1992) 'Lexical systems and lexical domains as measures of accessibility, consistency and efficiency of lexical information in dictionaries', in H. Tommola *et al.* (eds) 441–8.

Thelen, M. and Starren, P. (1992) 'Languaging-up the dictionary maker: Neologisms and dictionaries', in M. Alvar Ezquerra (ed.) 391–415.

Thomas, G. (1992) *Linguistic Purism*, Harlow: Longman.

Thomas, J. (1995) *Meaning in Interaction: An Introduction to Pragmatics*, Harlow: Longman.

Thomas, P. (1992) 'Treatment of compound terminology entries', in H. Tommola *et al.* (eds) 185–92.

Thompson, D. (1992a) 'Making room for the compound nouns in small monolingual English dictionaries', in M. Alvar Ezquerra (ed.) 417–23.

—— (1992b) 'Television as a source of material for English dictionaries', in H. Tommola *et al.* (eds) 541–8.

Thomsen, K. T. (1994) 'On the hardship involved in

creating a labelling system for usage restrictions in a comprehensive monolingual dictionary', in W. Martin *et al.* (eds) 378–83.

Tickoo, M. L. (ed.) (1989) *Learners' Dictionaries. State of the Art* (Anthology Series 23), Singapore: SEAMEO Regional Language Centre. [16 papers by 17 authors.]

Tollefson, J. W. (1991) *Planning Language, Planning Inequality: Language Policy in the Community*, Harlow: Longman.

Tomaszczyk, J. (1988) 'The bilingual dictionary under review', in M. Snell-Hornby (ed.) 289–97.

Tommola, H., Varantola, K., Salmi-Tolonen, T. and Schopp, J. (eds) (1992) *EURALEX '92 Proceedings I–II. Papers Submitted to the 5th EURALEX International Congress on Lexicography* (Studia Translatologica A.2), Tampere: Yliopisto. [72 papers by 91 authors.]

Tono, Y. (1989) 'Can a dictionary help one read better?', in G. James (ed.) 192–200.

—— (1996) 'Using learner corpora for L2 lexicography: Information on collocational errors for EFL learners', *Lexikos* 6: 116–32.

Towner, G. (1995) 'Creating an English Anagrammicon', *English Today* 11, 3: 25–8.

Trapido, J. (1980–1) 'Theatre dictionaries: A view from inside', *Dictionaries* 3: 106–15.

Trask, R. L. (1994) *Language Change*, London: Routledge.

Tribble, C. and Jones, G. (1990) *Concordancing in the Classroom*, Harlow: Longman.

Ungerer, F. and Schmid, H.-J. (1996) *An Introduction to Cognitive Linguistics*, London & New York NY: Longman.

Urdang, L. (ed.) (1988) *Computer Applications in Lexicography*, (thematic issue) *Lexicographica International Annual* 4: 1–144. [9 papers by 14 authors.]

—— (1996) 'The uncommon use of proper names', *International Journal of Lexicography* 9, 1: 30–4.

Vancil, D. E. (1993) *Catalog of Dictionaries, Word Books, and Philological Texts, 1440–1900*, Westport CT: Greenwood Press.

—— (1994) *Incunable Dictionaries. A Checklist and Publishing History*, Terre Haute IN: Indiana State University Cunningham Memorial Library.

van der Meer, G. (1996a) 'How alphabetical should a dictionary be? The case of *high* and its combinations in some dictionaries', in A. Zettersten & V. Hjørnager Pedersen (eds) 183–97.

—— (1996b) 'The treatment of figurative meanings in the English learner's dictionaries (OALD, LDOCE, CC and CIDE)', in M. Gellerstam *et al.* (eds) 423–9.

van Ek, J. A. (1988) *Threshold Level English in a European Unit/Credit System for Modern Language Learning by Adults*, New York NY: Prentice Hall.

van Niekerk, A. E. (1992) 'The lexicographical treatment of neoclassical compounds', in H. Tommola *et al.* (eds) 379–85.

van Roey, J. (1988) 'Work in progress: A parallel-lexicon of English–French "faux amis"', in M. Snell-Hornby (ed.) 161–9.

van Sterkenburg, P. G. J. (1992) 'Electronic onomasiology: Van Dale greater dictionary of synonyms', in H. Tommola *et al.* (eds) 519–26.

Varantola, K. (1992) 'Words, terms and translators', in H. Tommola *et al.* (eds) 121–8.

—— (1994) 'The dictionary user as decision maker', in W. Martin *et al.* (eds) 606–11.

Veisbergs, A. (1996) 'False friends dictionaries: A tool for translators or learners or both', in M. Gellerstam *et al.* (eds) 627–34.

Veldi, E. (1994) 'Onomatopoeic words in bilingual dictionaries (with focus on English–Estonian and Estonian–English)', *Dictionaries* 15: 74–85.

Vogel, C. (1979) *Indian Lexicography* (A History of Indian Literature 5,4), Wiesbaden: O. Harrassowitz.

Vossen, P. (1992) 'The automatic construction of a knowledge base from dictionaries: A combination of techniques', in H. Tommola *et al.* (eds) 311–26.

—— (1996) 'Right or wrong: Combining lexical resources in the EuroWordNet Project', in M. Gellerstam *et al.* (eds) 715–28.

Wachal, R. S. (1994) 'The dictionary as grammarian: Part-of-speech definitions and labels', *Dictionaries* 15: 159–70.

Wadsworth, R. W. (1989) 'Lexicographers as closet authoritarians', *Dictionaries* 11: 81–95.

Wakelin, M. F. (1987) 'The treatment of dialect in English dictionaries', in R. Burchfield (ed.) 156–77.

Walker, D. A., Zampolli, A. and Calzolari, N. (eds) (1995) *Automating the Lexicon. Research and Practice in a Multilingual Environment*, Oxford: Oxford University Press. [Introduction and 11 papers by 14 authors.]

Walter, E. (1992) 'Semantic set-defining: Benefits to the lexicographer and the user', in H. Tommola *et al.* (eds) 129–36.

Warburton, Y. (1986) 'Finding the right words: An account of research for the Supplements to the *Oxford English Dictionary*', *Dictionaries* 8: 94–111.

Webster, J. (1992) 'Text analysis and lexicographical

research: Implications for Singapore English', in A. Pakir (ed.) 172–86.

Wells, J. C. (1985) 'English pronunciation and its dictionary representation', in R. Ilson (ed.) 45–51.

Whitcut, J. (1989) 'The dictionary as a commodity', in F. J. Hausmann *et al.* (eds) I: 88–94.

Wiegand, H. E. (ed.) (1990) *Dictionaries and their Parts as Texts*, (thematic part) *Lexicographica International Annual* 6: 1–161. [3 papers by 3 authors.]

—— (1992) 'Elements of a theory towards a so-called lexicographic definition', in F. Dolezal (ed.) 175–289.

—— (1996) 'Textual condensation in printed dictionaries: a theoretical draft', *Lexikos* 6: 133–58.

Wierzbicka, A. (1985) *Lexicography and Conceptual Analysis*, Ann Arbor MI: Karoma.

—— (1992) 'Semantic primitives and semantic fields', in A. Lehrer & E. F. Kittay (eds) 209–27.

—— (1995) 'Dictionaries and ideologies: three examples from Eastern Europe', in B. Kachru & H. Kahane (eds), 181–95.

Williams, J. (1992) 'The question of plagiarism and breach of copyright in the dictionary-making process (with particular reference to the UK)', in H. Tommola *et al.* (eds) 561–70.

—— (1996) 'Enough said: The problems of obscurity and cultural reference in learners' dictionary examples', in M. Gellerstam *et al.* (eds) 497–505.

Willinsky, J. (1994) *Empire of Words: The Reign of the OED*, Princeton NJ: Princeton University Press.

Winer, L. (1991) 'Ethnic lexis in an English creole dictionary', *Dictionaries* 13: 65–74.

Winston, P. H. (1993) *Artificial Intelligence* [3rd edition], Reading MA: Addison Wesley.

Woods, D. J. (ed.) (1985) *Language Standards and their Codification: Process and Application* (Exeter Linguistic Studies 9), Exeter: University of Exeter Press. [7 papers by 7 authors.]

Wynar, B. S. (ed.) (1986) *ARBA Guide to Subject Encyclopedias and Dictionaries*, Littleton CO: Libraries Unlimited.

Xue, Shigi (1982) 'Chinese lexicography past and present', *Dictionaries* 4: 151–69.

Zettersten, A. and V. Hjørnager Pedersen (eds) (1996) *Symposium on Lexicography VII. Proceedings of the Seventh Symposium on Lexicography, Copenhagen 1994* (Lexicographica Series Maior 76), Tübingen: M. Niemeyer. [18 papers by 21 authors.]

Zgusta, L. (1971) *Manual of Lexicography*, The Hague: Mouton.

—— (ed.) (1980) *Theory and Method in Lexicography: Western and Non-western Perspectives*, Columbia SC: Hornbeam Press. [10 papers by 10 authors.]

—— (1984) 'Translational equivalence in the bilingual dictionary', in R. R. K. Hartmann (ed.) 147–54.

—— (ed.) (1986a) *Problems of the Bilingual Dictionary*, (thematic part) *Lexicographica International Annual* 2: 1–161. [Introduction and 11 papers by 12 authors.]

—— (1986b) 'Grimm, Littré, *OED*, and Richardson: A comparison of their historicity', *Dictionaries* 8: 74–93.

—— (1988a) *Lexicography Today. An Annotated Bibliography of the Theory of Lexicography* (Lexicographica Series Maior 18), Tübingen: M. Niemeyer.

—— (1988b) 'Copying in lexicography: Monier-Williams' Sanskrit Dictionary and other cases', *Lexicographica International Annual* 4: 145–64.

—— (1989a) 'The role of dictionaries in the genesis and development of the standard', in F. J. Hausmann *et al.* (eds) I: 70–9.

—— (1989b) 'The influence of scripts and morphological language types on the structure of dictionaries', in F. J. Hausmann *et al.* (eds) I: 296–305.

—— (1991) 'Probable future developments in lexicography', in F. J. Hausmann *et al.* (eds.) III: 3158–68.

—— (ed.) (1992) *History, Languages, and Lexicography* (Lexicographica Series Maior 41), Tübingen: M. Niemeyer. [3 papers by 5 authors.]

—— (1996) 'The lexicographer's creativity', in M. Gellerstam *et al.* (eds) 323–36.

Zimmermann, H. (1983) 'Multifunctional dictionaries', *Linguistica Computazionale* 3: 279–88.

Zöfgen, E. (1991) 'Bilingual learner's dictionaries', in F. J. Hausmann *et al.* (eds) III: 2888–903.